Rodanthi Tzanelli is a leading analyst of how cinematic, tourist and political mobilities are complexly intertwined. In *Heritage in the Digital Era* she powerfully dissects five cases which exemplify many new intersecting mobilities within the digital era.

— John Urry, *Distinguished Professor of Sociology,*
Lancaster University

This is a fascinating and timely book. Tzanelli takes us on a grand cinematic tour across the world in a penetrating discussion of the digital re-invention of heritage. The backdrop of these cinematic stories is the recovery of an original condition of human innocence and purity. But innocence is not to be had as politics and power are never far away.

— Vassos Argyrou, *Reader in Social Anthropology,*
University of Hull

Heritage in the Digital Era

What happens to traditional conceptions of heritage in the era of fluid media spaces? 'Heritage' usually involves intergenerational transmission of ideas, customs, ancestral lands and artefacts, and so serves to reproduce national communities over time. However, media industries have the power to transform national lands and histories into generic landscapes and ideas through digital reproductions or modifications, prompting renegotiations of belonging in new ways. Contemporary media allow digital environments to function as transnational classrooms, creating virtual spaces of debate for people with access to televised, cinematic and Internet ideas and networks.

This book examines a range of popular cinematic interventions that are reshaping national and global heritage, across Europe, Asia, the Americas and Australasia. It examines collaborative or adversarial articulations of such enterprise (by artists, directors, producers but also local, national and transnational communities) that blend activism with commodification, presenting new cultural industries as fluid but significant agents in the production of new public spheres.

Heritage in the Digital Era will appeal to students and scholars of sociology, film studies, tourist studies, globalization theory, social theory, social movements, human/cultural geography and cultural studies.

Rodanthi Tzanelli is Lecturer in Sociology at the University of Leeds. Her interests centre on globalization, cosmopolitanism, identity, media and tourism. She has published five books, including *The Cinematic Tourist: Explorations in globalization, culture and resistance* (2007) and *Cosmopolitan Memory in Europe's 'Backwaters': Rethinking civility* (2011).

Routledge advances in sociology

Heritage in the Digital Era

Cinematic tourism and the
activist cause

Rodanthi Tzanelli

LONDON AND NEW YORK

First published 2013
by Routledge
2 Park Square, Milton Park, Abingdon, Oxon OX14 4RN

Simultaneously published in the USA and Canada
by Routledge
711 Third Avenue, New York, NY 10017

Routledge is an imprint of the Taylor & Francis Group, an informa business

British Library Cataloguing-in-Publication Data
A catalogue record for this book is available from the British Library

Library of Congress Cataloging in Publication Data
Tzanelli, Rodanthi
Heritage in the digital era: cinematic tourism and the activist cause /
Rodanthi Tzanelli.
   p. cm. — (Routledge advances in sociology; 93)
Includes bibliographical references and index.
1. Tourism and motion pictures. 2. Tourism in motion pictures. 3. Culture
and tourism. 4. Heritage tourism. 5. Mass media—Social aspects. 6. Digital
media—Social aspects. I. Title.
G155.A1T934 2013
302.23'1—dc23   2012034245

ISBN: 978-0-415-64380-1 (hbk)
ISBN: 978-0-203-07995-9 (ebk)

Typeset in Times New Roman
by Deer Park Productions

Printed and bound by CPI Group (UK) Ltd, Croydon, CR0 4YY

For Majid and mother – better this time

The artistic imagination shapes the 'unconscious memory' of the liberation that failed, of the promise that was betrayed. Under the rule of the performance principle, art opposes to institutionalized repression the 'image of man as a free subject; but in a state of unfreedom art can sustain the image of freedom only in the negation of unfreedom' (Adorno 1953: 182).

(Herbert Marcuse, *Eros and Civilization*, New York: Beacon Press, p. 121)

Contents

Figures

Acknowledgements

This book benefited from ongoing face-to-face and virtual dialogues with John Urry (Chapter 3), Majid Yar, Spyros Sifakakis, Nick Emmel and Nick Ellison. The master's class in *Globalisation and International Social Change* and my doctoral student, Jane Reas, provided inspiration. All film stills were purchased with the financial support of the School of Sociology and Social Policy at the University of Leeds. I am grateful to Naveen Selvadurai for granting me permission to use his photograph of Zodiac Heads; Getty Images for the photograph from New Zealand's protests; and the Photofest team for their help with film stills.

Part of Chapter 4 was based on ideas presented in *Cosmopolitan Memory in Europe's 'Backwaters': Rethinking Civility* (2011), which I published with Routledge and 'Cultural intimations and the commodification of culture: sign industries as makers of the "public sphere"', *The Global Studies Journal*, 2008, 1(3): 1–10. 'The Da Vinci node: networks of neo-pilgrimage in the European cosmopolis', which was published in the *International Journal of Humanities*, 2010, 8(3): 113–28, was used in Chapter 3. Aspects of a critical intervention published on *Open Democracy* (14 March 2012) under the title 'Avatar's "development" predicament' and on *Rodanthi's Artsite* (2012) informed Chapter 6. The British Academy project 'Reciprocal Orientalisms: understanding Thessaloniki's Ottoman past through multiple narrations' and its inspiration, my family, provided unexpected help and insight for the present book's films and theorization.

Abbreviations

AD	Angels and Demons
CCM	Captain Corelli's Mandolin
DA	Driving Aphrodite
DB	The Devil's Backbone
DVC	The Da Vinci Code
HFD	House of Flying Daggers
KK	King Kong
LOTR	Lord of the Rings
LWW	The Lion, The Witch and The Wardrobe
MBFGW	My Big Fat Greek Wedding
MLIR	My Life in Ruins
PC	Prince Caspian
PL	Pan's Labyrinth
ROTK	Return of the King
SSH	Silent Hill: Homecoming
WR	Whale Rider

1   Rethinking heritage
Cultural industries and global kin

Staging the debt

Shakespeare said once that the world is a stage. Each of us has a little role to play in its cosmic drama and traverses the world in search of transparent meanings. Yet, the Shakespearean stage is a Western stage with a particular brand of cosmopolitics in which humans lament their loss of purity. The Shakespearean cosmic stories convey ideas standing beyond the ephemerality of petty political polarities and host the dramaturgy of human sociality. Where place is rumoured to be 'untouched' by the corrosive passage of time, the West visits to recover and preserve its essence in polaroid and digital cameras as testimony to 'man's' common cause. The visit rebuilds this commonality even as the exotic man's achievement and uses it as tribute to a glorious age that has already been transformed en route to new domains.

This collection of essays is about the paradoxical projection of such archetypal tales of human sociality on the big screen and their undemocratic uses by various interest groups. By 'cosmology' I refer to the structured views we are acculturated to embrace as natural givens, but also the competences we acquire in the socio-cultural environment that generates these worldviews (Goldman 1964; Mannheim 1968). The ways in which human experience is socially ordered and framed invites an understanding of the dynamics of social relations and processes of social ordering (Campbell 1964; Sahlins 1996; Herzfeld 2008). The movement from the Shakespearean terrain of art to the anthropological plane of politics is highly problematic in real life-time: it allows social actors to place their contrived 'common past' in the service of suspect projects. The politics of lamentation for the demise of the original human condition is an attempt to retrieve the time of pure reciprocity before genocides and wars in the name of exclusive units. Remembrance necessitated the institution of recuperative mechanisms that withstand but serve the pressures of 'real politics' – a process adopted today by the media, which contribute to ritual remembrance.

Remembrance mechanisms are responsible for the rise of 'heritage' and 'legacy' discourses. These regulate communal narratives of cultural and intellectual property in contemporary industrial settings, where transnational, national or regional agents have to agree on the use (consumption) of tangible and intangible heritage. The functionalist dilemma is a clandestine structural question that collapses into biological discourse: as both Smith (1995: 98) and Habermas (1996: 495) warn us, the 'nature' of culture is not a metaphor but a political model of belonging. In line with strategic oscillations between ethno-racial and civic understandings of citizenship, the oscillation between 'legacy' and 'heritage' guides identity battles in the era of global digital reproduction. Legacy is a gift of a chattel or an item of personal property by will (Duhaime.org): this presents the act of transaction as intergenerational reciprocity, forming a continuation with heritage as the process of inheriting, whereby the beneficiary (heir) is legitimated as an actor in transactions by kinship affiliation. Inheriting refers to pure exchange (Mauss 1954): the 'gift' of will becomes magically inseparable from the donor that transfers it only to those with whom (s)he shares in bloodline (Shohat 1992: 109). Mobility tropes (the historical movement of customs and traditions through time) meet in one of modernity's great traumas: the colonization of new lands and the reconfiguration of human episteme through new intercultural encounters (see Fabian 1990; Argyrou 2005; Loomba 2005). In contemporary consumption milieus, such histories are resurrected every time the debt to colonized cultures acquires value as cultural capital to validate claims over 'heritage'. Notably, the same claims guide the institution of creativity through intellectual property regulation (Wall and Yar 2010: 257).

This symmetry transforms the industries of film and tourism into a slippery ground for intercultural exchange: once 'lending' one's property to film industries, their actors change the native environment by simply shooting scenes in locales, trading in relevant merchandise and setting up websites that reinvent native environment. The practice is then replicated by filmed localities for a variety of commercial and socio-political reasons. These interactions resemble Sahlins' (1985) 'structures of conjunction': though planned by knowledge economies, re-presentations may trigger quite unexpected cultural misunderstandings based on the function of heritage. Heritage used to promote inward-looking practices in disorganized ways: artefacts, crafts, landscape, legends and music were not really audiovisual manifestations of the community's past. But their display in the media and tourist trade is followed by claims over their authentic inception-production, even though some degree of staging for visitors manifests their constant reinvention (MacCannell 1973; Chhabra *et al.* 2003; Chhabra 2005). The debate is clearly not about what is authentic or whose culture is represented but who is entitled to possess and use 'the genuine article' (Harrison 2005: 3). Where media and tourism (especially 'cinematic' or 'film-induced' tourism [Beeton 2005; Tzanelli 2007b]) generate significant revenues, a variety of interest groups (the nation's political representatives, rival countries) strive for custodianship of the visited sites and artefacts. In search for global monetary and political recognition these groups adapt foreign ideas of 'native traditions' to their own interests (Steiner 1995) and proceed to 'substitute an image of the past for its reality' (Hewison 1989: 21; Hewison 1987).

Touring and travelling are examined through theory to elaborate on the novelty new (media) technologies introduce in the experience of travel itself. As such, this chapter reflects on the importance of multiple professional mobilities *and* emotional immobilities in the original enactment of these imaginary travels – first in film and then in the digital domain and on (tourist) location(s). Professional mobilities present us with a partial picture: to fully explore the contribution of media industries such as film, cyberspace and tourism in the production of public spheres, we need to examine the responses of local, national and other transnational agents. Appadurai (1990) suggests that we reconsider the binary oppositions colonial history bequeathed us: 'global' versus 'local', South versus North or metropolitan versus non-metropolitan. Instead, we should try to understand how 'flows' or 'scapes' sweep through the globe, carrying capital, images, people, information, technologies and ideas. As these flows travel through national boundaries, they form different combinations and interdependencies, mutate and split cultural imaginations into 'nation' and 'state', constructing and reconstructing public spheres. Resorting to Arjun Appadurai's scapal theory I examine the development of multiple public spheres. Within these spheres the old reference framework of the Enlightenment regulates conceptions of 'high art' and 'Europe'. At stake is the memory of a past that retrieves and restores the unity of our 'damaged' world despite the prevalence of digital simulacra.

To look at the mediatized genesis of public spheres we must consider the ways new alliances between artistic labour and craftsmanship nourish contemporary social imaginaries. Castoriadis' (1987) distinction between the institutional and the radical (social) imaginary suggests that the human resources of cultural industries rather than the industries themselves are this book's focus. New audiovisual markets operate as diagnostic domains for the causes and effects of human disenchantment, promoting a hermeneutics of recovering and restoring human pasts in search of new function. More controversially, individual studies highlight precarious collaborations and shifts between the two imaginaries in national domains. Anna Collard's (1989) identification of the ways communities tend to describe things they never experienced such as distant pasts of occupation, oppression or genocide as a form of misremembering is pertinent here: such historical regressions often mark turning points in self-perception while also allowing for the maintenance of archetypal normative divides ('us' versus 'them'). Re-enchanting identities through historical 'excavation' and audiovisual hybridization guides cinematic narratives and films that become implicated in the politics of community building. Audiovisual mergers of Eastern and Western pasts in *Battlestar Galactica* (2004–9) show that not even science fiction and horror genres escape this fate. Addressing what preserves human nature in interplanetary and interspecies journeys, the series explored real American concerns over terror, torture and risk via an array of characters symbolizing race, gender, disability 'defects' and virtues. A similar memory trope binds the book's chapters and is explored through themes of war, genocide and forced mobilities – pivotal in the production of pilgrimage and thanatotourism in contemporary cultural industries. The trope refers both to old Grand Tourist itineraries, their professionalization (travellers as colonial administrators) and implication in chains of media production (Seaton 1999: 132; Tzanelli 2008b: chapter 4).

The mobility of the tourist gaze refines some themes introduced in *The Cinematic Tourist: Explorations in Globalization, Culture and Resistance* (Tzanelli, 2007: 2–3). Building on Urry's (2002; Urry and Larsen 2011) conception of the 'tourist gaze', I explained that 'cinematic tourism' and the 'cinematic tourist' are not uniform conceptual tools but theoretical models internally differentiated by the moves and motions of travel through and after film, as well as the cinematic production of travel and tourism. I identified four types of 'cinematic tourist' and respective 'cinematic tourisms' in:

a)   representations and simulations of tourist mobilities within cinematic texts;
b)   the act and performance of film viewing and interpretation;
c)   virtual travels (web surfing) and constructions of 'tourist' online; and
d)   film viewing that transforms into embodied visits of the cinematic stage.

Here I re-evaluate this typology from the perspective of both symbol creators (directors and actors) and representatives of the public spheres to which their movies contribute in various ways. Their forms of agency unite through enactments of 'pilgrimages' that refer back to the audiovisual matrix of the movies. I discuss directors, actors and social movement groups that simulate cinematic texts as pilgrimages. Such pilgrimages combine references to the monetary capital of the films (e.g. their value as audience or tourism generators) with emotional and spiritual investment in values that exceed this capital. The link between cinema, tourism and social movements is not coincidental: all three promote blends of what Nietzsche saw in the Apollonian and Dionysian 'spirits', or intellect and emotion respectively. I return to this later.

From both a social movement and creative labour perspective, I establish a dialogue with scholars who focus on the secularization of ritual. MacCannell's (1973, 1989) explorations into tourist quests for authenticity even in the staging of custom, Cohen's (1996 [first published 1979]) exploration of visitor experiences as rituals, and Graburn's (1983) accommodation of consumerist and spiritual practices in visits to sacred sites provide a useful template for my thesis (Meethan 2002). However, my focus on the sacralization of landscapes in digital domains also suggests a departure from these theories in that it emphasizes the diversity of 'roots' and 'routes' (Clifford 1997) that heritage and ritual cinema generates. I look at the ways such rituals endorse interpretation, rather than blind reproduction of these roots and routes. 'Place' and 'time' go hand in hand in global economies of 'sign' (Lash and Urry 1994): many European countries look to landscapes as cultural heritage steeped in legend, mythology and history but the transposition of them onto the big screen triggers new processes of meaning-making (Prentice and Guerin 1998; Edensor 2004; Edensor 2005; Thompson-Carr 2012). Thus, whereas I use some European constants as starting points, the study of individual cases suggests disparity and reproduction of these tropes in equal stead and often within the same cultural space.

An adjacent theme running through the studies is the performance of 'thanatotourism' by various parties involved in this phenomenon. Thanatotourism or 'dark tourism' in and through film organizes human visits to locations 'wholly or partially motivated by the desire for actual or symbolic encounters with death' (Lennon and Foley 2000; Halgreen 2004: 149; Sahlins 1996). The consumerist desire to visit and 'devour' the exotic essence of 'other' sites generates them as tourist and media-ethnographic topographies (Fabian 1990: 70; hooks 1992). In these sites – virtual or actual, digitized or painted – old cultural meanings also die. As a form of cinematic tourism, thanatotourism may also be a simulated practice – whether this happens in the film or 'on location'. Thanatotourist rituals are constitutive of the creation of new public spheres by cultural industries, their agents and agonists (quite often, social groups in filmed locations that enter global heritage display). *Thanatos* as death is a well developed sociological and anthropological subject in which Durkheim and Weber saw an opportunity to ritualistically create society as an apparent external force, a humanocentric order and a mediator between materiality and spirituality (see Weber 1985; Bloch and Parry 1982; Árnarson 2007; Walter 2008). Dann and Seaton (2001) note that slavery as 'dissonant heritage' has left its mark on tourism across the world. Cinematic tourisms stretch this observation further: the passage from the death of colonial heritage to the 'death of the real' (digital simulations) (Baudrillard 1983: 53) sees the rise of a society that lives through simulations. But simulations of what? Scholars who view the trauma of death from genocide as a by-product of modernity (Bauman 1989) and national identity (Edmunds and Turner 2002) mostly focus on European and Western traditions. As Seaton (1996) has noted, thanatotourism dates back to Grand Tourist motivations and the European colonization of the world. Bauman's (1998) distinction between Southern 'vagabonds' and Northern 'tourists' may be rigid in terms of classification but allows us to examine such types in terms of status (e.g. destitute migrants versus rich professionals). The tendency to universalize Western 'types' in Baumanesque theorization is, however, less acknowledged. Bauman's classification is rooted in socio-linguistic traces of Europeanized antiquity: vagabonds are analytically homologous to the Hellenic *alítes* (*aláomai* = to wander), the peripatetic strangers who endeavour to satisfy their theoretical (*theoría* = God's view) needs (Vardiabasis 2002). In Europeanized Plato's *Kratylos* the vagabond roams the world looking for the Truth – a futile exercise, given that 'truth' is in the eye of the beholder. Viewed through Bauman's typology, today's privileged professionals in cultural industries are anomic *alítes*, ego-enhancing (Dann's [1977]) tourists) theoreticians who conceptualize the world via a camera-like mourning vision. Where 'love of death' informs landscape pilgrimage, it becomes a topophilic rite (also Tuan 1974). We come full circle here: not only does the rite reconstitute identity through conceptions of land as heritage, it also reiterates the privilege of Western European humanity to master nature.

Topophilic rites promoting rural innocence reach their digital apogee in the enclaves of postmodernity – global cities (Eade 2001; Sassen 2001). The city has long been considered a repository of phantasmagorical images, readily available to global *flâneurs* and tourist visitors for inspection, consumption and reproduction.

The Western city's propensity to image-making resembles Benjamin's recognition of Arcadian urbanity in Asian spectacular customs (Patke 2000). As a 'system' in its own right, 'a single field with multiple attractions to carry out in its complex and changing totality' (Amendola 1999 in Savelli 2009: 150–1), the city accommodated filmographic narratives of mobility while generating surprising connections with as unlikely industries as fashion. Transitions from Fordist industrial production to postindustrial reproduction enabled cityscapes to embrace nostalgic narratives of rural innocence and unspoiled authenticity. Nevertheless, the modern city is not a religious mausoleum fixed in time but a representational vortex inviting entrepreneurial innovation in which local culture and heritage are fused with multisensory, participatory mobilities and experiential engagement with landscapes. The city is also a nodal point in the production of new commercial empires in which other cosmologies become enmeshed. I view globalization through the cracks of cultural and economic organization in inter-firm and inter-state networking and alliances (Hardt and Negri 2000). Such malleable intra-state, transnational 'empires' sustain developmental interdependencies between global centres and peripheries and constant movement of people and ideas between them (Ritzer 2010). The decision of officials in the Andalusian town of Júzcar, Málaga, to paint its historic buildings blue in preparation for the release of *The Smurfs* (2011, dir. Raja Gosnell), an animation film in which picturesque villages hide portals to New York's phantasmagoria, is one such example (Bovingdon 2011).

The spectacle of late modernity (Debord 1995) supports the urban emphasis on a tourist-like gaze working from above and afar (Szerszynski and Urry 2006; Edensor 2004). But in urban milieus creative labour forms new alliances and solidarities across capitalism's hierarchical spine – from leading artists to common manual workers. The shift from imagining mechanical solidarity through technological reproductions to forging organic solidarities in social milieus is a mobility phenomenon in its own right (e.g. Albrow 1997). It may encompass image trade we associate with cultural industries (film, tourism) but also the formation of social movements striving to correct the ethical basis of this trade. These globalizations 'from above' and 'from below' (Kellner 2002) are in fact systemic components of European modernity. They guided the confusing institutional organization of imagined communities into nation-states that failed to recognize how their civilizing practices replicated the social rationale of 'common folk' (Herzfeld 1992; Herzfeld 2005). The suggestion that globalization eviscerates national and local scales (Virilio 1997; Sassen 2003; Herod 2012) demands an important corrective. This corrective resonates in the mobilization of *technopoesis*, 'the totality of practices and processes of "self-making" available to a community and embodied in the artefacts, techniques and technologies available to a culture' (Hand and Sandywell 2002: 208), by various social groups for the promotion of disparate causes. In the era of digital reproduction, *technopoesis* – a term signifying the human mastery of nature – can be both kinship-based and transnational in context.

Rethinking kinship through network theory

Undoubtedly the technological revolution has reinforced exchange inequalities, producing reactive responses (Castells 1989). This book examines those centring on intersecting notions of digitized heritage: the transition from 'organic', tangible and material registers to intangible print and digital ones has been among UNESCO's priorities since the beginning of the twenty-first century. The organization places more emphasis on conventional divides of tangibility/intangibility. As tourist and media industries are among the foremost income generators in glocalized milieus – especially for small nations – the monograph's focus is very timely. This is so because such industrial mobility complexes intersect with modernist versions of environmentalism that relies on science – something countering any pretensions that they preserve 'nature' intact (Szerszynski 1996). Moreover, their modernist versions of environmentalism become implicated in meaning-making processes that transnational institutions and nation-states alike aspire to universalize. The interdisciplinary literature on media production and tourist practice is informative, as it forges useful connections between literary texts, cinematic adaptations, film trivia, rumours and the customary stories cinematic fans and tourists contrive en route to their desired destination or on location (Aden 1999; Crouch 1999; Crouch and Lübbren 2003; Crouch *et al.* 2005; Reijnders 2011). The merging of informative media discourses with the immediacy of other communication styles such as gossip refers to the persistence of an oral culture in a 'secondary orality' (Ong 1987: 130). We face a cultural map very different from the one proffered by 'the Manichean rhetoric of developmentalism' (Martín-Barbero 2000: 33–4). This map accommodates discontinuities and wrong timings, secret approximations and exchanges between modernity, tradition and their postmodern nemesis, between urban and rural spaces.

Urry (2004: 208) speaks of 'places that die' to explain the shift from land (tangible forms of *heimat*) to landscape (its transformation into an ideal based on novel technologies of the eye). The shift marks a replacement of concerns with representations as such with the ways these representations are produced, conserved or modified (Mitchell 1994). Controlled by national centres, such hermeneutics valorize culture in the technological spaces of late modernity, where imagined communities circulate ideas and customs for global consumption. Inflections of supra-cosmological scripts through native knowledge affirm the survival of custom in the face of global socio-economic change, promoting a multisensory 'tourist gaze' that travels faster in media spheres. Urry uses the story of Venice as a simulacrum that has to be authentically experienced. The use of Venice as a reproducible icon is affected by the city's perception as an ecosystemic lagoon merging nature with culture. The tourist and media mobilities defining its cityscape clash and collaborate with its fixed identity as European heritage, but also as property of Italy's nation-state.

How are we to understand the interplay of the predicament of fixity and mobility in this context? Life in the city certainly framed in European cosmological terms the mastery of nature and human nature (Argyrou 2005: 7). However, the

Aristotelian qualities of the frame appear to guide civility norms outside the European space, in Eastern city-states. Ironically, even Aristotle's Hellenic Europeanness is discussed today as a racialized simulacrum in academia (Bernal 1991) – a question I revisit in Chapters 3 and 5. The European hegemonization of the world was achieved in the universalization of the European sociosphere through the generation of global mobility chains. As Dann and Parrinello (2009) have argued, the prevalence of 'tourism' as a form of social action originates in European modernity. The European image of the 'nation-family' shows the importance of natural symbolism in cultural belonging. Family memories partook in the democratization of the image though tourist rituals (Sontag 1990), but authoritarian regimes subjected to populist abuse the nation-family's image after the recognition of paid holidays (1939) as a universal right, just as Europe was sliding into totalitarian self-destruction (Dann and Parrinello 2009: 28; Spode 2009: 70). This old principle of kinship informs contemporary professional mobilities mediated through technology, guiding practices of strategic alliance in industrial environments.

Again, the origin of travel in the pedagogical and administrative milieus of the colonial era is a good starting point. Cohen's (1996) identification of 'diversionary' tourist interest in advertising that promotes 'authentic reproductions' suggests that just as our theoretical academic mobilities, such professional mobilities have always been based on simulations. The claim that guidebooks and brochures depicting the developing world confirm 'what Westerners have historically imagined the other to be like' (Silver 1993: 303) becomes banal in today's digital environments (Hand 2012: 35). A more pertinent question concerns the conditions of marketing and its impact on contemporary mindsets, as well as the role new media play in them as 'technology'. As technology is a process of 'social and cultural instantiations of ideational innovation' (Fischer *et al.* 2008: 521; Fischer 2004), it is part and parcel of our ongoing mastering of natural resources as well as our symbolizations of it. Following the invention of the press, digitizations of image and sound enabled large-scale reconstructions of transnational and global communities of interest, assent and emotion but also the emergence of new forms of leadership that are not limited to charismatic nation-state personalities (Zeitlyn 2001). Late modern *technopoesis* is articulated in the interstices of national and cosmopolitan identities through distant communications and in disembodied forms that revise leadership paradigms. This advocates an analysis of human networks and connections in the new technological environments (e.g. Thrift 2007), but also their continuities with older frames and modes of belonging (Herzfeld 2007). Once more, we draw on the nature of social organization as nature.

Digital *technopoesis* bestows upon professionals a new sort of aura, transforming them in Rojek's terms (2001:121) into 'staged celebrities' through calculated presentational strategies and self-projection that bestows 'pop monumentality' upon them. It has been suggested that such professionals should be viewed as members of the new transnational 'epistemic communities', groups or networks of experts with shared beliefs or ideas about specific issues that might occasionally influence or be drawn into national and regional policy-making (Haas 1992). But there have also been suggestions that we look to the 'axiom of amity' (Fortes 1969) to examine the social production of leadership, even in digital milieus: operating like symbolic families, digital and digitized alliances acquire 'patriarchs' or 'matriarchs' that assert their status through symbolic exchanges. Although such exchanges can become monetary, the primary value in the digital field is that of 'pure' reciprocity: I give and you give back, and our respective debt is organized in a concise time frame (de Certeau 1985: 193; Zeitlyn 2003: 8). Honourable transactions secure long-lasting friendships in the interest of all parties. In this schema *technopoesis* emerges as auxiliary to symbolic capital accumulation for the leader and the group as a whole. We see an overlap of fixity and mobility in these 'mediapoles', which also regulates the 'tourist technological body' (Parrinello 2001). Both a 'natural artefact' and a cultural prosthesis, the technological body of Baumanesque media tourists asserts its social nature when it becomes subjected to the rules of reciprocity.

In this process of reputation-building a great deal of intra-group and cross-group 'borrowings' – legally known as 'thefts' and 'copyright infringements' – are likely to take place. The 'Dialectic of Enlightenment' (Adorno and Horkheimer 1991) casts this old custom (e.g. see Campbell 1964: 38 on the defence of the nuclear household interests and Herzfeld 1985: 52 on the honourable logic of animal theft in small communities) into a discourse of artistic authenticity. Such practices die hard in contemporary industrial environments: media corporations and lead artists 'steal' from each other all the time, as the following case studies attest. *Solomon Kane* (2009, dir. Michael Bassett and based on Robert E. Howard's pulp magazine character Solomon Kane [1928]) is one example of such digital borrowings. Set in sixteenth-century England, the film follows Kane's religious battle with the Devil's reaper across a country ravaged by diabolical human Raiders. The film, produced by a consortium of French, Czech and British companies and mostly filmed in the Czech Republic, figures a combination of Jackson's and Del Toro's digital innovations that conveyed the theological basis of previously published literature and artwork. A closer look at the cast reveals however that the makers of the film also used actors with established performative repertories (e.g. Max von Sydow, as usual, plays the fearful ruler whereas Pete Postlethwaite and Alice Kringe as devout Protestants practically reproduce their roles in *Silent Hill: Homecoming* [2006]). The mobility of artists and technological crafters (e.g. visual effects) across cinematic markets as well as synergies with different (or even rival) groups can also result in artistic reproductions.

Idioms of 'connection', 'networks' and 'flows' have become powerful metaphors in multiple socio-cultural contexts both in quotidian and academic life (Strathern 1996). Albertsen and Diken, who endorse such models, recognize that 'works cannot exist … without artists, their biographies and struggles of interest' (2003:8) but proceed to examine artwork as existing independently from human communication. Throughout this chapter I refer to 'technology' as a collection of reproducible knowledge appealing to reason (Aristotelian *logos*) to articulate (*articulare* = connect, bend, join) *techne*. In European philosophy *techne* defines the birth of knowledge with the help of *maieftiki* (childbirth). Yet, this Socratian metaphor for dialectical self-analysis clearly presents conscious self-understanding as 'nature'. Notably, in traditional ethnic contexts *techne* is synonymous with 'craft' acquired through apprenticeship, a form of tacit knowledge that presents artisanship as naturalized domesticity. Such domestic reproductions became reinvented and appropriated in professional contexts of technological artisanship. Hollywood's recent technological advances have further changed the economic conditions of cinematic production 'which can now be artisanal as well as capitalist' (Mulvey 2006: 343). At the same time, the value of social networks that guides Putnam's theory (1993) is transformed via new media routes, in so far as new digital communities are not always bound by regional or national belonging (Gauntlett 2011: 138).

Benjamin (1973: 91; Laing 1978: 55–68) claimed that the transformative potential of art is not illuminated solely through a study of changes in artistic mentality but by developing a critical-reflexive stance towards the specific techniques and styles we employ to do such work. McLuhan's (1964) argument that we may find the message in the medium complements this thesis. Film-making necessitates fusions of art (sustained by iconic creativity and story-telling akin to literature and history writing [White 1973]), and craft (sustained by technological manipulation of image and sound), allowing for critical montage of tradition in a semi-ethnographic style (Lange 2007; Kien 2008). Intimate engagement with the cinematic background allows directors to speak from the heart before they use their head, processing encounters with the world into poetic narratives (Peirce 1998). Blends of art with craft partake in poetic productions of identity, but the interpretative production of meaning depends on the cultural agents (Archer 1995). Such interpretation may, for example, allow cultural agents to operate outside traditional conceptions of community but may also become auxiliary to central power by enabling the allegorical breakdown of highbrow-elite and lowbrow-folk divides. Because of its power to reduce complex ideas to seamless images, film-making can also reproduce structures of community-building. Cinema valorizes national culture, enabling its integration in the international arena – an image-making practice modern societies share with older communities (Campbell 1964: 211–2). 'Artwork' becomes a social domain in which labour and craft can entertain *legitimation* they lack in everyday understandings of artisanship (Herzfeld 2004: 5), achieving global recognition as exhibits that are mobile, modern and reproducible without losing their auratic status (Mannheim 2003; Mannheim 1968: 292–309; de la Fuente 2007: 413). Differentiations and definitions of cinematic *techne* as 'creative' or 'knowledge' labour (Miége 1987 and 1989) cannot account for the ways artistic/aesthetic and professional expressions of identity and autonomy function in creative industries, even at institutional level (Golding and Murdock 2000; Hesmondhalgh 2007).

I view the work of art in the era of digital reproduction as the outcome of deliberative actions of various human groups (Melucci 1995; Tsagarousianou *et al.* 1998; Delanty 2000) and propagate the study of the worldviews they uphold rather than focusing on inanimate things or networks *per se* (e.g. see Hennion and Latour 1993). The *act* of 'networking' on the other hand foregrounds my study of human-digital networks. The transition from national communities and terrestrially organized orders to digital networks and transnational communities is not straightforward. The very idea of a community defined by similar 'interpretive' interests is hazy when the actors are not immediately identified (Schrøder 1994). In its labyrinthine network of websites the Internet allows individuals and various communities of interest (from collegial allies in creative industries to nation-states) to reinstate or reorganize terrestrial social orders, while also 'educating' and recruiting others in their cause (Horst 2009; Miller 2009). Such networked cultures enable the construction of collective and individual public 'faces' that can expand and join more sub-networks (Wellman *et al.* 2003; Boyd and Ellison 2007). Digitization allows cyberspace to project globally national heritage in intangible forms (as in ideas and designs inspired by the past) and formats (as in photography and videos of national landscapes) (Strathern 2004). Miller (1987) refers to the 'humility of objects' to describe the ability of material things to 'frame' (as in Goffman 1975) habitus in unnoticeable, yet powerful ways. Digital framings of such ideoscapes include the articulation of distinctive aesthetic dispositions that appeal to localities, individuals and even states and transnational communities (Geertz 1973, 1980).

Smith (2008), who recognizes in Geertz's work some formalist principles and a cosmology befit for a movie (the 'narcissistic male ego' [Geertz 1973: 419]), is a useful starting point. All great works of art refer to big questions such as love, hate, death or destiny: 'the more significant and long-lasting the theme, the better the guarantee of the life of the work' (Tomashevsky 1965: 65 in Smith 2008: 174). DeNora's music-sociology which sees 'art' and the 'social' as co-produced corresponds to the habit of anthropological authority to seperate out representations and the represented (Clifford 1983; Smith 2008: 172). Argyrou's (2005: 91–2) invocation of Heideggerian metaphysics as part of the history of European thought generates vital connections between idioms of tourism and the culture of moving images: a 'world picture' is in effect the world conceived and grasped as a picture. Such pictures can become generalized and promoted as *alítheia*, a form of truth that negates oblivion (*a* = non + *léthe* = forgetting). Yet as I explain below, artwork can indeed manipulate remembrance of the 'truth' in dissimulating ways.

Archplots: Oriental craft, European art and the category of 'human'

Leaps to the interpretive universe of art are also consistent with the social context in which symbolic creativity takes place (Goldman 1964; Mannheim 1968): hence, a discussion of the film's content should connect its underlying archetypal story to the social values its creators and actors profess to uphold in that particular conjunction of circumstances; and by turn, to link these values to grander normative themes underlying the foundations of Western and Eastern civilizations.

Cosmologies are projected on the big screen as 'archplots', the movie's central scenario that sustains unity of action within the story. My interdisciplinary project aims to link cinematic 'archplots' (McKee 1999: 3–4, 41–2) to anthropological studies of 'cosmology'. The stories we choose to narrate are unique hybrids of experience and knowledge rooted in collective pasts, but also interpretive vehicles of change (Herzfeld 2008; Alexander 2006). Wearing my sociological hat I will argue that this book's movies stand at such a crossroads between interpretive systems, structures and human agency (Archer 1995). My aim is to tease out of these systemic, structural and agential forces something more than a uniform Marxist critique of media capitalism: rather than merely lagging on the institutional surface of such enterprise (which I do not intend to ignore) I want to understand why both its infrastructural and superstructural components seem to refer back to familiar ideas of human progress and creative interpretation that Enlightenment traditions bestowed upon the 'postmodernist' or 'liquid modernist' condition (Bauman 2000b).

The '-ism' suffix is important: rather than speaking of epochal claims as such (Weber, 1978a: 11, 1978b: 18–25), I tie these to the artistic sentiment they produce – paramount for a study of 'archplots' and 'cosmologies' alike. Cultural theory takes this leap for granted (Dyer 2006) whereas social and political theory notes its practical uselessness, perpetuating the war with it (Giddens 1984; Cohen 1989). In such disjunctions theory subjugates artistic sentiment to economic imperatives the same way certain branches in social movement analysis flag instrumental over value-oriented reason and emotion (Bakhtin 1984: 7). Decades ago the renowned post-Weberian scholar Campbell (2005) identified in the modern consumerist spirit a 'romantic ethic' scholars of nationalism had already tied to tropes of identity, authenticity and uniqueness (Guibernau and Hutchinson 2004). Such field leaps are easily accommodated in mobilities literature (Hannam *et al.* 2006: 3, 14) but are acknowledged in passing by globalization theorists who examine the genetic relationship between media systems and agents in relation to consumerist imperatives (Castells 1997, 2000). Other scholars posited this disjunction in terms akin to those produced by 'artistic sentiment': thus Derrida's logocentrism and its feminist nuances ('phallologocentrism') produce a neo-romantic discourse even in controversies over the digital will to power (Derrida 1976: 107–8; Sandywell 2011: 461–2). This activist discourse proclaims the 'end of history' in conjunction with a decline in the ethics of experience – whether these manifest as the dominance of writing over speech or are mediated over face-to-face contact (Derrida 1997). At the same time however, the reliance on Marxist materiality stretches or contracts our temporal horizons to such an extent that we remain dependent on evolutionary biology for any ethical corrections to reality.

The dependence of social theory on this cosmological-biological model makes a peculiar reappearance in artistic archplots that counterpoise the good beginnings of the history of nature (as divine work) to its evil endings (as man's/woman's work). Evil is crafty but good is noble and aesthetically beautiful. This archplot is about permutations and variables within human nature, which is marred by technological warfare and turned into a terrorizing demon. It is not coincidental that all the archplots of this book unite behind the image of an evil Oriental influence – or that they tie this to realist European and transatlantic political events. The story of Enlightenment, art, culture and modernity at large is plagued by the guilt of sin against Edenic perfection (Argyrou 2005: 144–57). Craft promotes sensory dissimulation from the original condition, demoting the Edenic couple to human copies that proliferate. Ethnic and racial studies embrace this archetypal tale in an attempt to build 'global analyses' of the destruction of human recognition as if the priority is the 'experience' of racism (Dikötter 2008; Law 2010; Tzanelli 2011a), when in fact the end is to provide a picture of reality. Even the call to embrace a new 'critical mobility paradigm' seems to follow this pattern in as much as it seeks to reinstate the unity of humans with nature and the more general environment. What reinstates the plight of 'sin' is the knowledge that what is discussed is more a global perspective that presents the world as a picture – and us at its core, travellers on a mission to learn more *about it but never from within* (Ingold 2000: 218–9). The roaming traveller of (post)modernity is a rootless demon stubbornly rejecting what all rooted humans recognize in 'home', allegedly *plagued* by the incurable nostalgia only war and economic rupture can cause in the eyes of a 'civilized humanity' (Lowenthal 1985; Gregory 1998; Butler 2006). We could recall how Derrida's (2002) suggestion that UNESCO break away from its Hellenic Kantianism recycles an essentially Western call to responsibilization and indebtedness towards the archive of alternative world-views. Sadly, even radical Derridian cosmopolitics views vagabond 'others' from a tourist stance but fails to notice its ocular angle.

Although from a methodological point of view cinematic detachment allows the world to be less of a context and more in context, the very medium promotes de-mediation as both a valorizing and re-enchanting process (Ingold 2000; Strain 2003). Man's *syn*-opticism is wilfully translated into God's *pan*-opticism through cinematic de-mediation, while also allowing in some cases audiences to read form as content (Strain 2003: chapter 1; Argyrou 2005: 98). Methodologically, the concept of form, which is 'curiously and contrary to Bourdieu's basic episte-mological position ... imported ... from artistic discourse or other disciplines' (Albertsen and Diken 2003: 13) is taken here to work in unison with the cultural content of the product but not in overlapping ways. The basic premise of the present studies is that artwork's hidden structures are both reinstated and revised by individual artists in creative and marketable ways but local idioms may haunt the enterprise, retaliating for poetic slights that are offensive in specific cultural contexts. Artwork is a cultural process and a product, and like culture, it should be treated as a context in which 'behaviours, institutions or processes ... can be intelligibly – that is thickly – described' (Geertz 1973: 14). One such example is the phenomenological make up of dark forces in the *Lord of the Rings* (*LOTR*) trilogy, which is part of Chapter 3's *problématique*. The trilogy informed a stream of Orientalist representations, among which we may account King Leonidas' (Gerard Butler) battle against Persian 'god-King' Xerxes (Rodrigo Santoro) and his equally monstrous army in *300* (2007, dir. Zack Snyder and based on Frank Miller's 1998 comic series). The demonic appearance of Persians in the film provoked reactions in Iran leading to its banning within the country. The Iranian Academy of Arts submitted a formal complaint to UNESCO against what was perceived as an 'attack' on the historical identity of Iran, with Persians represented like freaks: the black 'terrorists of today' (*Payvdad* News, 16 March 2007). Here the hermeneutics of American artists and of Iranian institutions may be focusing on the same artwork's principal narrative but their combined 'thick description' also uncovers the follies of Western specificity. As much as they strive to talk about *the human*, cultural industries end up discussing the ethical vicissitudes of Western human nature that was globalized over the last few centuries.

The emergence of the new discourse of 'political economy' in the world religion's stead certainly attested the hegemonization of the known world by the West (Nederveen Pieterse 2005: 386). At the same time, however, it did not eliminate the Christian spirit but populated instead the new economies of sign and space with its derivative moral grammars (Weber 1985; Mignolo 2002). These grammars consolidated the 'denial of coevalness' (Fabian 1983: 39), the temporal coexistence of different cultures and world views: where in Renaissance thought the infidels were neither primitive nor distant in time but merely spatially divided from Western European civilization, Enlightenment translated space into time and embraced both in terms of wisdom (Mignolo 2002: 933). The new knowledge economies Lash and Urry (1994) discuss are offspring of these biographies of coevalness: their post-Hegelian ethos strives to preserve pre-modern enchantments in digital domains, on the big screen and in discourses of a much-awaited 'postmodernity'. These days cinema becomes cosmologically implicated in a globalized 'activist cause' by lending its simulatory medium (digital technology) and its performative art to activism in which even its makers feel compelled to participate.

Of course, we should not disregard the cultural basis of such 'activist causes'. To adapt Argyrou's commentary (2005: 3), the economy of memory of such causes (especially those led by Western upper-class artists) reflects 'the convenient disregard of history and culture in understanding the naïveté of activist conviction'. I would add that overemphasizing such histories in (post)modern milieus might also support some convenient solitary amnesias or promote the substitution of pervasive guilt with activist ritual that regresses to even older pasts or reinvents communal presents (Tzanelli 2007a). Alternatively, where century-old traditions are threatened by uncertain revisionisms even the world of arts and letters wages war against film-making. Roland Emmerich's Anonymous (2011), which suggests Shakespeare was a fraud and Edward de Vere, the seventeenth Earl of Oxford, the true author of his plays, is such a case. The critiques ranged from historical and architectural 'inaccuracies' to lies, exploding to a discourse on the corrosion of English literary heritage, with many literati proffering their opinion on the limits of the director's 'poetic licence' (Shapiro, 4 November 2011). The furore culminated in Stratford-upon-Avon, Warwickshire, where Shakespeare's name was being removed from signs in a campaign against a new film. Dr Paul Edmondson, head of knowledge and research at the Shakespeare Birthplace Trust, nicely encapsulated this in his statement: 'Shakespeare is at the core of England's cultural and historical DNA and he is certainly our most famous export' (BBC Coventry and Warwickshire, 25 October 2011). Here legacy and heritage ought to form a plausible continuity for the tourist, as for insiders they define the global identity of the place. Clashes centring on such intersections of tangible (landscape) and intangible (literature) heritage (Yudhisthir 2004) involve the mobilization of intellectual debts (who did what first) and can easily reproduce discourses of blood delineations.

The role of emotions in the production of archplots and their reproduction as activist cosmologies presents human rebellion against divine orders as a moment of insanity. This is a problem that reappears in some academic work that considers 'emotion' (Ahmed 2004) – rather than unprocessed 'affect' (Thrift 2007) or feelings (Karatzogianni 2011) – as the polar opposite of reason, rationality and positive action. A peculiar regression takes place today in postmodern milieus, whereby emotion is consigned to pre-modern forms of religious organization (the religion-state) and reason rules modern civility (the nation-state and the economic pursuits of the transnational communities of my study). My argument is that the two modes of 'knowing' constitute the double preconditions of creating and disseminating (products, ideas, images and meanings), as well as symbolizing such creations. Consequently, I view 'mobility' as an epistemic concept, not an ontological one, which adheres to post-Kantian understandings of human faculties (Chukwudi Ezze 1997 in Mignolo 2002: 936, 952; Burnham 2005). Mobility theory speaks of 'affordances' to examine the range of choices available to humans within their particular world but examines subjective experience of the environment as its inextricable part, explaining very little about its situated meanings (see Michael 1996: 149 in Urry 2007: 51). Emotional triggers and responses are part of this epistemological question and they can provide useful insight into the value and uses of audiovisual art by various actors in the activist field.

Emotions such as patriotic love (Chapters 2 and 4), resentment and *ressentiment* (Chapters 3, 5 and 6), joy (Chapter 4), fear (Chapter 5) or guilt (Chapter 6) do not comprise the focus of this monograph, but are useful signposts to various mobilities inspired within and from films, their tourist legacies or activist motivations. Again, film theories provide connections between spectatorship, reception and terrestrial action through the phenomenology of 'experiential' engagement (McGregor 2000: 28). 'Experience' is, like all human contact with the world, a mediated experience. Virtual worlds should not be located solely 'in some enclosed cyberspace: they exist in human culture, knowledge, and values as well' (Kellogg *et al.* 1991: 430; Tzanelli 2007a: chapter 1). Acting on cinematic narratives in politically organized ways corresponds to the ways movie-watching induces subjective engagement that involves emotion and reason (Sobchack 1992). As the unfairly vilified Russian formalists remind us, 'the emotions a work of art excite are its chief means of holding attention … and call forth, as it were, the personal interest of the reader [and viewer] in the development of the theme' (Tomashevsky 1965: 66). The generation of emotions from unprocessed feelings reflects Charles Peirce's 'thirdness' (1998), a conscious cognitive engagement with unattainable experience that can support political engagement but usually exceeds narrow political partisanship. I therefore read reactions to film-making as a by-product of 'refined [aesthetic] sensibility', to paraphrase Smith (2008: 175), rather than 'pure experience'.

'Plotting' the book

The book examines five core representations of enchanted spaces through global cinematic successes: the first considers the locus of Western European civilization through post-Enlightenment encounters with Antipodean others (New Zealand); the second relocates primal Christian demons in the heart of Catholic Christianity (Italy); the third moves to Europe's and the West's professed 'cradle' (Greece); the fourth regresses to Europe's colonial exteriority (China); and the fifth considers the spatio-temporal coordinates of Europe's ethno-racial foundations (Brazil). The creative industries involved in such cinematic re-enchantments thrived on synergies that I examine with some degree of detail in individual chapters. However, the binding theme of these studies is the ways European and Western 'others' articulate responses in the digital fissures of postmodernity, revamping or re-inventing notions of 'heritage' and 'legacy'. Another focal point is the struggle of some leading symbol creators in these cultural industries to induce, endorse or respond to such articulations, which may be culturally specific but retain their global(ized) resonance (on 'glocalization' see Robertson 1992). The multiple agents that overdetermined the production and dominant interpretations of the films are presented with caution, as Hollywood and its satellites exercise their own control over cinematic production (Altman 1999: 102–5). The book's 'case studies' outline how various creative agents and their reactive nemeses (the Church, the state, the old national communities) counter-pose or subsume postmodernization into ideas of 'human imperfection', denying relocations of progress outside the European birthplace of epistemology. Notably, the mobility paradigm from which some of my academic interlocutors speak might elevate capitalist progress to a remedy for the imperfections of non-European people. The Western mobile human reproduces and trades in myths, whereas his/her uncivilized relatives perform them in instinctive ways. Often, postmodernization is reduced to cosmetic practices, bypassing equality, fairness and justice altogether (Nederveen Pieterse 2006a). But as the trope of injustice is haunted by the self-imposed Western/European debt to indigenous primordialities (Argyrou 2005) we must use it as stepping-stone to an analysis of the contexts in which the 'drama' takes place.

Chapter 2 examines how culturally situated worldviews survive in the technological spaces of late modernity in the context of the *LOTR* and *The Hobbit*, two cinematic enterprises that established New Zealand as an international tourist destination. It traces the narrative threads of the literary and cinematic plots in European cosmological themes (suffering, the battle between good and evil), arguing that the production process enabled imaginative cinematic travel by the makers of the films that drew upon culturally situated memories connected to New Zealand's colonial past. At the same time, however, this new media industry encouraged the production of new transnational social formations. This is explored in three different forms: the first involves the loose but steady communication of relevant literary, cinematic (audiovisual) and digital (Internet) texts that transformed the actual stage of the enterprise (New Zealand); the second involves the formation of new alliances and communities of interest; the third involves the actual structures of the *LOTR* industry – more particularly, a controversy over employment rights induced by an Australian union which sparked strikes and protests against the relocation of *The Hobbit* shootings outside New Zealand (2010). The chapter explores how the ensued scapal clashes in fact became enmeshed into an audiovisual matrix that invited a sort of pilgrimage to New Zealand's cinematic sites. The pilgrimage confirmed New Zealand's dual cultural and political belonging in a postcolonial world – as member of a national polity comprised of conflicting groups, and a global community of competing institutions (states) but related cosmologies (rooted in colonization).

Chapter 3 begins by examining how the *Da Vinci Code* (*DVC*), a novel by Dan Brown, and its cinematic adaptation (2006) came to operate as a 'node' for European capitalist networks of corporeal and virtual travel. Re-examining the convergence as well as the divergence of patterns and practices of early travel and contemporary tourism, I discuss the centrality of technologies of 'gazing' upon other cultures and collecting cultural signs to the global networks of contemporary (digitized or corporeal) travel. The film and the novel assist in the interpellation of a new type of traveller, what is termed here a 'neo-pilgrim'. The mobilization of neo-pilgrimage by global tourist networks also indicates a kind of staged cosmopolitanism originating in conceptions of the cosmopolitan as the epistemological subject of Enlightenment. Contrariwise, the cosmopolitanism of the *DVC* and its sequel, *Angels and Demons* (*AD*, 2008) democratize the consumption of what used to be regarded as 'high culture', reserved exclusively for the old, aristocratic elites of Europe. The *DVC* node breaks away from established codes of authorship in cultural production while debating the emergence of a new service class of professional travellers whose fleeting visits to museums, galleries, luxury hotels and boulevards operate as both unacknowledged touring of commoditized European heritage and an aspect of personal self-betterment and self-education. The chapter explores the ways the audiovisual and digital matrix of the genre challenged conservative visions of heritage based on the Christian tradition and European civilization via ecofeminist and anti-racist discourses. The ideoscapal conflicts singled out for exploration (heritage sanctity sustaining cultural hegemonies) appear in other similar fabulist scripts that promote cinematic pilgrimage to ancient-mythical sites (*Silent Hill*, *SSH*, 2006). The recurring trope of 'theft' of public image that permeates such narratives suggests connections between the archetypal tale of Edenic fall and the futures of image production and mobility in cinematic tourism planning.

Chapter 4 uses as a starting point *My Life in Ruins* or *Driving Aphrodite* (*MLIR/DA*, 2009), a film starring Canadian-Greek Nia Vardalos as Georgia, a tourist guide in Athens who is immersed in Hellenic classicist education and regards Greek popular culture and foreign tourist habits with contempt. The film articulates a clash between imported (Western) understandings of European civility, education and heritage with the modern Greek ethos for the 'good life', thus highlighting the gap between popular (natural) and elite (manipulated) tourist habits. Being created and financed by artists with Greek connections raises questions concerning the dynamics of a transnational imaginary that is neither 'purely Greek', nor foreign, but dialogically constructed in meeting points for its various agents. This aspect of the chapter explores the dynamics of a transnationally crafted Greek 'cultural intimacy' – more precisely, the public staging of non-existing intimate aspects of 'Greekness'. There are some unmistakable political extensions to this fabulist script: some scenes were shot at the Acropolis with the support of the Greek Film Institute and the Greek government, making this film the first to utilize a renowned world heritage site as a stage. The chapter follows the logic of this choice as a strategy of urban tourist regeneration but also as an ambivalent ideological statement on the uses of heritage sites by media industries. In tandem, it asks some difficult questions regarding the prioritization of Greek metropolitan tourist and media growth, tapping thus into wider issues regarding regional, national *and* global heritage hierarchies. As the film reproduces blended forms of pilgrimage in a classical-come-modern Greece, it reconsiders transformations of a tourist gaze steeped in European history into a plural gaze directed on forms of Mediterranean *habitus* that potential cinematic tourist hosts vie to domesticate for commercial purposes.

Chapter 5 debates the ways two famous Chinese artists, Yimou Zhang and Ai Weiwei, enact imaginative forms of travel in their artwork in highly specific styles, supporting forms of pilgrimage to sites and signs associated with Chinese culture and their personal memories. This pilgrimage combines visions of high art with popular and folkish culture, producing 'technological craft' in globally marketable forms. The urban profile of both artists endorses a visual political agenda that translates fixed forms of national authenticity into globally intelligible ideas. The chapter highlights how key artistic aspects of the *Beijing 2008* Olympics were partly defined by their contributions and how these convey their socio-political and cultural outlook as artists. Focusing on some key moments in their careers, the study follows the rationale informing the protests against human rights violations both in the *Beijing 2008* context and following Ai Weiwei's imprisonment by the Chinese state in 2011. Against this background the chapter highlights a second background that supports China's cosmopolitan openness through tourist and media growth but also the cosmopolitanization of its artistic communities that produce Chinese versions of 'world travel'.

Chapter 6 considers how James Cameron's *Avatar* (2009) operates at multiple interpretative levels: on the surface, it examines the vicissitudes of First World development through a visual-discursive simulation of anthropological records on indigenous encounters with the 'civilized world' (the film's story). Its mediation of such themes through reflections on human ontology (the disembodied emancipation of its central hero) suggests also an ambivalent take on the role of technology in human progress (as a force that allows for either the preservation or destruction of Arcadian universes such as that of the film's fictional land of Pandora). The film revisits themes present across Cameron's career, including the role of technology in human progress and narrativity. *Avatar* invited criticism for its developmental subtext, with some analysts going as far as to accuse its makers of racism. The chapter takes a closer look at the cinematic narrative itself in relation to its audiovisual and digital offshoot (the official website and its overall digital popular culture) but also the native political background around which the film was produced. The digitization of Pandora's landscape produced an alternative journey to a simulated world, an Arcadia for virtual tourists. But as the makers of *Avatar* became involved in Brazilian developmental projects (Brazil is cast as the cinematic backdrop of Pandora, the Arcadian world of *Avatar*), the cinematic narrative allegorized some political dilemmas involving indigenous relationship with the land and the communication of different worldviews. Against this political background, the chapter places another that emphasizes the uses of *Avatar*'s simulated landscapes as tourist capital in China. These scapal meetings (Brazilian social protests against developmental projects 'harmful' for communities, Chinese regional tourist planning, the *Avatar* industry's economic growth and its makers' mobility narratives as world travellers), however dissimilar and disconnected, refer back to a development metanarrative (archplot) both emphasizing and vilifying 'mobility'.

Methods from epistemology

Naturally, my primary material involves Internet sites that market the films and relevant consumption, including tourism. To carry out such interdisciplinary work I mobilized existing research methodologies from sociology's cognate disciplines (paradoxically, this compels me to posit method and epistemology both as heuristic tools and objects of analysis). Although computer-mediated communication alters considerations relating to space and time, we can still use small-scale ethnographic modalities to sample more diverse or dispersed and larger samples (Mann and Stewart 2000: 42–7; Fischer *et al.* 2008: 527). Tracking down relevant material involved a snowballing-like technique: initially, I visited the Internet Movie Database (IMDB), a major online database for information on films, crew, Hollywood agents involved, and a repository of movie critiques as well as international viewers' comments. Wikipedia entries on individual movies also helped me track down relevant material, including film reviews and other websites. Although such web pages are constantly altered or occasionally unreliable in terms of authorship, they allow consistent interpretation and rearrangement of materials through time because the movies and their industry act as constants. After my epistemological excursus in the previous sections it would be naïve – and dangerous – to disregard how semantic content rather than location (keywords as classifiers) necessitates human interpretation: though not hostile to the new technologies, most relevant methods software presents limitations when it comes to meaning inference or use of digital knowledge

(Fensel *et al.* 2002). Inversely, audience reception theories also have their limitations, as they adhere to the rationale of 'willing subordination' to media materials or 'strategic passivity' (Williamson 2006; Barker and Mathjis 2007) – a trend that reappears in the 'tourist gazing' literature for similar reasons (MacCannel 2001; Daye 2005). My mobilization of kinship rationales to understand digitally mediated ordering of human relationships attests to the usefulness of old social frameworks in new research without glorifying them as methodological or epistemic tools (Zeitlyn 2003; Read 2006).

Official and unofficial review material sketched a general idea about the marketing of the films and their political and commercial impact. I translated such observations into relevant keywords that I used to track down holiday and other sites that mobilized the narrative content of the story to generate global communities of interest. In turn, these sites defined my analytical and interpretive frame, suggesting that I do not disconnect online mediations of cosmopolitan knowledge from conventional readings of the history of cosmopolitanism; and by turn, that relevant technological changes have consequences not only for the images we produce but also 'for the *activities* of producing, storing, displaying and distributing them, as well as the conventions that regulate these activities' (Hand 2012: 97). Hence, as a subject technologically mobile and globally 'connected', I cannot completely excise myself from the context I study but can, at least, examine and critique its structures 'from within'.

Cinematic 'text' and socio-political 'context' thus coexist in my analysis, actualizing the European-Oriental nodes of contemporary audiovisual markets. To conceptualize the social as a pre-given set of 'variables' is to render it 'mysterious' and unexplainable, when in fact all 'social process' refers to making, valuing and consuming art, the things 'people do together' (Becker *et al.*, 2006: 3). Musical mediation in art highlights the synergy between score-makers, musicians, recorders, classical instruments and their digital renditions (Hennion and Latour 1993). But considering how film soundtracks are, by their maker's admission, visualizations of cinematic narrative, their analysis can be placed in the social extensions of the European-Oriental nodes of art. Among the chosen films I have included some major cinematic adaptations of novels and computer games. Building on conceptions of social simulation, Baudrillard (1997) and Bourdieu (1984: 103) consider literary works as markers of class that both legitimize and manipulate mobilities of taste (*status*): democratized consumptions of their 'essence' might lead to social rearrangements but always secure the structural preservation of hierarchy. Cinematic fluidity has been significant in the production or reproduction of precisely those (old and new) communities I study in this book. We cannot actualize such communities in home-readings of novels (see Dudley 1992; Egan and Barker 2006; Barker 2009: 390). In tandem, participatory openness has some limitations: the Internet is still a positional good as only a portion of the global population owns or has access to a computer and connection (Lax 2004: 226). However, audiovisual and digital renditions of literature can challenge such social structures, replacing old conceptions of status-as-class with new ones (e.g. virtual or cinematic mobilities).

Of course, film is a highly malleable and polyphonic medium when it comes to interpretation. When it comes to the generation of meaning, the same principles apply to digital and natural environments, with human interpreters providing many alternative viewpoints. Whether we consider Ingold's (1993) suggestion that the world is an unfinished project or Mitchell's (1994) argument that landscapes partake in constructions of social meanings, we end up with a plural thesis. Mediascapes construe a second-order vision in the director's eye and a third-order one in audiences, producing a mobility system in which various consumers and producers become involved (this, incidentally, is the demonized mobility of romantic social theory). Cosgrove and Jackson (1987) focus on European ways of seeing; steeped in methodologies of 'uncovering' hidden meanings, European hermeneutics inform the work of some of the directors I discuss. Cinematic landscapes and interconnected websites appear in this methodology both as audio-visual objects and as machines of meaning-making, extending the principles of network theory so as to embrace both actors and their products (see Aitken and Dixon 2006; Edensor 2005; Beeton 2005; Ren 2011). My examination of some YouTube material or official movie site video clips posted online by movie-makers is viewed as an attempt to induce various affects that organize emotional responses under certain circumstances. As opposed to that I examine image stills from movies for their 'retrieving effect' and their subsequent implication to emotional organization of mobile communities (of viewers, activists, travellers and artists) (Elliot and Urry 2010: 33).

The dynamic nature of meaning production in articulations of political and cultural, individual and collective citizenships makes the assessment of such work difficult, as no community remains fixed in (cyber-)ethnographic time (Bauman 2000b; Urry 2000, 2003; Gray 2003; Haldrup and Larsen 2010; Urry and Larsen 2011: 22–3). 'Structuralist hermeneutics' (Alexander and Smith 2001) can still find plausible uses in methodologies of the Semantic Web, allowing the analysis of modes of experience, feeling and ways of 'being human' (Smith 2007). For all the benefits scholarship reaps from an engagement with (post)modern cosmologies of mourning, it is wiser to highlight how preservations of, and ruptures from, tradition inform every work of art as well as its techno-poetic conditions (Jacobson 1971). Art both necessitates and rejects the human mastery of nature because of its participation in the domination of the magic of the 'original world' (Malinowski 1948, 1922). The book examines the recuperative value of e-topian paradises that compensate for the collapse of the divine cosmopolis into a simulatory 'hell' (Hand and Sandywell 2002). The retrieval of these non-existing paradises of human and divine harmony by film-makers, their audiences and ethno-national communities runs through the studies, asserting the power of specific visions of the '(post)modern human'. My methodological framework grows out of a critical discursive tradition pioneered in the West (Fairclough 1992) but couples this with insight that anthropological sensitivity to social minutiae can offer. My production of a 'double hermeneutics' (as in Giddens 1987) eventually fosters a dialogics that fragments tradition outside national borders, at once deconstructing Western media frames and native knowledge.

The traditions in which such artwork originates partook in utopian and Arcadian discourses of modernity the 'postmodernist turn' in arts appears to preserve, via routes of adaptation (Herzfeld 1986; Bloch 1986; Jameson 2005). Deconstructing such texts, contexts and readings from within might allow for the production of a 'methodology of the spectacle' that looks both to Eastern and Western routes of knowledge.

2 Heritage entropy?
Cinematic pilgrimage in New Zealand (2010)

Introduction

Recently, New Zealand's heritage discourse underwent changes: the cinematic adaptation of *The Lord of the Rings (LOTR)* (2001, 2002, 2003; dir. Peter Jackson) transformed the country into a cosmopolitan destination for Tolkien fans, movie lovers but also eco-tourists and post-tourists enjoying simulacra. The literary creations (*The Fellowship of the Ring* [1954], *The Two Towers* [1954–5] and *The Return of the King* [1955]) of J.R.R. Tolkien (1892–1973) instigated competitions around their custodianship as cinematic adaptations. The first film's world premiere (10 December 2000) was held in London as a compliment to the 'Englishness' of Tolkien and his Middle Earth (Sibley 2006: 506). The films' reception was affected by their simultaneous English (Tolkien's work), New Zealand (the cinematic locations) and Hollywood (financing) sources (Barker 2009: 376) – but how? Looking past the cinematic and literary 'text' into contexts of reception necessitates more than an examination of tourist and fan cultures. New Zealand's cinematic simulations were compared with Tolkien's *English* literary authenticity, and a brand-related international conflict focused on the monopolization of *LOTR*-related tourist revenues: in the UK Canterbury advertised *LOTR* actor Orlando Bloom's Canterbury origins while the city's surviving medieval gates and towers became iconic reminders of Tolkien's mythology in the city council's brochures to attract global tourists. Warwickshire has been sporadically recognized as Hobbit-like countryside (Barker 2009: 382), and even today some Yorkshire areas harbour similar rumours. Lancashire also enhanced its marketability on the basis of its iconic similarity to the rural landscapes of the films, reclaiming thus what New Zealand had 'stolen' from Britain. In the Antipodes New Zealand's Matamata (the 'true Shire') and Ruapehu (Mordor) incorporated in self-presentations both Lancashire's naturalistic iconography and Canterbury's architectural and ethno-nationalist claims, whereas Auckland became a global advertiser of Jackson's 'authentic' cinematic stage with the foundation of *LOTR*-themed museums and exhibitions (Tzanelli 2007b: 68–81). Jackson's digital retrieval of Tolkien's utopia turned into an object of international discord, revising old colonial conflicts (England versus New Zealand).

Tolkien's writings became embroiled in rumours involving unacknowledged or unauthorized authorial 'borrowings' and 'likenings', with cinematic extensions.

Figure 2.1 Canterbury City Library poster advertising the Canterbury Roman Museum. Credit: Rodanthi Tzanelli, 2006.

J.K. Rowling's profitable *Harry Potter* novels and their cinematic adaptations (2001–11) are replete with such literary and visual references to Tolkien's *magnum opus* but no explicit reference is made to them. Likewise, George R.R. Martins' *Game of Thrones* novels (1996–ongoing) and their spectacular HBO cinematic adaptation (2011–ongoing) were built on Tolkien's and Jackson's paradigms. The question of symbolic creativity and its referential networks merits analysis in a separate monograph. Suffice it to mention here that when such scenarios do not develop outside Western colonial legacy they are about the politics of cultural globalization. The Tolkien–Jackson legacy has evolved into a solid heritage trope in New Zealand, endorsing a matrix of diverse mobilities the little Antipodean country strives to control in a global community of stakeholders.

This chapter is concerned with the consequences of techno-national traditions for the development of tourist industries into memory apparatuses and the integration of imagined communities in the cosmopolis of late modernity. Beck (2002: 21) contends that globalization and cosmopolitanization do not exist in entirely polarized ways or take place only across national boundaries but are processes that change national societies from within. I investigate how J.R.R. Tolkien's and Peter Jackson's creations contributed to one such socio-cultural transformation from within through interventions from without.

I view cosmopolitanism as the ethical aspects of globalization (Nederveen Pieterse 2006b: 1248) and cosmopolitanization as the process through which these become morally (cosmologically) situated.

My spyglass is placed on the artwork of New Zealand's foremost director, Peter Jackson, and that of two other directors (Guillermo Del Toro and Andrew Adamson) involved in the enhancement of the country's international prestige as a tourist destination and multimedia hotspot. Despite these film-makers' identity as professional world travellers, their artwork became implicated in what I shall term 'heritage entropy', a strategic fusion of racially embedded heritage with hybrid (cinematic) legacy (see Hannerz 1990 on rootedness). Peter Jackson is strongly connected to this because of his ethno-civic identity (born in New Zealand) and the episodes surrounding disruptions in the filming of *The Hobbit* in New Zealand in 2010. These protests, which addressed re-definitions of the conditions under which film industry contractors can claim rights as employees, attest to the ways cinematic tourism develops as ethnically bounded property in post-colonial political formations. The expansion of the *LOTR-Hobbit* media enterprise into an industrial network also encompassing *native* tourist and media services meant that a relocation of the shootings would threaten hard-earned national achievements. Keeping the *LOTR-Hobbit* enterprise at home would allow the country to capitalize on Jackson's iconic connections between New Zealand and Tolkien indefinitely. New Zealand's nationalization of Tolkien preyed on strategic oscillations between legal/civic and ethnic/cultural understandings of tradition – or legacy and heritage. Such oscillations were enabled by the transformation of Tolkien's novels into cinematic epics that were in fact recognized by global audiences as such (Barker 2009: 277–9). The material traces of those epics (Hobbiton's authentic cinematic stage) then reconfigured New Zealand's national character.

'Entropy' is a process that turns (*tropé*) inwards (*en*), a practice induced by external interventions that aggravate nationalist affective labour through scopic practices such as those proffered by cinema (Graml 2004). But this involves emotional mobility, a form of *existential* travel *within* that translates generic aesthetic categories of nature (e.g. Porteous 1996) into culturally situated worldviews (belonging) (Hochschild 1983; Thrift 2007). Theories of 'anchorite pilgrimage' (Adler 1992: 408–13) recount how a voluntary departure from the social cosmos in early Christianity transformed into a secular (tourist) ritual of late modernity – a phenomenon reflected in today's 'find-the-ring' adventure tours in New Zealand and Jackson's fascination with Tolkien. Romantic sublimation forged a link between individual and collective experience in proto-nationalist environments (Anderson 1991: 146; Smith 1984), replacing godly presence with ideas of 'nation' and 'heritage', while bestowing upon them an originality religions reserve for holy icons. If tourism is an ego-enhancing process, tourist iconography bears the potential to bridge representations of the community's kinship with the idea of (home)land (Dann 1977; Herzfeld 2005: 108). Thereafter, heritage and originality merge into a self-referential schema appealing to biological images of the 'nation-family' to forge exclusive memberships (Morley 2000; Tzanelli 2011a, 2011b). The contribution of cinematic simulacra such as those created by Jackson to New Zealand's redefinitions is one such example: following the *LOTR* economic miracle, imagological reproductions of Tolkien's *Hobbit* myth constructed a non-existent native 'paradise' for selling to global cinematic and tourist gazes.

My *problématique* shows how anthropological debates upon 'cultural invention' connect to sociological debates on the potency of simulation to produce not just subjectivities (Baudrillard 1983) but also (individual) expressions of collective identities. Artwork stands here for symbolic creativity that speaks the language of national worldview even better when its exponents are excised from the cultural context they symbolize. A legally foolproof domestication of the colonial literary heritage of J.R.R. Tolkien was achieved through its reduction (and re-invention) to an audiovisual complex (in reality transnational in its inception). The argument that New Zealand protesters made in view of the imminent loss of jobs if Warner Bros moved the *Hobbit* production outside the country drew on such visual reductions. This act involved an interpretation of foreign ideas (J.R.R. Tolkien's) and transnationally produced images (Peter Jackson's and his associates) that emerged quite independently from any intentions its symbol creators might have had. The country's position in a volatile global tourist economy and its entrenchment in Eurocentric discourses of civility remained pivotal to the profitable domestication of histories of European cosmologies, even when cinematic ventures such as those of the *LOTR* and the *Chronicles of Narnia* (*The Lion the Witch and the Wardrobe* [*LWW*] 2005 and *Prince Caspian* [*PC*] 2008, dir. Andrew Adamson) changed its economic and cultural status. New Zealand's heritage entropy was heralded in 2010 by an Angelus Novus (Benjamin 1992: 249) from Mordor, aspiring to build its future on a techno-cultural exclusivity that was *de facto* the creation of a global community of artists and workers.

In what follows I sketch two different processes of cultural production but also the way they intersect: first, I look at the content and social conditions in which Jackson's and his network's symbolic creativity takes place. This highlights the rationale and function of his alliances as well as their place in the independent production of similar global flows or scapes in New Zealand (Appadurai 1990). Second, I examine the mobilization of the symbolic creativity of such artists in the promotion of a different political cause in the 2010 *Hobbit* strikes and protests. I place emphasis on the protests rather than the labour strikes. Although the strikes are also part of contemporary scapal clashes, they invite separate analysis by sociologists of work. Publically available materials on them are filtered by multiple political agendas at which I can only hint here. A whole new book would have to be written on that, which would marginalize some pretty central questions of this chapter.

Memory's 'golden palette': forging techno-national traditions

New Zealand's heritage entropy highlighted its distinctive national character or *habitus*. As inculcated and embodied praxis, *habitus* (Bourdieu 1977) finds symbolic extensions in the material creations of communities and their individual members (Wagner 1975). Oscillating between ideological fixities and tourist liquidities (Bauman 2000b; Urry 2002), national *habitus* comprises the material, embodied and emotional complex of culturally situated attributes (a simulacrum in itself, no doubt). Today, New Zealand's national character is marketed in two seemingly conflicting ways: the first draws upon Maori human and natural resources, producing a distinctive ecosystemic discourse that conflates ethnic with natural capital; the second capitalizes on the cinematic genres of the *LOTR* and *Narnia*. Representations of Maori 'heritage' as homogenous in the tourist trade cunningly accommodate the (today discredited) anthropological traditions of ideological diffusionism and long-distance migrations that once eschewed the development of alternative paths to modernity in the country (Hanson 1989: 891–3; Herzfeld 2002). Early anthropological appreciation of Maori esoteric greatness (comparable to Christian theosophical traditions) or alleged entrepreneurialism (comparable to 'European hunger' for discovery and innovation) are strategically embraced to enable the theft of a literary tradition from New Zealand's former colonial masters, embedding it into a *native* technology and marketing it to global tourists (Blok 1981; Greenwood 1997; Chatterjee 1993: 3–5). Jackson's digital shift from Tolkien's Catholic literary subtext to New Zealand's tourist landscape is pivotal and guided his creative industry's artwork. The cosmological superscript of the works from which his transnational community worked was not fully erased but became enmeshed in commoditized interpretations of old ideologies and customs.

Consider how today New Zealanders pride themselves on their 'do it yourself' character that stresses their versatility and entrepreneurialism (Perkins and Thorns 2001: 198), mimicking (Bhabha 1994) European discourse while simultaneously erasing internal social divisions between Maori (native tribes) and Pakeha ('whiter' settlers, today the socially privileged groups) (Amoamo and Thompson 2010: 37). New Zealand's political discourse develops on such divides, which thrive upon class and status distinctions in the global arena, also producing varied forms of citizenry within the nation-state. Thus, heritage entropy was reinstated in late October 2010 by Prime Minister John Key's claim that the arrangements of his government with Warner Bros to re-examine the legal status of media employees in New Zealand 'was commercial reality. We did the business' (NZPA, 1 November 2010). Key drew upon narratives of New Zealand's 'DIY culture' originating in Pakeha colonial mimicry (Handler 1985; Linnekin 1991) to justify his party's decisions to distinguish in the new employment bill between creative employers and contractors. His policy towards retaining a US$670 million production in the country aimed to save the reputation of New Zealand's tourist industry, even at the expense of labour rights. The replacement of one stereotype (of New Zealand as the sheep-farming relative of 'civilized' nations) with another (New Zealand as the land of business transactions and technological craftsmanship) is part and parcel of a global 'rumour' circuit, to evoke Hutnyk's (1996: 216) apt metaphor for Calcutta. And just as Calcutta's image as the site of poverty 'is one whose maintenance suits dominant interests' (*ibid.*), so are New Zealand's 'character rumours' implicated in global hegemonic battles. Key's intervention in creative industrial processes involved the manipulation of circumstances and belongs to the sphere of national politics.

Here I am more interested in ways blended creative labour, upon which film-making depends, revise old paradigms of 'craft'. I suggest that the lead artists of the twenty-first-century cinematic ventures that connected New Zealand to capitalist world centres created their masterpieces as critical tourist-like *pilgrims* to a national utopia originating both in childhood memories and the country's ideological colonization by European models of progress and civility (Graburn 1977; Bauman 1998; Herzfeld 2002). Jackson's artwork enabled the construction of alternative models of self-narration for New Zealand that were perceived and used by national agents as strategically viable and politically empowering for the country (Clifford 1988: 183), including a re-branding of Tolkien's ethno-nationalist stories, which were populated with white, happy village Hobbits and Arcadian worlds threatened by dark forces. Jackson's 'hard yakker', the ANZAC Kiwi slang for 'hard work' I examine later, derives from the Aboriginal word *yaga* (Sibley 2006: 271, 475). Combining the emotional and bodily properties of creative labour, 'hard yakker' is akin to Hochschild's (1983) and Caves' (2002) blends of artwork with a managerial ethos we encounter in professionalized environments. Instead of examining such talk as part of *démodé* folkish movements we might sociologically consider its function in contemporary artistic labour.

In the *Hobbit* and *LOTR* context such national traditions were filtered through the multicultural voices of its agents to such an extent that new (political) agendas revised their original purpose. The *LOTR* transnational *technopoesis* began with the cinematic *adaptation* of Tolkien's fantastic story by Jackson, his wife, Fran Walsh, and scriptwriter Phillipa Boyens; (in the early *Hobbit* stages) prospective director Guillermo Del Toro; proceeded with Jackson's cinematic directorship and was completed with manipulations of New Zealand's physical landscapes in Computer Generated Imaging (CGI). Digital manipulations of New Zealand nature require the involvement of many CGI technicians and artists, mainly under the supervision of Jackson's Weta Digital which has become globally famous now due to its involvement in Jackson's Tolkien adaptations but also after its Oscar award for its work in James Cameron's *Avatar* (2009; see Chapter 6; Sibley 2006: 277, 324). Lead artist of the film John Howe and Jackson remarked on New Zealand's 'otherworldly landscape' that becomes 'one of the principle factors of the story' (Jackson in Brookley and Booth 2006: 215). However, the function of local flora and fauna has been rather instrumental in the *LOTR* movie-making, as it guaranteed the production of an international blockbuster (Radner 2005: 8).

The selection of Wellington studios and locales for the production of the first part of the *Hobbit* as well as Jackson's broadcasting of the 'work behind the scenes' and relevant Hobbiton shots (The Hobbit, Production Video 1, 5 November 2011) might be the outcome of the awkward post-2010 (protests) climate in the country. A series of six videos on the production of the movie were uploaded on YouTube: they included production narratives, digital artwork tips and shots in various locations in the country. Partly a digitized travel diary and partly a cinematic pilgrimage to national land, they work as narratives of simulated landscape with the value of 'land'. This 'land' served as a heavenly multicultural Babel of art and craft, successfully creating in such a small country the illusion of a global community (also Bourdieu 1993). Intentionally or not, the post-national coexists with the national in these videos in harmonious ways that cannot be achieved in real(ist) political time. Jackson and his associate's digital artwork are examples of 'motility', a mode of appropriating a field of possibilities relative to the movement so as to use them effectively in personal projects (Kaufman and Montulet 2008: 45; Sheller 2012).

It is then understandable why 'getting that texture of Middle Earth' in New Zealand's wilderness was deliberately matched in one of the videos with fabricated maps of New Zealand as 'Middle Earth' (The Hobbit, Production Video 5, 23 December 2011). Marketing imperatives aside, projecting a dissimulation of his 'Middle Earth' as New Zealand and locating artistic labour in Wellington's Stone Street Studios presents Jackson as a grounded cosmopolitan who 'does business' with foreigners but does not neglect his homeland or the needs of common folk (the industrial workers and technicians who figure in his introduction of the movie's settings) (Hannerz 1990; Hannerz and Löfgren 1994). Elijah Wood's (Frodo Baggins) confession that today Hobbiton, where he arrived more than a decade ago, is steeped with nostalgia endorses this emotional labour (Hochschild 1983). Here it is as if art collaborates in reproductions of original *technopoesis* with the help of the 'craft' of basic labour. There is no indication in the documentary that the technicians are from New Zealand, but the homely setting of the narrative (that signifies 'nation' in the minds of most New Zealanders today) cleverly works in this direction. The reverence with which land is treated in the shootings of the *Hobbit* is playfully presented in archaic terms (Piopio in Te Kuiti is 'the land of dinosaurs' and the Ruapehu region replete with 'ancient vegetation' and 'archetypal landscapes'), but in the spirit of contemporary conservation norms the crews observe with care (The Hobbit, Production Video 6, 1 March 2012). In *Hobbit's* post-national utopia the scholar can still find some relics of the old primordial tropes of nationalism (Gellner 1983: 125; Anderson 1991: 146; Smith 1999, 2000; Herzfeld 2001: 171–2). This biopolitical arrangement (Foucault 1997b) leads us straight down the nation's underbelly, where colonial histories are ingested and national suffering is displayed in palatable ways for the tourist gaze: as professional migrants, filmmakers are mobile human labour, but as citizens they are symbolically fixed; their work fuses travel experience with situated cosmologies, reflecting 'an ongoing (re)construction of praxis and space in shared contexts' we associate with conventional and auto-ethnographic tourism (Edensor 2001: 60; Graburn 2001: 151, 2002: 26). Cinematic tourism is thus not just tourism induced by film (e.g. Beeton 2005), but also an existential journey to one's *heimat* – the affective core of 'home' humans carry with them even when they are on holidays (Dann 2002; Tzanelli 2007b: chapter 1).

Peter Jackson, who was named a national hero (Zanker and Lealand 2003: 66) for drawing global attention to New Zealand's landscape and knighted for his contribution to the Kiwi film industry in 2010, grew up in Pukerua Bay, a coastal town near Wellington. His specialism in slapstick horror comedies and science fiction in his early career, his experience in working as Wellington's Evening Post photo engraver and his foundation of Weta Digital make him the perfect example of blended art and craft that today figures in New Zealand's digital advertising campaign (100% Pure New Zealand 2, undated; Sibley 2006: 59). Jackson's early career slips into 'gory' post-colonial discourses (his Cannes debut with *Bad Taste* [1989] tells the grotesque story of Derek's triumphant elimination of Lord Crumb, an 'Old English' alien leader aspiring to control Zealand's people) symbolizes a sort of otherworldly 'colonial pollution' of native human landscapes (Woods 2005: 25–7). The symbolism of contamination (aliens turning locals into automata) allows one to read *Bad Taste* as a political satire encompassing the control of human nature and cultural landscape. The politically overt discourse was consciously repudiated in his later work, in which Jackson claims to seperate political conviction from artwork (Sibley 2006: 90). But such old stories die hard in contemporary games for global cultural flow control: today, integral to the country's national branding, the '100% Pure New Zealand' campaign builds on earlier representations of 'green and clean' New Zealand (Dürr undated: 1), incorporating in its discourse native filmmakers as pure ethnic capital. Otherwise put, motility strategies employed by directors and media industries were eventually reciprocated in an equally marketable fashion by cultural industries such as tourism based in, or affiliated with, New Zealand. This phenomenon, which reflects a physical spatialization of the Bourdieusian 'cultural capital' thesis, allows 'heritage entropy' to enter a global field of commercial possibilities to enhance national prestige.

The fact that Jackson employed the very technologies Tolkien critiqued in his novels to do and *sell* this art under New Zealand's *brand* suggests a cunning subversion of European cosmological superscripts. *Avatar*, which also mourned the destruction of indigenous ecosystems and tacit knowledge by the ruthless machine of progress, was also visually narrated though a 'machine' (CGI) Tolkien would have condemned. In contrast to Tolkien's austere mourning, suffering and comedy (the esoteric-spiritual and the embodied-slapstick) were blended in the *LOTR* cinematic narrative, problematizing European cosmological binaries that bestow exclusive seriousness upon the didactic. Jackson's professional experience with comedy-slapstick and horror, two genre *categories* that operate as European cosmological superscripts at two ends of the social spectrum (folk-working class and elite), enabled him to appeal to wider audiences while establishing his own work as art (Langford 2005). Here the categories of subjectivity and self-identity are mediated through an aesthetic reflexivity that is instantly recognizable in Western contexts, which elevates mobility and tourism to status symbols (Beck *et al.* 1994; Urry 1995: 141; Desforges 2000: 929).

But Jackson's camera-work also focused on the natural wonders of his *heimat* to explore a declining ecosystem in which the Hobbits are integrated and to which they give voice. This nostalgia is especially pronounced in his masterly distant shots of Middle Earth – New Zealand's tangible heritage that makes great profit in the tourist trade. Endorsing a tourist pilgrimage 'from above' (as professional migrant) and 'afar' (from Hollywood), Jackson is emblematic of urban intelligentsia that commercializes pre-national (pastoral) communitarianism through natural allegory. If Benjamin (1973) is right to argue that art's transformative social potential is achieved through a critical-reflexive stance towards the specific techniques and styles we employ to do artwork, Jackson's venture stood at a Faustian crossroads between nationalist and capitalist imperatives. However, before we fully explore the politics of the *LOTR-Hobbit* enterprise, we need to have a closer look at the content of industrial creativity *per se*: text makes no sense without context and vice versa; cultural borrowings and synergies are the bread and butter of cultural industries and its diners love to operate as a community of 'thieves'.

Reading allegories of disenchantment: Jackson's mobility matrix

The cinematic text

In terms of structure, the *LOTR* script is a by-product of a Western European attachment to antithetical pairs. Its archplot was compared by Jackson himself to the old *Star Wars* movies that operated on archetypal ideas of 'secrecy/revelations' (Sibley 2006: 412). More specifically, *Bad Taste* (1988–9), which marked Jackson's career biography in this direction, foretold the masterful thanatourist strokes of the *LOTR* and the *Hobbit*. Jackson's work on the *LOTR* and now the *Hobbit* draws upon earlier Pakeha cosmological themes that debate indigenous emotional connections to the land and the spiritual battle between good and evil (Geertz 1973; Sahlins 1996; Graburn 2004). Tolkien's literary allegory on social disenchantment was mirrored in the end of Hobbit and Elfish eras due to the rise of warfare that destroys natural resources to provide 'compensation on the symbolic level for the political and economic processes that have destroyed the traditional fabric of ... societies' (Spurr 1993: 132; see also White 1978: 153; Smith 2008: 174). If Tolkien's *LOTR* and *Hobbit* recorded Europe's traumatic experience of the Second World War that saw the rise of an Orwellian machine and natural destruction (an inference he denied at the time [Tolkien 1999: xvii]), Jackson's script promoted New Zealand's cosmological equivalent by translating ideas of natural destruction into an allegorical demise of New Zealand's Hobbit-like original socialities. Jackson's epic war battles in *The Two Towers* and *The Return of the King* have a nostalgic feel ingrained in New Zealand histories of involvement in the battle of Gallipoli (1915) – that ill-fated struggle on the Turkish beaches that filled the Mediterranean shores with dead Allied soldiers and which is celebrated in New Zealand and Australia as a nation-building moment to the day (Moorhead 1973). Not only did the Allied defeat of the Australian and New Zealand Army Corps (ANZAC) enrich English language with new terms and words, it also created 'the belief that the people from the two countries were different from those originating from the United Kingdom' (Slade 2003: 779).

Jackson's home place (Wellington and Pukerua Bay) from which most of the *Hobbit* shootings are coordinated is related to New Zealand's post-ANZAC acquisition of Dominion Status (1907) and the emergence of late modern thanatotourist practices tied to sacralized sites (Mulgan 1967: 15). Legends of native heroism were cast in European Hellenocentric myths: in them New Zealand soldiers figured as ancient Greek heroes, 'good' forces in the war against the villainous Oriental hordes of the Ottoman empire. The ANZAC episode connects to Jackson's life-long interest in the First World War (his grandfather was a soldier and subsequently a professional world traveller) and has reportedly inspired the creation of Nazgûl sculpture and scenes (Sibley 2006: 11–12). It is an episode that also generates unmistakable links to Tolkien's first-hand knowledge of the Second World War as a Somme veteran. At the same time, there is a 'canonical' (Ben-Ze'ev and Lomsky-Feder 2009) distance between Tolkien's and Jackson's generations. This corresponds to first- and second-hand testimonies of thanatotourist journeys. The process of producing serious horror out of second-hand knowledge involved successive reworkings of scenarios that allowed transitions from comedy to serious drama: reportedly, even Mordor's faceless Black Riders originate in Jackson's earlier humorous spooky cinematography of *The Frighteners* (1996) (Sibley 2006: 306). Critical distance from Tolkien's intimate viewpoint and the 9/11 tragedy in the US amplified the effectiveness of Jackson's symbolic creativity in various ways.

Tolkien and Jackson's 'structural nostalgia' (Herzfeld 2005: 150) – the return to a long-lost solidarity both the state and its subjects invoke in the face of modern fragmentation – reproduced earlier European discursive imports. In Jackson's case, such imports dictated the replacement of colonial with neoliberal imperatives to enable circulation of his artwork in global capitalist networks without taking him away from his 'muse': New Zealand's landscape (Woods 2005: 67; Sibley 2006: 396). At a discursive level we do not have a simplistic replacement of native cosmologies by the 9/11 Western trauma, as others have suggested. Jackson's adoration of the 1950s' and 1960s' historical epics (*Quo Vadis*, *Spartacus*, *El Cid* and *The Fall of the Roman Empire*) and Western Orientalist renditions (*The Golden Voyage of Sinbad*, *Sinbad and the Eye of Tiger*) certainly point to Western influences akin to the literary paradigms explored by Said (1978, 1993). A closer look at Jackson's biographies of creativity suggests the replacement of one distant discourse with a proximate one, based on New Zealand's experience of modernity (Robertson 1992; Sibley 2006: 32–4). The *LOTR*'s nostalgia echoes the country's cosmological blends of 'land', which inspired a century-old native film industry steeped in Maori myths and legends (Sibley 2006: 43). Jackson, who admits that he first came in contact with such legends as a child thanks to his mother's diegetic talent (*ibid.* 179), turns such legends into a mourning thanatotourist site.

In this cosmological scenario the Maoris respected and mourned their dead, had a 'close, spiritual relationship with the land ... loved [their] land and identified with it perhaps more closely than any other race' (Hanson 1989: 894). Tolkien's and Jackson's protagonists demonstrate the same attachment to their home, longing to return to it after the end of Sauron's Dark Age. Jackson depicted Sauron as a Panoptic Eye when Tolkien does not represent him anywhere in his work. The Hobbits are forced migrants symbolizing Jackson's family history: his extended family network were post-First World War migrants from the UK and he grew up with stories of war suffering that fed into his artwork (Sibley 2006: 6–13). Under Orc tutelage they serve as reminders of colonial slavery, positioning us as thanatotourists (Dann and Seaton 2001). At the same time, European utopias of indigenous harmony populated the screen with Shire marketplaces, festivities and local pubs in which the happy folk enjoyed a good pint. Alongside these emotional fixities, Jackson granted global mobilities of myth and fabricated histories a realist feel – something he intended from the start of the venture (Sibley 2006: 360, 390). Thus, Maori greatness granted *The Return of the King* with an emotive 'happy ending': released from the ring's burden, Gandalf, Frodo and their friends depart on their long-waited migratory sailing to a place no Hobbit ever reached. This ending corresponds to Pakeha glorifications of the Maori-Hobbits as world travellers and matches Tolkien's chronicles of civility into which the movies are discursively locked. We might consider how the conception of the 'Hobbit' image originates in Jackson's fascination with alleged 'natural wonders', such as gorillas that feel and love – a quirk that was creatively employed in *King Kong* (*KK*, 2005). *KK* was also filmed in New Zealand with the help of WingNut platforms for the reconstruction of New York and the use of natural landscapes. The *LOTR*'s hairy but adoring Hobbits are attached to Middle Earth as land, just as the Maoris are connected to New Zealand's sea and land.

Jackson's digital narrative stripped natural worlds off of their trees, transformed garden images into a mass of Isengard mines and crowned the Saruman's kingdom with a tower. *KK's* allegory of natural retaliation against Western postmodernity (a giant gorilla cut loose in New York) must have evoked the terrorist horror in its viewers. But whereas Kong's physical mass asserts nature's primacy in *KK*, Sauron's corporeality is challenged in *LOTR*: there Jackson visualizes evil through a shadowy impersonal 'presence', aerial vultures, flaming volcanoes and a 9/11 surveillance allegory in which the 'Dark Lord' is a giant eye (Tzanelli 2011a: chapter 6). From the outset the Moria sequence and Frodo's treks through the slumps to Mount Doom were designed as a journey through deathly sites (Sibley 2006: 494). And as the release of the second *LOTR* film almost coincided with the 9/11 tragedy, Modor's 'two towers' (Gelder 2006) – one natural and the other a technologically constructed site in New Zealand – symbolized an emerging 'ecosystemic racism'. Just like the Eastern terrorists of the Western hemisphere, the *LOTR* 'enemy' has no face, is surrounded by lesser beings with animal instincts and uses modern technologies in destructive ways. Western audience pools had to be appeased: so Frodo's arrival at the gates of Mordor was matched with hordes of Asian-looking warriors sworn to fight on Sauron's side. Dressed like Arthurian knights but with heavy Arabic headscarves (a nomadic custom) that leave only their kohl-painted eyes uncovered, these fierce warriors are queer Eurasian hybrids. Frodo's passing remark that we cannot know whether these warriors were coercively conscripted hints at Bush's 'War on Terror'

(Kellner 2006). Such ambivalent uses of gender and ethnicity as archetypal tools correspond to real representations of outlawry in both positive (folklore) and negative (state-regulated law) terms across different cultures (Melosi 2000: 296; Tzanelli 2008b: 101). Plays on binary oppositions of concealment and disclosure are filtered through Western oculocentric norms: the evil 'eyes' of Mordor are instituting a regime of non-European 'counter-law' that is nomadic, dangerous and elusive – the mythical surveillance 'Eye' that steals people's phenomenological descriptors (Lyon 1994; Erickson 2006; Tzanelli 2011a: 126–9). At the same time, the *LOTR* world is based on combinations of historical detail and late modernity's high technology, thus displacing oculocentric norms to artistic domains (on technology, see Jones and Smith 2005).

Yet, for all its Western subtext, there is counter-specificity in the trilogy that looks to New Zealand's narratives of sublimation (Bell and Lyall 2002). Leotta (2012: 181) notes that in 2002 New Zealand was among very few countries in which tourist flows were hardly touched by terror. Thus the *LOTR* surveillance regimes might be better matched with native discourses of environmental surveillance and protection (see Cubitt 2006: 67 in Leotta 2012: 187 on Aotearoa). New Zealand is a non-European exotic site, ancient enough to enclose mythical horror: Shire's romanticization and Mordor's demonization *are New Zealand* as a national *topos*. A Kiwi version of 'human' emerges from this ambiguity that resembles European conceptions of humanity. Thus the action of 'dark forces' in the *LOTR* trilogy reflects an indigenous distinction between European philosophy's *ánthropos* (from *ánō* = up and *thrōskō* = stare at), which denotes a being aspiring to reach the upper level of 'truth', and *vrotós* (*vivrōskomai* = being consumed, perish), which denotes the perishable, malleable side of human nature (Tzanelli 2008b: 149). Spirituality corresponds to the first human type and is represented by the magical world of Middle Earth whereas perishability is the dark world and its creatures that are born of earth (Orcs). The *LOTR*'s evil creatures become then a suspicious rendition of Maori *whenua* 'the placenta afterbirth which is inextricably connected to the land' (Leotta 2012: 189). In this respect, the trilogy's 'two towers' might not be sites of Western terror but 'holy mountains' of spiritual significance. Aoraki/Mount Cook, a famously marketed World Heritage Site in international tourism that figures in the second *LOTR* film, the *Hobbit* movies and on the '100% Pure New Zealand' website suggests that Mordor sites are, in New Zealand, aspects of a national brand rather than Westernized sites of terror (Morgan *et al.* 2003; Thompson-Carr 2012: 39, 41). In short, the *LOTR* spirituality has a domestic context we cannot ignore.

However, the religious feel of the narrative – a tribute to Tolkien's Catholic background – defines most of the principal characters, including those that stand between Christianity and paganism. Jackson's early interest in the so-called 'Swords and Sorcery' fantasy subgenre provides the essential link here (Sibley 2006: 312–3): this trend is best represented by the trilogy's good wizard, Gandalf. Gandalf the White's traits and emotions (irascibility, forgetfulness and tiredness) made the character more human than his aloof counterpart, Gandalf the Grey (Sibley 2006: 464). Jackson himself was aware of Tolkien's religiousness and some religious Tolkien fans thought that he tried to preserve the spirit of the novels. Gandalf's 'stirringly poetic affirmation of life after death' like Lazarus and Jesus himself, as well as Weta Digital's conception of his battle with hellish Balrog, are examples of the plot's Christological arc (Greydanus, undated). Human crossings with the paths of the dead and the knowledge that the elves are Orcs' predecessors suggest more connections with the trope of Satan's 'Fall' from Paradise. Aragorn (Viggo Mortensen) was deliberately portrayed as a 'reluctant hero' who comes to terms with his fate as the new crown, whereas Arwen Undómiel's (Liv Tyler) presence in earlier parts of the trilogy matches ethologically the purity of the Virgin Mary (Tzanelli 2008b: 171). Arwen dreams of her union with Aragorn and their offspring – a dream for which she forsakes immortality. The 'cult' of 'white motherhood' as a racial/ethnic ideal is part of the 'iconography of domestic service' and in the *LOTR* trilogy betrays the role of Western visual imports (McClintock 1991: 7, 18). Marketing aside, Arwen's character is framed by the ambiguity of her denouncement of divine spirituality. Despite her role as Aragorn's motivator, she is the only mythical female character in the story who loses her immortality and expresses excess of emotion, especially by physically manifested suffering (e.g. *contra* Galandriel [Cate Blanchett]). Her ethographical counterpart, the fearless Éowyn (Miranda Otto), also serves similar extra- and intra-textual purposes. The two ideal females are modelled on the sacrificial trope of nationalism, and serve as mediators between realist facts and literary fiction. Hence, despite any native cultural specificities, European traditions are present in the *LOTR* trilogy in character ethographies that treat emotional intimacies on a par with the love of land. The trilogy's female characters *are* land, emotional and ethological renditions of heritage.

Figure 2.2 Rivendell as digitised Augustinian 'city of God'.
Credit: New Line Cinema/Photofest.

Heritage imagery became implanted in the Rivendell shots, where Aragorn pays homage to the broken sword of kings. The site itself was digitally produced as a simulated 'City of God' (Augustine, 1948), amply illuminated and other-worldly. The city, which is populated with statues of ancestry, is also the intimate terrain in which Árwen waits for Aragorn's safe return. It seems that Jackson and Walsh toyed with gendered allegory, both reinstating and challenging feminine and masculine essentializations. Gender stereotypes also become implicated in characterizations of the four Hobbit fellows: Meriadoc-Merry (Dominic Monaghan) and Peregrin-Pippin Took (Billy Boyd) project a happy yet naïve demeanour appealing to comic genres, often associated with feminized 'kitsch art', slapstick and the 'embodied grotesque' (Binkley 2000). However, their hero-ism in battle looks to masculine themes of sacrifice for a common cause that we encounter in nationalist discourse (Tzanelli 2008b: chapter 6). Frodo's and Sam(wise) Gamgee's (Sean Astin) more serious characters produce a similar in-betweenness through their dedication to each other and an everlasting 'bromance' (brother romance). However, like their peers they present equally strong masculine traits in battle. Character liminality and indeterminacy might be a way to symbolize exoticism through familiar phenomenologies with which global viewers can associate.

The *LOTR* and the *Hobbit* scores are part of such ethological plays as much as they are constitutive of the overall narrative. The centripetal mediator in the *LOTR* and the *Hobbit* music is a very small group of human actors including award-winning Canadian composer Howard Shore and Jackson. Co-ordination at this senior lever is necessary as the music acts in the story simultaneously at discursive and emotional levels, binding image, sound and human affect into consciously interpreted plots (emotions). A great deal of interpretative work is necessary for such artwork, as the composer himself beautifully illustrates on his personal website. 'To a composer', states Shore who has been presented with the Canada Governor General's Award in the Performing Arts, 'music is very much what you see'. Shore composes and dreams in a setting close to the forest: a relevant video on his website recreates the stereotypical conception of the lonely genius who is fully absorbed by artwork, ordered and disciplined like the classi-cal music background of the clip. We watch the artist writing on a piece of paper his new music piece – 'a feeling' and an 'internal type of sight … a memory, really'. Here Shore's appeal to European visual aesthetics is extended to embrace modes of painting. The articulation of composure as an inner journey and a constant struggle also speaks the language of artistic pilgrimage (Adler 1989), especially as it is visualized through the composer's walks in fields and forests (Howard Shore Official Site, undated). This casual ritual was in fact part and parcel of Shore's *LOTR* music-making (Sibley 2006: 425). It is significant that the music was not used in the *Hobbit* protests, even though the composer clearly connects it to the movies' narrative: the *LOTR*'s organic aspects were image-based whereas the music could more easily be perceived as a 'foreign' product. Styles of art become associated with 'styles of social being and with patterns of perception and thought' (DeNora 2000: 1; Becker 1982), and perhaps such a hybrid creation bore no relevance to the activist cause.

Shore worked with New Zealanders (David Donaldson) and artists renowned for their folkish styles. All along there were shifts from literary and pictorial art to embodied (acting, singing) and technological craft (digital manipulation of image and sound). However 'fluid' in its definitions, the *LOTR* 'epic genre' does not hinge exclusively on visual images but endorses instead audiovisual engagement with cinematic artwork. Binding the primary category of 'poetry' (Altman's [1999: 50–1] starting point) to digital and instrumental *technopoesis*, the music encompasses human experiences of companionship, bravery and sacrifice, thus rebranding the emotional and moral grammar of nationalism in global consumer contexts (Anderson 1991; Barker 2009: 381). For example, the score ('May It Be', *Fellowship of the Ring*) performed by Enya, whose Irishness appeals to Tolkien's borrowings from Celtic traditions, encapsulates the cinematic shift from land to landscape while speaking of the hero's lonely travel through the darkness. The singer's contribution was favoured by Shore who thought that it 'felt natural. She sounds beautiful' (Adams 2011: 166). Gender and ethnicity drove musical representations of myth, and sealed the love of Aragorn for Árwen. The semi-religious feel of the music was strengthened in Shore's composure of the *Hobbit* soundtrack, where the group of Middle Earth fellows chants a hybrid of ecclesiastical and ancient Greek theatrical lyrics. The sepulchral audiovisual atmosphere of the *Hobbit* trailer nicely ties Shore's European classical artwork to Jackson's background in horror and slapstick genres. Even closer to the heart, young Bilbo's 'unexpected journey' is also a musical journey that marks the beginning of a Hobbit rebellion against Sauron's evil orders.

Scholars highlighted parallels between the *LOTR* music and the Wagnerian saga *Der Ring des Nibelungen*. The connection, which refers back to Middle Earth as Tolkien's symbolic European topos, provides the music's so-called mythical *motive/motif* (e.g. structurally significant musical fragment) and is acknowledged as such in the official companion to Howard Shore's scores (Adams 2011: 8–9). We may view such *motifs* as the musical equivalent to character portrayal in novels and films – an ethographical (= *habitus* description) device of sorts. In this respect, Shore's music illuminates Middle Earth from an anthropological point of view, casting rhythmic variations as cosmological narratives. The composer places emphasis on hidden numerical messages such as the trinity of trinities that have figured in mythologies around the world: his *LOTR* mark is that the second musical phrase contains exactly nine notes (Dean in Adams 2011: 83). The nine theme is often found in the music for the good creatures of Middle Earth whereas its monsters have more *aleatoric* (performatively indeterminate) tones befit of Isengard's and Mordor's industrialism (*op. cit.* 90–1). The monsters' pattern is the five beat, a 'viral' theme that bleeds its way into other themes and cultures – often scored for any assortment of anvils, metal bell plates, bass drum, taiko or distressed piano and always reserved for Sauron, Orc and Ringwraith scenes. Of particular significance are the Eastern tinted harmonic inflections of evil and the use of relevant instruments (e.g. the Moroccan *raita*), which translate into an ethicized European 'hermeneutics of suspicion'. The Elvish cultures borrow from this idea in 'Gilraen's Song', which foretells their diminishment: choral passages in Aragorn's visit to his mother's monument are feminized while retaining some Eastern-flavoured chromatic inflections. Contrariwise, ideas of 'home' and safety are rendered with a shade of melancholy or joy through Celtic rhythms: the Shire 'hymn setting' is evocative of Western religious music and other folk tones from around the world (*ibid.* 26–7). Part of the European-Eastern commercial node of media industries, Shore's artwork ties his musical trilogy to the cultural futures of colonial history.

At the same time, the music also enmeshes the structural principles of Hollywood screenwriting as it figures themes that appear at the beginnings and ends of narrative cycles. Two-step figures from the first film (*The Fellowship of the Ring*) reappear in the third film. Gollum's mediating role in the trilogy (as corrupt Gollum and good Sméagol) is articulated through the cimbalom's primitive stride and epic tunes in significant moments of personal struggle throughout the story (*ibid.* 230). Contrariwise, for Galandriel's and especially Árwen's themes a female chorus intones a set of angelic stanzas (*ibid.* 45). As the story looks to the end of the mythical world, female voices become more frequent and combined with Eastern rhythms. The music of Lothórien uses the *maqāb hijaz*, an Arabic mode not unlike the Western Phrygian (used in ancient church modes) in order to communicate both antiquity and exoticism. An adapted *maqāb hijaz* mode over drone-like harmonies in low strings and a female chorus compose the ceremonial 'Lament for Gandalf', matching thus actual customs of mourning in Eastern and borderline European societies (Tzanelli 2011a: 1). Fabian's (1983: 39) observation on the missing Western coevalness applies to Shore's understanding of ancientness. At the same time, it is worth remembering that his artwork was subjected to the needs of cultural acclimatization within Tolkien's genre.

Thus, the Moria scenes present Dwarf music through virulent and masculine Māori choruses that, according to Jackson's own directive, should sound 'like voices from the depths of Hell' (Adams 2011: 57). Producing his own transformation of 'land' to 'landscape', Rohan's music was created to present 'the nation's art and architecture … its connection to the natural world' (*ibid.* 60). Likewise, the music of the Ents employs wooden instruments that 'bristle and crick like branches' to replace melody with natural texture (*ibid.* 115). Tolkien's attribution of redemptive motivations and actions to the good side compelled Shore to embellish his work with 'amen' cadences and sad tunes. Such clear themes begin to overlap and comingle in the second film, producing new hybrid themes with Gandalf the White's role as mediator between life and death, and different cultures, reflected again in gendered musical themes. In the final movie, this hybridity becomes more focused on the narrative's climax (in Mount Doom where the ring is destroyed) in overlapping themes of sacrifice, lament and snare drums in five-beat pattern (*ibid.* 344–5). The departure of the Fellowship seals the story in soft harmonics, chords and whistles: as much as the 'Journey to the Grey Havens' is the music of loss, it is also the story's solidification as Western history.

Renouncing Eastern *motifs*, the 'Journey' merges myth-making and history-writing, as is the case with most humanist discourse (White 1973; de Certeau 1988).

The website and video game industry

The magic of the movies finds some continuation on the film's website and official blog (The OneRing.net). Significantly, to date it makes no reference to New Zealand's official tourist sites, whereas the reverse has become the norm. The start page prompts visitors to buy the DVDs, watch the trailer or enter the main site, which is framed by Shore's soundtrack. The main page opens with the broken sword of Elsinor, which is assembled like a visual key to the movie. The page suggests different paths: to buy the extended version of the trilogy, buy merchandise (e.g. a 'Frodo Lives' shirt), visit a 'Media Trivia' gateway or buy relevant video games. The page is populated with news about the *Hobbit* casting and links to the relevant Facebook page in which thousands of fans are posting comments. The Facebook page includes a series of image stills of the *Hobbit* setting from the movie, including some familiar faces from the *LOTR* trilogy, which strengthen the connection between the two franchises. This 'assures us that the upcoming films will be visually and tonally consistent with The Lord of the Rings trilogy and will include a bit of humour thrown in as well' (The Hobbit on Facebook, 2 February 2012).

The romance of the *LOTR* website and the *Hobbit* videos stands in stark contrast to the content and rationale of its video game industry. Brookley and Booth (2006) discuss the limited interactivity that augments synergistic connections between films and video games in ways similar to my conception of 'sign industries' (Tzanelli 2007b: chapter 1; also Chapter 1, this volume). Discussing the 2003 Christmas release of the *Lord of the Rings: The Return of the King* (*ROTK*), they outline strategies of profit-making optimization through links between cinematic text and video game narrative (e.g. highlights of game players' experiences of heroic action). There is no doubt that video games draw on cinematic aesthetics (see King and Krzywinska 2002 in Brookley and Booth 2006: 216) but an exclusive focus on political economy does great disservice to considerations of the creative context. We must consider traditional divides between active and passive roles in game playing or narrative control in unison with the archplot such digital cultures propagate: this would focus attention on the way war histories lose their initial significance in leisure milieus – a more important statement for the needs of the last section of this chapter. Succinctly put, *ROTK's* 'deep play' (Geertz 1973) is a world of suffering and salvation just as its Tolkien counterpart, but which is now replete of the romantic spirit of consumerism that nationalist structures bequeathed to our digital modernity (Campbell 2005). The game progresses through inserted cinematic clips from the *LOTR* trilogy (figuring as 'rewards' in each stage), which culminate in Gollum's oath to 'kill the master' and 'swears on the precious'. The *LOTR's* narrative of 'evil' fighting human goodness within Gollum is organized by the tale's magician, Gandalf, who gives directions and Gimli, who provides training (Brookley and Booth 2006: 222–3). Hence, the mastery of danger is masculinized just like the custodianship role of New Zealand's landscapes. Rather than focusing on 'active interactivity' in game playing, I contend that the *ROTK* archplot actually reproduces the role of the anchorite traveller of late modernity, constructing a cosmological frame of action in experiential terms (Graburn 1983; Adler 1992; Urry 1995). The focus should not be video gaming itself but the cosmological premises on which 'sign industries' are grounded (see Ang 1996: 12).

The *War in the North* video game, developed by Snowblind Studios and released in 2011 in Xbox 360 and PSP3 and PC DVD versions (see Amazon.com for all versions), develops along the same cosmological lines. The official website 'introduces player[s] to the Northern reaches of Middle Earth, in a realm where survival depends on Fellowship' (LOTR website, undated). Again, the game invites up to three players to engage in combat with Middle Earth enemies (Orcs), by developing and upgrading skills and weapons. The game is marketed as the first to promote solidary action that follows 'mature and brutal combat of J.R.R. Tolkien's Middle Earth – forcing player [sic] to play together or perish!' The pedagogical subtext certainly refers to the film franchise, especially the first film (*The Fellowship of the Ring*) (see Brookley and Booth 2006) but it also promotes geographically situated narratives of dark, exotic wilderness that we encounter in tourist industries. The digital manipulation of combat grounds produces a dystopian environment that stands in contrast to New Zealand's bright natural environments.

Among the hyperlinked posts on the *LOTR* site we find a short video on the selection of locations for the film (The Hobbit on FB, 20 July 2011). This video is the first example of the ways the 'axiom of amity' (Fortes 1969; Herzfeld 1985; Zeitlyn 2003) operates in digital-cinematic networks. The video, which was posted in 2011, follows some presentational conventions that we will encounter in James Cameron's documentary on Belo Monte (Chapter 6, this volume). But there are only hints as to the environmentally-friendly attitude of the crew that match the *LOTR* work on locales (Sibley 2006: 413). Unlike Cameron's explic- itly political motivations in the Belo Monte documentary, Jackson's narrative of location-hunting conforms to Graburn's (1983) idea of commercialized tourist pilgrimages with no explicit political motivation. In the *Hobbit* video, narratives of cinematic pilgrimage have been incorporated into location-hunting and global coordination logs, where one can hear about MacKellen's tiring visits to London, James Nesbitt's planned journey to America and other professionals' holiday plans. Professionalized individualism rather than political conviction frames the video (Giddens 1991): several professionals, including Jackson himself, stress lack of time from work commitments. Location hunting (e.g. in the South Island) becomes the video's narrative core, revising the old rationale of 'touring' outside organized labour time (Eade 1992; Weaver 2005; Baum 2007; Urry and Larsen 2011: 89). Embellished with emotion, the video follows Jackson's hunting with the helicopters in the rhythms of Shore's epic melody.

Holding a digital camera, Jackson becomes from the helicopter's vantage point the digital eye of God that scans native landscapes. But on the ground, together with his multicultural community of peers, he marks new sites, wanders, stumbles upon bushes and trees and toils like a backpack traveller. A playful simulation of his own cinematic script that looks at Middle Earth from heaven, Jackson provides CGI-free shots of Mount Cook which speak the language of aerial tourism (Szerszynski and Urry 2006; Duval 2007: 236–7, 239–42). 'We are going to go to some places very, very few people have seen ... people think it's such a small country, we've seen everything' Jackson protests in an intermitting shot in his office. Although the video endorses 'armchair' tourism through connections of action, spectatorship and desk labour, like Jackson's simulated *LOTR* pilgrimage it also functions specifically as an introduction to the *Hobbit* world of travel with a purpose and a premonition of the things yet to come within the cinematic narrative. Significantly, the first official *Hobbit* trailer adheres to the rules of Hollywood narrative intertextually: young Bilbo's story figures in it in such a way that it corresponds to the cinematic beginning of the *LOTR* enterprise. The trailer's ending figures a shining ring emerging from piles of dirt in a dark cave, and Bilbo in a background that is filled with light. The crypto-Platonic allegory of goodness, which is attracted to light, and evil, which hides in the dark, plays with old camera techniques of illumination. As the trailer concludes, we see again the creepy figure of the 'evil' Gollum hissing from a narrow passage to Bilbo about the role of Bagginses in the ring's story. This circular narrative revises Tolkien's linear plot, coercing viewers to review the future from the vantage point. This point is provided by a past that Bilbo mediates through his own biography of travel (also Desforges 2000). Connecting the heritage of Bagginses' family chronicles to the adventurous touring of Bilbo-the-'backpacker', produces Middle Earth's collective memory through the digital lens (Halbwachs 1992).

The emotive potential of Jackson's movies becomes relevant to the *Hobbit* controversy if we consider that 85 per cent of the population in New Zealand lives in urban areas. Its landscape and endemic flora and fauna 'constitute a powerful source of nation pride' (Dürr undated: 4) and an aspect of its national character that sells well to eco-tourists, adventure tourists and backpackers. Under considerable market pressures, the environment has become further implicated in an ethno-national programme of conservation to which countries with rare ecosystems need to demonstrate commitment. Tolkien's and Jackson's Arcadian principles became implicated in this protectionist discourse, which commenced with the British colonization of non-European lands but became politically constitutive of high civility standards (Fairburn 1989; MacKenzie 1997). To this one may add the significance of the Foreshore and Seabed Act for New Zealand, which aimed to resolve conflicts between Maori (native populations) and Pakeha (New Zealanders of European descent) competition over the uses of land, which contributed to its deterioration. The Act, which declared that the land in question was owned by the Crown, allowing the Maoris (its traditional custodians) to apply for guardianship only of certain areas, sparked protests that almost overlapped with the *LOTR* filming. The Act was investigated by the United Nations Committee on the Elimination of Racial Discrimination after complaints by the principal Maori iwi tribe, but its suggestions are yet to find implementation in the country (UNHCHR, 2005). In the context of an up-and-coming cinematic tourist industry, the decision to exclude Maori tribes from land control remained highly controversial, with accusations that it promoted covert racism in favour of profitable nation-building running rife. Film-making in the country and its by-products (tourism) do not operate outside such controversies.

We need only look at representations and policies that framed the filming of *Whale Rider* (*WR*, 2002, dir. Niki Carro) to consider how conservative discourses on local ecosystems become solidified even in mobility environments. Textually, *WR* conveys such policy concerns through intergenerational conflict, by gendering Maori 'heritage' both through the protagonists' contested visions (Koro's obsession to identify a male successor) and his granddaughter's (Paikea) determination to change his mind (as the 'whale rider' she feels that she embodies heritage). Such scripts debate the power of colonial legacies over interactions even within indigenous communities (Sinclair 1992). Just as Jackson's earthly people, *WR*'s characters acknowledge that they are born of the sea and will return to it, thus emphasizing the spiritual value of 'land' and its naming as the basis of tribal identity (Thompson-Carr 2012: 39). Koro's *reiputa* (a whale ivory pendant, which populates today ethnological museums around the world) is also his honour (only the chosen successor can retrieve it from the bottom of the sea). The unexpected union of the pendant with Paikea reinstates the order of intergenerational transaction: the girl serves as a mobility instrument, a *hau* that asserts the system of giving that Mauss explained in his anthropology of gift and giving. Contextually, the film is situated in a 'first people' counter-movement that promotes films 'made by Maori and set in the Maori community' (Barclay 2003: 8), thus promoting tighter links between landscape, land and human capital (Turner 2002). This movement would adhere to visions of the seashore as a magical place and a livelihood factory rather than a Pakeha space of leisure. It is otherwise understandable why the film was inserted into global flows that made the Whangara community of the filmed sites a tourist destination (Leotta 2012: 118–20). *WR*'s tradition was embedded in mediascapes in ways similar to the *LOTR* franchise – even though not with equally spectacular results. Experiencing landscapes from within is thus communicated to cinematic tourists, strangers 'from without' with interest in the exotic. As I proceed to explain, this strategy is constitutive of New Zealand's cinematic network, which presents important cosmological affinities.

Cosmological affinities

Guillermo Del Toro's evil

The theme of the unjust suffering of the vulnerable (connected to the European traumas of genocide, displacement, memory effacement and forced migration) informed the search for a *Hobbit* director before Jackson's appointment to the post in 2010. The first selection, Guillermo Del Toro, is remembered as the charismatic maker of *Pan's Labyrinth* (*PL*, 2006) and *The Devil's Backbone* (*DB*, 2001), two cinematic allegories of Spain's precipitation into self-destruction (civil war) narrated from the standpoint of vulnerable or abused humans – a running theme in Del Toro's work since his 1993 Cannes debut with *Cronos* (1993). Jackson's and Del Toro's friendship must have informed the original quest for a new *Hobbit* director; as members of a transnational artistic community both directors trade conventional understandings of kinship with forms of belonging conditioned by professional interests. Engagement with auratic spooky themes guided their earlier work (e.g. Jackson's *The Frighteners* compares with Del Toro's more austere apparition in *DB*). The *LOTR-Hobbit* plots comply with both directors' engagement with the horror genres as well as with Howard Shore's acclaimed soundtrack career in horror films (e.g. *The Fly,* 1986; *The Silence of the Lambs,* 1991; *Crash,* 2004). Jackson's know-how career is also reflected in Del Toro's artistic dexterity with sketching and make-up.

Del Toro's biography also immediately suggests a link to Tolkien: born in Guadalajara, Mexico (1964), he was raised by his grandmother who was a devout Catholic. His involvement with film-making began early, despite objections in his ultra-conservative native environment. Studying scriptwriting with Mexican director Humberto Hermosillo and becoming founding member of the Guadalajara-based Film Studies Centre and the Mexican Film Festival, he slowly became involved in global professional networks (*The Guillermo Del Toro Collection,* DVD guide: 2007: 1). For a decade he supervised special effects for his company, Necropia, and through it he met leading producer, Bertha Navarro and her brother, Guillermo, who served as her regular director of photography. Del Toro's epistemic network matches Jackson's, which includes a blend of traditional and post-kinship connections. His three principal films were published as a DVD trilogy after the *LOTR* success in 2007. Whether this is a manifestation of the axiom of amity or just a promotion technique on the basis of personal biography, the collection provides valuable information corroborating my argument towards a cosmological likeness between Del Toro and Jackson.

A revision of the vampire genre, *Cronos* sketches a baroque character, Jesus Gris (Federico Luppi), who lives among antiques with his granddaughter, Aurora (Tamara Shanath). When he discovers an artefact that belonged to a sixteenth-century alchemist, he enters a metaphysical limbo as a living dead who lives off human blood and through his contact with the artefact. Del Toro's ethographical narrative capitalizes on Christianity's archaic ambivalence towards its protagonist, Jesus, a 'living dead' who merges the profanity of the rotting human body with the sacredness of its divine soul. Jesus Gris' Catholic conscience defines *Cronos*' cinematic dialogues and monologues which culminate in the destruction of the artefact (and thus Jesus Gris) so as to protect his granddaughter from his thirst for blood. Third age is thus portrayed in the film as ossified time, an anthropophagic heritage based on patrilineage. *Cronos*' self-destructive *hau* makes space for younger generations in what appears to be an autobiographical theme in Del Toro's cinematography.

Alchemy's presence ties this personalized plot to a human archplot of Enlightenment progress that can be achieved only when earlier antiques of magical gold-mining are replaced with tacit knowledge of the natural world – and by extension, metaphysical (or demonic) *poesis* with rational *technopoesis* and experimentation. Del Toro's influence by the Hammer-Universal 'vivid' but 'Gothic colour palette' and his engagement with James Whale and David Cronenberg (*The Fly*, 1986) allowed him to mix in *Cronos* organic and mechanical forms of being, mirroring Jackson's artistic split between nature and culture. The audiovisual themes of horror and suffering allow artwork 'to turn the horns', righting the wrongs of a colonial machine that stole the two respective nations' 'childhood'. Mechanical-as-organic views of the world are present in Del Toro's and Jackson's artwork memory-making through a European philosophical analogy of God as nature-maker and clock-maker (Argyrou 2005: 2). Del Toro's attention to magical 'evil' artefacts (e.g. mechanical insects with living cores) discusses the management of nature as human hubris. *Cronos* set Del Toro's signature by successfully resolving binary distinctions between memory as a less legitimate means of establishing the past, and history, 'the destroyer of a more authentic, existentially rich memory' (LaCapra 1988: 17; Herzfeld 1987; Sutton 2000; Gibbons 2007: 54) through the phaneroscopic lens of cinema (Peirce 1998).

The audiovisual stylistics of *Cronos* but also *DB* and *PL*, appear to borrow from the traditions of Europe's Great Masters (*chiaroscuro* shots that illuminate only the faces of the protagonists) but also film noir (*Cronos*' music echoes that of the scores from the interwar and post-Second World War film industry). Del Toro himself admits influences by later painters such as Goya but for *PL* in particular he pays homage to illustrator Arthur Rackham (*The Guillermo Del Toro Collection* 2007: 9). Del Toro's thanatotourism was extended in *DB*, which was filmed in a combination of confined space and flat countryside. The cinematic landscape is filled by the historical depth of the parable, asserting the importance of symbolic modernism in his artwork. Filmed after his difficult collaboration with the American film industry in *Mimic* (1997), *DB* and *PL* better conveyed his interest in genetic manipulation and the ways ghosts of the past haunt us. *DB* is connected to his desire to make a film about what he regards as an 'unfinished' Mexican Revolution. The plot practically speaks of wars within families, 'an intimate war where brothers kill brothers'. Displacing this desire in the years of the Spanish Civil War in an orphanage, *DB* follows the encounter of ten-year-old Carlos (Fernando Tielve) from a republican family with the ghost of Santi who was murdered by a greedy adult orphan, Jacinto (Edurado Noriega). The orphanage is run by sympathetic leftist Carmen (Marisa Peredes) and a romantic poet-scientist Dr Cesares (Federico Luppi), who assume the place of dying Old Republicanism. The orphanage's children are the 'people' who are oppressed by Franco's fascism (Jacinto) in 1938.

The story's narration by old Cesares (a ghost himself after his murder) creates a chain of associations within the story, including Carmen's suffering 'phantom limp' (a metaphor for her self-hatred and shame), Santi's haunting desire for revenge and Jacinto's hateful greed. *DB*'s death of old age also links to *Cronos*' ending. The film is framed emotionally by the possibilities of Nietzschean *ressentiment* (1996: 55) to turn into self-destructive reality. 'What's a ghost? A tragedy

Figure 2.3 Protecting the young and vulnerable: the *DB*'s narrative of the Spanish
        (civil war) orphanage as a cosmological statement.
Credit: Sony Pictures.

condemned repeating itself in time? An emotion suspended in time? Like a fading
photograph?' asks Cesares' phantom at the start and end of the film. The myth of
'eternal return' is thus symbolically connected to family chronicles through
photography but the cinematic genre itself fosters other mobility connections too
(Sontag 1990; Larsen 2005; Hand 2012). Despite the intended use of CGI in his
previous films, Del Toro affirmed his tendency to emotional monumentalization
(Nietzsche, 1980: 17–18) when he explained that his films 'depend on location'
(TheOneRing.net, 25 April 2008). Rife with thanatotourist content, Cesares'
statement becomes implicated in the interpretation of liminal experiences such as
sightseeing and memory-making (Bærenholdt *et al.* 2004): Madrid (first war
target during the Second World War and dictator Franco's stronghold), Aragon
(largely erased from Spanish history during the Francoist period) and Castile (the
architect of Spanish nation-building), Del Toro's cinematic locations are both
Spanish heritage centres and international business and tourist attractions. Just as
Jackson's, Del Toro's style produced a mediatized gaze that promotes pilgrimage
to historical sites and signs firmly embedded in inter-national tourist economies
(Lash and Urry 1994: chapter 6).

   PL is in many respects Del Toro's coming of artistic maturity. The film is an
audiovisual thanatotourist journey to dark lands and legends: it follows the director's very own Frodo, Ofelia (Ivana Baquero), who is uprooted to a remote military outpost commanded by her stepfather (Sergi López), a general in Franco's

Figure 2.4 Princess Moana's otherworldly paradise is a dream beyond Ofelia's death. Credit: Picturehouse/Photofest.

army in 1944. She lives her own dark fable in which she confronts monsters after her discovery of a neglected labyrinth behind the family house. In the labyrinth she meets a Pan who presents her with three tasks that will reveal her true otherworldly identity as princess Moana. Just as in *DB*, the beginning corresponds to the cinematic ending, whereby human Ofelia is revealed as the cocoon of an immortal princess in an underground Arcadia. Yet, the story is framed by nature's wonders, blending fairies with insects, mud with frogs and a Resistance movement as the nation's 'body' that is protected by woods and mountains. Just as in *DB*, a female housekeeper (Maribel Verdú) and a freethinking doctor (Alex Ángulo) are Resistance collaborators whereas Ofelia herself figures as a war martyr (killed by her evil stepfather while protecting her newborn brother). Ofelia's pregnant mother (Adriana Gil) seems to represent the ravaged 'national intimacy' the sexist general-husband treats as his son's 'vessel'. Unable to dream anymore when he removes Ofelia's magical mandrake from her bed, she dies in childbirth. 'Dreaming' is revealed as the nation's 'radical imaginary' that totalitarianism crushes.

Del Toro's monsters in the film include the 'Pale Man', a freakish Rackham-inspired anthropophagous creature that Ofelia narrowly escapes. The monster's

Figure 2.5 Del Toro's 'Pale Man' as ethnicized allegory of the evil (eye).
Credit: Picturehouse/Photofest.

strangely embodied way of seeing (its eyes are located in its palms) allows it to locate and devour humans. The Pale Man's hands are a sort of Aristotelian 'tool of tools': they invert Islamic interpretations of 'Fatima's Hand' as the Hand of God and a family of divine characters (Cooper 2009: 79), turning the sanctity of alterity into profane matter. The Pale Man (white like a dead vampire, faceless like a terrorist and spiritually 'dark') is an Oriental Saruman, at once part of the nation's intimate domain and its abject enemy within (also Tzanelli 2011a: chs three and six). The faun in *PL* became a Pan in the film's global distribution, consolidating Pan's global marketing through images of the (Cretan) Minoan maze.

Del Toro's faun granted primordial depth to standardized European crypto-colonial narratives that viewed ancient Greece as the birthplace of Europe's civilization and constructed a white-Aryan lineage for European empires (Bernal 1991; Tzanelli 2010b). The story's true monster is, of course, Ofelia's stepfather, Captain Vidal, who kills her to reclaim his son before he is executed by Resistance fighters. Allegorizing the coming of adulthood and the loss of innocence (the otherworldly portal opens, according to the faun, only when innocent blood is shed – a double metaphor of sacrifice and female menstruation), *PL* is at the same time the cost humans pay for their mastery of nature. The mythologization of heroism in history appears to attract Del Toro and is clearly matched with his hermeneutics of folk myth: an ancient tree revived by Ofelia's bravery concludes the story. The tree is Moana's 'small trace of her time on earth, visible only to

Figure 2.6 European renditions of the faun as Pan speak the horror language of natural evil. Credit: Picturehouse/Photofest.

those who know where to look'. The all-seeing Pale Man is replaced in this concluding remark with the power of human hermeneutics to shape a better world. Javier Navarrete's soft classical piano and violin notes, a typical early Del Toro 'touch', crown *PL*'s European thematic. Like Tolkien, Del Toro admitted an influence of Catholic cosmology ('It's true what they say – once a Catholic, always a Catholic' [*Guardian*, 17 November 2006]) but also like Jackson he highlighted the role of his family in his artistic pursuits.

Del Toro's creativity has a Christian sacrificial focus (the narrative node of *PL* and the *DB*): in another interview he revealed how the Pan's Mexican background was replaced in the cinematic script's final version with Spain (*The Guillermo Del Toro Collection* 2007). Spain's experience symbolizes Del Toro's homeland's colonial history of racial discrimination, civil war and genocide (Tannenbaum 1966). Camera-work and dream-work are informed by memory regression in his esoteric journey: Spain (Mexico's first colonizer) experienced in the twentieth century what Mexico had suffered at the hands of British colonists a century before. Akin to secondary revisions of unprocessed experience (Gourgouris 1996: 262), Del Toro's little heroes/heroines are both the nation's perverted childhood (children represent primal purity not innocence, he claims) and its future, which is damaged by a malicious archaic presence (the orphan's warden, the Pan/faun). The experience of directing *Cronos* and *PL* facilitated Del Toro's transition to Hollywood with *Hellboy II* (2004), which figured

Ron Perlman as the superhero, a regular in Del Toro's previous movies. The superhero genre satisfied the director's fascination with comics design (Kike Mignola's cult series) and connected the ways he reminisces about his family's past (Gibbons 2007: 76) to what Spiegelman (1988) has termed 'commix', a mixing of words and pictures to tell a story that is anything but comical. His fascination with supernatural spells placed on children informed his archplots for similar reasons: children are unprocessed 'otherness', malleable beings closer to nature. In 'commix' nemesis is graphically inscribed as the tragedy of innocence through encounters with devils that appear to be harmless or even funny. Del Toro's cinematic Hellboys remind us that radical evil can be of service and 'infinite destruction can be invested in a theodicy' (Derrida 1998: 13). Just as Jackson's evil Sauron-Leviathan that devours innocent mythical creatures instantiates the goodness of New Zealand's Hobbit Paradise, Del Toro's Faun and Devil present Spanish character as pure evil that ought to be condemned by the global viewers this drama educates (de Pina-Cabral 2008:243-5). Matching Jackson's nostalgia, Del Toro had revealed in early interviews how the *Hobbit*'s 'palette' was going to be 'more golden', just like Tolkien's wide-eyed world facing the prospect of the First World War 'so there is a loss of innocence and a darker tone as the book and the film progresses [sic]' (TheOneRing.net, 25 April 2008). This blend of darker tones with innocence has become a sort of 'brand' in New Zealand's artistic node. Working between allegories of power and empowerment crafts phanasmagoric tales that use literary pasts for new cosmetic purposes, as the next case suggests.

Landscape and childhood in Andrew Adamson's artwork

The recuperative hermeneutics of such movie-making that looks to primal innocence – of Hobbits, elves or orphans – also figures in the work of Auckland-born Andrew Adamson who directed *LWW* and *PC* – two cinematic adaptations of C.S. Lewis' allegorical biopic of the Second World War's impact on childhood. I do not argue that Adamson generated these allegories but that he transferred in his cinematic updating Lewis' cosmological constants. I thus expand the artistic complex of this chapter to include J.R.R. Tolkien's longstanding friendship and rivalry with this Protestant author and lay theologian, backing the argument that visual adaptations of their works in a former colonial country is of cosmological significance. The New Zealand director, known for his blockbuster animations *Shrek* (2001) and Academy-nominated *Shrek 2* (2004), lives and works today in Los Angeles. His digital expertise won him a place in *Batman & Robin* (1997) and *Batman For Ever* (1996) as visual effects supervisor. With a family background in technology (his father was an engineer), an unfulfilled desire to be educated as an architect and a successful career that commenced in US-based Pacific Data Images, Adamson is a case comparable to that of Jackson. *LWW* (co-directed with Chris Miller and Raman Hui) and *PC* entertained global recognition with a worldwide gross of US$745 million and US$419 million at the box office respectively (Box Office Mojo, undated).

LWW's cosmological melancholy is situated in the Blitz chaos of the Battle of Britain that the novel's four young protagonists escape through a wardrobe (the passage to the wintry world of Narnia). There, the children encounter various mythical creatures (including a faun and Aslan, a lion) and a White Witch claiming to be the 'Queen of Narnia'. The witch pursues the children who find out a story foretelling her end when two sons of Adam and two daughters of Eve sit in the four thrones. Matching in numbers the prophecy's prediction, the children appear in the story as both symbols of innocence and unavoidable 'Fall' from God's grace, offspring of the 'Original Sin' stuck in a cold kingdom – a fragile theological limbo. *PC* builds on this plot, following the return of the children to the Kingdom to aid prince Caspian (Ben Barnes) in his struggle for the throne against his corrupt uncle, King Miraz (Sergio Castellitto). The visual narratives follow Lewis' theological hermeneutics, toying with whiteness and darkness as symbolic opposites embedded in a digitally manipulated natural environment. Lewis' very magical portal (located in the English countryside) is symmetrical to Tolkien's allegory of disenchantment, generating ample possibilities for movie-making along the same cosmological lines. But the plots also seem to borrow from other ancient mythologies that point to New Zealand's affiliations with Europe.

This blend is visually plausible, both to knowing and less informed audiences, as a fairy-tale template – a European formula akin to Shore's love of musical renditions of *Niebelungen*. The soundtracks of the films were created by *LWW* Global-nominee Harry Gregson-Williams and follow the same *motif* that incorporates

Figure 2.7 Out of Hellenic mythology? Reading Adamson's visual stylistics as a European statement.
Credit: Walt Disney/Photofest.

Figure 2.8 Edmund and Aslan the lion against a digitally manipulated natural background.
Credit: Walt Disney/Photofest.

shifts from the heroic otherworldly passage to the dark feel of a militarism that is
musically infused with muted trumpets. Gregson-Williams fused the use of
instruments used in ancient folk music and the solo voice choral textures with
electronic music (Burlingame, 5 October 2006). In an interview the composer
also admitted that the religious themes are 'hidden away within a musical
subtext! Actually, Aslan's theme had religious overtones in *LWW* and I carried
that forward' (Schweiger, 6 May 2008). The Chronicle's musical allegory resembles Shore's shift from soft whistles to pompous epic tunes but Gregson-
Williams' work is not a copy of the *LOTR* scores.

Digital manipulations of nature in the films render ideas of childhood purity as
natural property in Lewis' footsteps. The filming of *LWW* necessitated constant
relocations within New Zealand (from Auckland to South Island) and outside
(Poland and Prague and National Park České Švýcarsko). Post-production CGI
efforts were handled in Los Angeles and effects house Rhythm & Hues handled
the bulk of the visuals (IGN Film Force, 16 February 2005). Location-hunting
lasted for about eight months and included stops in Ireland, China and Argentina
before New Zealand, Slovenia and Poland were chosen (NarniaWeb.com,
29 March 2008). The decision to film most of the picture in Europe allowed
shooting during summer both in European countries and New Zealand (Hunkin,
5 February 2007). The decision was made on practical grounds (lack of big stages
in New Zealand's cities and weather). Adamson's determination to stay faithful
to the original story also presents location choice as auxiliary to New Zealand's
link to Europe. His participation in the epistemic network that Jackson manages
becomes evident in Weta Digital's involvement in the Narnia industry. Here transnational and national bonding overlaps in professional labour initiatives: *The Crafting*

of Narnia (2008), a guide written and designed by artists from the special effects house, chronicles the stunning concept drawings, designs and props that helped Adamson shape the world of Narnia. Detailed photography, hundreds of drawings and sculptures, and commentary from the artists and craftspeople of the workshop, shows how Weta Workshop was involved in *LWW* and *PC*.

Just as Jackson, Adamson encapsulated a dying green rurality from his urban techno-cultural stronghold (Williams 1974; de Pina-Cabral 2008: 246): *PC* used as filming sites Mercury Bay on the Coromandel Peninsula (North Island) and Paradise (South Island), a privately-owned horse ranch about an hour's drive from Queenstown. Adamson appears to remark through '100% Pure New Zealand' that 'there's not an area of Europe that hasn't been felled and re-grown at some point, so finding an old growth forest is very difficult. In New Zealand, the whole west coast of the South Island is covered with ancient forests' (18 May 2008). A product of Zealandish suburbia, Adamson commemorates cinematically childhood holidays in the scenic Coromandel Peninsula (100% Pure New Zealand 1, undated.), a counter-cultural enclave in the 1970s and currently a lifestyle alternative for urban dwellers east of Auckland. Here the personal is tied to the national in ways akin to Del Toro's memory work that encloses histories in technological frameworks. However, Adamson's words were extracted from another interview (Hunkin, 5 February 2007) and use on the '100% Pure New Zealand' website. In this interview the director speaks highly about the country as a place of commercial opportunity.

From this extensive analysis of the network's leadership one may conclude that individual expressions of structural nostalgia for an irretrievable topos communicate with national(ist) sentiment only under certain conditions: in principle, the camera forges genealogical continuations between personal and collective memory (Connerton 1989; Halbwachs 1992) while blending narrative with image and sound, *inviting audiences* to do the hermeneutic work. In practice, however, such interpretations might be monopolized by various centres that legislate upon the uses of iconic narratives for tourist growth and political self-aggrandizement. This endorses memory's value as a social activity not only in configurations of hermeneutic work but also as a model of socialization that thrives on histories as much as it is nourished by myths of origins and cohesion that we encounter in post-Enlightenment tropes (Mizstal 2003: 12; Habermas 1996; Pensky 1989). What belongs to the 'nation-family' stays in the family – a peculiar antinomy that disregards the production of the *LOTR* industry across national planes. As I explain below, by amplifying remembrance-like rites based on artwork's affective labour, the '*Hobbit* wars' threatened New Zealand's global reputation as a tourist destination.

The 'labour' of national memory-work: striking as touring

All three directors are business travellers and members of the new transnational 'epistemic communities' (Haas 1992). This identification is akin to Bauman's 'tourist' (1998), which supports precisely this 'distant' cosmopolitanism social theory associates with high status and economic privilege (Erskine 2002; Delanty 2006; Gauntlett 2011). In New Zealand's case, epistemic nodes such as that emerging from a group of films rich in animatronics and unspoilt landscape were formed around a post-colonial narrative of national excellence in the tourist trade, capable of reproducing the European urban phantasmagoria (Patke 2000: 4–5) outside Europe (Auckland as Orcland) and an Augustinian-like 'city of God' outside the city (Matamata as Hobbiton). There is no doubt that the *LOTR* industry produced a 'mediated centre' when cities such as Wellington became New Zealand's 'Welliwood' (Peaslee 2011: 49), but the assumption that this applied across the country or even for the whole city may be wrong.

Peaslee, who suggests that Matamata-Hobbiton operates as a 'boundaried space', locates such productions in media spaces, but his discussion of Matamata folk as uninterested in *LOTR* tourism's impact on self-narration conceals local resentment for the influx of strangers behind a discourse of innate hospitality ('character') ('why the fuck would we care?' he otherwise quotes from the interview [2010: 67]). He explains that locally managed Hobbiton tours present a local family (the Alexanders) both as displaying commercial innocence in their dealings with the *LOTR* location hunters and as the *original founders* of the cinematic-tourist location – a crafty move that represents the *LOTR's* inception as peripheral family creativity. The very practice of offering tours to global visitors is the sign of a cultivated 'expert class' able to offer more than what travellers find in a tourist guidebook (Bourdieu and Darbel 1991: 52 in Earl 2008: 403). Here, native 'knowledge of the field' becomes a manifestation of peripheral socio-cultural mobility that can be favourably compared to the unjust monopolies of the national centre. A similar strategy informed, in 2010, the national centre's 'cosmetic cosmopolitan' policies that sought to produce a gloss to overlay local realities (Nederveen Pieterse 2006b: 1250). As in 2010, rural enterprise took a back seat nationally, and national branding was threatened by the *Hobbit* controversy, with protesters visually mobilizing Jackson's marketable pilgrimage to rescue their jobs. If we consider that at its peak the *LOTR* production employed approximately 23,000 workers; that in 2000–1 the local film industry doubled the numbers and the trilogy provided global visibility to corporations such as Air New Zealand, generating about NZ$283 million for the Aoteara economy alone, the *Hobbit* strikes begin to make sense from an economic point of view (see Mathijs 2006; Lawn and Beaty 2006; Tzanelli 2007b; Peaslee 2011).

Cosmetic cosmopolitanism, which strategically feminizes and racializes the desire for pedagogical inclusion in the global polity, is embraced by communities that are considered 'underdeveloped' and in need of recognition. The child-like innocence of Hobbits, coupled with a protectionist discourse over native nature, already stereotypes national landscapes as property, creating a pool of interest groups vying for its custodianship. Here we can place the transition of heritage entropy from the individual to the collective level: reproducing heritage formulas fills the recognitive gap by techno-poetic means while disqualifying or valorizing native knowledge regimes (Hobart 1993: 2; Azcárate 2006: 99) – but quite often achieving the former in the guise of the latter. The rationale is roughly this: if others will not recognize us as an equal and autonomous community, then we will empower ourselves with some sort of affirmative action. As 'signs' with fixed local meanings, natural locations are only conditionally shared with outsiders such as tourists or businessmen, as the Maori case suggests (O'Regan 1990; Strang 1997; Hinch 1998; Thompson-Carr 2012). The *LOTR-Hobbit's technopoesis* (Hand and Sandywell 2002: 208) can be mobilized by various interest groups, including the labour masses. Here, heritage entropy exemplifies the autopoetic potential of national memory in the distinctive but communicating domains of state policy and capitalist reproduction at both superstructural (cinematic narrative) and basic (labour of creative industries) levels.

Affirmative action uses a blend of tools and means in the battle that satisfy both native (e.g. lands and their traditions) and imported (e.g. cinematic landscapes or dominant ideas of art) notions of the 'authentic' (Chhabra *et al.* 2003; Chhabra 2005). Whereas these can become inserted into global flows of authenticity (e.g. American film studios as authentic sites [Peaslee 2011: 43]), they maintain solid connections with the site of cinematic pilgrimage the rebels claim. Today New Zealand's heritage is simulated in its numerous official and unofficial tourist websites that sell what foreign interest groups might naturally envy. But this merits discussion in another essay. Suffice it to note here that territorial claims on open land are framed these days in terms of spatial representations that emerge from simulation regimes as Couldry (2003b) and Peaslee (2011) remark. Mediated representations of simulations have become in today's global economy a form of cultural capital in the most conventional Bourdieusian fashion (Couldry 2003a). Unlike Couldry and Peaslee, who considered rituals in media/tourist regimes, I examine how such rituals informed political rites in the *Hobbit* protests. Re-interpreting the scripts of Jackson and his associates, these strikes became a 'movie' in their own right, asserting heritage entropy in global mobility fields (also Minca and Oakes 2006). Global media assisted in the staging of the strikes and the protests to such an extent that it is difficult to establish clear causal timelines or identify instigators.

Such digital communications allowed the promotion of a newly discovered national authenticity and 'cultural intimacy' (Herzfeld 2005: 3). Cultural intimacy, the self-acknowledged aspects of one's cultural vulnerability to external spectators (tourists, media), calls for vigilant supervision by the community that claims monopoly in their selective commoditization. 'Community' and nation-state might overlap in terms of social action to enable both interpretive achievement by independent actors and political mobilization by the national core (Habermas 1989c: 118–19; Delanty and O'Mahony 2002: 50–3). We cannot view the democratic and institutional domains as watertight compartments: the public sphere remains open to institutional manipulation, such as that achieved by interest groups during the *Hobbit* controversy. However, such models can establish causalities theoretically; 'hard facts' point to less organized action that is not politically viable or useful even for its performers. Take, for example, how Labour MP Trevor Mallard raised in Parliament a modified national flag figuring Warner Bros' logo in the place of the Union Jack ('New Zealand's sovereignty is finished',

Figure 2.9 Protests in New Zealand: Gollum as New Zealand's property.
Credit: Marty Melville, Getty Images/Flickr.

he told the house in protest for the *Hobbit* bill [Murray, 29 October 2010])
and compared it with the Gollum banners of protesters pleading 'Save my
Precious Home!'

Such emotional declarations transcend the boundary of economic interest,
allowing New Zealand's national melodrama to enter the Mines of patriotic
Moria, where claims to a postcolonial heaven and patriotic suffering are cleverly
instantiated to both achieve internal unity against external enemies and morally
educate the global cinematic tourist. The language of moral instruction replaces
here the intimate Aristotelian didactic with the distant gaze, fusing Jackson's or
Del Toro's craft into New Zealand's DIY *techne* to secure global compassion
(Aristotle 1996; Tolstoy 1960). The globalization of the *LOTR* staging as well as
its implication in the politics of marketing authenticity and 'heritage' becomes
evident in its regeneration as a theatre play in the UK, when Theatre Royal Drury
Lane digitized an educational pack for young schoolchildren wishing to learn
more about Tolkien's 'original' story (Theatre Royal Drury Lane, 2011). Such
initiative certainly plays the card of authorial authorship: without blindly reproducing the old tropes that consecrate works of art, it uses the postmodern
discourse of hybridity to validate the author as 'original' celebrity in mass cinematic production (Glass 2004; Earl 2008: 409).

New Zealand's *LOTR* spectacle capitalizes on memory signs without original
meaning to produce marketable forms of identity, pluralizing thus collective self-
narration (Bakhtin 1981: 16). But nation-building hinges upon this cinematic

fiction that travels in mediascapes to represent it as exclusive national *property* in ideoscapal domains (Appadurai 1990). Just as Jackson's covert reflections on the global Islamophobic surge, his compatriots' love for Middle Earth enables discursive replacements of history with myths to manage changes in national identity (also Collard 1989). Historical and mythical pilgrimage to other sites becomes a nation-building process in globalized settings. Mallard's defying gesture, for example, is a media-induced national pilgrimage ('the flag/Hobbit land belongs to us!') that in conventional tourist terms conceptually conflates the tourist-pilgrim's experience with the revered tourist objects (Wang 1999: 351; Albertsen and Diken 2003: 2; Hennion and Latour 1993). This vocabulary might seem straightforward to outsiders but to New Zealand audiences remains bifurcated: on the one hand it can appear to endorse Western separations of the natural world from humans, but on the other it can be read as human ancestry's natural insidedness (a Maori vision) via the European tropes of nationalism (Sinclair 1992; Cosgrove 1993). National normativity suggests that the pedestal on which a nation rests its semi-religious images cannot host just any artefact, nor can any stranger be granted rights to re-arrange its displays (Lowenthal 1985: 252).

This is why the *LOTR-Hobbit's* emotional core found interpretive resonance in the *Hobbit* social movements. These movements involved affective labour that preached against forgetting the history of colonialism (Labour Opposition's argument), strategically supporting transitions from market economics to colonial politics (Schiller 1991; Mackay 2004: 61). Both external-systemic and internal-structural impositions contributed to this transition: the economic recession hit hard the creative arts, leaving mega-corporations such as Metro Goldwyn-Mayer (MGM, established 1924, originally co-financing the *Hobbit* with New Line), the home of *James Bond* and part of Hollywood's heritage, struggling to complete promising projects. Debt holders such as Icahn, Anchorage Advisors and Highland Capital Management aimed to take over the studio, and equity owners such as Sony feared that they would 'have their stakes wiped out'. Gary Barber and Roger Birnbaum, co-CEOs for Spyglass Entertainment now managing MGM, declared themselves 'honoured and inspired at the prospect of leading one of Hollywood's most iconic studios into its next generation' (Nakashima, 4 November 2010). But as MGM became a shiny auction item, corrupt practices of transaction entered the picture, with knock-on effects in the Antipodes: rival stakeholders including Time Warner and Lion's Gate valued MGM differently, whereas Icahn was sued by Lion's Gate for opposing its merger bid with MGM, then backing it after buying a large chunk of the company's debt.

Restricted budgets invited all parties involved in the *Hobbit* production to re-evaluate self-promotion and preservation means. Though with a small population, New Zealand prides itself for its film industry workers at all levels, from actors to animators, because they grant it a global 'face' (Williamson, 27 October 2010). Post-colonial political formations better actualize labour segmentation, reserving primary markets for cosmopolitan artists and using indigenous or migrant populations who lack Jackson's international fame to fill their secondary ones (Doeringer and Piore 1971; Bonstead-Bruns 2007). In 2005 the Supreme

Court had ruled in favour of long-term workers in New Zealand, recognizing them as employees regardless of the type of contract they had signed. At the time special effects worker James Bryson had taken legal action against Jackson because he was made redundant, claiming that he was an employee rather than a contractor, and he won the case (Satherley, 1: 29 October 2010). This legal background would act as a precedent in the controversy and an inconvenience for Warner Bros. The state sought to settle this through the so-called 'Hobbit Amendment Act'. Domestic policies dressed up the deal with a neo-liberal rhetoric of profitable cleverness that was not equitably profitable: Key's concessions to the foreign studio included in the deal an offer of NZ$25 million (about NZ$15million in tax breaks), making the overall arrangement anything but favourable to regional development, especially in those regions from which creative industries would recruit labour for their projects. The appreciation of the New Zealand dollar from being worth 50 US cents to 75 US cents since the conception of the *Hobbit* project, would have placed Warner Bros at a disadvantage prior to the Amendment (NZPA, 1 November 2010). Drawing on moral economy debates that examine recognitive struggles where just distribution is hindered by hidden (e.g. class, status) value hierarchies (Sayer 2000), Labour Minister Kate Wilkinson explained: 'we were not prepared to see thousands of Kiwi jobs disappear and ... the hard work of the many talented New Zealanders who built our film industry put at risk' (*Telegraph*, 29 October 2010).

This globally reported manoeuvring contributed to the development of social entropy into a performative script: thousands of New Zealanders took to the streets to protest against Warner Bros' threats to move the production elsewhere. In tandem, Oscar-winning *LOTR* technician Richard Taylor told protestors that he hoped the *Hobbit* would stay in New Zealand and read a letter from Jackson thanking the crowds for their support. BBC News reported him saying: 'The created DNA is here; this is where Middle Earth was born and this is where it should stay' (Child, 25 October 2010). This granted Taylor and Jackson leading roles akin to those we tend to associate with celebrity politicians who are able to draw more attention to causes otherwise lost on account of their weak support (Street 2004). The protesters, who were dressed as characters from J.R.R. Tolkien's tales and held Gollum posters (Child, 25 October 2010), visually legitimated New Zealand's branding over the entire *LOTR* culture (a strategic reversal of marketing cultural essence to foreign tourists [see Beeton 2005]), emotionally underscoring such commercial endeavours (Lury 2004). The *Hobbit* project was now engaged in a downward spiral, a cause designed to 'take back' the history that had been 'stolen' (Gabriel 2004: 149) from the nation by foreign manipulators of impressions. No longer identifying with indigenous traditions *per se*, the protesters romanticized Tolkien's fictional rurality instead so as to save the *Hobbit's heimat* from corporate 'intruders'. Ironically, the protests sanctioned hierarchical divides within the nation by simultaneously romanticizing the Hobbiton periphery and valorizing its urban centres (Wellington, Auckland, Christchurch), presenting the protesters as rurality's 'protectors'. In line with the political and artistic leadership's 'Keep the *Hobbit* in New Zealand' stance, the protests tied common European themes of manliness to civilization and the nationalist dogma (Bederman 1995).

Jackson's artwork in the *Hobbit* protests has symbolic value that exceeds the meaning of the *LOTR* trilogy. Just as the work of art emerges from the belief system of the field of art – its 'magic' – to partake in a domination system (Bourdieu and Wacquant 1992: 247), protest artwork communicates a constellation of meanings very specific to the cause (Löfgren 1989; Hannerz 1996; Hannerz and Löfgren 1994; Titley 2003: 5). The cultural context in which this digital mediation of heritage takes place is appropriate for a return to the analysis of the *hau* (gift), a Maori concept applicable to the new mobilities paradigm: Mauss (1954) and others (Sahlins 1972; Davis 1992) highlighted that because donors and gifts are bound in a magical way, the recipient of the gift is *obliged* to reciprocate the giver's gesture. In 2010 a foreign corporation threatened to withdraw from such a relationship, 'donating' instead Jackson's digitized (auratic) creation to the country's former colonial masters (UK) or a neighbour (Australia). The collective belief that grounds the artistic-come-political order of the *Hobbit* protests (e.g. Bourdieu 1998) is the rebirth of New Zealand as 'Middle Earth', a para-nationalist misrecognition of cinematic landscapes as national 'land'.

In this context the banner of Gollum communicates an ambivalence embedded in the *LOTR* and *Hobbit* literary/cinematic narratives: an earthly product like the Orcs that lives in mud and dirt, the Gollum is now treated by its 'neo-colonial

Figure 2.10 The earthly make of Orcs points to convergences of European Christian and Maori cosmology in Jackson's fantasy-horror genre.
Credit: New Line Cinema/Photofest.

Figure 2.11 Gollum as a double allegory of rebellion.
Credit: New Line Cinema/Photofest.

masters' as proof of New Zealand's 'Fall' from European grace (Herzfeld 1986; Tzanelli 2008b). Gollum is New Zealand's Jesus Gris, born human and of dead lands – a thanatotourist gift to Western civilization that was treated with disrespect and now must assert its magical belonging to New Zealand's people. Akin to global traveller cultures, Gollum faces exile from what has served as 'home' for centuries: the Antipodean Eden. Such hermeneutics can incorporate an antithetical scenario, in which Gollum's associations with primordial evil are countered by his pleading good nature in the banner. They certainly corroborate observations on split representations of the criminal (Gollum as thief and victim) and the nomadic nature of social movements ('terrorists' with a good cause) (see also Melucci 1989). One may even argue (*contra* Bourdieu [1992]) that the practical necessity of reading such visual signs as New Zealand 'property' submitted to the scholastic needs of tourism in the country – a leisure mode originating in Europe. Protesting as touring became prerequisite for a native 'cinematic pilgrimage' in New Zealand (on art see Bourdieu and Wacquant 1992: 87; Albertsen and Diken 2003: 5–6).

The ascent of the county's Angelus Novus binds transnational *technopoeia* to national *autopoeia*. Otherwise put, the work of a transnational group of artists allowed both New Zealand's political leadership and its working people (in the

LOTR-Hobbit tourist and media industry) to recreate a plausible form of native self-narration. In this narrative a colonial product (Tolkien's literary work) was legitimately appropriated by Peter Jackson's cinematic industry, enabling thus the discharge of a debt suspended in time. A past stolen by the colonial centre could now be reclaimed in money *and prestige* (Habermas 1989c: 183; Luhmann 1992, 1999; Duvenage 1999: 8–9; Tzanelli 2007a: 255). The cinematic lens became the collective lens of memory, backing a strange emulation of *WR's* desperate search for the missing *reiputa*, token and sign of virulent leadership. This process developed quite independently from the intentions of Jackson and his associates as a by-product of the country's desire for global recognition, external action by a foreign union, and a global pool of workers fighting for job security in the global economic recession. None of these factors worked independently and the importance of their effects cannot be accurately retrieved. Individual affiliations of *LOTR-Hobbit* actors with the former colonial centre were silenced whereas Jackson was awkwardly pushed to demonstrate some solidarity with his 'betrayed' compatriots. This statement corroborated with the director's artistic beginnings in anti-colonial narratives. However, such early endeavours cannot account for his later artwork and should be better understood as the assertion of New Zealand's cosmological *urtext* as much as Jackson's spontaneous siding (Goldmann 1964; Mannheim 1968; Luhmann 1990).

The *urtext* amplified interpretative possibilities, inviting global media contributions. In late October 2010 the *Guardian* reported that a British woman of Pakistani origins was refused a part in the scheduled films for not being 'light-skinned' enough. A spokesman for the film-maker's company, WingNut Films, allegedly said the crew member who uttered this was an independent *contractor* who was sacked (Child, 29 October 2010). Jackson himself suggested in an interview in late 2009 that the selected actors 'have to have a particular type of physical appearance and sensibility... you have to find the *right humans* to translate into those characters' (THR.com, 23 December 2009). We could regard these British comments as reciprocations of the Kiwi hostility but there are also marketing imperatives we must consider. Tolkien's racist depiction of white Middle Earth (where no good creature has darker skin tones) dictates contemporary fandom norms, continuing to destroy global solidarities dictated by history's moral grammar on purely commercial grounds (the heroes' visual appeal).

It seems that the organized strikes over contractual work commenced with the Australian Media, Entertainment and Arts Alliance's initiative. But relevant Hollywood reporting stressed how the dispute erupted when *English-speaking actors' syndicates* 'issued "do not work" orders in solidarity with local organizing efforts' (Handel, 20 October 2010), aligning Australian action with New Zealand's historic archenemy: Britain. Australia's economy depends on the country's self-presentation as an ideal tourist and migration destination, displaying an all-around attractive package in northern European markets with which it collaborates. Government-funded cinematic projects such as *Australia* (2009, dir. Baz Lurmann) are analogous to the *LOTR* tourist miracle, but not with the same global glamour. Even the *LOTR-Hobbit* principal agents appeared at a loss with the whole upheaval. Jackson and Boyens,who are also unionized, stressed in a joint interview their disbelief at how Helen Kelly, head of New Zealand's Council of Trade Unions, made some unsavoury comments about the workers (a 'lunchtime mob') she vouched to protect (TVNew Zealand, 21 October 2010), questioning her commitment to New Zealand's cause. Political segmentation in New Zealand certainly amplified the conflict (e.g. see ideas of Nuer segmentary politics in Evans-Pritchard 1937, 1940). Thus media interventions in the *Hobbit* controversy conformed to neo-liberal models of governance, whereby capital investment safeguards (iconic) *property* while demarcating it as a state-controlled 'good' (Freedman 2008: 33, 40) – an oxymoron, considering neo-liberal objections to market monopolies. In some journalist discourse falling back on kinship meta-phors in the face of suggested corporate threat also transformed New Zealand's heritage entropy into a rational-emotional by-product of prestige-hunting within a post-colonial community of rival nations (Gluckman 1963; Barth 1969; Herzfeld 2009a). By the latter I mean that some external reports allowed readers to assume that the core of the *Hobbit* controversy was not about employment rights but scapal monopolies: which country would claim Jackson's creativity and the privileged mobilities it generates.

Inadvertently or not the victim of this mayhem became New Zealand's credi-bility as a media-tourist destination, but Economic Development Minister Gerry Brownlee added fuel to the fire by reiterating how an Australian union 'put at risk' the jobs of 'our workers', clearly casting now the whole dispute into the old ethno-nationalist mould of 'us' (natives) versus 'them' (foreign industries) (Satherley, 2: 29 October 2010). There is no doubt that natives found work in these media and tourist industries, but at the same time we must acknowledge the presence of global labour flows that might have become implicated in national protests. Just as is the case with film extras in films, protesters are in the viewer's field amorphous masses until the camera presents some as heroes, victims or villains. The importance of viewpoints is pronounced for example in the various shots of the protester who paraded the Gollum banner – a man with an indigenous Maori 'profile'. One could easily fix on this case (or indeed that of the rejected Indian applicant) to highlight some general truths about conflations between the country's human capital, land and digital landscape (the 'native' Gollum) and critique the presence of 'environmental racism' (Blanton 2011). Interpretations aside, a constant in the case is provided by its impeding consequences: when they evolved from international protests against a problematic bill to national outbreaks ('*Hobbit* jobs for New Zealanders'), New Zealand's movements threat-ened the country's much-needed stranger traffic (*fremdenverkehr*) (Spode 2009: 69): media and cinematic tourism. Jackson's creative labour was subsequently used by those who wanted to control it to amplify the 'labour of national memory-work' (Gabriel 2004: 149–50), transforming a group of films into expressions of patriotic commitment to marketable-invented memory (Anderson 1991: 193; Huyssen 1995). The affective core of Zealandish memory-work complied with immaterial and cybernetic forms of labour fostered by creative industries, 'flexible and precarious networks of employment and commodities increasingly defined in terms of culture and media' (Hardt 1996: 4). But even this angle may be part of the script of the movements. Just like the *LOTR-Hobbit* script, the protesters' battle spoke of peace-loving Arcadian creatures. These creatures are threatened with extinction by a (corporate) Dark Lord and have to fight to save their happy Shire. This repeated simulation is the emotive heart of 'heritage entropy'.

The 2010 marches fulfilled a crucial symbolic role as a form of secular pilgrimage to signs and sites of *LOTR* memory. Protesting in urban spaces (Wellington, Christchurch, Auckland) that store the *LOTR* spectacle effectively infused processes of work with cosmological meanings borrowed from European Christian traditions, opening up possibilities for various audiences to conflate secular *communitas* with nationalist commitment (Eade 1992: 19) or racist scenarios better suited to Tolkien's novelistic text and context. Striking addressed remuneration/recognition gaps by corporate visitors (resembling normative expectations of native guests from tourists-visitors to donate or spend money in pilgrimage sites), whereas the protests were headed by political leaders and marked by special clothing (just as pilgrims who follow a religious leader in special attire) (Graburn 2004: 132). The strikes temporarily withdrew the 'hospitality' from corporate strangers for which New Zealand prides itself, blocking business traffic in the country. They fostered a visual *entropy*, domesticating the *LOTR* enterprise as a good rightfully belonging to the 'nation-family' and legally worshipped by a global community of tourists-pilgrims (Bell 2002; Dann 2002: 7; Savelli 2009: 141; Lanfant 2009: 113; Tzanelli 2011a). Strike and protest endorsed the denial to serve and recognize strangers-visitors, allowing protesters to translate instead a colonial brand into New Zealand's new hybrid tradition (Brandist 2002: 123; Alexander 2006). This turned a legal issue (working conditions) into a discourse of kinship (jobs for Zealanders). Yet, ultimately, to remember Geertz (1973: 450), such localized causes go down in histories of revolt more as dramas of cosmic proportions, paradigmatic human events able to move the global heart.

3 The *Da Vinci* 'node'

Networks of neo-pilgrimage in the European cosmopolis (2006–8)

Power geometries and the ethics of intersectional mobility

Urban phantasmagorias addressed to terrestrial and virtual tourists, web surfers and cinematic audiences enclose the horror of the unknown, the 'stranger' who traverses their domains and destabilizes fixities of tradition (Bauman 1991: 56). The stranger is a mirage of a being 'without a home', always 'multiplying masks and "false selves" ... never completely true or completely false' (Kristeva 1991: 8) – but always present in narratives of belonging. Just as in horror films, the stranger is constitutive of social 'monstering', at once an object of fear, revulsion (as in monsters) and fascination (Latin *monstrate* = to show) (Wood 1986). This chapter explores the psychodynamics of feminized strangerhood as a tourist and cinematic phenomenon, capable of raising objections both in literary and ecclesiastical domains. Focusing on *The Da Vinci Code* (*DVC*, 2006, dir. Ron Howard), *Angels and Demons* (*AD*, 2009, dir. Ron Howard,) and *Silent Hill: Homecoming* (*SHH*, 2006, dir. Cordy Rierson) as well as their popular cultures (websites, computer game and tourist itineraries), it explores the reproduction of some pervasive themes of strangerhood across popular and elite artistic registers. Following closely Massey's (1993) call for a consideration of power geometries, I examine the temporal and spatial mobilities of gender and ethnicity as ideal types in consumption induced by cinema.

These mobilities are part of entrenched understandings of Western civilization. The cosmetic nodes of the city as a museum and as a safe stronghold produce a social meta-genre (see Tudor 1989; Langford 2005: 167) in which ideas of supernatural and secular 'threats' and 'risks' are never quite managed by technology. In all three films the city serves as the civilizational backdrop, a marker of identity but also a space contravening the fixity of pre-industrial ritual and custom. Figuring heroes and heroines in adventurous journeys, the films support cosmopolitanism that is debated institutionally both as a shallow and profound endeavour. In what follows, I outline the ways in which secular mobilities actively redraft the story of human rebellion against narratives of divinity that is both patriarchal and paternalistic, but also how the defenders of a withering religious humanism respond to this change. Ironically, de*monstrating* their own textual orthodoxies as a reliable source of knowledge and cosmic order, defenders of the

Christian establishment construct their own counter-movement that contests the transgressive energies of feminist literary-cinematic ideoscapes. This paradox corroborates contemporary mobility cultures that promote flows of art, ideas, humans and products, as well as the virtual and imaginative environments in which these develop (Appadurai 1990; Hannam *et al.* 2006; Sheller and Urry 2006; Urry 2007). These mobilities encourage further ideational movements or what we might acknowledge as multiple hermeneutic chains of represented heritage signs on the big screen – by internet businesses, viewers, photographers and scholars (Giddens 1987; Friedberg 1995).

The films as mobility narratives

In 2004 Charis Atlas Heelan from Frommer's was suggesting to readers of Dan Brown's popular *The Da Vinci Code* to experience the story 'literally, with a literary tour' (16 December 2004). The suggestion was deceptively straightforward: literacy has been a social skill historically tied to the legitimation of hegemonic orders – the priesthood of the Middle Ages, the feudal elites of the Renaissance, the national elites of the Enlightenment. As a vehicle of value dissemination, it has been the *sine qua non* of a cosmopolitan belonging initially streamlined into promising ideological structures of modernity (industrialism, capitalism, nationalism and other 'isms' that left indelible marks on world history). McLuhan's work (1962, 1964) on the history of the media and Anderson's 'imagined communities' thesis (1991) among others have suggested that the paradox of literacy, in its print and audiovisual forms, was that it democratized knowledge the very moment it became complicit to the emergence and preservation of political centres. Jardine and Brotton (2000: 8) suggest that artistic and other material transactions made the boundaries between East and West thoroughly permeable in the Renaissance. However, to date people may acknowledge the coexistence of various worldviews and still limit their narrative of belonging to European sites and sacred histories (Wills 2001).

In effect, Heelan was highlighting how the *DVC* engaged in a similar paradox: while opening up literary and embodied experience to the masses, it was repressing the knowledge that this 'staged' democratization (by media conglomerates, cultural industries) had structural limits (it was *not* for the poor immigrants, for example) and served particular interests (of capitalist networks). We may remember Glücksmann's critical investigations into the ambivalent function of this democratization, especially where the economic value of tourism/leisure looked to cement collective mentalities while ensuring the 'healthy' reproduction of a workforce controlled by centralized authority (Spode 2009: 70). One wonders how the globalized coordinates of late modernity truly differ from those of earlier priestly impositions, and how we can secure the institution of inclusive polities. Brown's novel (2004, first edition 2003 by Doubleday) was yet another exposition of the quest for the 'Holy Grail' that intertwined such histories with fable. The marriage of historical with fabulist elements produced a magical recipe that captured many readers' imagination: not only did it guarantee the success of the novel, it also provoked a debate about the very foundations of Christianity, which was further disseminated when in 2006 the novel became a film.

The Da Vinci Code

The *DVC* tells the story of an investigation started by symbologist Robert Langdon (Tom Hanks) and cryptologist Sophie Neveu (Audrey Tautou) around the murder of Louvre curator Jacques Saunière (Jean-Pierre Marielle), Sophie's grandfather. The old man left a trail of codes and symbols, eventually linked by Langdon and Neveu to a heretical theory. According to this theory, Christ and Mary Magdalene had a child, Sarah, whose lineage survived with the help of the millenarian cult the Priory of Scion. Chased by the French police and Vatican spies, Neveu and Langdon depart on a journey across Europe determined to solve the mystery of Magdalene's offspring. An eccentric British researcher, Sir Leigh Teabing (Ian McKellen), deciphers Da Vinci's masterwork *The Last Supper*, guiding Langdon and Neveu through a series of mythical and actual places to the true meaning of the 'Holy Grail' (the union of Christ with Magdalene) and its potential to shake the foundations of Christianity and reveal its irreducibly patriarchal past. The plot crafts its polemics on the idea that an unrecognized wedding survived across centuries in apocryphal texts and came back in late modernity to 'pollute' the sacred domains of classical art discussing archetypal themes of divinity.

The feminization of art and its haphazard mobilities in search of independence and escape from the Church's anathema are a theme that dominated early feminist debates (De Beauvoir 2007: 350). This theme of deviant mobility is combined with the role of Langdon and Neveu within the cinematic narrative as virtual travellers of at least two types: connoisseurs of European art and history, and pilgrims of a long-lost religious site (the burial chamber of Magdalene). As such, Langdon and Neveu are collectors, desperately seeking 'signs' of cultural history and long-lost religion. Readers and especially viewers of the *DVC* are vicariously taken along for a ride as virtual sign collectors and corporeally travelling *neo-pilgrims* to these unexpectedly interdependent sites. I subsequently use neo-pilgrim as an ideal type of cosmopolitan tourist. The cinematic and material projections of this type through capitalist networks (its transformation into embodied tourist), assists in its democratization. This democratization is owed to contemporary links between creative arts and commerce, with whole sectors within creative industries that were not commercial in the past (e.g. performing arts, broadcasting) having become commercial. Modern economies are consumption based, and 'social technologies that manage consumption derive from the social and creative disciplines' (Cunningham 2005: 293). This drives the analysis of the *DVC* knowledge economy in the next section.

Angels and Demons

Brown's *Angels and Demons* (Corgi, 2001) also became a controversial film. It is a mystery set in the awe-inspiring Rome, an Eternal City recognized today as the home of the Vatican's earthly Eden. It follows Dr Vittoria Vetra (Ayelet Zurer) from the European Organization for Nuclear Research (CERN) and Robert Langdon (Tom Hanks) in their attempt to save the world from disaster, which leads us through some of Rome's best tourist markers. The focus on Rome makes the narrative spatially more compact and claustrophobic than that of its cinematic prequel. Conceptually, *AD* is more manageable, like a weekend abroad in a 'global city' (Eade 2001). Even the bishops and priests visiting the Vatican for the election of the new Pope are represented in the film as mobile subjects, photographing and video recording the premises and exchanging impressions about the place on their mobiles. *DVC*'s sequel presents Father Silvano Bentivoglio and Vetra initiating the Large Hadron Collider and creating three vials of suspended antimatter particles. Father Silvano is murdered and one of the vials goes missing while the Catholic Church prepares to elect the next pope. Carmelengo Patrick McKenna (Ewan McGregor) assumes temporary control of the Vatican but the *Illuminati*, an organization of rational convictions based on Enlightenment traditions, kidnap the four *preferiti* (candidates for the pope's role) before the conclave enters seclusion, and threaten to murder each one of them every hour and destroy the Vatican at midnight using the vial as a bomb. With Father Silvano's diaries as a guide and the assistance of the Vatican's *gendarmerie*, Langdon and Vetra depart on a frenzied attempt to uncover the secret identity of Father Silvano's confidant and secret murderer. Initially a step behind the killer who ritualistically executes the *preferiti* and marks them with ambigrammatic words/signs (earth, fire, water etc.), they eventually discover that former military pilot McKenna is the real culprit. His agenda is to become the next pope and repress scientific interpretations of religion (for full plot see IMDB, undated and Wikipedia, undated). The battle of religion with science frames the narrative in a style akin to critical theory's elaborations on the development of a European public sphere (Habermas 1989a). In this respect, the film explores the contemporary dissonance between secularism and religion and questions the inclusiveness of both.

Global impact and cultural flows

Creating two thrillers of religious revisionism, centuries-long conspiracy, murder and the lust for power has been in equal ways a 'blessing' and a curse for Brown. It certainly transformed the *DVC* into a stunning global phenomenon with sales of over 40 million copies since its publication around the world (*Guardian*, 28 March 2007; *First Great Western*, December 2006: 51), at least US$200 million earnings (*Guardian*, 27 February 2006) from the book and US$77 million in cinema takings in only the first week of its release in North America (Williamson, 8 June 2006). It entertained unprecedented popularity, especially in China, which has claimed the film's world premiere over Cannes (China National, 17 May 2006), and coerced the Vatican to appoint an official debunker of its scandalizing content (Owen, 15 May 2005). In Samoa the government censor banned the *DVC* from cinemas and all local television stations. The move, backed by the scandalized Samoan Catholic Archbishop prompted Magik cinema owner Maposua

Rudolf Keil to cast such interventions as a violation of 'people's fundamental rights' (Radio New Zealand, 21 May 2006). The notorious court case against Dan Brown for his alleged copyright infringement relating to *Holy Blood, Holy Grail,* a book by Michael Baigent and Richard Leigh released in the 1980s, only served to make the novel and film more popular (CBS News, 13 March 2006). The court case, lost twice by Baigent and the now late Leigh, adds an interesting twist to my reading of the *DVC* as a paradoxical cosmopolitan statement. This point, to which I return in a latter part of the chapter, ties the literary-cinematic narrative to the history of democracy. The number of websites the film and the book generated is ever-growing as a Google search shows (from 1,800,000 in January 2007 to 6,630,000 in August 2008 to 7,290,000 in June 2009).

As Brown's prequel was also transposed from the literary to the pictorial domain, feelings in some religious communities still run high; despite reassurances the producers provided to the Church and Tom Hanks' mobilization of charm to win the crowds, Brown's name was enough to make sure that the doors of the desired religious locations would remain shut to Howard's crew. Cardinal Tarcisio Bertone, the Vatican's secretary of state, said: 'Boycotting this film is the least we can do'. Franco Zeffirelli, director of *Jesus of Nazareth,* told the Corriere della Sera: 'Dan Brown is a rapscallion. The Vicariate has done well to deny them access' (*Telegraph*, 17 June 2008). If *AD* involves four murders of cardinals, for the Vatican the *DVC* has already 'turned the Gospels upside down to poison the faith' and churches into sets for 'mendacious films' (CBS News, 19 June 2008). Claiming that Hollywood is populated by anti-Catholics, Catholic League topper Bill Donohue declared a 'holy war' against *AD* studios with the booklet *Angels & Demons: More Demonic than Angelic* (2009) – a new polemic following his supposed victory over New Line's adaptation of Philip Pullman's *Golden Compass* (2007, dir. Chris Weitz) (Siegel, 6 March 2009). There have been suggestions that no sequels were made to *Golden Compass* because the film failed to excite audiences and critics (Heritage, 15 December 2009), but its US$85 million (£52 million) profit in America is a good start and we may have to look more closely at the case to understand its discontinuation. Pullman's suggestion is that, if nurtured, childhood curiosity can kill the institutional religious control of free thought. Pullman's childhood preserves the mystery of cosmological unities between human, non-human and inanimate things – and hence the pagan foundations of mobility. Locating this in the domain of human reproduction (children as offspring of Original Sin, which in the plot is further stretched in Miss Coulter's [Nicole Kidman] pregnancy out of wedlock) could only add fuel to the fire. Pullman's materiality of nature suggests a political-aesthetic order hostile to Cartesian polarities on which Catholicism thrives, looking instead to cosmological domains in which ontological differentiations between nature and culture do not exist (McLean 2009: 216). Pullman's epistemology seems to take non-European ontological realms very seriously indeed – a dangerous act for a Church that spent centuries trying to extricate unChristian indigenous beliefs in exotic colonies. Samoa's principal censor repeated for *AD* his 2006 decision on the *DVC*, banning the movie from the cinemas (Samoa

Observer, 21 May 2009). At the time Howard responded that Donohue's witch-hunting failed to recognize the film as a work of art 'taking liberties with reality'; or, that the film was populated 'with references to struggles within the Church between faith and science [but also] support for the pursuit of science at the highest levels of the Vatican' (Howard, 21 April 2009). Notably, Howard also mentioned that the 'faith versus science' debate over embryonic stem cells appeared in the film, thus hinging his enterprise on issues of creation.

There are two hidden but interlinked references to such anathemas: one hints to the significance Brown attributed to Madgalene's apocryphal texts (alongside her sexuality) for Catholicism – and by extension, his suggestion that women were excluded from an allegedly inclusive religious agenda. The second reference gestures towards opening up an exclusive cultural domain, once reserved for connoisseurs of 'high culture' and 'history proper', to the masses of literary/cinematic tourists. As horror films, the *DVC* and *AD* touched an extra nerve: Brown's and Howard's narratives outline concerns about the body as a split site, hosting sexuality and inviting torture. The ambivalence of bodily pleasure underscores both movies' diegesis of ritualized murder, sex and procreation, matching twenty-first-century changes in sexual values and practices and the relocation of sexual intimacy in the marketplace (Featherstone 1991; Giddens 1992; Beck and Beck-Gernshein 1995; Plummer 1995; Bernstein 2001; Bauman 2003).

But the *DVC* also became a significant node in various intersecting (socio-cultural, economic and political) networks – hence the title of this chapter as I seek to decipher how the *code* became such an impressive *node*. If the book generated significant tourism, inviting visits to some of the key locations of the novel (initially Parisian sites with a lustrous history and cultural ambience,) the cinematic adaptation of the novel, which visualized the protagonists' journey across Europe, produced tourist networks, providing a plethora of possibilities for visits to many other places mentioned in the book: the Louvre's *Mona Lisa*, the Pyramid, Saint-Sulpice and Chartres Cathedral in Paris, Rennes le Château in Aude, *The Last Supper* and Sforza Castle in Italy, Rosslyn Chapel in Edinburgh, the Temple Church, Westminster Abbey and Lincoln Cathedral (Westminster in the movie). In 2008–9 it was *AD's* turn to create more 'cinematic tourism'. A guide in one of the cinematic locations bears testimony to the reproduction of this phenomenon when he says that 'he takes at least one hundred tourists a week on an "Angels and Demons" tour – and no one objects' (CBS News, 19 June 2008). *AD's* cinematic markers (notably the Four Rivers in Piazza Navonna) present Europe as a nodal geohistorical point where the Danube in Europe, the Nile in Africa, the Ganges in Asia, and the Plate in South America converge, but the story promotes the symbolic destruction of this myth. A suggestion of fused cultural horizons, this point angered some more the institutional guardians of European cultural purity, betraying how anti-globalist intransigence survives even at the heart of cosmopolitan domains.

I set out to explore how the *DVC's* intersecting networks and narratives of neo-pilgrimage construct our identity as 'cosmopolitan travellers', seeing and collecting 'cultures' from above, from afar, as possessions from outside. But I will also move on to argue how the self-same cosmopolitan knowledge, with all its paradoxes, informs the cinematic narrative's reinvention of history from a feminist point of view. In the next part I examine some elements of contemporary tourism and how signs are central to the networks of contemporary travel, in particular how the *DVC* necessitates a '*Da Vinci* node' within extensive networks of globalizing relationships. Cosmopolitanism is examined here as a facet of 'mobility cultures' of transient business, professional pursuits and middle-class tourism that relates education and self-betterment to leisure. This is already part of the language of knowledge economies, and mediascape theorists such as Appadurai or Urry purport to shed light on socio-economic structures that generate agency through flows of ideas, products and human movement. It is also part of the lexicon of a 'liquid modernity' (Bauman 2000b) – incidentally, also Urry's starting point – that promotes individualism and entrepreneurial talent as both the apotheosis and the downfall of the postmodern subject. The mediascapes of this chapter reside in Internet extensions of the *DVC* node, which are managed by various independent actors.

The third part of the chapter explains that the language of global flows remains incomplete without an examination of the ideological and material immobilities that defined the history of cosmopolitanism and which did not escape Brown's pen. This necessitates a return to the cinematic narrative and its literary core, to show how 'sign collection' informs the art *and* practice of history writing. The *DVC* literary node, the foundation of the material node of tourism and capital – of art-as-practice in short – radicalizes knowledge because it attacks conventions regarding authorship. Here I pay attention to the gendered and racialized dimensions of knowledge the institution of the Church safeguards to this day. Religious knowledge facilitated the migration of exclusivist medieval traditions to the modern age of reason. In turn, modernity revived Hellenic-European modes of belonging and fused them with Christian pedagogy, generating new patterns of inequality. The *DVC* and the *AD* debate these histories through representations of religious etiquette and hierarchy but also through modern academic and scientific erudition, sparing praise neither for traditional theosophy nor for contemporary philosophy. In the concluding part I recapitulate my observations to provide an alternative 'social theory' agenda through the arts that promotes ideas of intersectionality (class, ethnicity, race and gender) in the study of tourism mobilities. There I move on to add the third film to my analysis, because its popular culture has instructive value for this study of multiple mobilities. Whether we situate this agenda in the counter-cultures of modernity or recognize it explicitly as a postcolonial critique of subaltern exclusion (Gilroy 1993; Bauman 1991; Spivak 1999, 1993), it is worth noting in advance that it has been attacked for its promotion of mobilities.

Staging cosmopolitanism: neo-pilgrimage in Europe

The types of tourism that the film presents worked as a mould which *DVC* tourist industries used to reproduce ideal types of tourist. The types were subsequently promoted online and in corporeal forms. The *DVC* industry emerged from the cinematic mobilization of a distinct collection of 'signs' (Urry 2002: 3) imaginatively arranged in a new order (Ateljevic 2000: 381). The old order, on which new empires of signs were built, points to the early phases of travel. I refer to the history of the so-called Grand Tour, a rite of passage for predominantly male youths of upper middle-class and aristocratic families during the eighteenth and nineteenth centuries. This was part of the pedagogical training they would receive before 'manning' the administrative orders of the British empire. The Grand Tour was constitutive of Enlightenment conceptions of cosmopolitan knowledge that valorized classicist education (of the ancient civilizations of Greece and Italy) over the study of African and Middle Eastern civilizations. I use gendered and racialized references consistently here to stress their presence in my archaeological analysis of cosmopolitanism and to establish further links between that and what Said (1978) and others (Loomba 2005) examined as 'Orientalism': knowledge of the 'other' was a medium of control (administration of colonized 'races') reserved for the highest ranks of colonial hegemons (the upper classes of European metropoles) who were invariably *white men*. As Urry implies in earlier work (2002), just as Grand Tourists figured as modern 'producers' of specific versions of our humanity, the first professional makers of the 'tourist gaze' were cosmopolitan businessmen (e.g. Thomas Cook) marketing opportunities to enjoy otherness in safe ways (organized travel). Travel books, the first medium to democratize travel for the middle classes, defined the contours of cosmopolitanism long before film and the Internet: they formed a referential matrix in which on-site experiences could be embellished with fabulist colour to merge 'truth' and 'fiction' into one vision of other cultures that remained out of reach, even for the greatest part of the better-off metropolitan masses (the old and women).

Likewise, we should not assume that cinematic messages develop in a sociocultural void; on the contrary, they comprise representations of existing consumer experiences that circulate within contemporary culture. It has been suggested that socially constructed images and experiences of place and culture (Rojek 2000: 54; Shields 1991) are not directly the product of tourist industries, but are overdetermined by various 'non-tourist practices, of film, TV, literature, magazines' (Urry 2002: 3; Taylor 2001) and other consumption processes. There have been many other forms of such travel, as people travel elsewhere through memories, texts, guidebooks and brochures, travel writing, photos, postcards, radio and film. In the nineteenth century it was principally written texts, including guidebooks, that were crucial for imaginative travel; in the first half of the twentieth century photographs and the radio were central (Sontag 1990); while in the second half of the twentieth century film and TV became the main media for such travel (Tzanelli 2004a; Tzanelli 2007b; Beeton 2005). The interconnectedness of all these different phases and sectors of creative industries confirms how tourism begins with cultural 'signification' (Culler 1988; MacCannell 1989; Urry 2002; Wang 2000). By the same token, the *DVC* signs did not belong to any pre-established order, but their simultaneous de- and re-contextualization generated a new sign order transferred from Brown's story to the big screen and then to various tourist networks, including the Internet. As MacCannell (1989) has suggested, mediated versions of tourist locations generate 'markers' of places in the form of images. Film has this function: it ascribes meaning to locations through imagining, making them desirable destinations through 'imaginative travel' (Urry 2007).

My repeated use of metaphors such as 'node' and 'matrix' suggests interconnections of policies (tourism industries) and practices (writing), enabling me to link Orientalism to early visions of cosmopolitanism and then to deconstruct such connections through the 'disorganized capitalism' thesis (Lash and Urry 1987) and its revisions (Lash and Urry 1994). Following Marx's (1976) elaboration of labour and value, Harvey terms capital a 'value in motion' (1999: 83–4). Harvey critiques its chameleon nature, the way it circulates in different social domains and networks, as well as how these networks communicate and complement each other. Although this chapter concerns (cinematic and actual) travel mobility, it also notes the global mobility of capital and its interdependence with diverse mobilities (Urry 2007: 212). This capital mobility is unidirectional and multidirectional at the same time: it generates new forms of cultural tourism while it presupposes old (travel agencies, hotel chains) and the new (Internet) capitalist networks, such as those implicated within *DVC* tourism. Virilio (21 October 1984: 156) observes how the 'nodal' has succeeded the 'central' in electronic environments of 'tele-localization', enhancing a 'technocentric' logic that eradicates secular oppositions of the city/country and the state: we are a global village now. However, unlike Virilio's anti-humanist stance that runs through actor-network theory, my take on networks stresses human agency evolving over time.

We may talk about a *DVC* 'economy of sign and space' (Lash and Urry 1994) – networks that do not function on the basis of a prefixed relationship, save that most of them are recognized by humans as part of European cultural heritage. The *DVC* phenomenon complemented organized societal spaces with flexible structures assembled through flows of cultural signs (Castells 1996; Urry 2003). The communication of these flows was 'chaotic' in that it was not direct and controlled by state apparatuses or single hierarchies, but ordered with the help of a US-financed film: first, through the reduction of the diverse *loci* of European cultural heritage into interchangeable and easily quantifiable 'abstract' signs (also Adorno 1991; Adorno and Horkheimer 1993). This was assisted by the mercurial nature of virtual mobility management, which resides in 'scapes' of global structuration, where even corporeal travel can become redundant. Second, the *DVC* sign potential was mobilized by various tourist providers to construct a type of tourist that appears to promote European cosmopolitan values.

Viewing positions and cinematic tourism

Langdon and Neveu proffer versions of cinematic tourism: devoted to their investigation and consumed by intellectual curiosity and determination to solve the mystery of the Grail, they echo the passion of the Grand Tourist to be educated and transformed by the corporeal experiences of travel (Brodsky-Porges 1981).

Langdon (a Harvard academic) and Neveu (a government agent) immerse in European culture through a painstaking analysis of early modern documentation on science, the holy scripts and a study of art history in order to fulfil the purpose of their travel exploits. Every time they visit a new location the camera situates them geographically (with a caption at the bottom of the screen); their visits to cultural sites are often followed by a brief history of that place. The cinematic technology incorporates travel guide techniques: it equates the movement of the protagonists in an imagined European space to narratives of culture and history that entrepreneurs such as Thomas Cook used in nineteenth-century guides and we find today in Rough Guides. As Neumann states, there is usually a 'public discourse' that precedes and 'frames' visits to places 'repeatedly mark[ing] the boundaries of significance and value at tourist sites' (1988: 24). Throughout the movie Langdon and Neveu display a double identity as middle-class profession-als and as tourists for a day. They exemplify the modern mobile subject of airflight travel who visits liminal spaces such as the train station or the airport (Urry and Larsen 2011: 29). Standing between the new elites and the new service class of transnational knowledge economies, they represent social change.

The transposition of this version of globalization theory onto the big screen is recognisable by viewers of most cultures and social identities: 'viewing posi-tions' thus partake in the marketing of the film, popularizing elite production (reading history) and consumption (visiting sites) of 'signs'. As contemporary mobile subjects, Langdon's and Neveu's engagement with apocryphal and philo-sophical aspects of Christian doctrine helps them to transcend an emotionally neutralized study of European culture, reminiscent of the early phase of the Grand Tour (Towner 1985), and to engage personally with the mystery they investigate. The shift of experiential perspective resembles a rite of passage (van Gennep 1906; Turner 1974), and transforms the fictional protagonists into pilgrims of the elusive sacred sites that they trace. Hence, the *DVC* endorses the idea of the tourist as a 'secular pilgrim' in quest of experiential authenticity (the acquisition of the Holy Grail) (MacCannell 1973; Cohen 1973, 2003). The presentation of this quest 'culturally legitimates the practice of (sight-seeing) tourism' (Cohen 2003: 101), transforming film viewers-as-tourists into collectors of particular kinds of signs, interlinked with each other to demonstrate high cultural capital (Bourdieu 1977, 1984). It is a new 'tour' that the *DVC* describes and legitimates, but it is a 'tour' nonetheless.

If anything, the director's cinematic gaze encourages the subjectivization of viewing experience, which is linked to feminine/feminist ways of seeing *and* interpreting (Kaplan 1986; Mayne 1995; Friedberg 1995). The positioning of the protagonists within the story however counters this vision, sustaining a gendered hierarchy of knowledge constitutive of the history of cosmopolitanism. This hierarchy is also debated in the cinematic adaptation of *AD* that pairs Langdon with Vetra. In *AD* Vetra assumes the side of natural science in opposition to Langdon's hermeneutic humanism that is more associated with feminist scholarly move-ments in the West. In opposition to *DVC's* radical critique, *AD* addresses some familiar socialist feminist themes on labour mobility to counter essentializations that freely occurred in the first film (see Weedon 1987; de Lauretis 2007: 263). The director and the cameraman's intentions aside, the cinematic tourist experience is not 'simulated' (Baudrillard 1983) in similar ways by all *DVC* tourists: as Edensor argues, 'tourism is a process which involves an ongoing (re)construction of praxis and space in shared contexts' (2001: 60; Graburn 2001: 151).

There are many different places dependent upon the performances that occur within them (Bærenholdt *et al.* 2004). Established *DVC* suggestions for the consumption of place and culture may be challenged on location. The prevalence of the gaze in this analysis does not intend to downplay other sensory experiences as analysed by various scholars (Veijola and Jokinen 1994; Cloke and Perkins 1998; Crouch and Desforges 2003). It is just that my main concern is not tourist performances as such but the prevalent norms, practices and patterns consolidated in the staging of the *DVC* tourist experience by networks of international tourist providers, of companies, churches and states (see MacCannell's notion of 'staged authenticity', 1973). The theatrical stage that *DVC* tourist networks promote is linked to the ocular character of their cinematic node. Marketization practices that reside in the *DVC* and its emerging tourist networks interpellate, call into being, a cosmopolitan subject keen to gaze upon, experience and enjoy European culture and history in a detached fashion that sets them apart from the locales they visit. This cosmopolitan tourist is what I call a *neo-pilgrim*, a pilgrim overwhelmed by secularized religious sublimation, just like Adler's 'anchorite' pilgrim who looks for spiritual purity in the wilderness (1992: 408–13). Unlike the anchorite pilgrim, the *DVC* neo-pilgrim does not seek solitude in order to experience the sublime, but welcomes the tourist systems of luxury hotels such as the *Ritz* (a cinematic attraction visually embedded in Langdon's and Neveu's tourist trajectory) and of organized tours within the filmed locations. Much like Bauman's (1998) tourist, the privileged neo-pilgrim is able to play at their pilgrimage, be a pilgrim for a day, and hence is another example of contemporary 'post-tourism', the 'knowing' tourist (Urry 2002). This interpellation is symmetrical to Langdon's and Neveu's cinematic function as fleeting visitors of European heritage markers: thus, the cosmopolitan *tourist* and the cosmopolitan *expert* begin to converge to democratize elite consumption.

Virtual and embodied journeys in 'Europe'

There are many examples of how in this node various travel guides interpellate the neo-pilgrim. The primary locus of this is the Internet, which is full of virtual tours, such as that offered by GoogleEarth. Such tours allow one to visit these filmed places virtually, but also to take the fictional routes of the novel's various characters. The experience of zooming in and looking at satellite aerial photos of these sites transforms one into a 'virtual *flâneur*' (Tzanelli 2006a), a type of traveller who experiences a digital space-time compression, enabling them to stay at the heart of global developments while retaining territorial distance and anonymity as is the case also with round-the-world travellers (Germann Molz 2004: 171). This virtual *flâneurie* is promoted by other tour(ist) providers that advertise the

DVC online: Fodor's invites cinematic viewers and Brown fans to 'travel the roads' taken by the protagonists of the novel, linking thus the literal to the pictorial/cinematic narrative. The site operates as a secondary node as Fodor's article is followed by a hyperlink to a variety of terrestrial tours of the key locales. *First Great Western* travel magazine takes a step further by linking *DVC*-led tourism to other instances of film-induced tourism in London (December 2006: 26). Films such as *Notting Hill, Howard's End, Creep, Mission Impossible* and *Match Point* figure in an illustrated article on famous cinematic locations. At the bottom of the page an Internet address is provided for those who would like to 'map' or visualize their travel trajectory. The same strategy is adopted by Heelan in his online article for Frommer's (16 December 2004), which also underscores the significance of numerous travel novels for the development of global tourism. A Traveller's Guide to London (2006) follows the same practice, while advertising the book and tours for foreign visitors. GotoParis.com, a website that specializes in 'discovering France', offers 'designer tours' for *DVC* fans, alongside the stereotypical night clubbing, shopping and 'Paris romantic evening' options, making the whole experience an exercise in consuming places but where the places now include unexpected religious and cultural sites indicating cultural taste.

DVC tour providers are located in various places, such as Denmark where the website Panoramas (2006) hosts photographed images of the cinematic locations, and even New Zealand (Da Vinci Code Tours 2006) that, following the *LOTR* success, began to promote its cultural image online as the home of Tolkien's 'Middle Earth' (Tzanelli 2004a). The New Zealand *DVC* tours are accompanied by references to their potential for 'self-discovery' even though they stand between 'fact and fiction' (*ibid.*) – yet another allusion to their simulatory function. British Tours Ltd (2006) places more emphasis upon London's key locations, combining a presentation of their place in the cinematic and literary narrative with their place in English history, and VisitScotland.com does the same for Edinburgh's religious history and culture. Just like the New Zealand reference to simulation, the site stresses the hybridity of cinematic discourse, noting how 'the art of film editing allows in some cases widely separated locations in Scotland to come together to represent a single place' or to revisit particular locations because of their 'dramatic ambience'. Rosslyn Chapel is listed as a magical location which figured in as diverse cinematic registers as those of the *DVC* and *Trainspotting* (1996), transforming anonymous communities into recipients of global tourism.

The placelessness of the Internet is ideal for developing new unexpected collections of 'signs' of the unique places that literally cannot be elsewhere, and are begging to be collected after the appearance of the film. Whether we choose to see this as a manifestation of 'global fluids' (as in Bauman 2000b) of images and ideas or 'ideoscapes' and 'mediascapes' (as in Appadurai 1990), such Internet marketing promotes a form of cosmopolitan knowledge that mobilizes specificity in the name of a constantly malleable global culture. Not only is this culture easily accessible to anyone with an Internet connection, it is also invites revision: from blogs where users post comments on products and experiences to the Web 2.0 interactivity and collaborative content generation, Internet users figure less as passive recipients of a globalization from above and more as its creative agents from below (Harrison and Barthel 2009). Thus, I do not seek to adopt a deterministic view of Internet marketing of cinematic tourism, only to examine this marketing from the viewpoint of professional symbol creators and the creative industries within which they move.

It is worth having a look at one such Internet user-turn-entrepreneur who displays the versatility of the upper service class and its bourgeois-bohemian status (Brooks 2000) that fuses the liberal idealism of the 1960s with the ideology of individualism of the post-1980s era. Sacred Earth Journeys (2006) is a website located in Canada which advertises combined tours to Paris, London and Edinburgh. The tour leader who figures online is Mark Amaru Pinkham, author of *The Guardians of the Holy Grail*, 'Templar Knight' and 'co-director of the North American branch of The International Order of Gnostic Templars' founded by himself and his wife. He is a devoted traveller to India and other countries and has studied the Hindu scriptures and the Theosophists of India who wrote on the secret history of earth. His links with Andean esoteric societies and his dedication to the occult (in the past he has led an expedition in search of a secret monastery in the Andes à la *DVC*) propelled him to establish in 1994 Soluna Tours Sacred Journeys, a commercial company that organizes tours for those seeking spiritual experiences by visiting sacred sites in other countries. Pinkham advertises his Scottish ancestry, which allegedly 'dates back to Prince Henry St. Clair' whose family built Rosslyn Chapel. He promises to deliver a series of lectures on the history mobilized by Brown in the film on location, thus bestowing the tour with the aura of erudition and authority through lineage. One could also see in Pinkham a sort of Orientalist scholar who appropriates cultural signs, histories and identities of ancient Oriental civilizations, treating them as environments that can be managed in mystical rituals akin to those of Gaia (Argyrou 2005). The ultimate aim is to demonstrate that he possesses the identity of a cosmopolitan adventurer who is interested in creating personal genealogies for economic returns but who is even more interested in their value as social capital (Bourdieu 1993: 77; also Giddens 1987 on professional individualization). As Rojek (2001: 13) notes, such a biography is able to produce celebrity discourses similar to those we find in popular beliefs in 'the divine right of kings'. Pinkham's hazy genealogical connection to Arthurian legend replaces old auratic authorial frames with the postmodern discourse of experiential tourism (Earl 2008: 409).

The *DVC* brand of cultural capital primarily rests in the civilizational roots of Europe, as the marketization of cultural authenticity is prominent in Paris tours, addressed mainly to American *DVC* tourists. Paris is still considered the cradle of 'high culture' on the other side of the Atlantic – a view of European sophistica-tion that has dominated Hollywood cinema for decades. Tour providers repeat-edly call upon the ideal type of neo-pilgrim, suggesting that in this way tourists can 'distinguish themselves from the herd' by 'making their museum visit the contemplative experience art was intended to provide' (Paris through Expatriate Eyes, 2006; Paris Muse, 2006). Cultural capital can thus be acquired through collecting this particular set of signs, making this sign collector a 'sophisticated traveller' rather than a 'common tourist' (Buzard 1993). Jeff Steiner's Americans in France, a site that uses the *DVC* as a path to acculturation for American visitors in Europe, promotes traditional tour options that involve roaming the Paris sites as well as enjoying a minibus tour and a cruise down the Seine. The main page is however surrounded by hyperlinks to *DVC* products sold on Amazon.com and research around the *DVC* story that involves the blending of historical records with occult philosophy and 'break the code' tourism. The simulation of Langdon's and Neveu's attempts to 'break the code' figure in most of the online tour options (Kunkle, 14 May 2006), especially those addressed to American tourists. But Jeff Steiner, an American who has lived in France for a long time, prefers to present himself as someone who provides 'the "straight" info, no rose coloured glasses and you decide if France is right for you' (Jeff Steiner 2001–6). In 'over 4000 pages of personal info about living and travelling in France', Steiner combines the experience of a cultural tourist with the talent of a Grand Tour travel writer. Thus the *DVC* is mobilized in the articulation of counter-Europeanism (e.g. the discourse of American matter-of-factness as a self-stereotype versus European sophistication) to redirect attention to American cultures of mobility (Morley and Robins 1995: 80).

Neo-pilgrimage and social theory

This figure of the neo-pilgrim can be viewed as constitutive of formulations of the contemporary cosmopolitan. There are many different notions of the cosmo-politan. Vertovec and Cohen (2002) have identified six main conceptions: as a socio-cultural condition (Appadurai 1996); as a philosophical view or worldview as in Beck's 'cosmopolitan manifesto' (2000); as a political project to build trans-national institutions (Kaldor 1996); as a political project for recognizing multiple identities (Held 1995); as a mode of orientation to the world (Hannerz 1990); and as a set of competences which allow one to make one's way within other cultures and countries (Friedman 1994). The cinematic spectacle suggests that in contem-porary societies we come to know places but from afar. Air travel is the best expression of the shift in the relationship of place from land to landscape: air travel affords a god's eye view, a view of the earth from above, with places, towns and cities laid out as though they are a form of nature. In Ingold's terms, air travel generates 'map-readers' rather than 'wayfinders' (2000). While wayfinders move around within a world, map-readers move across a surface of the globe as imag-ined from above. Air travel colludes in producing and reinforcing the language of abstract mobilities and comparison thus promoting the expression of an abstracted mode of being-in-the-world and colonizing from above. Through this mode places get transformed into a collection of abstract characteristics in a mobile world, ever easier to be visited, appreciated and compared from above, but not really known from within (Szerszynski and Urry 2006).

This indirect engagement with other cultures echoes the nineteenth-century ethnographer's translation of experience into graphically arranged knowledge of the 'other' (Fabian 1983: 106–7). The *DVC* endorses both nineteenth-century and contemporary modes of knowing the world, forming continuities between them, especially because some scenes in the film are characterized by a detachment of human agency from visual diegesis. To act and to see, the political and the cogni- tive, become artificially separated: high-angle and distance shots of cultural sites may be granting viewers an omniscient perspective, but also transform landscape into the principal actor of the story. This tension was transferred into the commodification of the *DVC*, which simultaneously invites tourists, virtual or not, to re-enact the cinematic adventure but also to spend time gazing and enjoy- ing the filmed cultural sites. The marketed tourist imagination is societally arranged and 'learned' (Strain 2003: 265): viewing unfamiliar cultures from afar (the airplane, the Internet) provides both a sense of security and the thrills of sanitized adventure. In the staging of tourist consumption, the *DVC* ideal type of cosmopolitan tourist appears to operate in an 'aesthetically reflexive' manner, monitoring rather than passively accepting a predetermined place in the social world (Beck 1992; Beck *et al.* 1994; Lash and Urry 1994: 5–6). Cinematic and actual *DVC* tourists may be seen as participants in a new version of the 'public sphere' (Habermas 1989a) that is performed, 'staged' with the help of new media (Thompson 1995). The aesthetic reflexivity of the cosmopolitan tourist resembles the romantic form of the Grand Tour(ist) gaze that emphasized privacy, solitude and spiritual growth through an intense engagement with the observed object (Urry 1995: 137), but also the mediated gaze of Internet touring, which reinforces this privacy while encouraging communication (Kozinets 1999; Baym 2000).

The cosmopolitan tourist is interpellated through *DVC* tourist networks: by drawing attention to the aesthetic experience of visiting cinematic sites, tourist industries promote the creation of interlinks between all these tourist sites that are scattered over the European continent. This is assisted by the hegemonic European convention to use the idea of culture 'in opposition to notions of that which is vulgar, backward, ignorant, or retrogressive' (Jenks 1993: 9; Eagleton 2000: 32; Meethan 2003). This tourist type clashes with literal meanings of *kosmopolítis*, the subject that inhabits the space of the aesthetic (*kósmos* as beauty). It is no coincidence that the Kantian *sensus communis*, the moral universe of human solidarity and togetherness, frequently figures in critical accounts of cosmopolitanism: Kantian beauty is supposed to foster social bond- ing, and its moral principles would go against the individualization of the aesthetic experience. Arendt's critique of the individualization of action, which is not grounded in social co-presence and an agreement with others supported by dialogue (Benhabib 1992), could be read against a critique of the consumerist logic that characterizes modernity (Bauman 2005; Davis 2008: 56). It has been argued that this social vision corresponds to a neo-liberal, 'thin' cosmopolitanism rooted in Enlightenment understandings of the concept related to mobility, travel and 'societal pluralization' (Delanty 2006: 31; Erskine 2002; Stevenson 2002). The *DVC* cosmopolitan tourist of the tourist networks is viewed from this perspective as a subject who pursues visual pleasures of collecting sites/sights, endorsing the values of an empire of capital (Hardt and Negri 2000). And yet, this individualized mode of seeing, thinking and touring the world virtually (online) and actually (by air travel) is ingrained in the democratization of tourist consumption.

Thus this democratization may not be truly democratic, given that such ways of being in the world apply to the developed countries but are inaccessible to the dispossessed masses of the developing world, where air flight and Internet connection are a luxury at best. The public sphere of mediatized political cultures (Castells 1996) may be promoting a form of aesthetic reflexivity, but it does not resolve such social divisions. I do not aspire to reiterate the argument supported by theorists of methodological nationalism that take the nation-state as an exclusive starting-point in reflections on inequality. As Beck (2002: 21) notes, globalization and cosmopolitanization do not exist in entirely polarized ways or take place only across national boundaries, but are processes that change national societies from within (Sassen 2000). The democratized consumption of the *DVC* network both transcended national boundaries and incited a variety of responses within states that operated as hosts of *DVC* signs. In the case of France, in which cultural heritage is safeguarded by the state and defines national identity, the inscription of the *DVC* myth over established understandings of high culture artefacts might have generated some resentment in French citizens against cosmopolitan tourists and consumers, but it also led to the incorporation of some *DVC* signs into local tourist advertising (CBS News, *The Early Show*, November 2004; CBS News, 12 November 2004; McGrath, 30 May 2006). Take for example a staffer at the Louvre's information desk under Pei's glass Pyramid (the alleged tomb of Magdalene), who 'has no advice for the daily trickle of curious fans. "After all", he sniffs, "the book is fiction"' (Bly, 21 October 2004). Such comments reiterate the urgency to draw clear-cut distinctions between authenticity and unauthorized (by those who regard themselves as legitimate heirs of this culture) reproduction, or the unanimously recognized cultural capital of France and the banal artefacts of contemporary cultural industries.

The urgency to protect these artefacts also secretly genders and sexualizes their heritage status, promoting the sort of universalisms even feminist scholarship cannot always escape. All the more reason then to revisit these sites and highlight the reasons behind the urgency to maintain these sclerotic boundaries between 'art', 'fiction' and even the academic disciplines that study them (Hall 1992; MacRobbie 2006: 527). But at the same time there are Parisian hotel managers today who are keen to provide their own 'critical tours' of the story, thus legitimizing the working of a *DVC* node and network that provides services to cosmopolitan consumers and tourists. The same ambivalence informs the reactions of some priests to the newly constituted *AD* node: 'You never get a priest coming up and yelling at you "get out you heretics"', a tour guide explains. 'Sometimes they might be a little bit edgy because they know it's "Angels and Demons" but at the same time I think they are aware that it's, you know, a work of fiction and that it's bringing people into their churches' (CBS, 19 June 2008). The tension exemplifies Beck's 'cosmopolitan crisis' (2002: 27) that begins with the unexpected appropriation of a revered cultural heritage resting at the heart of Europe proper and results in its reinvention for external audiences and hosts alike

(Tzanelli 2007b: 146–7). It is a crisis that generates debate around the role of literacy and its surrounding hegemonies. In this case the hegemonies are represented by a Catholic Church that would not admit in European Christianity any pagan or Oriental elements, frequently present in Brown's novel. We need only couple the comments of the Louvre's staffer with those of a life-long parishioner at the Church of Saint-Sulpice in Paris, who exclaimed to a reporter that 'it's all wrong. The description of the artwork, the architecture, the documents in this church … secret rituals – I don't know, because we never had any secret rituals in the church' (CBS News, 12 November 2004). Following the cinematic adaptation of the novel, the agitated parishioner decided to put on the wall next to the obelisk a notice: 'Contrary to fanciful allegations in a recent best-selling novel, this is not a vestige of a pagan temple. No such temple existed in this place. It was never called a Rose Line. It does not coincide with the meridian…' (Sacred Destinations, undated). The clash between the determination to preserve artwork's aura (Benjamin 1992: 217) and the need to trade in mechanical reproduction, leads to the emergence of new forms of culture.

The history of the Louvre's Pyramid points to the clash between a broader discourse that prioritizes facts and another that opens up the domain of history proper to accept fiction. I.M. Pei's material intervention in the architectural integrity of an essentially classical project (the Louvre) promoted the fusion of France's classicist (and imperialist) past with a modernist vision of the world (Heyer 1993: 275–8, 282) that bears the potential to liberate territorially bounded, nationally insular and Orientalist visions of identity from their stifled history of prejudice. The project of implanting such bold structural forms in a Second Empire survival that entertains universal recognition for its cultural rootedness gestures towards the hybridization of a culture that is exclusive by definition – for women, immigrants and any other form of 'vagabond' identity that does not neatly fit into national archetypes of belonging. Pei's Pyramids has been a controversial project since its announcement in 1985 as one of President Mitterrand's most ambitious *grand projets* (Great Buildings Online, 2008). The pluralist vision of the social it upheld explains why the *DVC* story has inflamed the Church and a political establishment that continues to support its unity and continuity with the state. The French president's conviction that 'humankind cannot be separated from nature' and that we all have a duty to protect it as our very own 'sustainable garden' (Argyrou 2005: 75) speaks the same ambiguous language of environmentalism that the Pyramid symbolizes. In this environmentalist discourse the European debt to the past was from the outset a debt to the gendered and multicultural properties of 'Mother Earth'.

Such revisionism was not unilaterally produced by Brown but was effectively mediated on the big screen through his novel. French history is visually rewritten through the projector the moment Langdon arrives at the Louvre with the suspicion that Magdalene's resting place is the mythical inverted Pyramid – a discovery that suggests a cinematic resolution. Here we may recall Benjamin's (1989: 50) observation that the material text might be subjected to standardization through constant reproduction (print, digital) but the literary text is unique in its existence

Figure 3.1 Tom Hanks on the Louvre's Pyramid in the *DVC*.
Credit: Columbia Pictures/Imagine Entertainment/Photofest.

at the place where it happens to be. But whose version of events should we believe on this occasion – and whose sanctity is at stake? This resolution operates as a departure on a debate between the politics of Pei's creation and its mobilization in popular culture (Religion Facts, 2008b). This necessitates a return to the *DVC* cinematic narrative, which uses Pei's artistic (material) creation to outline the vicissitudes of cosmopolitan exclusion anew: first, by prioritizing the role of women in cultural production and democratizing its consumption; and second, by connecting the discourse of gendered authorship to that of racialized exclusion.

Alternative scripts: cosmopolitanism and gender

Here we can establish connections between the cultural and the political – for, as a conception of the world, cosmopolitanism originates in the way in which a supposedly ancient Greek cultural idea was transformed into a political project. I follow this trail for a while, because it supports some interesting observations regarding the quality of cosmopolitan visions that inform both a predominantly male academic discourse and a commonsense engagement with the world – what a post-Kantian tradition recognizes as 'practical reason' (Honneth 1979; 1991: 32–72). The ancient Greek *polítis* of the *kósmos*, a product of Western-born classist misconceptions, misses the exclusivist Hellenistic understandings of citizenship and polity. The 'world citizen' of the Hellenic orator Isocrates (436–338 BC) to whom the concept is attributed, was supposed to speak Greek, think Greek and act as a Greek (*Panegyricus*, para. 50) in the context of the Alexandrian *imperium* (Inglis and Robertson 2005). Those who did not conform to Isocratian expectations were non-humans – beings whose meaningless 'bar bar' language confirmed their barbarian state. The alien tribes of the Eastern and Southern imperial borders were 'exotic' in the most meaningful sense – they stood outside human culture. This cosmopolitan is supposed to embrace the world by colonizing it, intellectually and materially. It is no coincidence that the ideal of the *kosmopolítis* later assisted in the presentation of modern Greek nation-building to the rest of the world as a pedagogical project with religious overtones. It is held that Cyril's educational mission to the Slavonic tribes was arranged by Patriarch Photios (861) for their conversion to Christianity, a civilizing mission the nineteenth-century Greeks named the 'dissemination of the good word'. The rhetoric of Christian 'dissemination' was addressed to Balkan peoples the modern Greeks wanted to incorporate in their new empire (Tzanelli 2008b).

This genealogy of cosmopolitanism is not entirely disconnected from the key cultural and institutional forms that brought nations to life (Smith 1981; 1995), their histories, discontinuities and adaptations. It is also the story of globalization narrated from a structural point of view but with an eye to the uses structures find in new environments. For a sound historical sociology, cultural hybridity should be seen as an everyday condition, whose existence is constantly being denied within national spaces, traditionally defined through boundary erection. What has certainly accelerated hybridization is 'the new middle classes and their cultural and social practices arising in the context of migration and diaspora and the new modernities of the "emerging markets"' (Nederveen Pieterse 2004: 88). Pinkham's *Sacred Journeys* initiative is a striking example of the tranformative power new technologies and the markets they create have on cultural traditions: by merging elements from different religious traditions, his enterprise produces a new 'cultural grammar' (*ibid.* 54–5). The circuits of cultural signs he adopts do not flow in one direction but are broadcast, googled and emailed in many directions and often in bilateral ways (Appadurai 1990: 7; Mackay 2004: 72; Sinclair *et al.* 1996: 5).

The interpretive trajectory of the *DVC* is a celebration of this phenomenon. The tale itself is replete with references to the early history of Christianity – never mind the protests of pedantic scholars that Brown got historical facts wrong when he used the Council of Nicea (325) as a historical landmark in his narrative. Such protests suspiciously mirror the resentment of common folk in France that cinematic simulacra steal, sell and reproduce France's high culture – characteristic of authoritarian populism that in Italy's 'Eternal City' (*AD*'s stage) once dictated combinations of cosmetic conservation with political censorship (Herzfeld 2009a: chapter 3). Unfortunately, the same practices informed Catholic policies over the centuries, making the Vatican a state within dictator Mussolini's state. The meeting in Nicea to which the *DVC* polemically refers, was intended to resolve both theological and administrative issues that threatened the unity of the

Roman empire as a spiritual kingdom – a perfect analogy of nationalist discourses of boundary fixing that informed global authoritarianisms and totalitarianisms. Brown worked as a fabulist historian to single out and rework a particular point from this story: both in the novel and the film the amateur historian Sir Leigh Teabing explains to Sophie how the early Church consolidated its power by destroying the pagan 'sacred feminine' and making the mortal prophet Jesus (a version of Allah's prophet) into a divine being (Religion Facts, 2008a). So, complaints of historical inaccuracy aside, Brown made a point that flew in the face of malestream cosmopolitan manifestos: ancient, early Christian and modern nationalist understandings of the cosmopolitan, exclude from citizenry all those humans who are not male Christians.

Brown's project appears to promote the ecofeminist paradigm in so far as it views the organized destruction of female nature (Magdalene's obliteration) and the subordination of archetypal women through institutional discourse as inextricably interrelated phenomena (Argyrou 2005: 57). As the historical diegesis in the *DVC* attests, different legal approaches were concealed behind universalist pretensions that only native men enjoy full socio-political citizenship rights. Such citizenships were discursively constructed around gendered geometries of power: the public sphere became a *de facto* male territory, as opposed to the private sphere (of family, home), which was populated by passive, secluded femininities (Pateman 1989; Lister 1997a, 1997b; Evans 1997; Walby 1990, 1994; Yuval-Davis and Webner 1999; Lister *et al.* 2007; Tzanelli 2011a). Leading female figures in the *DVC* (Sophie and her ancestors) and *AD* (Vetra, the elusive physicist) are, after all, presented as either in need of protection by political clubs or of instruction by erudite men: cosmopolitan knowledge has a male face, as opposed to its reproductive side (Sarah's line in the *DVC*), which is exclusively female.

A racialized dimension of exclusion complements the gendered, if we take into account the protestations of Muslim scholars that the 'code' (Jesus' divinity) was broken over 1,400 years ago in Islamic scripts (namely, the Quran) (The Religion of Islam, 10 February 2007). Such protests target the Eurocentric spirit of modernity that failed to acknowledge the traditions of the Arab-Islamic world. Building on the physics of Aristotle that *AD*'s cinematic plot debates via Vetra's contribution, the Christian-Latin scholars of the Middle Ages recognized Averröes' 'carry-on philosophical spirit' but forgot his intellectual opponent's (Avicenna) 'oriental teachings' (al Jabri 1999). This philosophical rupture is embedded in the contemporary logic of Western motility that appropriates and markets Oriental mysticism in leisure and travel but demonizes or excludes what does not fit or contradicts its political premises (Mignolo 2002: 950; Kaufman and Montulet 2008: 45; Nederveen Pieterse, undated). Here, the Eastern argument about Western prejudice might also clash with contemporary Western claims to Oriental patriarchy, and widen the political gap between the two some more. A fusion of horizons on equal terms remains an unachievable aim, according to Islamic theosophical proponents (Dallmayr 2001), whereas even for some Western radicals political authorship remains a male, white privilege, revealing misogyny and Islamophobia as two intertwined cosmopolitan paradoxes (see de Lauretis 2007: 363).

The *DVC* cinematic narrative revises this history: Da Vinci's masterpiece *The Last Supper* is transformed into the carrier of a code that overwrites conservative Christian discourse, dominated by male divinity, by a progressive femininity which is pagan and secular. It propagates the idea of a 'woman' (Magdalene) of non-European lineage, a woman immigrant who takes refuge in France out of necessity, to escape persecution, just like contemporary female migrants who cross boundaries to flee political disasters (e.g. Bauman 1998). Ironically, the very moment the *DVC* promotes a critical reversal of 'the figure, which organizes the practices of a society' (de Certeau 1986: 24), it destroys its deconstructive validity by relocating the 'migrant' in the space of contemporary racial persecution: Europe. Adhering to hegemonic narratives of masculinity some European national centres use(d) in order to fix ethnic – especially Islamic – and gendered identities even in global consumption spaces, the *DVC* allegory debates the ethics of mobility (Herzfeld 1985; Cresswell 2001). If indeed politically Islamic 'hyper-veiling' (cultural concealment) developed as a response to the Western colonial gaze, Western unveiling of the Orient developed as a tourist gaze (MacMaster and Lewis 1998: 123, 126).

The transition from this discourse to a second-order one, in which high culture is replaced by popular culture, also illustrates both the paradoxical nature of a cosmopolitanism replete with political clashes and unfair overwritings and the endless educational possibilities the literary and cinematic touring of other cultures opens up for all: Langdon himself clearly states in his opening lecture that symbols (just like tourist, and any other type of cultural signs) find various uses in different contexts. But when examined closely, Langdon's pursuit of the truth (*alítheia*) is part of a Western apparatus. This is corroborated by the appearance in his PowerPoint presentation of the swastika, a Hindu symbol whose original religious meaning was overwritten by Nazi ideology and came to signify in post-Second World War Europe 'evil', or that of the 'blade', the symbol of manhood used in military uniforms to signify rank. This militarization of masculinity can also be read against Teabing's exclamation that Magdalene's alleged prostitution was a fabrication by the Church establishment that sought ways to smear her reputation – a note matching the insurgent feminist literatures of Woolf, Austen, Elliot and the Brönte sisters (de Beauvoir 2007: 355). The *DVC* begins thus to operate as a nodal point for a post-national form of collective identity that resides at the centre of the novel's narrative, the alleged tomb of Magdalene: the Pyramid.

From then on, material and literal references operate in chains of signification to deconstruct exclusivist traditions of literacy, at once gendered and racialized. Magdalene's social identity refers to contemporary modalities of power, if we consider how sexuality has formed a dominant discourse of privileged control in Western sites (Braidotti 1992: 185). *DVC*'s main cinematic referent is the visual and discursive rearrangement of *The Last Supper's* protagonists (Jesus and Magdalene-Apostle) as an embodied unity, a couple. Sir Teabing proceeds in front of Sophie and Langdon 'to digitally remove Magdalene from the polluting domain of prostitution and to place her in the loving arms of Christ – the head of a sacred gathering that is revered as an artistic artefact in actual domains of cultural pilgrimage today (the painting). One may claim that Teabing's technological intervention presents contemporary historical discourse as mediation between the digital craft of virtual travelling in art spaces and the art of evidence-mining or erudite interpretation of artwork: an *alítheia* (also Kvale 1997: 49–50). Teabing's fiction is technologically mediated, just like Brown/Howard's manipulation of Pei's artefact, which becomes literally and literarily impregnated with Magdalene 'the secret Saint'.

Ironically, on a metalevel even Magdalene cannot escape nature, which, in De Beauvoir's terms (2007: 356) is both 'herself and her negation, a kingdom and a place of exile [where Magdalene's essence resides today, according to the *DVC*]'. The very digital mobility of feminine narratives that are instantly reproducible and therefore never 'original' in a Christian sense, accounts for the Vatican's urgency to address the Howard/Brown simulacra of religious history with such vehemence. Repeating the tale of Original Sin (Sahlins 1996) in the form of a theft of the religious establishment's right to interpret Catholic textual heritage, the *DVC* legitimizes the practice of profitable cinematic simulations that can be globally disseminated, further promoting the pursuit of self-interest and leading to fragmentations of the social order. The more the interpretations, the

Figure 3.2 Digital mastery of art as a form of intersectional hermeneutics: Sir Teabing's reading of *The Last Supper* in the *DVC*.
Credit: Columbia Pictures/Imagine Entertainment/Photofest.

more powerful the rebellion humans organize against the earthly custodians of divine orders. *DVC*'s liberal humanist narrative finds an even more challenging continuation in the fictional scientific plane of *AD* where the Vatican itself, as material and intellectual heritage, is saved by a *homo hermeneut* (Langdon) and a female scientific genius (Vetra). The couple weaves gendered mobility into theory-informed action, commonly associated with post-structuralist feminism (de Lauretis 2007: 365) and memory-work as a 'method of lives lived out on the borderlands, lives for which the central interpretive devices of [dominant] culture don't quite work' because they belong to intimate human spheres such as those of the family (Kuhn 1995: 8; Tzanelli 2011a: chapter 6; Ali 2012).

Precarious hermeneutics: the politics of gender/sexuality in social research

The effemination of otherness was a strategy used by European, colonial power centres to construct hierarchies of human nature. Just as modern air travel supported the disconnection of seeing from knowing from within, so a particular (conservative) version of scientific positivism supported the disconnection of observing from experiencing. From this perspective, the *DVC* story is also paradigmatic of early feminist battles regarding ways of 'doing social science': it popularizes a scholarly debate upon traditional divides between '*male*stream research' (dominated by the positivist approach, doing things through numbers and rigid planning) and feminist objections (dominated by the interpretivist approach, doings things through participant observation and open planning) (Oakley 1998; Argyrou 2005: 120–1). As a popular counterpart of feminist history, it provides viewers the opportunity to know through unlearning patterns of prejudice, without forgetting their history. The *DVC* capitalist node takes this a step further, inviting viewers to become performers of this knowledge through their own journey of the sites and the fabulist heroes' adventures – a step towards a positive feminization of tourist markets.

But there is more to the story's political trajectory, in the *DVC* novel and the film ideas of authorship and authority go hand in hand, reminding us that global modernity may be dialectical in its specific moments (Giddens 1990) and dialogical in its global scope but 'power geometries' (Massey 1993, 1994) remain entrenched in the social processes that comprise its mechanics (Tomlinson 1999: 63). Here, the cultural facets of cosmopolitanism begin to converge with the political ones, especially as Langdon, a male academic of the American intellectual establishment, appears to be sceptical of the validity of hidden religious records. The cosmopolitan paradox of exclusion in an inclusive political agenda is read in the story of the Holy Grail, the human (rather than divine) union of Jesus and Magdalene. Da Vinci, the old and wiser Sir Teabing explains to (a slightly dismissive) Langdon, set the male and female counterparts in opposite but simultaneous union in his composition to produce the code that grants women passage to human history. Even though Magdalene is placed by the painter on the right hand of Jesus, the place of honour, readers would take for granted that she is just another male disciple of Jesus (a 'scoptoma', Teabing explains: 'The mind sees what it chooses to see'). So, the *DVC* can also be viewed as a pedagogical project, an attempt to retrain our mind in reading signs that are thrown at us in new arrangements – an interesting alternative to conventional sociological teaching on the interplay between structure and agency.

The film is populated with signs that refer to the 'sacred feminine' – from Langdon's historical overview of world religions to the Venus star carved in the dead body of Jacques Saunière, to its interpretation by Teabing and Sophie as a confirmation of Magdalene's 'royal blood' (Sang/real). Ironically, even Louvre's pyramid (otherwise read as yet another iconic blade) ends up hiding the feminine underneath it (Magdalene's burial place). Place this against the history of witch-craft, to which Teabing refers: *The Witches' Hammer*, a book instructing the clergy 'how to locate, torture and kill all free thinking women' operates as the historical counterpart of Langdon's dismissive comment on the unofficial history of the Chalice ('this is an old wife's tale!'). Teabing and Langdon voice two complementary faces of history writing: one that concentrates on facts and evidence (the historicist, 'scientific' approach) and the other that acknowledges its poetic and fabulist nature, and tries to do justice to any hidden polyvocalities of the past (de Peuter, 1998).

Gender complementarity is revised in *AD* scenes shot in the simulated library of the Vatican, in which Langdon and Vetra consult Galileo's *Discourse of Truth* (*Diagramma Veritatis*). Visually restaging the fragility of truth (the manuscript presents Galileo's repressed views on the solar system), positivism is now assigned to the female scientist whereas the old art of hermeneutics is presented as a male academic skill. As a preferred cosmology, the shift from biology to physics attempts to speak of the evolution of the universe as a single unfolding process in feminist terms (Argyrou 2005: 57, 154–5), but the very presence of second- and third-order manipulation of reality through Vetra's technological knowledge also counters this (Hand 2012: 129). Cinema's cosmic projection of *DVC's* ethics of care works in the same direction, by universalizing the particular while enchanting Magdalene's tale. The slip from ecofeminism to deep ecology is at the heart of *Avatar*'s development predicament too, as we will see in Chapter 6. This acquires more resonance when we consider McKenna's sugges-tion to Langdon that he should consider how much the priest's garments suit him: hermeneutics (of recovery) stemmed from the art of interpreting biblical texts and was originally reserved for privileged male priesthood. As the newly elected pope makes Langdon permanent custodian of Galileo's *Diagramma*, the heritage of Western knowledge retains its gendered face.

The audiovisual complexity of the second film generates new contradictions: following *AD*'s release, Golden Globe and Grammy Award nominee for *DVC* Hans Zimmer claimed in a joint interview with Howard that the theme from 'CheValiers de Sangreal' represented a 'musical identity for Langdon's journey', serving as 'the backbone' for the cinematic sequel's score (Filmtracks, 5 October 2009). The composer's scores for both films bear many similarities in what has been identified as 'consistent masculine choral bombast and propulsive bass

Figure 3.3 Playing with gendered hermeneutics: Aylet Zurer (Vetra) as science and Robert Langdon (Tom Hanks) as human science.
Credit: Columbia Pictures/Photofest.

ostinatos on pulsating strings or synthesizers' (*ibid.*). Conveying the constant build-up of emotion in the face of suspended resolution of the mystery, *DVC*'s music was so tense that the British Board of Film Classification granted it a 12A certificate only after the producers (Sony) made significant changes to its audio content (Scotsman.com, 7 May 2006; Live Journal, 24 May 2009). *DVC*'s and *AD*'s bone-crunching sound effects which nearly damaged their box-office takings appealed to the conventions of the horror genre. Zimmer's abrasive musical edge in them followed his previous soundtrack stylistics (*Gladiator*, 2001; *The Dark Knight*, 2008; *Batman Begins*, 2005; *Frost/Nixon*, 2009). However, the apocalyptic archplot of *AD* further accentuated the role of electronic ambiance that is present even in the lengthy 'Science and Religion' score, fronted by Joshua Bell's melodic violin – an intentional classical addition to a film claiming intellectual and metaphysical depth. An addition to the music's trivia is that Zimmer hid in his scores an ambigram to match the brands impressed on the *preferiti* by the murderer. Just like the classical tunes he used in key moments of the story, this centuries-old past time has European roots, as author of *Wordplay* (1992) John Langdon's and Brown's inspiration attests in *AD*'s extras (*AD* DVD 2009). Just as Magdalene's tomb, musical signs are begging for discovery by experts so that they acquire a public face.

Cinematic interplays between hidden (private) and revealed (public) stories also point to a shift from modern narratives of sexuality (causal, linear and driven, 'constructing sex as a category of "truth"' [Plummer 1995: 132; Attwood 2006: 79–80]) to postmodern ones that are uncertain and dialogically emerging. Art and pornography 'are caught in a cycle of reciprocal definition, at which each depends on the other for its meaning, significance and status' (Nead 1992 in Attwood 2002: 96). As a trope associated with twentieth and twenty-first-century emancipatory movements, pornography is situationally understood better as a clash between artistic propriety as originality and populist perversity as reproduction. For better or worse, Howard's visual repertoire alludes to such debates by placing Sophie and Langdon in front of Mona Lisa's enigmatic portrait in the sacred space of the Louvre.

Oscillating between uses of the human body as a surface of inscription (of violent acts [Butler 2007: 372–3)) and an object of 'thick description' (of Western civilizational predicaments [Geertz 1973]), Howard provokes institutional resentment at the most fundamental level. On that we may recall that in *AD* Langdon's entrance to the Vatican is marked by his comment that Pius IX's alleged 'great castration' of the statues decorating the preamble represent Catholic vandalism on artistic heritage.

Teabing explains to Sophie and Langdon that the Council of Nicea, the official face of history, rejected the Gospel of Philip, and any other Gospels that challenged Jesus' divinity, because of its references to Christ's preference for Magdalene and their sexual relationship: the term 'companionship' that frequently figures in biblical texts, Langdon explains to Sophie, should be interpreted as 'marriage' and procreation. Official history also denied Magdalene any claims to authorship: her own Gospel was written out of Christian records (its demotion to 'apocryphal' and 'mystical' texts casts it as the secret, intimate aspect of Christianity), discarding the fact that she was the chosen successor of Jesus. In this revelation we may see a narrative thread binding the *DVC* to *AD* via more recent politicizations of Catholic hermeneutics – notably, Vatican II's *Declaration on the Church's Relations to Non-Christian Religions* (Jewish, Islamic, Hindu and Buddist). The Council's split over the uses of Catholic tradition in interpretations of ancient scripts brought to the fore the Church's stance over the persecutions of the Jews in Europe, questioning anti-Semitism, Nazi genocide on one hand and the institution of allegedly Jewish-controlled Freemasonry (woefully confused in *DVC/AD* pop culture with the *Illuminati*), deicide and forgiveness on the other (D'Costa 2010).

Magdalene's tale permeates correct interpretations of tradition with racialized conflict. In debates over the *Declaration,* conservative constituencies also stressed that sacred interpretations should not be confused with the 'detached [and comparative] academic style of the history of religions' (*op. cit.* 494) à la Langdon and Teabing. This deliberate demarcation of divinely ordained originality legitimates elitist European frameworks of artistic authenticity over the know-how experimental frameworks of science and the traditions of social methods and epistemologies. In this respect, the *DVC/AD* narrative discreetly highlights African and Middle Eastern contributions to the foundations of Western European science – a debt to intellectual migrations into the Renaissance and Enlightenment domains that repeatedly shook even the Western academic establishment (for the controversy see Bernal 1991, 1995). It is clearer now why just as the Italian priests of today, the *DVC*'s Apostle Peter appears as the usurper of someone else's human rights, a competitive male asking his master if he chose his female companion over 'them' (the Apostles). As a continuation of his ambivalent historical role in *DVC*, *AD* locates the terrorist bomb in Peter's tomb in the Vatican necropolis, imposing an Orientalization of sorts on religious history via Irish MacKenna's agency. *DVC* is populated with men who seek to eradicate Magdalene's bloodline: two prominent examples are Bishop Manuel Aringarosa (the delegate of Opus Dei) and his surrogate son, Silas, a self-disciplined Albino monk whose marble muscular body stands in the narrative both for the militarist ethos of religion and the Aryan European ideal. Silas' excessive whiteness is an apparent defect: rather than reproducing the harmony of gender and racial order, it defies it, siding with otherworldly creatures such as vampires that appropriate human sexuality. His coloured purity borrows from racist discourse (e.g. Dyer 1993) and subverts it only to reinstate the power of intersectional inequalities.

A second-order discourse would also cast Aringarosa and Silas as the godly 'Father' and his divine 'Son' the 'State' betrays when it arrives at their doorstep in police uniforms to murder them like common terrorists. In a critical take on the Freudian myth, it is the 'Son' of Opus Dei that falls instead of succeeding his Father. The cinematic syntax presents both bodies symmetrically and hierarchically arranged like villainous deities the viewers can easily juxtapose to the Divine Trinity of Teabing, Langdon and Sophie, and to inspector Fache's (Jean Reno) secular power. The betrayal of the sacred feminine extends to historical hermeneutics when Teabing reveals himself as the 'Teacher' whom Silas actually served as Opus Dei's delegated murderer. In this respect, the decision to keep Brown's original novel title for *AD* is rife with intention: as embodiments of good and evil, angels and demons are products of an interaction between Persian Zoroastrianism and Judaism (O'Connor and Airey 2007: 56), another fusion of original traditions the Catholic Church regards with suspicion. The Orientalization of danger in contemporary terrorist discourse comprises part and parcel of this representational complex that toys with colour, degrees of able-bodiness and social conformity.

Although both films service a mandatory Hollywood 'happy ending', the lingering suggestion that they are about the politics of human violence counters the formula of definite resolution: something sinister is left unsaid and undone for posterity. This deferred articulation is best reflected in Teabing's invitation to Sophie to break the code that will put an end to the 'suffering of the poor, those of different colour and women' under the threat of a gun. This perplexing move, which is symmetrically extended to McKenna's determination to protect the Church from science by terrorist means in *AD*, couples the poetics of history with the politics of violence, placing the cosmopolitan agenda of Pai's architectural miracle in a visual linguistic framework. Both cinematic metanarratives are violently iconoclastic and both build on an archplot in which the enemy resides within the auspices of home. This enemy safeguards what they regard their own and circulate only what might intimidate their enemies or might destroy their image in paradigmatic ways. Terrorism associates spectatorship with shaming (which is reserved for effeminate groups in sexist nationalisms), whereas action restores honour and faith in oneself and one's community (the sole path to self-ascribed civility) (Tzanelli 2011a). Ironically, relocating the faceless terrorist at the heart of Christian civilization reproduces European ocular philosophy's primary opposite of light and goodness (darkness), attributed by European theos-ophists, artists and colonizers to non-European others.

From gender to race: Oriental terrorism

Revising the 'Dialectic of Enlightenment', the constant slippage in gender and ethnicity that informs the *DVC* and *AD* exposes socio-cultural communicative fields as context-bound products rather than practices fixed in time and divinely ordained (Ricoeur 1974; Herzfeld 1983; Habermas 1972 and 1989a; Pellauer 2007: 59). The Satanic envy towards God is presented as *de jure* deviant desire with affective and embodied dimensions (Campbell 1964: 354; Turner 1982): just like prostitutes who do business with disempowered men, reproducible digital art corrupts weak humans *en masse* with apocryphal suggestions relating to Christian histories. Vetra's impersonation by an Israeli home name in *AD* is anything but coincidental in this respect, as it challenges theological discourse centring on Jewish craftiness as the demise of Jesus (Tzanelli 2008b). As fully recognized citizens of the nation-state and 'integral segment of the city's [Rome] soul' (Herzfeld 2009a: 58), the Jewish people stand for the ambivalence of human nature but also the double debt to a giving God and a commercial Devil. In a move which was sure to annoy the Vatican, the organizers of *AD*'s premiere in Rome got performers to dress as Vatican Swiss guards (*Daily Mail*, 5 May 2009). Not only did this marketable simulation of tradition complement Zurer's spec-tacular appearance in the event, it also attacked the anti-Semitic stereotypes of duplicity, cunning and betrayal Christian traditions perpetrate. Relocating the cinematic stranger (Hollywood's machinery and its feminine 'icons') within the civic replica of God's kingdom on earth, would be viewed as an insidious replacement of one imagined community (national and religiously homogenous) with another (transnational and mostly secular in pursuits). Of relevance here is the myth of Hollywood's invention by Jews who, feeling impeded from mobility into Eastern aristocracy, migrated westward and invented the modern illusion industry as their own unholy spectacular empire (Lin 2002: 402). Significantly, *AD*'s Vatican retains this glamorous public face throughout, framed by millions of pilgrims, tourists and TV journalists.

We need only recall that the makers of *AD* tried (unsuccessfully) to avert new Vatican criticism by focusing the plot on an act of terrorism at the Vatican but framed this around a more amiable relationship between science and faith. As a plot involving *Illuminati*'s revenge for ancient persecutions of scientists, *AD* attributes ungodly resentment to the proponents of modern reason – a clever reiteration of Kantian and Nietzschean arguments on the role of time and reason on emotional calculation (Bowles 2003). Dan Brown's website (undated; also Book Browse 2001) already cultivates a less amiable link with conspiracy theories about the *Illuminati* cult, including the infiltration of the British Parliament and US Treasury, secret involvement with the Masons, affiliation with Satanic cults, plans for a 'New World Order' and the resurgence of their ancient pact to destroy Vatican City. The *Illuminati*, which were indeed recruited among lawyers, government officials and scientists, embraced Enlightenment philosophical ideas proffered by Immanuel Kant (1724–1804). Their covert associations with the father of European nationalist theory, Johan Gottfried Herder (1744–1803), and a major European intellectual, Johann Wolfgang Goethe (1749–1832), also extends their influence to the emergence of European political modernity. At the same time, the *Iluminati* propagated myths of self-origins in India and Persia, thus generating theosophical links with European Orientalist traditions based on Aristotelian theory.

Notably, the claim that their cult was behind Italian Renaissance and post-Renaissance art and science cast them as progenitors and founders of Western civilization, stripping the Church and the nation-state of their missionary humanist genealogy. The comment a Swiss guard addresses to Langdon concerning the role of the Vatican as a 'state within the state' in *AD*, but also Langdon's pointed remarks that the Vatican operates like a corporation with its own bank, are attacks on institutionalized religion. The cinematic narrative alludes to Italy's contemporary managerial ideology. This ideology routinizes attributions of blame and responsibility within the Italian polity, 'reducing ethics to a numerical audit' (Herzfeld 2009a: 66) while at the same time ironically reinstating the Roman stereotype of theft performed by the Eternal City's moral custodians: the Church. Such accusations of corrupt managerialism are irreparably related to the city's fascist legacy that looms like a ghost in *AD*. This is further supported by the *Illuminati*'s persecution by the Nazis and their association with left-wing ideology, which place them at the heart of European discourses of suffering and salvation. Such discourses borrow from the Judeo-Christian moral grammar that translates metaphysics into politics (Tzanelli 2008b: chapter 6). Yet, implanting threat and risk into the Vatican's heart (McKenna was adopted by the Pope after an Ulster bombing that killed his parents) is more problematic. McGregor's impersonation of an Irish Catholic bigot and a villain does little to dispel enduring ethnic stereotypes of civility and civilized boundaries dating back to colonial discourse (Curtis 1971; Tzanelli 2009: 62–3). It is no wonder that Howard's second film provoked Catholic devotees enough to make them attribute the badge of original theft (Satan's destruction of the godly paradise) to Hollywood. Centro Studi sulle Religioni director Massimo Introvigne (2012) makes a relevant insinuation when discussing the 'fiction' of the *DVC* purges, Eco's *Foucault's Pendulum* (1988), *Lara Croft: Tomb Raider* (2001), and relevant comics and computer games that play with *Illuminati* histories. His view is that contemporary *Illuminati* personalities were 'sexual magicians, hypnotists and occult masters' (*ibid.*) – in other words, manipulators of impressions akin to the troublesome movie-makers who traffic Vatican heritage abroad. Ideological mirage and carnal pleasure already separate the search of absolute truth from utility, reserving instead conceptions of the non-utilitarian *kósmos* (beauty) for the custodians of Christian heritage (Burnham 2005).

Even producer Brian Grazer's acknowledgment that *AD* 'looks at what would happen when you have an act of terrorism designed to undermine [the] belief [faith]' contradicts his suggestion that the movie has 'no political undertones' (Bowles, 27 October 2008). To further complicate matters, the second bishop's murder is St Peter's Square is framed by demonstrations against stem cell research, asserting thus human interventions in divine and public order alike. The fear but also the eventual spectacle of explosion over the Vatican's starry sky are part and parcel of a twenty-first-century 'graphic revolution' (Boorstin 1962) that defies the cosmic order propagated by political institutions. In *AD* the apocalyptic moment is watched from below by crowds of Roman passers-by who simultaneously assume the function of unmediated cinematic viewers. Ironically then, as an emulation of the 'risk society' thesis (Beck 1992), *AD*'s scientific modernization promotes a form of reflexivity that leads to questioning and reproducing a deficit in democracy through a detached vision of disasters most humans cannot control. In the post-9/11 climate, *AD*'s simulations of a lethal particle explosion over the Vatican's heritage becomes a 'replacement discourse' (Henry and Milovanovic 1996: 204) for the tale of aerial terror, a suggestion that secular knowledge produces an ethnic-like economy of otherness easily digitized, broadcast and reproduced. Henry and Milovanovic suggested that replacement discourses 'should retain a vision of society as [an] emergent outcome of human activity' (1996: 205), a mobility complex that in our case combines as mundane activities as traversing the piazza or rushing from one building to another (Langdon and Vetra's endless chase for signs and culprits) with the movement of weapons of mass destruction. Criminological replacement discourse retains this vision by engaging in a study of the complex relationship between the process of social change and the ways in which it is narrated by contemporary social agents – including cinematic viewers and makers. *AD*'s mysterious particle itself is a replacement discourse in which the technology replaces God's eye and awe is produced by the simulacra of a Satan ready to appropriate divine dominions.

The biblical language of theft and appropriation is anything but innocent when related to artistic multi-products plagued by copyright wars and accusations of defiling sacral sites for commercial purposes. In the context of copyright violation, Brown's artistic creativity suggests that we consider how 'theft' also involves unconnected births of similar ideas in parallel intellectual constellations – ideas whose similarities are revealed only by unexpected clashes (legal or not). This is the legal language of cosmopolitanism – of social contracts and pacts that seal peaceful togetherness of individuals as beings in a polity (Benhabib 1992). It is the sacralized vocabulary of nationalism that dates back to print invention and artefact branding, for which we are called to action, just like the protesters in New Zealand (Eisenstein 1979; Anderson 1991). At the same time, however, this language unveils the significance of acknowledgment, a reinvention of the moral (Christian) language of reciprocity as a secular duty all authors of post-Enlightenment convictions still ought to observe.

Brown's liberal stance as a broadcast storyteller allowed for easy conflations of his persistence that he owed nothing to his colleagues with Howard's determination to simulate revered Christian sites, making both liable to accusations that they support corporate profit-making that violates the laws of Man and God (Yar 2005). Howard's favourable comments on the reconstruction of St Peter's Basilica and the Sistine Chapel in Los Angeles for the shooting of *AD* (Singh, 7 May 2009) bypass these complaints and assert the triumph of cinematic reproductions over discourses of heritage originality. On this Howard matches Langdon's comment: antimatter is a new rendition of the 'moment of creation' that is represented on the Sistine Chapel's masterly cupola depictions of the birth of the world. Just as the *LOTR* production necessitated the replacement of former sacralized sites with the technological matrixes of transnational urban nodes (Sassen 2002), *AD* articulated its visual enterprise outside exclusive zones of authenticity monopolized by powerful institutions such as those of the state and the Church. Partaking in a budding industry that welcomes tourists to God's temples, cinematic fans to the Louvre and web surfers to the films' official websites replaces affective attachment to Christian heritage with the fleeting pleasure of consumption – a normative shift befit for aficionados of cinematic *monstrosities*.

It has been noted by others that 'a generic model of the original sin informs the long Roman conjuncture of corruption and civility' (Herzfeld 2009a: 54–5). The rule of law is literally observed in the Eternal City in the aesthetics of personal interaction and artistic creativity that encourage conflations between civility with *civiltá* (urbanity). In this respect, even the tourists are obliged to pay their dues to holy images and buildings to contravene the workings of the Devil which invites visitors to sign the pact of tourist pleasures. Christian debt is about redemption, a temporal and legal process cinematic tourists and makers ought to observe. However, a *de facto* intermingling between theological and mercenary cultures interferes with the Catholic mission of salvation. As a result, even the normative foundations of the Vatican's complaint that the *DVC/AD* industry consolidated neo-pilgrimage in religion's stead do not exist entirely outside the workings of the 'popular'.

Stealing our joy: the Satan of technological (post)modernity

The *DVC* controversy raised some questions regarding the Church's relationship with the media that even the Vatican's official newspaper *L'Obsservatore Romano* debated in light of *AD*'s release. Although its spokesmen tried to ameliorate tensions, the dismissive comment that Howard's film 'is a videogame that first of all sparks curiosity and is also, maybe, a bit of fun' (BBC News, 7 May 2009) suggested uneasiness and even resentment for its success. In this section I explore relevant cosmological narratives that point to inter-industry linkages between hardware media technologies and entertainment industries (Barnet 1994; Lin 2002: 403). I begin with a brief overview of the *DVC* and *DN* websites but proceed to introduce a third film into the analysis, *SHH*. The ideoscapal conflicts I single out (heritage sanctity sustaining cultural hegemonies) also underscore how *SHH*'s fabulist script promotes a form of cinematic pilgrimage to ancient-mythical sites. *SHH*'s thanatotourist script stemmed from cosmological permutations of the idea of 'theft' and 'easy gains' in popular culture – in particular the Konami code in computer gaming. I contend that the Konami code revises the archaic codes of individual respectability and honour (Peristiany 1965). Such codes remain widespread even in contemporary discourses of social prestige and recognition. On this we may consider Dan Brown's copyright problems and J.K. Rowlings' borrowings from Tolkien in *Harry Potter* as another version of the discourse of mobility: both acts destroyed someone else's image to build that of someone else. Just as in the *DVC*, *SHH* and the Konami code mobilize gender and kinship values in culturally meaningful ways. Their claims to theft overdetermine the histories and the futures of image production and mobility – and as the *Hobbit* case suggests are of immense importance in tourist planning that is based on digital mobilities.

Silent Hill: Homecoming (originally *Silent Hill V*) is the sixth instalment in the *Silent Hill* computer game series, a survival horror genre developed by Western developer Double Hellix Games. The game, which was first announced by Konami as part of their E3 press conference in 2007 but released in North, Central and South America in 2008 and in Europe in 2009, follows soldier Alex Shepherd's journey back home (Shepherd's Glen, named after a distant ancestor), where he finds his mother in Catatonia and his brother missing. His investigations into what happened lead him to discover the cult of Silent Hill, which is connected to the deaths of Mayor Bartlett and Dr Fitch by monsters in otherworld versions of the same locales. Alex finds out that both persons have a missing child and that his father was involved in town intrigues. However, he is incapacitated by the Order, a cult that worships Silent Hill's god and has kidnapped his mother. Alex goes through various tribulations and important decisions that determine the course of the game, to eventually meet his father who reveals that instead of serving as a soldier, Alex was secluded in a mental hospital. Thereafter Alex's father is murdered by a monster known as 'Bogeyman' (the film's analogous Pyramid Man). Alex also discovers that the town was cursed when 150 years ago its four founding families broke away from Silent Hill's order to move to Shepherd's Glen on the condition that every 50 years they sacrifice their children in a preordained fashion. More recent game installations borrow from the original plot but develop characters involving an escaped convict (*Silent Hill: Downpour*, 7 March 2012), a man mourning his wife who visits an otherworldly asylum (*Silent Hill*, 20 March 2012) and a book in which the player finds all their memories imprinted (*Silent Hill: Book of Memories*, 27 March 2012) (for more information see Amazon.com).

The plot appears to borrow several key features from heritage discourse: first it combines the importance of autobiographical memory with the experience of thanatotourism in a rather gruelling style (Desforges 2000); second, it places emphasis on the value of progeny as a sacrificial token to gods, thus emulating Abraham's archetypal biblical tale of surrendering his bloodline as a trial of faith; and finally, it blends the monstrous appearance of otherworldly creatures with the ripping insertions of human madness in a digital environment that replaces reality with hyperreal chaos. The game seems to function as a digital rendition of Goffman's (1961) 'total institutions' that are staged with the help of Jake's mental breakdown. However, the very virtual background of the story replaces this chaotic effect with a cosmos ordered on the principles of landscape that is land – a heritage Alex carried with him since his birth. Almost all instalments of the game focus on a deserted American town with a passage to a dark dimension, an Otherworld that defies the rules of nature and logic. Characters suffer from delusions and nightmares that set them on a trail shrouded by mysterious occurrences. Incidents lead protagonists to uncover an ancient religious cult that publicly operates as a charity with an orphanage but actually kidnaps and drugs children, is involved in illegal trade of drugs and worships a deity. The cult's ancient goddess apparently failed to recreate paradise but will be resurrected in the future to complete this mission (Konami PlayStation 2, 23 May 2003). The plots correspond to Paul Virilio's observation that the 'hallucinatory utopia of communication technologies' (Der Derian 1999: 218) has an inherent darkness that generates eternal crises and social breakdowns.

Just as in *DVC* and *AD*, the genre employs the techniques we find in detective and horror films. These often figure an 'Everyman' or 'Everywoman', an ordinary decent person caught in virtual nightmare scenarios (Tzanelli 2004b: 53). The same tropes frame the cinematic story of *SHH* but with female protagonists whose biographies reiterate some feminist concerns I raised above. In fact, director Gun's interview on the transformation of the main film character into a woman reveals how some deep-seated gender stereotypes informed the work:

> Roger, Nicolas and I were willing to adapt Silent Hill 1 and thus tell the search for Harry Mason searching [sic] for his little girl in the city of Silent Hill. After putting all the dialogue of the game on a script, we realized that something was not right with this main character who [sic] was always crying and fainting. We had a choice between the harden a bit more, but turn it into action heroes, or to a woman, what was all the more interesting it made sense with all that was known of Silent Hill. Suddenly it became a film about motherhood, the Immaculate Conception, the witches. Silent Hill is actually a matriarchy and if you pushed the male out of our sight, there were only women and a problem Women [sic].
>
> (Ferry, 20 April 2006)

Just as with *DVC* and *AD* we are back to the ecofeminist realm – but with additional problems. Treating practices associated with feminine and ethnic properties as exotic necessitates a 'thick description' of their context that the film never provides (Argyrou 2005: 65–6, 70). Instead of figuring what the cult is up to we face a polarized, self-explained 'female' *habitus* through the movie's good and bad protagonists (and ghosts), and a hazy separation of science from backward shamanism. The movie opens with Rose (Radha Mitchell) and her husband's (Christopher Da Silva, played by Sean Bean) concerns about their adopted daughter's (Sharon played by Jodelle Ferland) sleepwalking and nightmares during which she repeats the name of 'Silent Hill'. Rose and Sharon set out for the foggy town of Silent Hill where they meet police officer Cybil Bennett (Laurie Holden). Meanwhile Sharon disappears and Rose and Cybil decide to look for her. In town, which is covered in ashen rain and haunted by regular ghostly alarms, they find out that a mining community disappeared a while ago under mysterious circumstances. As the first alarm rings, Rose and Cybil enter an Otherworld of monstrous creatures – among them the red Pyramid Man (Roberto Campanella). The creature, which is given shape by women's soul (Guns, 6 April 2006), represents the unconscious domain but the shape of its head suggests hidden analogies with *DVC*'s Orientalist feminizations of otherness.

Rose and Cybil discover a cult (the Order) headed by a woman named Christabella (Alice Krige) with a long history of witch burnings – another lateral link to *DVC*'s historical analysis of Magdalene's demonization in Christian tradition. Between events Rose finds out that her adopted daughter resembles strongly Alessa, a girl who was stigmatized because she came out of wedlock and was burned by the Order to appease a demon. The dead Alessa worked as a demonic vessel and dragged the town into its present dark state. The cult condemns Rose and Cybil as witches because of Sharon, and burn Cybil, but Rose manages to escape and reunite with her daughter who represents Alessa's remaining innocence and goodness. She is told that she must aid Alessa in her revenge against the cult by granting her entry into the Church, where they confront Christabella and her peers for their cruelty and religious conservatism. The conflict allows the demon to destroy the Church and its cult but Rose and Sharon survive. However, their return to Christopher takes place in a parallel dimension and they never meet. Thus the film's ending is ambivalent, implying that their actual 'home' might be a Christian-like Paradise or a hellish limbo (for full plot see Wikipedia and IMDB).

Apart from various CGI modifications to landscapes, the film was mostly shot in Ontario, Canada and included several scenes from lma College, a girl's private school that featured in three films after its closure in 1995, including di Caprio-produced *Orphan* (2009) that capitalizes on *SSH*'s plot (Bunnell 2010). Several versions of a rumour that the school was haunted by the evil ghost of 'Angela' further corroborate enduring demonizations of femininity by association with the occult and Satan. More pervasive is the near-sacralized discourse of the nuclear heterosexual family as all humans' earthly haven and preordained *telos* – another tradition bound to Christian hermeneutics. Despite some progressive commentary, the three cinematic narratives of the chapter hinge on ideas of protective parenthood that complies with patriarchal models of sociality and the persistence of kinship in social movements (McAdam 1988; McAdam and Paulsen 1993). The genre's music works in this direction with its emphasis on emotional engagement: in *SSH*'s horror tale the family's reproductive agents (mother, child) are threatened by metaphysical enemies. Composed by regular contributor Akira Yamaoka, the soundtrack (24 November 2008) envelops the plot in atmospheric electronic tunes that convey the macabre through scarce voice acting in high tension scenes. The only other piece of music used in the film is Johnny Cash's *Ring of Fire*. Yamaoka's scores were arranged by film composer Jeff Danna (*Resident Evil: Apocalypse, The Boondock Saints*), with some tracks appearing in almost identical form to their in-game counterparts, while others were entirely recreated (Wikipedia entry, 'Silent Hill', undated). Former sound director Yamaoka rated musical atmosphere as an indispensable element of the computer series, presenting its function as emotion-inducing for the player (*Silent Hill 3*, 2003). The blend of musical styles in various instalments range from pop to rock and are combined with electronically produced screams, screaks and drums (see, for example, Double Helix Games, 30 September 2008).

Of more interest here is the association of a cinematic genre propagating the chaotic social effect of feminine and ethnicized nature with an invention we trace to one of the founders of *Silent Hill*'s popular culture. Original game designers Team Silent worked for the Japanese entertainment corporation Konami (est. 1969, Osaka). The company has branches in Asia, Europe, Oceania and America and is famous for its contribution to the production of toys and entertainment games. I refer to the 'Konami Code' that is known in Japan also as the 'Konami Command'. The concept is used to convey a cheat code Kazuhisa Hashimoto used first to refer to his experience of developing the arcade game *Gradius* in the 1980s (NES version, 1986). In an interview in the Japanese game magazine *Dorimaga* Hashimoto explained that because he could not finish the game, he 'inserted the so-called Konami code in it' (1Up.com, undated). The code, which provides the player with advantages normally attained gradually through the game, was subsequently implemented in different versions in a variety of computer games, eventually attaining a special place in popular culture as reference to third-generation video game consoles (see Wikipedia for 'List of Konami code games'). In a community of video gamers, completing the digital journey with high scores demonstrates skill, and knowledge of such codes can be an asset.

Deception has been reductively attributed to Eastern racial profiles at various points in the history of Western civilization (Law 2010). European Christian narratives connected lying to *ponirós* (cunning), Jesus' Satanic nemesis that facilitated Eve's trafficking of knowledge outside Paradise (Tzanelli 2011a: 101–2). Bok reminds us that deception affects the distribution of power: lies add to the power of the liar and diminish that of the deceived, altering the choices of the deceived at different levels (1978: 19–28). In many cultures cheating is an interactive skill that allows for reciprocal and bilateral circulations of valuable goods, or merely serves recognition rituals institutionally condemned as illegal practices (Herzfeld 1985; Yar 2008). Zeitlyn (2003) notes that a symbolic idea of ownership in open source software endorses 'co-possession' as a form of sharing. But sharing also empowers givers who accumulate in reputation for generosity. Drawing on the Maussian thesis (1954) whereby giver and the gift cannot be neatly separated, Zeitlyn highlights the archaic *anthropocentric* origins of the new 'mobilities paradigm' (Strathern 1983, 1988, 2004). Technocratic regulations of such neotribal cultures correspond to older institutional replacements of everyday knowledge and experience with formalized rules of conduct, consolidating continuities with legalized discourses of power machines such as those of the state or transnational corporations (Sutton 2000; Strain 2003). Attempts by activists to strengthen claims of indigenous peoples to their own cultural productions through adoptions of intellectual property frameworks now inform the entertainment industry in more ways than one (Fischer *et al.* 2008: 532). Corporate enterprise acknowledges the power of such custom flows in its trade in covert ways that optimize sales or product marketing (Wall and Yar 2010: 260). One such symbolic acknowledgment is the use of what is known as 'Easter Eggs' – messages akin to the Konami code hidden in software in the form of videos, graphics or sound effects and intended as jokes or creative credits. Easter Eggs used by video game developers such as Rovio (*Angry Birds*, 2009–12) or corporations such as Google (e.g. regular April Fool's jokes) draw parallels with the Western custom of the egg hunt and the last Russian imperial family's practice of offering elaborately painted or jewelled egg-shaped artefacts (Hidden DVD Easter Eggs, February 2010).

Orthodox Russia's role in this custom constructs a bridge between East and West via religious philosophies of iconicity, material simulations of concepts (Nederveen Pieterse 2004: 75; Herzfeld 2005: 70–1). The visual narrative of the *DVC* and *AD* is also structured on successions of codes and surprises their protagonists interpret. In *AD* the Vatican is even sent an ambigram by the shadowy assassins, which points the guns at the *Illuminati*, perniciously suggesting two things at the same time: first that the Church can only handle codes that have a single meaning; and second that from the Church's viewpoint the founders of Enlightenment science and technology contrived a malicious Konami-like code to restore their honour at the expense of the Church (the irony being that behind the plot is hidden a Catholic peer). Within this we can discover the structural parameters of both movies' archplot (McKee 1999), which is equally ambigrammatic in its inception: we may attribute 'evil' to either side but ultimately the binary structure (light versus darkness, good versus evil) remains unchallenged; there are two antithetical camps locked in a cosmic battle (Ricoeur 1970: 43, 1974; Derrida 1976: 107–8; Ricoeur 1981). Constant use of visual symbolism by Hollywood's sign industry (including Zimmer's in-house joke) and the role of Brown's original inspiration (John Langdon) suggest more open interpretations of technology as a creative craft in an artistic sense. On the one hand appropriations of Easter Egg's old hybrid custom in new digital milieus continues to legally borrow from the meaning of old heritage registers as original property that ought to circulate within selected groups of users and under the custodian's supervision. On the other it may also contest this legal framework in the domain of leisure.

This is so because Konami codes may breach security applications and thus connect to copyright violations (O'Hanlon 2006) – the property of capital. Cybercrime scholars prefer to frame such issues in terms of piracy, especially where the theft of virtual artefacts leads to dilution of their value in global markets (Wall and Yar 2010: 263–6). Microsoft Office does not allow Easter Eggs in software as part of its Trustworthy Computing initiative to counter potential attacks on it (Osterman, 21 October 2005). Reversely, contesting technocratic regulations in video gaming can also be understood as a contentious attempt to challenge discourses of property – a conflation of indigenous movements over control of land and ethnic artefacts (cultural rights) with the right to possess and control assets, thus monopolizing commercial prestige (intellectual property rights) (Craig *et al.* 2011). The spirit of Catholic corporatization to which Langdon alludes in *AD*'s script highlights how even religious institutions partake in such practices, by transforming assets into 'heritage' and freezing them in time and space like a thing in need of protection (Shohat and Stam 1994: 15; Tzanelli 2009: 85). The urgency to control natural and virtual environments alike is nicely encapsulated in the Vatican's recent digitization of the Sistine Chapel without any reference to the profitable *DVC/AD* that added to tourist visits to Rome (Vatican, 2012). Despite the obvious use of digital craft to open the visual consumption of high art to global audiences and virtual tourists, the contribution of such cinematic enterprise was sidelined on this occasion.

Digital hermeneutics: the websites

This convoluted journey through the three films highlights an institutional dilemma: how can the Vatican (and indeed any Church aspiring to reach the hearts and minds of its people) preserve centuries-old traditions in the face of sweeping cultural change? On purely pragmatic grounds, losing footing in digital modernization leaves the temples of God empty, giving the opportunity to cinemas and Internet salons to reconstitute the public sphere outside the metaphysical domain. The fictional *Illuminati*'s determination to remove such a religious prerogative is a danger that cinematic agents might realize. This suggests that we browse the *DVC* and *AD* websites – today maintained by Sony Entertainment – to speculate on the ways cinematic industries partake in the threat of tradition. Deliberately or not, their digital hermeneutics contribute to an overall movement towards audiovisual secularizations in marketable ways, setting discourses of authenticity against those of reproduction (Crossley 2003).

The *DVC* website opens to a gallery framed by a solemn repetitive track invoking both ecclesiastical and marching music. Staging the *DVC* popular culture as a sort of audiovisual mourning, it invites visitors to partake in a digital thanatotourist journey, and become traveller-investigators akin to Langdon and Sophie. Following the stylistic conventions of the old book and Renaissance scholastic manuscript, the pages and hyperlinks toy with dim lightning (a visual metaphor for hidden truths). The centrepiece of the start page is an image of Langdon and Sophie that the web designers have cleverly superimposed on Da Vinci's *The Last Supper*. The film's DVD version covers the face of Judas Iscariot, but not those of Peter and what Teabing recognizes as 'Magdalene', possibly using their characters to rewrite the tale of treason. Judas is after all the hidden devil in Leonardo's detail, a faceless villain on the *DVC* website, a terrorist.

Leonardo's painting was intended as an encapsulation of sinister confusion and agitation at the announcement of Judas' upcoming treachery, visually articulating a divine challenge to Jesus' twelve human disciples (Cooper 2009: 121). Teabing (the painting's cinematic analyst) functions as the website's absent presence, the voice exclaiming in a calligraphic script: 'Watch the *Da Vinci Code* Gallery and embark on your own quest for the hidden truth! Search through some of Da Vinci's most famous works of art for hidden symbols. If you succeed in finding all six symbols you will unlock a secret'. The discourse is a perfect example of the hermeneutics of suspicion, the language of humanist devils that defy surfaces and a perfect specimen of Eurocentric ideology (Dallmayr 2001: chapter 2).

This ambiguous start is further convoluted by the presentation of the plot, its characters and news highlights. The site visualizes this page from above, through the shot of a pensive Langdon standing on the illuminated glass Pyramid. The newsmatrix (found under 'News') is thus the audiovisual reproduction of the cinematic resolution: the movie's publicity itself tells you everything you need to know. 'Da Vinci's Gallery' provides a flash tour through some of the polymath's most important works, commencing and concluding with Mona Lisa's enigmatic smile. As the film's and one of classical art's unbroken codes, Mona Lisa is the true digital face of artistic reproduction in the *DVC*: splintered into millions of pixels on Sony's website, and hidden in one of Christ's followers on the left side of Langdon on the start page of the movie's site, it invites viewers to explore new meanings.

Figure 3.4 A Hitchcockian moment: Gioconda's enigma as background to the apocryphal history of Christianity (Langdon and Sophie as foreground).
Credit: Columbia Pictures/Photofest.

Bakhtin noted how laughter operates as cosmological supra-philosophy in folk traditions associated with feminine domains of reproduction and defecation – bodily mobilities in short (Murashov 1997: 207; Papathanasiou 2007: 179). But a hint of smile communicates the uncertainty of intention and a controlled behaviour adhering to the principles of modern civility. Mona Lisa's digital reproduction is thus characteristic of feminine irony, playfulness and even resentment towards Da Vinci as Giaconda's original spectator with attention to detail. Da Vinci employed *sfumato* in this painting, a blurring style that nicely conveys the ambivalence of feminine strangerhood. This uncertainty is also anything but irrelevant for modern science: over a decade ago Harvard neuroscientist Margaret Livingstone explained that Mona Lisa's smile 'comes and goes' because of how the human visual system is designed to capture shadows and motion peripherally rather than by looking straight at images (BBC News, 18 February 2003). Peripheral vision discards the details central vision processes as colour or fine print, thus functioning as the locus of interpretations of mobility (Blakeslee, 27 November 2000). Mona Lisa's enigma is both a rendition of *sfumato* and a visual critique of European hermeneutic traditions that morally classify the world in obscured and illuminated domains: incorporating in this normative illusion both the image of Magdalene (the Eastern Black Madonna) and of the Virgin Mary (sexuality and purity), Mona Lisa's smile supports the post-Kantian interdependency of hermeneutic mobilities and moorings (Urry 2007; Uteng and Cresswell 2008; Kaufmann and Montulet 2008; Nussbaum 2010). Magdalene is the Christian Khali of positivist religion, a fallen Eve who bit the digital apple and condemned the human race to reproduce itself through Edenic simulacra indefinitely (also Argyrou 2005: 131).

By the same token, the visitor is introduced to the 'Symbol Logic' page and the 'Anagrams' that depend on a popular game, Sudoku. It is explained that in these puzzles the numbers one to four are replaced with symbols taken from *The Da Vinci Code*. Sudoku's history itself propagates fusions of Eastern and European intellectual traditions: invented as a leisure activity by retired American architect Howard Garns (c. 1979), it has a convoluted archaeology dating back to nineteenth-century French puzzles based on 'magic numbers'. The game was truly popularized in 1986 by the Japanese puzzle makers Nikoli under the name Sudoku (single number) (Hayes 2006; for complete history see relevant Wikipedia entry under 'Sudoku'). Various studies attributed the puzzle, which has a Japanese name, to the mysteries of the Land of the Rising Sun but the computer software for the game was developed by a judge from New Zealand, Wayne Gould (Smith, 15 May 2005). It has been noted that Sudoku puzzles facilitate applications of principles commonly presented in introductory classes in mathematics and combinatorial optimizational systems of linear equations (Scott Provan 2009: 1). Combinatory mathematics corresponds to the philosophical principles of relationality in human sciences. It is not coincidental that on the *DVC* website each page opens with a cylinder – one of the film's most important message carriers through the centuries, according to symbolologist Langdon. In this schema the European traditions of interpretation depend on the mathematical combinatory traditions of African mathematics – the source of all modern scientific knowledge. This apparent fusion of traditions also bears testimony to a productive communication between Eastern and Western cosmologies as well as its continuous role in postmodern mobility circuits (Brandist 2002; Alexander 2006; Nederveen Pieterse 2006a; Sheller and Urry 2006).

The *DVC* sign industry is steeped in politics, setting a precedent for other filmmakers to follow in the presentation of relevant digital merchandise. It is telling that, as opposed to *DVC*, Sony abstained from developing a website for the second film. Firm opposition in ecclesiastical circles in the case of other progressive cinematic narratives could easily block *AD* sales and colour its global reception in negative ways. *SHH*'s marketing bypassed this sensitive issue by casting its enterprise as popular culture detached from immediate Church matters, a dark 'fairy tale' rather than social critique. Religious debates necessitate the employment of hermeneutic tact even the most qualified speakers cannot always manage. The *DVC*, *AD* and *SSH* cases demonstrate that there is no such thing as innocent film-making, rather, cinema and its digital merchandise articulate viewing positions capable of offending because they invite open interpretations. Exemplifying the vicissitudes of cosmopolitan pedagogy, such flows of art can legitimately reintroduce questions of cosmological sensitivity from the standpoint of those traditions cinematic simulacra question. A devout pilgrim may ask: is the Vatican's digital Sistine Chapel not a site waiting to be discovered by the Catholic visitor?

Conclusion

It is said that Wordsworth's poem *The Brother* signifies the beginning of a time when people stop belonging to a culture and increasingly can only tour it, so as to compare, contrast and collect, to see Venice and die (Buzard 1993: 27; Szerszynski and Urry 2006). A specialized visual sense characterizes the modern world. Urry repeatedly quotes E.M. Forster (2004, 2007) in his environmental aesthetics who wrote: 'Under cosmopolitanism... Trees and meadows and mountains will only be a spectacle, landscape not land' (1931: 243). The language of abstract characteristics is a language of mobility, the expression of the lifeworld of mobile groups of tourists, conference travellers, business people or environmentalists. In this mobile world abstraction might detract from direct engagement and replace this with formal agreements – as in packaged neo-pilgrimages of educational nature minus European history's unpleasantries (the mass murders of colonialism, the bigotries of Orientalism, the hatred of Christian preaching) or glorified stories of repression minus authorial antagonisms and corporate policies. But it may also enable critical engagement with distant environments, enlarging public spheres through *scholé* (Lanfant 2009). To use an appropriate pun, the European system of mobility can be a 'godsend' if used properly by its global managers even in difficult, disorganized conditions.

This chapter examined one node in this set of mobile processes: the books, the films, the virtual and the physical travel interpellated through and by their self-expanding global fluids. This produced various kinds of position, especially that of the cosmopolitan collector of signs of European culture – a collector originally male and Christian, but now also female, pagan and even Muslim, if we are to believe the Quranic scholars. This move, achieved through the democratization of European Christian history and its coupling with the literary art of social poetics (a diachronic production of social bonding through Magdalene's non-European bloodline), constantly reinvents the notion of the Athenian cosmopolitan. More specifically, visitors to places can be knowing and playful cosmopolitans for a day, engaging in forms of playful and reflexive pilgrimage under certain structural conditions. The films, their novels and their digital cultures resurrect this genealogy of democracy to operationalize a cosmopolitan node that seeks to counter Europe's classicist roots and Christianity's ambivalence towards its pagan others. Their neo-pilgrims are constructed through various intersecting networks to engage with yet another sign system of global tourism and travelling cultures. In this case some out-of-the-way churches and religious sites become, for a short while, signs of cosmopolitan taste – that is, until the next global fluid sweeps into town and blows them away.

4 Projecting European heritage

The Acropolis in *Ruins* (2009)

Turning the page: global Greek imaginaries of mobility

The Athens depicted in *My Life in Ruins* (*MLIR*, 2009; aka *Driving Aphrodite*, *DA*) is known through an array of conflicting representations including noise, smog, migrant groups, dirty industrial buildings and squares, and the twin vantage points of Plaka and the Acropolis. This human and automobile mayhem cannot be properly conveyed in travel books but is constantly alluded to in global routes and rumours. The imagery of this ancient city – a cosmopolis of European modernity in its own right – fluctuates between what Hutnyk saw in Calcutta as 'a definition of obscenity' (1996: 8) or a cornucopia of joy, and an Apollonian school for contemporary cultural tourists who, though diminished today in numbers, continue to pay homage to its ancient civilization like the old Grand Tourists (Brodsky-Porges 1981; Towner 1985; Urry 1995; Urry and Larsen 2011). *MLIR*'s insertion into this network of neo-pilgrimages brought together different phantasmagoric nodes from the European margins (Greece) and the Western media centres (Los Angeles, Chicago and Canada). Even today amid the most debilitating global economic crisis that bankrupt Greece faces, Athens, site of the second twenty-first-century Olympics and a regional telecommunication and transport node, ranks among what we call the 'global cities' (Eade 2001; Sassen 2001, 2002; Duval 2007). But as much as it appears self-evident why Athens was chosen as the primary stage for the shooting of Nia Vardalos' 2009 film, the cosmological and geopolitical depth of the case invites closer inspection.

The initiative's most prominent agent is an excellent start in our investigations of this node. Nia Vardalos (born in 1962, Winnipeg, Manitoba) is the daughter of Greek-Canadian bookkeeper and homemaker Doreen, and Constantine 'Gus' Vardalos, a land developer. After many small roles in television (*The Drew Carey Show* [1995–2004] and *Two Guys and a Girl* [1998–2011]), Vardalos gained overnight success with her movie about a woman's struggle to find love in *My Big Fat Greek Wedding* (*MBFGW*, 2002), which was based on a one-woman show she had previously written and starred in. Although an independent film with a US$5 million budget, *MBFGW* became a sleeper hit grossing over US$368.7 million worldwide, the fifth highest-grossing movie of 2002 in the United States, with US$241,438,208, and the highest-grossing romantic comedy in history

(Fretts, 11 April 2003). The film earned Vardalos an Academy Award Nomination for Best Writing, a Golden Globe Nomination for Best Actress in a Motion Picture Musical or Comedy and a Screen Actors Guild Award Nomination. After *Connie and Carla* (2004), a musical about two women pretending to be drag queens, and her directing debut in *I Hate Valentine's Day* (2009) her next notable step was *MLIR*. The film grossed US$8,500,270 in the United States (The Numbers, 22 July 2009) and US$1,549,303 in Greece in its first three-day opening weekend, where it came first in sales (Box Office Mojo, 2009). Set among the ruins of Ancient Greece, featuring Delphi, Epidaurus, ancient Olympia, and the Acropolis, the film speaks the double biopolitical language we encountered in the *LOTR/Hobbit* epistemic node: once a Greek always a Greek, but if you want to make it to the big time insert yourself in global artistic networks. In *The Dialogue,* an interview series with producer Mike DeLuca, Vardalos (2006) talks about how her experiences in *The Second City* comedy troupe helped her as an actress and a screenwriter, and how the unofficial tell-the-Greek word-of-mouth program had a hand in catapulting her movie to such great heights.

As much as it is a film about Greece, *MLIR* includes a bit of the 'Maple Leaf', as it is embellished with scattered references to the Great White North: Canadian tourists are repeatedly seen wandering archaeological sites in red-and-white attire, while Vardalos' parents and husband pop up in separate cameos because 'they're good luck … and it's just great to have this moment where we're all (saying), "Hee, hee, we're on screen together!"' (CTV News, 1 June 2009). Winnipeg is also referenced by way of the number 204, which is both the Prairie capital's area code and the number of Vardalos' hotel room during the filming of *Connie and Carla*. Behind the scenes Vardalos notes she had a lot of help from friends, including long-time collaborators Tom Hanks and personal mentor Rita Wilson as well as her *Second City* buddy, Rachel Dratch, who supplies some improvised gags. Vardalos is an example of embodied knowledge akin to the craft of ethnography: not only does she use her background as a graduate in acting to write, she also spies on others and engages in performative monologues in which she brings character interaction to life. Her technographic ethos 'demythologizes the rhetoric of the electronic sublime' (Vannini *et al.* 2009: 473) in the tradition of comedies about everyday life rather than dystopian visions of sci-fi futures. 'Everything came from a place of authenticity', she admits, highlighting the importance of the banal in inner journeys (Vardalos 2006). Bakhtin speaks of internal 'microdialogues' that enable dialogical Selves to come into consciousness through engagement with 'real, imagined, historical and generalized others' (de Peuter 1988: 39; Tzanelli 2008a: 15), Desforges argues for a tourist Self that is relationally and reflexively produced through personal biography (2000: 931), and Williams (1965) attributes the uniqueness of creative workers to their dedication in transmitting their expressive journeys as experience.

Mobilizing her own experiences and family chronicles also conveys Vardalos' self-recognition as what she calls 'an invisible minority' – not white or ethnic but someone in-between. This ethno-racial indeterminacy is also reported as constitutive of the protean, semi-European nature of modern Greek identity (Herzfeld 1987;

Todorova 1997). Just as other great European diasporas such as the Irish, Greek expatriate communities recycle such narratives that originate in British colonial discourses. In them Greekness within and without Greek dominions retains an elusive primordial authenticity that is European because of its phenomenological whiteness and Christianity (Gallant 2002: 16–17, 35–45; Tzanelli 2008b: 40). Vardalos comes from a Christian Orthodox environment, and despite her open-mindedness she recognizes that she cannot quite escape her roots (on Greek-American communities see Moskos 1999: 110). But Bernal (1991) reminds us that ancient Greek history also dies hard in global official registers. Alongside such intimate Greek self-presentations as Vardalos', the old Athenian Hellenic clout persists, infecting global Greek communities with confusion about their identity. The actress' confession that it has been 'a dream' of hers to shoot in Greece and 'tell Greek stories' (*My Life in Ruins* poster 2009: 5) point to a familiar convergence of migrant 'routes and roots' (Clifford 1997; Sheller and Urry 2006).

This history provides *MLIR*'s background, arming its nerdy protagonist with a post-Enlightenment argument in which Europeans were the spiritual children of Hellas, and ancient Greek civilization the cradle of Europe. In this respect, the film historically mirrors the persistence of metropolitan Greeks in calling themselves *Neo*hellenes or modern Hellenes (Leontis 1995). At the same time, Vardalos presents through the protagonist's transformation into a replica of Greek cultural intimacy (Herzfeld 2005) the Greeks' condemnation to 'heritage blindness' via obliterations of more recent transformations in their fictionally uniform culture (Lowenthal 1985: 249). Otherwise put, Vardalos' artwork is organic in its routes and roots. I use organic in the Durkheimian sense (1997 [1893]) as a deliberative model of belonging that applies to those allocated a place in the Greek imagined community and a badge they often mobilize as critical outsiders. Thus I also understand organic as a Gramscian term (Gramsci 1971; Hall 1996: chapter 13) that complies with the ecological model of memory in so far as Gramsci's 'organic intellectuals' remember histories from which they emerge as subjects (Ricoeur 1993: 147; 1981: 325). The organic dimension of such memories allows for the strategic subversion of fixed cultural models and histories, because art-making and global communications of artistic forms recreate them, thus pluralizing their interpretations. The work of such artistic crafters blends first-hand (organic) accounts of the places they visit and represent in their work with accounts fabricated in the industrial milieus of tourism and the media (Hesmondhalgh 2007: 83; Daye 2005: 14). We examined the consequences of modernity's double break with religion in the context of the *Hobbit* protests that dictated a peculiar re-enchantment of (New Zealand) nature through digital imagery (Gollum). In Vardalos' case we find a similar eco-systemic rationale through organic simulations of an expatriate's domestic sphere (Athenian culture) – a sphere she does not really know from within. Indeed, in *MLIR* we can speak of representations of a global Greek imaginary as much as we can examine the film as a simulation of organic socialities. The meaning-making ritual is enacted for the sake of Western viewers and Greek expatriates, especially those of the second and third generation who long for some re-enchantment of 'Motherland's private sphere' (see also Argyrou 2005: 85–6 on modernization). Again we move within the sphere of collective action that is actualized through imagined journeys by extensive kinship networks: Greeks beyond borders (see McAdam 1988).

MLIR's melodramatic plot echoes that of *MBFGW*: Georgia (Vardalos) is an American academic who has lost her teaching job in Athens and has taken instead a job as a tour guide. Unfortunately, the tourists who cross her path in Athens are bored with history and archaeological details and want to shop and visit Greece's beaches instead. Thanks to an unlikely friendship she forms with the bearded bus driver Prokopis (Alexis Georgoulis) on one of the tours, plus daisies, an ice-cream cone, the history of syrup, and the Oracle at Delphi, Georgia may have a shot at finding her *kéfi* during a four-day tour (see IMDB, 2009 on *DA* for a summary). The film (dir. Donald Petrie) was released in 2009 under the new title *Driving Aphrodite*, which also invited associations with Cyprus as the land of 'sea and sun' (Sharpley 2004). Although it is not a sequel to *MBFG*, it was released in Italy as *Me Mie Grosse Vacanze Greche* (My Big Fat Greek Holidays), thus adding confusion over its marketing as a completely different film (IMDB, 2009 – trivia). The visual marketing of *DA* (suntanned Vardalos in a pink frame for the first poster) and the cerebral signs of *MLIR* (Georgia amid global tourists at the Acropolis as the alternative poster's background) addressed a variety of cinematic tourists.

The film's website, hosted today by Fox Searchlight (undated), promotes this hybrid mobility: prompting visitors to find on Facebook 'which goddess they are', the generic pink poster addresses audiences of particular gender and sex orientation. From there we enter the main site, which includes the usual props: the cast of characters, movie crew, partners and various image stills projected via a digital camera. The homely feel of the movie, which Vardalos never stopped stressing, is reiterated via the family tourist medium *par excellence*: photography (Sontag 1990; Chalfen 1999; Larsen 2005). Internet artisanship remediates the domesticity of family albums and memories (Hand 2012: 135, 164). Bringing together a variety of interviews on the making of *MLIR* and connecting to a variety of sites (including Facebook, Twitter and g+1) produces a cinematic node akin to that of *DVD* and *AD*. The European roots of travel are asserted in the trailer, which includes the first scenes of the film (explored below) but also images of the white and blue island, Greece. There is no better introduction to the following section than Vardalos' own article in *Huffington Post* (8 June 2009) on the deeper meaning of such blends: 'Women don't go to the movies – huh?' she blurts out in the title. She proceeds with the conviction of a studio executive that her script should have a male lead and contrasts this to several box office successes that had women in leading roles (*Sex and The City, Mamma Mia* and the *Obsessed*). In another confession sure to attract attention she cunningly sniffs that the movie may not be playing everywhere, but audience members found it. 'We don't have billboards, or giant newspaper ads, or skywriting. So I've been Twittering, loading homemade videos onto YouTube: "My Life In Ruins, Really!" and blabbing to anyone who makes eye contact with me.' Vardalos' transition from artistic heritage to crafty marketing guides contemporary tourist mobilities and responds to 'prosumerist demand' online (Toffler 1980). The DIY streak characterizing her professional pursuits matches the biographies of Jackson, Adamson and del Toro while re-gendering the face of cultural cosmopolitanism (Qiongli 2006: 386). It is precisely this presentational technique to netizens and prospective *MLIR* fans that produces the archplot of a mobile Greek persona that masters late modernity's 'feminine craft' (Tzanelli 2011a: 82).

Ruined or disorganized? From cinematic archplot to national cosmology

MLIR's archplot is the stereotyped character of global Greece: a cunning, racialized agent getting by in a ruthless world in which (s)he has 'lost her marbles' to the powerful. This agent switches gender according to the task at hand: (s)he circulates reputable discourses in public but resides in the domestic hearth of the family. *MLIR*'s archplot is constitutive of modern Greek cosmology's global cultural intimations, which are not uncritical mimesis of commodified signs, as their local and national communicators are always-already components of the global sign industries: they perform a function similar to that of formal organizations (Hollywood, tourist industries). Such cultural intimations might also become expressions of *ressentiment* (Nietzsche 1996), an acknowledgment that economic power rests with formal organizations, when screened nations remain trapped in global political and economic structures (Parsons and Smelser 1957).

The communicators of cultural intimations retain clear insight into the injustice of the economic structure within their cultural horizon (Sayer 2000). However, Greece's rather disorganized economic structures make 'bad pals' with the global disorganized capitalist system (Lash and Urry 1987). The struggle for power (otherwise known as 'market competition') that guides the agendas of formal cultural industries becomes a struggle for recognition for the filmed place (Honneth 1995). Struggles for power are valorized processes that in Greek culture project a 'poetics of manhood' (Herzfeld 1985), whereas struggles for recognition are tropes of feminine vulnerability. Industrial transactions of the *MLIR* kind promote negotiations of these two models of social action and blends, not only because state agents have to enter agreements with female businesswomen but also because negotiations take place in the artistic domain. Conservative divisions of labour tasks demote artistic work to unessential or peripheral labour performed by women or neurotic men (Molotch 2004) and reserve technological labour for those who conform to normative models of hegemonic masculinity (Connell 1987, 1995). Both in contemporary permutations of Athenian cosmology and in *MLIR*'s archplot, Greek agents display the familiar traces of resentful self-valorization social theorists recognized in black domestic labour (Rollins 1996). Georgia the tour guide, a neither white nor ethnic other, and Athens the global city with a fading prestige, partake in homological meta-symbolism: they serve global tourists while cursing their bad luck and those they find unhelpful to their dreams (Tzanelli 2011a: chs two and three on the margins of Greece).

Ressentiment feeds on insecurity induced by micro-globalization (Knorr Cetina 2007: 65–6) – local inflections of worldwide socio-economic changes that shake the foundations of entrenched identities and histories. As a by-product of 'structural nostalgia' (Herzfeld 2005: 150), the longing for manners lost in the whirlwind of progress, *ressentiment* is overdetermined by generational dissonance, assisting in the symbolic transcendence of systemic constraints through strategic destruction of reciprocities within localities and nation-states. Yet, structural nostalgia can also be mobilized strategically *a fortiori*. Kaufman (2002) notes that in contemporary societies 'motility capital' assists humans to overcome the temporal and spatial constraints of their environment (Urry 2007: 38). In this respect *ressentiment* can become a motivator for action also in younger or more open-minded social groups to compensate for capital deprivation elsewhere.

The same practice found ample use in Greece in marginalized regions (Herzfeld 1991 on Crete; Tzanelli 2011a on Northern Sporades and Tzanelli 2011b on Thessaloniki), which compensated for lack of access to resources withheld for metropolitan beautification by adopting a precarious performative stance associated with ethno-racial and gendered difference (Butler 1993: 225; 1997: 16). The will to self-mobility is an agential decision that may be subjected to or obstructed by external forces (Crossley 2002). So, while we are speaking about Athens, we may keep at the back of our mind the second biggest city of Greece, Thessaloniki, which is rather marginalized in such global media initiatives despite its buoyant art scene and its interesting locales and monuments that can be used in movie-making. Technological mediations of guarded cultural idioms, artefacts and traditions often partake in developmental initiatives, and *MLIR* is a case in point. Flying in the face of any pretensions to universal togetherness, this strategy is part of the cosmopolitan pragmatics social theory aims to 'rectify' (e.g. de Sousa Santos 1995) by consigning the political dimensions of cosmopolitanism to a limbo between Enlightenment and Romantic ideals. Greek *ressentiment* maps an emotive geopolitics of globalization to support abstract hegemonies and systems and solidify liquid borders and identities (Agnew 2007).

The Acropolis is a World Heritage site of significance for Greeks. The formulas of heritage proposed by UNESCO take into account what national centres consider worthy for conservation and global display (Harrison 2005: 3–4), but the European *urtext* on which this seemingly democratic model rests can be manipulated by those who monopolize power (Delanty 1995: 5). Thus, politically insignificant nation-states such as Greece willingly destroy internal reciprocities with those who have little symbolic capital to contribute to a globally reputable national image or who have enough to snatch customers away (Tzanelli 2008b: chapter 3). Among UNESCO's relevant listing criteria for the Acropolis we may count its recognition as 'a masterpiece of human creative genius', an 'outstanding example of a type of building, which illustrates a significant stage in human history', 'exhibiting an important interchange of human values' (UNESCO criteria i, ii and iv). But the city's insertion in digital extensions of capitalist networks (Castells 1996) enables – indeed urges – global trafficking of such heritage markers. As the symbolic centre of global Hellenism but also political centre of the

Greek state, Athens controls budgets, corporate connections and national opportunities. Athens is symbol and actor of Greece's 'gardening state' (Bauman 1992) that nourishes those areas it likes or purposely allows useful weeds to grow elsewhere and kill costly initiatives. These complex interconnections of global and local conditions came to haunt the uses of Athenian Acropolis as a 'boundaried' media space (Couldry 2003b) that must exclude other national regions from national tourist policies, in search of global recognition. *MLIR*'s colourful poster, which can now be accessed online, shows how Athenian political agents and Vardalos entered a 'pact' on the uses of the Acropolis as a mediated centre. By the end of the 2000s, the Acropolis had eventually achieved the status 'of a monument anchored and bounded on a particular site, but ... mobile and multiply situated' (Yalouri 2001: 20). As a 'reservoir of meanings' (Nora 1989: 56), the Acropolis belongs simultaneously to the world of tourist signs and heritage fixities, inviting global hermeneuts to play a game of definitions.

The idea of hard bargaining defined the actions of Greece's powerful Archaeological Council (KAS) in 2006–7, when Vardalos directly contacted the then Minister of Tourism Fanni Palli-Petralia and the Culture Minister Giorgos Voulgarakis to obtain permission to shoot *MLIR* on the Acropolis (Smith, 18 October 2008). Both Petralia and Voulgarakis held posts in two important service industries in the country which require the blended self-presentational skills I presented above. Here we can read a plot of empowerment that Geertz recognized in Balinese cockfighting: a strategy of personal and collective development treading the boundary of illegality even the nation-state adopts despite its public protestations to the contrary (Herzfeld 1992, 2005). 'It was a lot of dinners and handshaking, a lot of requesting permission and really assuring them that we would leave the ruins exactly as we found them', states Vardalos in an interview (*My Life in Ruins* poster 2009: 5). Notably, Fanni Palli-Petralia declared that the site would not close to tourists during filming, thus allowing various visitors to take autographs and pictures of the authentic cinematic stage (*Daily Times*, 13 October 2007). Since the 1960s, when the *The Guns of Navarone* and *Zorba the Greek* used Rhodes and Crete as backdrops, no major film had been shot in the country. The fact that recent Hollywood blockbusters *Troy*, *Alexander the Great* and *300* (all related to Hellenic history) were filmed elsewhere might also have to do with Greek anti-Americanism dating back to the junta (1967–74) but it certainly relates to the lack of tax alleviations the government was previously prepared to give to film-makers. Yet, it seems that even the permanent nationalist suspicion that Hollywood's 'Elgin' will appropriate a European heritage lawfully guarded exclusively by Greeks cannot stand up to the pressures of a tourism-dependent national economy. Despite Greek warnings that no ancient stone should be moved and no cinematic enhancement should be made to the archaeological site, Vardalos' enterprise was supported by the conservative government of Nea Dimokratia and the Greek Film Centre, whose website today proudly hosts photos of the shooting (see HFCO website).

It is not coincidental that *MLIR* marks this change in policies towards foreign film-making in Greece: Tom Hanks and his half-Greek partner, Rita Wilson (also co-producers of Vardalos' previous hit, *My Big Fat Greek Wedding* [2002] [Tzanelli 2004b: 54]), are the film's executive producers. Wilson also appears in the film as Irv's (Richard Dreyfuss) dead wife Elinor. The presence of two diasporic Greeks must have helped to grant the whole enterprise concessions only those who vaguely belong to the Greek imagined community could secure. One may compare this display of Greek bargaining skills to the shameless swindling of foreign film crews and tourist visitors on the Greek island of Kefalonia by locals, who recognized the exploitative potential of *Captain Corelli's Mandolin* (*CCM*, dir. John Madden) back in 2001. Mirroring stereotypical perceptions of the Greek character, the Kefalonian entrepreneurial spirit manifested itself when the *CCM* stage team reconstructed the old Argostoli (capital of Kefalonia) in Sami, and visitors and tourists began to photograph themselves in front of cinematic facades. This confirmed that the stage exuded the essential historical authenticity for the film, as even the old generation of locals admitted. A Kefalonian printing company took shots of *CCM*'s stage and reproduced them as 'Old Argostoli' postcards for tourist consumption 'without bothering to explain that the images shown were of a film set that would only be there for a few weeks' (Clark 2001: 95; see MacCannell 1973). Today, in *CCM*-induced tourist resorts, foreign visitors can enjoy 'staged' dancing *à la Zorbas the Greek* that local restaurant owners, inspired by the film's dancing routines, organize for their customers (Tzanelli 2007b: 114). This time, Athens had the chance to 'set the record straight' by offering the original stage to the altar of cultural industries in a professional manner. However, the role of Vardalos and Palli-Petralia in the story did not seem to deviate much from the Greek cosmological canon: two cunning ethnic women managed to traffic Greek goods abroad successfully, prostituting a sacralized European site (e.g. mediating it through foreign simulacra).

MLIR deviated from the obvious theme of the insider's knowledge (*MBFGW*'s Toula trying to escape the constraints of Chicago's diasporic custom), by shifting focus to the open memory scapes of tourism (*MLIR*'s Georgia is as free an agent as a professional migrant can be). As Chapter 3 manifests, media mobilities are often overdetermined by fixities within ethnoscapes and ideoscapes, with gender and ethnicity or race as cases in point (see Appadurai 1990). In *DVC* and *AD* the cosmetic nodes of the city-museum and the city as a safe stronghold (as opposed to marginal rurality) produce a social meta-genre (see Tudor 1989; Langford 2005: 167) thriving on the impossibility of controlling supernatural danger. In *MLIR* the threat to established civility norms is located in the impossibility of controlling embodied nature (or 'character'), stereotyped intimate habits ethnic humans allegedly share in the communal enclaves they worship as their heritage and which they perform in liminal tourist spaces. Turner's (1974: 74) overused conception of *communitas* in tourist studies applies to the emancipatory female story in cinema *à la Shirley Valentine*. It is understandable why *MLIR*'s meta-genre rests on that of comedy, which is by turn articulated through the embodied performativity feminist theory connects to the discursive limits of sex – and gender (Butler 1993, 1997). The fact that Vardalos' mentor, Wilson, was previously involved in horror films corroborates Vardalos' abject and sexualized

Greek normativity in this particular film but also in other interviews (Vardalos, 2006). Comical but serious, such convoluted paths are part and parcel of artistic cockfights that hybridize histories of culture. *MLIR*'s script is based on Mike Reiss' travel experiences but Vardalos edited the first version (IMDB, 2009). Consulting producer for TV series (including *The Simpsons*), the Harvard graduate brought to the story an outsider's view. His engagement with the comic/ comics genre certainly injected novelty into fictional Georgia's drama.

MLIR also merits analysis because of its gendered archplot, which centres on embodied emotion as pedagogy – an update of the tired Grand Tourist ritual. The story's embodied pedagogy presents Georgia the guide as a human being *en route* to self-discovery – an ideological constant in contemporary mobilities literature (Papastergiadis 2003; Urry 2007: 36–8; Uteng and Cresswell 2008). *MLIR*'s neo-pilgrimage successfully accommodates visits to ancient temples and modern bars, beaches and souvenir markets, matching the sacred sites of culture with the profane domains of reproduction. The ambivalence of such mergers resides in global structuration processes in which trafficking practices link to embodied hedonism (sex), consumption of fakes and copies but also the global circulation of culturally demarcated sites (Williams 2006 on the trope of pornography across media sites). The film debates these issues through representations of Greek culture's poles in Hellenic antiquity and Byzantine Christianity (standing for profitable temporal stillness) on the one hand and Ottoman rule on the other (standing for illegal, abject but also modern mobilities). Anthropologists have considered Byzantium and Ottoman Greekness as part and parcel of an 'inside' view of Greek culture (Herzfeld 1987: 114) but the internalization of these two tropes and their coexistence with antiquity produced a more uniform self-presentation to outsiders *vis-à-vis* the Mediterraneanist discourse of tourism.

The oscillation between the crypto-colonial trope of civilized Hellenism (Herzfeld 2002) and the colonial exotic of Greek Mediterraneanism portrays the country's insertion into a European-Oriental node of media capital. This oscillation is the new form of Greek 'glocalization' (e.g. Just's [1995] global projections of Hellenism in local settings) and applies both to the *MLIR* industry and the Greek state's strategy of media and tourist growth. In terms of genre, the film presents little deviation from Vardalos' expertise in romance comedy, but in terms of context there is some degree of innovation. Embodied knowledge and comedy frame the gendered and racialized nature of *MLIR*'s tourist mobilities while speaking a universal language of tangible and intangible Greek heritage most viewers recognize. The Greek decision to allow shooting to take place in one of Europe's most acclaimed heritage sites also betrays some propensity to innovation. The replacement of the dominant discourse of sanctified glocal heritage (the Acropolis' 'global fame and local claim', to remember Yalouri's [2001] apt subtitle) with one stressing the dialogics of mobility (the Acropolis as the domain of media and tourist flows) actualizes a form of 'practical Mediterraneanism'. Just as with the generic 'practical Orientalism' – 'the translation of hegemonic ideology into everyday practice so that it infiltrates the habitual spaces of ordinary experience' (Herzfeld 1997: 96) – practical Mediterraneanism is a philosophy of the margins, inviting enterprise in contemporary industrial environments such as those of tourism. Both the *MLIR* industry and Greek agents capitalized on an ecological complex constitutive of Greek practical Mediterraneanism involving physical ecologies of movement (landscapes and natural sites), symbolic but embodied movement (Greek *habitus* and custom) and a media movement through which they manipulated the first two in search of global recognition (Vannini *et al.* 2009: 466). The cinematic text is thus constitutive of the cosmic context of production, speaking a Greek ecumenical language with all its ethno-racial nuances and limitations.

Understanding cinematic text through Greek cultural contexts

We cannot pass cinematic diegesis in silence, as tourist mobilities are based on audiovisual traffic. *MILR*'s opening credits are designed as a moving postcard image offering previews of touristy urban Greece. The protagonist's voice (Vardalos as Georgia) suggests that visitors come to this 'cradle of civilization' to reclaim their soul – 'find their mojo'. Yet, the images of Athens feed back into reductive ideas of Greece that inform media and tourist policies and global imaginaries to the day. The tangible background is enmeshed in the experiential background, encouraging conflations of human nature with landscape. The first scenes widen such representations, with distant shots of ancient ruins from the viewpoint of Georgia's pretty balcony and a sign stating that we stand at 'The Gates of Athens'. The audiovisual narrative does not settle, but develops: from Georgia's balcony we are transferred to the *bouzoúki* player stationed outside her place, then the neighbourhood *períptero* (a typical Greek corner kiosk-mini market), the noise of taxi horns and a group of Orthodox priests who obstruct her way to work. This array of images and sounds stands for the cacophonies but also the exoticism of Greek urban modernity in which Christian *Romiosýni* (modern Orthodox Greekness), Hellenic glory and Oriental Ottoman custom co-exist (Faubion 1993). It is not just the *bouzoúki* ambiance that destructs but also Georgia's confession that Greek culture is dominated by ideas of *kéfi*. This Turkish word is often translated as mere fun or mirth – indeed *MLIR*'s hermeneutics present it as 'joy'. But Loizos and Papataxiarchis have noted that *kéfi* is part of the practice of male heterosexual self-presentation, 'a state of pleasure wherein men transcend the pettiness of a life of calculation' (Loizos and Papataxiarchis 1991a: 17) or 'the spirit of desire that derives from the heart' (Loizos and Papataxiarchis, 1991b: 226). *Kéfi* used to acknowledge the agency of male desire as well as its performative nuances in public.

The film celebrates Greek *kéfi* through embodied pedagogies that relate to dancing – a stereotypical tourist ritual in the country. A characteristic of *eğlence* or *gléndi*, informal gatherings during which men would have the chance to showcase embodied knowledge through dancing (Cowan 1990), *kéfi* became constitutive of modern Greek folk *habitus* as affectionate self-stereotyping. Notably, female public self-presentation used to be punished as prostitution

(Lazaridis 2001: 76): hence, Georgia's reserved manners and fixation on history and archaeological heritage figure in the film as the pinnacle of Greek conservatism. *MLIR*'s generic *syrtó*, a dance style Georgia ends up performing on the tour bus towards the end of the film, was also originally involved in the politics of collective self-presentation. These dance styles, attributed to migrations of Greek artistic communities from Turkey (1920s), became for Greek authoritarian regimes (1930s, 1960s) another way to discuss phenotypal extensions of moral community pollution (Stavrou Karayanni 2004: chapter 5). The dialectics of 'open' (suspect) and 'closed' (safe) memory scapes, which have always been overdetermined by gendered ideas of propriety (Herzfeld 2006: 54–5), are now negotiated in discourses of gendered tourism. Therefore my reference to 'practical' Mediterraneanism corresponds to professional artistic alignments with practical action, a way of knowing and acting upon historical representations of marginality through processed experience.

The film is also not blind when it comes to the global context in which Greek tourism operates: in terms of labour opportunities, Georgia, who arrives in Athens for a one-year teaching post at the University of Athens but ends up in Pangloss Tours as a guide, represents unlucky job hunters in the era of global recession. In terms of heritage politics her orientation is coupled with the guarded mobility of Greek antiquity after the economically disastrous Athens 2004 as I explain in the following section. However, here it is worth noting how her disgruntled commentary on her bad luck is replaced with a lax attitude when she secures 'her man'. By the end of the film, Georgia drops her invitation to join the University of Michigan and begins to resemble more *MBFGW*'s Toula, a computer geek in the making who marries the good guy and has kids like a good Greek woman (see Tzanelli 2004b: 55). From this angle *MLIR* appears to endorse social conservatism, which clashes with Georgia's original independence. It is quite possible that the actual culprit is the determination to contrive a happy ending that transposes the American myth of the 'melting pot' (Alba 2000) in the Athenian context. The ending is also flattering for a city that took a big hit in recent foreign human rights reports on xenophobia (Tzanelli 2011a: chapter 6).

Georgia also conveys her in-betweenness through the generation of endless ethnic typologies of cultures and social groups for which she caters: the 'tipsy' Australians, the 'obnoxious' Americans, the 'good-natured' Canadians, the 'miserable' married couples, the 'disgusted but still looking for men' divorcees, the 'comedians' of the group and 'the old people' (unkindly singled out for their disability and slowness). This disgruntled reaction is matched with Greek homophobia (e.g. Gator's [Jareb Dauplaise] gross attack by two gay men at a bar) in equally unflattering ways. In these instances the spirit of the script resembles that of *Borat* (2006, dir. Larry Charles), a comic cinematic travelogue that generated much controversy over what it was perceived as discriminatory representations, even though it boosted Kazakhstan's tourist industry (BBC Newsbeat, 24 April 2012). Just as *Borat*'s leading actor, Sacha Baron Cohen, Vardalos could be viewed as a sort of cultural insider with a licence to critique Greek *habitus* in humorous ways. As discursive practices of 'staged authenticity'

(MacCannell 1973) in tourist encounters are based on patterns of habitual misrecognition of host identities as pure and untouched by visitors, and of identity performance as a social reality, the two films exemplify audiovisual deconstructions of the tourist genre. Symmetrical denigration of foreign tourists, who are more interested in kitsch souvenirs (Binkley 2000) than ancient culture, produces a counter-discourse that Occidentalizes Western domains and the American custom of buying fakes in particular (Carrier 1995).

The native background in which Georgia operates is marked by colourful mannerisms exemplary of Greek 'cultural intimacies': her employer, Maria (Bernice Stegers), gossips about her lack of *kéfi* behind her back with Nico (Allistair McGowan), a colleague regularly employing cunning to extract more money from his customers. Untrustworthiness and gossip project Greece's disreputable heritage in racialized and gendered forms: whereas stealing and deceiving are stereotypically attributed to the country's Ottoman past (Tzanelli 2008b: 86), gossip is another 'feminized home art' in which only knowing insiders can partake (Gluckman 1963: 312, 314). A hotel concierge during Georgia's tour also displays a combination of lechery, sexual incontinence and passion for *Zorba the Greek*, producing a parody of male sexuality in the tourist trade (Tzanelli 2007b: 114). The hotelier is played by Ian Gómez, Vardalos' real-time husband who served as model for the Ian Miller (John Corbett) character in *MBFGW*.

Significantly then, the movie's sexual intimacy is located within the actress' real domestic hearth. Gómez (a New Yorker of Puerto Rican, Jewish and Greek extraction) and Vardalos' (Greek Canadian) immigrant roots and professional routes as artists are exemplary of global human mobilities (see IMDB, 2009). They forge the face of a Greek cosmopolitan memory standing outside the confines of the nation-state at a migrant crossroads (Papastergiadis 2005). Kinship connections aside, the choice of Gómez for this part in *MLIR* betrays how a generic Mediterraneanist *habitus* stands for ethnic specificity in cinema: the hotelier's dark lecherous mannerism is enough to signify phenotypal Greekness. The Greek personae's ethnic accents are part and parcel of this embodied authenticity nexus – in fact, Vardalos confesses in an interview (2006) that she finds everything said with an accent funny. It has been noted that strategic institutions of socio-cultural difference partake in the preservation of ethnic authenticity – of paramount value in *market* exchanges between East and West (Spooner 1986: 222–3). An intermediary businesswoman such as Vardalos can push this fictional discourse a bit further, to create novel hybridized representations (Nederveen Pieterse 2004).

Orientalist laziness returns as a discourse time and again: 'Greece was a happening 2,500 years ago', Georgia exclaims during a tour, 'and then [Greeks] discovered the nap'. Bargaining, cheating and swearing at tourists in Greek also figures as part of the native ethos of transaction. The humorous yet insulting suggestions of a souvenir shop owner (Takis Papamatthaiou) to an American group mobilizes an intimate language that Greeks historically employed in their interactions with their Anglo-Saxon colonizers (see Gallant 2002). Even the bus driver, Prokopis, appears as a typical Greek male, patronizing Georgia for her punctuality and uptightness. Clashes of *habitus* as embodied knowledge exemplify national and social characters in predetermined ways when history enters the picture: Prokopis' 'hairy' style (long hair and untrimmed beard) invokes the past intrusion of social movements from the West (1960s), when tourists-rebels were symbols of dirt (Douglas 1993; O'Brien 2008: chapter 6). Incidentally, Prokopis' nickname ('Poopi') and surname ('Kakas') literally mean excrement in Greek and Western contexts. This promotes some unsavoury conflations of disturbed cultural margins with disposable matter, making both a question of civility (Prokopis is unhelpful and speaks little in the first half of the film). The scenes of leisure bear a striking resemblance to stereotypical perceptions of hippy culture as decadent and apolitical – popular in foreign discourses of the West as the place of vice and lack of moral order.

The tour itself takes us through some renowned ancient Greek markers outside the metropolis, constantly cutting to aerial shots and graphic 'island style' architecture. As a result, viewers indulge in brochure images propagated by global tourist industries (Urry and Larsen 2011: 173). This distant vision is duly complemented by a proximate one that prioritizes dancing in Greek pop (*laikoús*) rhythms, plate-smashing, sexual innuendo and contrived jokes connected to Hellenic antiquity (Georgia's selling technique of antiquity to tourists). However, Georgia skips the scheduled stop at Thessaloniki's Archaeological Museum, making the southern part of the country the focal point of tourism. The shots at a generic beach communicate the joy of youth and cocktail drinking also through instant change to Western music tunes, suggesting that such liminal zones harbour the global. Even though the beach is the 'locus of an assemblage of ... behaviours and patterns of interaction outside the norms of everyday behaviour' (Shields 1991: 75), the west-northern norms that guide these shots are pretty prominent. The story's hybrid vision is better represented in *MLIR* not by Georgia but the tourists, who wander in Delphi with cameras and video recorders, either reproducing standardized visions or producing individualized or family versions of the tour (Larsen 2005). The Acropolis itself serves as a melodramatic stage in the movie, a picturesque background for the tourist gaze. As opposed to that, Georgia the narrator forms a double foreground of the film. This is so because she tells stories as a knowing insider but leads the tour as an outsider, actualizing Kvale's (1997) twin model of the researcher as a 'miner' (using inner knowledge) and a 'traveller' (using surface data).

Georgia's double role places cosmopolitan Greekness in a setting that can also be removed from its spatio-temporal specificity. The collapse of the group's 'joker' (Irv, played by Richard Dreyfus) at the beach party prepares the tourists and Georgia to engage with big questions about human existence upon return to the Acropolis. This way the possibility of Irv's death is connected to the film's thanatotourism: the monument transforms into a cosmic site as Georgia admits to others that she loves it not because of its connection to ancient goddess Athena but because the whistle of the wind becomes a meeting point of nature with human imagination – 'and for me, that's history'. Here, the Acropolis becomes a

Figure 4.1 Georgia (Nia Vardalos) as foreground to the Acropolis and its tourist crowds. Credit: Fox Searchlight/Photofest.

perennial Hellenic *topos* through the tour's embodied pedagogy that can be recorded and narrated in global media (Leontis 1995). It is significant that *MLIR*'s story ends with Georgia's admission that we 'cannot plan life' in a picture-postcard shot of Prokopis' kiss against the background of the moonlit temple. Just like Calcutta's reproduced banality through ideas of joy, human endurance and victory against all odds, *MLIR*'s Western cosmology portrays Greece's cultural externality as an alterity we thrive to manage in our personal travels (Hutnyk 1996: 185). *MLIR*'s romantic tourist gaze emerges from such solitary acts of contemplation, even in collective consumptions of place (Urry and Larsen 2011: 19). The tourist policies of Greece's capital are embroiled in this cinematic matrix, bearing testimony to its insertion into global developmental planning that exceeds the scope of its own 'heritage industry' (Hamilakis and Yalouri 1995). The romantic tourist and the mega-event tourist are two such paradigms in the twenty-first century, as Georgia's obsessional tour narrative attests. It would be very useful to have a look at this aspect of global tourist complexity from the standpoint of Greek policy-making on mega events and heritage.

Unpaid debts: cinematic characters and the activist cause

MLIR's romantic tourist attests to Greece's embeddedness in the global structures of mobility as a civilizational 'backwater' (Tzanelli 2011a). Early on, its labyrinthine island nature and its location between Italy and Asia Minor presented it as an alternative Venetian *raum*: Grand Tourists used it as a thanatotourist plateau, cultural pilgrims as a recuperative hermeneutic space, and postmodern neo-pilgrims transformed it into a digital narrative of sun, sea and antiquity. A Venetian Calcutta, at the start of the twenty-first century Greece presented ample possibilities for broadcasting, exploitation and political intrigue. This political background feeds into *MLIR*'s archplot in which a Greek imagined community reclaims a cultural debt from Europe and the West while paradoxically perform-ing its Oriental heritage through acts of theft, resentment and cunning diplomacy. Georgia's employer, Maria, bears a striking physical resemblance to the famous Greek socialist actress Melina Merkouri, whereas her attitude – characterized by gossip, plotting and back-stabbing – portrays her in devilish entrepreneurial colours. Placing a diasporic subject (Georgia) under cunning Maria's supervision subverts Merkouri's celebrity status, suggesting that the nation's global commu-nity and its labour are mistreated. Greece's disreputable socialist and feminized legacy is thus subverted in a movie that was filmed during the conservative 2007–9 term. Just before the dubbed Greek 'endgame' (bankruptcy) in a global recession (2011), both major political parties operated in an atmosphere of suspi-cion and mutual accusation that worsened with time. Criticisms aside, a movie with a modest budget had to tread softly in a minefield of embezzlement trials and successive ministerial falls. The humorous portrayal of cunning Maria who offers useful advice to Georgia diffuses any unwelcome criticisms by delivering ambig-uous messages. Not only is this vagueness constitutive of global discourses of the stranger as the locus of ambivalence (Bauman 1991; Kristeva 1991), it also cleverly plays on stereotypes of Oriental imprecision, faultlessly delivered by the offspring of global Greek migration histories (Nia Vardalos).

Melina Merkouri was born into an Athenian middle-class family of high stand-ing but she subsequently espoused left-wing ideas. She is known for her perfor-mance of the *femme fatale* who smokes and dances *zeibékiko* (a dance imported to Greece by Greek refugees from Turkey) like a man but sings love songs like a woman. Representing female attractiveness that is deviant because it threatens social order (Doane 1991: 2), Merkouri's cinematic 'sign' (Dyer 1982) simulta-neously undermined and reinstated conservative discourses concerning the place of women in society (Ryan and Kellner 1990: 2). Her aesthetic statement was of considerable ambivalence too: she remained self-exiled in France (the land of cerebral European art) for many years but never stopped cultivating a natural 'Oriental' ability that transformed her body into a unique Greek brand. Becoming universally known for her role in *Stella* (1955, dir. Michalis Kakoyannis) as the rebellious *bouzoúki* performer who defies the rules of conventional morality and drives men to commit crimes (Gledhill 1997: 28), Merkouri attacked familial stereotypes to grant Greek cultural intimacy with a public face. Her performance of *Ta Paideiá tou Peiraiá* (Children of Piraeus) in the famous *Never on Sunday* (1960, dir. Jules Dassin) speaks volumes about her alluring dark *habitus*. The film concerns a well-mannered American, Homer, who meets a sex worker (Ilya) in Piraeus and tries to change her ways. Homer, a lover of classics, is representative of the Western philhellenic face that aspires to discipline feminine Oriental

Greekness through education in classics and philosophy. The lessons, which last for two weeks, fall on deaf ears, as Ilya remains more interested in entertaining her male friends on Sundays (a provocative replacement of ceremonial Church communion) than learning about the Hellenic world the West reveres. This reiterates the principles of Oriental *flânerie*, which rely on the 'metaphysics of depth' (Tziovas 1986: 470), themes of strategic obscuring or illuminating those aspects of the Greek culture that can travel. Representing the life-loving Ottoman *kéfi* of a Greece that stands 'without columns' (Holden 1972), Merkouri operates in *MLIR* as an intertextual reference via Georgia's performance of the only Greek Oscar-winning song ever (*Ta Paideiá tou Peiraiá*).

Because the song proffers a musical narrative in *bouzoúki* rhythms it has been embraced now by all Greek sign industries including aviation, tourism, film and other audiovisual media. Although a product of what is often regarded as the most commercial and exploitative of cultural industries, genres such as that performed by Merkouri in *Never on Sunday* promote strong notions of authenticity as sincerity and honesty of creative expression (Negus 1995; Cohen 2002, 2005) – precisely what the industry of prostitution does in the marketing of sex. Merkouri is a 'condensation symbol' (Cohen 1985: 102 in Edensor 2005: 109), a multisensory icon projecting a Greek cosmopolitanism with Oriental folk properties. The famous soundtrack of the movie was composed by one of the greatest dissident artists of the junta, Manos Chadjidakis (1925–92), who won the Academy Award for his collaboration with Jules Dassin. Chadjidakis also wrote the trademark song for Kakoyiannis' *Stella*, *Agápi Poú' Gines Díkopo Machaíri* (Love, you became a double-edged knife) sang by Merkouri. During his exile in the United States, Chadjidakis completed several major compositions, including *Rythmología* for solo piano, his compilation *Gioconda's Smile* (produced by Quincy Jones), and the song cycle *Magnus Eroticus* (*Megálos Erotikós*), in which he used ancient (Sappho, Euripides), medieval (stanzas from folk songs and George Hortatzis' romance *Erophíle*) and modern (Dionysios Solomos, Constantine Cavafy, Odysseus Elytis, Nikos Gatsos) Greek poems, as well as an excerpt from the Old Testament book 'Wisdom of Solomon'. Despite therefore his progressive left-wing outlook, dislocation inspired Chadjidakis to merge Hellenophilic tradition with folk rhythms.

Ta Paideiá tou Peiraiá paints the feminized desire to 'have many children' that will grow and become 'the pride of Pireaus'. 'If I search the whole world, I will not find a port with the magic of Piraeus' that in the evenings fills with songs, the actress attests in front of the camera. The song is performed by a half-dressed Merkouri who admits that she loves all men and that every night she puts a charm under her pillow to dream of them. The black working-class woman of *Ta Paideiá tou Peiraiá* may be showcasing Greece's Oriental *habitus*, but its enclosure in a glass camera world produces a hermeneutics of recovery. 'Every night I wander in the port to meet strangers', the actress sings in a husky voice with an ambiguity that casts her both as a prostitute and a *flâneuse* – an urban wanderer collecting signs. A social actor and a detached spectator at the same time, Merkouri arrives at a self-understanding based on desire (Eve's fallible property) rather than unconditional giving. *MLIR* places Merkouri in a thanatotourist frame that is constructed across three dimensions: through the song's tourist-media value, the modest-come-'wild' cinematic academic (Georgia) and a bubbly artistic group (Vardalos, Reiss). The cinematic meta-frame is not merely the Acropolis but Greece surrounded by the Mediterranean's liquid nature: the sea.

Merkouri's artistic persona is representative of a Greek hermeneutics of suspicion (or 'metaphysics of depth') against patriarchal structures and the crypto-colonial system, and her political activism never supported forgetting: as a resentful voice of the subjugated, she actualized a historical revenge against those who divested Greece of its Hellenic honour. She turned the colonel's practice of stripping rebels of their citizenship on its head 'by demanding how a handful of colonels could deny them their birthright' in the last junta (1967–74) (Herzfeld 2005: 215). In the 1975 trial of the colonels she was recorded playing the journalist who humiliates Ioannidis (the junta's 1972–4 leader) with a question he found 'uncivil': 'How did you feel as Cyprus' torturer and undertaker?' (*Eleftherotypia History* 2010: 85). The dictatorship of Papadopoulos supported a national meta-narrative of European Hellenic whiteness and part of its policies was the preservation of the purity of heritage (Herzfeld 2002a: 13–15; Tzanelli 2008c: 499). But the controversy regarding the looting of the Parthenon, which has been around for about 200 years, gained in depth and passion in post-war Greece, especially in the political restoration period (1974–) during the rise of a Greek socialist movement that favoured Greek autonomy in the international political scene (Tilly 1984a). Coming out of a situation that plunged Greek political life into a dark age, the leadership of PASOK (Panhellenic Socialist Movement) heralded Greek liberation from the totalitarian handcuffs of the colonels' regime. As a post-restoration Minister of Culture for PASOK, Merkouri launched a battle for the return of the Elgin marbles in Greece (Yahoo Movies, undated). Her calculated (crafty) policy drew the attention of international institutions, such as the United Nations Human Rights Commission, to domestic concerns by successfully presenting the British usurpation of Greek heritage as a violation of human rights (e.g. Guest 1990). Her argument manipulated the Greek state's protection of prestige as Greek humanity's safeguarding. Ironically then, as a political actor Merkouri supported the discourse of racial property she contested as an artistic actor.

The famous Acropolis Museum in which the state aspires to host the Elgin marbles was Merkouri's initiative, but the enterprise was executed by generations of politicians from left and right (Yalouri 2001: 19–20). As an ongoing project, Merkouri's anti-Elgin activism would come back to haunt the organization of Athens 2004 (Tzanelli 2004c: 433) and again in 2010 with a new campaign before London's 2012 Olympics. The Western argument that even if Greeks had the spoils returned they would not know how to conserve them in a fumigated city (*MLIR*'s humorous hint) was a clear reiteration of the crypto-colonial canon with which PASOK and later the conservative Nea Dimokratia had to deal in the Olympic context. The Greek 2010 campaign points out in a relevant video clip (BringThemBack.org 2010) that a reciprocal gesture on the part of the Greeks might have set the record straight ('what would you Brits do if we stole the Big Ben to preserve in our empty Parthenon museum because London is very polluted?'). But it also represents a cultural controversy through an ecological vocabulary advocating new practices of 'regional warlordism' (expanding on Urry 2011: 148–9). In this schema, battles of civility are regulated by new city-states (Athens, London), free to delegate labels of barbarity to rival cities that cannot operate on set environmentally friendly standards.

Athens 2004 is a landmark in the global history of image theft that is enacted every four years in Olympic Games ceremonies. Shifting from narratives of media and tourist mobility (*MLIR*'s stance) to provisions of competence proof and secure temporary custodianship (the Olympic host's stance) reiterates the Olympic tradition as global heritage. Modern hosts struggle between commercial imperatives and rigid traditions in Olympiads, especially when public perceptions of risk (by natural disasters, riots and terrorism) become a sort of global 'testing' game. Then heritage tropes (Olympiads changing hands every four years) mirac-ulously transform into legacy agreements (Olympiads as material traces of a contract signed in front of a global community). Only Greece, the ultimate host and guest, the looted 'mediated centre', cannot escape the coexistence of heritage with legacy. In 2004, to save face from accusations of incompetence, the Athens Organizing Committee (ATHOC) invited NATO troops to 'guard' the Olympic athletes from potential terrorist attacks, thus also reciprocating the favourable comments on Greece's progress on the Olympics by New York Mayor Michael Bloomberg who presented Athens as the birthplace of the Olympic phenomenon (Tzanelli 2004c: 432). Perverted feelings of *ressentiment* could only be expressed in ceremonial aspects of Olympism that narrated the nation's dramatic comeback in the cosmopolitan arena (here one may also highlight Beijing 2008's resentful narrative in which, purified from their evident Islamic origins, several significant inventions [e.g. the compass, calligraphy] and the original discovery travels figured as exclusively Chinese history [Tzanelli 2010b]). Ceremony and politics complemented each other, as a pervasive Islamophobic discourse had already permeated the country's Olympic politics by the start of the 2000s (Antoniou 2003: 170; Tzanelli 2010a).

None of these issues are discussed as such in the movie but the Oriental phan-tom haunts its background: from Greece's Orientalist heritage (embedded in characterizations of its actors) to Athens' pollution problems (scattered in its jokes) to the recurring question of Olympic legacy (Georgia's passing comments en route to archaeological sites), we view a Greece struggling to put together its columns in a globally plausible pattern. Such seemingly innocent jokes refract twentieth-century political splits between a Greece 'belonging to the West', one 'belonging to the Greeks' (Clogg 1992: 179) and one marred by its Eastern legacy through an equally problematic narrative of a 'Hellenism beyond Greek borders' that Georgia-Vardalos represents in *MLIR*. Yalouri (2001: 69) reminds us that the Greek diaspora – otherwise dubbed 'ecumenical Hellenism' – has been the demagogical object of past Greek dictatorships that purposely recognized belonging to the Greek *yénos* (race) as part of belonging to its land. If not very careful, any digitopic mastery of the Acropolis as a cultural fusion of science and art risks turning heritage landscape, even in cultural industries, into a racialized token (Pine 1998 in Jamal *et al.* 2003: 155). For a country steeped in history and myth, such slips are ever easier, dragging expatriate travellers down with them despite any good intentions to 'develop' their imaginary homeland's potential.

5   Memory and protest

Yimou Zhang's and Ai Weiwei's artwork (2004–11)

Mobility and belonging in epistemic domains

Let us examine how the works of two of China's controversial artists – namely cinematic director Yimou Zhang and activist-architect Ai Weiwei – endorse imaginative forms of travel that render metropolitan Chineseness translucent across cultural planes. Once more, travel and tourism are differentiated experientially (Boorstin 1962; Bourdieu 1984). But whereas experiential creativity functions as a token of authenticity (presenting them as educated travellers, Grand Tourists of sorts), both artists declare attachment to popular culture and audience participation, thus advocating common tourist practices by technological means. I use the term pilgrimage here in recognition of the spiritual dimensions of both artists' journey but also to highlight its function as a human rite conducive to modern mobility cultures. Such analytical classifications conceal how the promise of demediation (experiential immediacy without technology) of travel experience is both 'standard to the marketing discourse of tourism [and] constitutive of the travel mythos as propagated by the very travellers' (Strain 2003: 4).

The mobility of ethnic style is a marketable feature in mediascapes, especially when it is tied to imaginative forms of touring foreign lands, as is the case with the Beijing Summer Olympics (2008) to which both Zhang and Weiwei contributed. Although the Olympics are not the chapter's centrepiece, they bind the two artists' passage from the private aura of ethnic artistic forms to the public domains of global fandom. I endeavour to show how, just as Vardalos, Zhang and Weiwei promote a form of organic art or artistic craft; and as members of a transnational epistemic community they were drawn into national and regional policy-making because their social identity and cultural status contributed to the Chinese Communist Party's (CCP) aspiration to enhance China's global political prestige (Haas 1992; Ong and Nomini 1997). Chinese policies strategically intertwined nationalist with cosmopolitan imperatives to this end (Conversi 2001; Drake 2003: 42). Following Den Xiaoping's post-Maoist reforms, Chinese nation-building began to promote in new knowledge economies mergers of middle-classness with symbolic skills that hinged upon hegemonic narratives of art, but on the domestic stage it endeavoured to control and repress such identities because they clashed with traditional communist values (Xu 2007). The zeal to revive Confucian teachings in more recent years consolidated this oxymoron, whereby organic knowledge was both promoted and destroyed.

From the Maoist era the educated urban youth and intelligentsia were forced to move to rural or industrial areas in the CCP's attempt to educate the peasantry and indoctrinate the middle classes into proletarian values. This phenomenon informs the biographies of Zhang and Weiwei. European social theory speaks of 'open' and 'closed' national cultures, domains of memory that define and are defined by the ethnic profiles of their human participants (Przeclawski *et al.* 2009: 173). This matches the relative 'openness or closedness of an media product' (Schrøder *et al.* 2003: 136): without denying the plurality of potential meanings in different global settings, taking the Chinese political context as an interpretative ground limits my readings of Zhang's and Weiwei's artefacts to a manageable size in this chapter. In China's case Maoist ideology structured ethnicity on class profiling and used this model to classify intellectuals as domestic heroes and internal migrant-outcasts.

Epistemological considerations

Both artists were called upon to enliven China's *technopoesis* (Hand and Sandywell 2002: 208). As Western cosmopolitics began to be imported through the country's colonial routes, knowledge technologies became more tightly connected to ideas of *kósmos* as visually manifested beauty in opposition to vulgarity (Jenks 1993: 9; Eagleton 2000: 32). In this respect, Zhang and Weiwei present us with some of the dilemmas we encountered in the *DVC/AD* controversy but from a non-European perspective. Artists transform *poesis* addressed to objects into *praxis* addressed to fellow humans (Lukâcs 1968) through personal journeys into what they relinquish in transnational creative contexts (fixed identity), supporting thus a subversive mimesis of power in paradigmatic ways. Distance from one's homeland – a separation of ritualistic significance that informs symbolic creativity – is *sine qua non* for the emergence of imaginative travel to the artists' *heimat*, turning them from citizen-members of the imagined community into strangers and tourists (von Wiese 1930 in Spode 2009: 69; Meethan 2003). In technological milieus such imaginative travel transforms place into a combination of abstract characteristics. Artistic journeys create allegories of place: as discourses that develop in public but away from their birthplace (*alloú* = elsewhere, *agorévo* = orate in the market or *agorá*), allegories are poetic mechanisms that find it easier to travel the world because of their inherent hermeneutic ambiguity. Allegory is a consequence of multidirectional flows: rural to urban, periphery to centre, home to foreign land, emotion to reason or back again. Allegory is part of a phaneroscopic process: it allows for the passage of immediate encounter to experience, transforming it into poetic reflection on what was left behind (Peirce 1998). Thus, although not currently addressed as such, allegorical labour in art is constitutive of methodological considerations in mobility literature (see, for example, Büscher *et al.* 2011, for a discussion of digital mobilities).

We may reconsider here Urry's elaborations on 'places that die' (2004: 208) to explain the transformation of tangible forms of *heimat* ('land' in his terms) into an ideal based on novel technologies of the eye ('landscape'), which travels faster in media spheres (MacCannell 1973; Morley 2000; Urry 2001, 2002, 2007: 265; McLuhan 1962; Anderson 1991). The traditionalist view of land that service classes embraced as 'heritage' in Western European contexts (on which see Thrift 1989), was identified by the engineers of the Cultural Revolution with peasantry. The onset of reforms by Deng was met with a challenge in attempts to recover 'selfless ethics' from the past and accommodate them in what today is recognized as the Chinese 'techno-nationalist' turn (Hughes 2006: 19–21). The trajectory of these successive reforms is traceable today in middle-class Chinese cosmologies that try to reconcile new techno-nationalist styles with older loyalties to 'nation' (*minzu*) and 'country' (*guojia*) (Larson 1993; Drake 2003: 38). Zhang's artwork stands at such ethical intersections. Also recalling Peter Jackson's case it is worth stressing once more that art exists at the technological level as articulation, a quasi-functionalist merger of word, sound and image addressed to global audiences, not just one's compatriots (Sandywell 2011: 37). For Weiwei and Zhang in particular the shift from land to landscape is autobiographical in context and transnational in means. Both artists mobilize the spectacular technologies (film, photography) social theory associates with the rise of postcolonial urban phantasmagorias and Western consumption milieus (Patke 2000; Berger 2008: 128). Reviewing the auratic through its supporting technologies is connected to both artists' biographies of political persecution and detention – hence their sociocultural identities.

Technological labour is a key aspect to their tourist-like pilgrimage, promoting a view of art originating 'from below' but eventually articulated 'from above' (on art and labour see Wolff 1984: 15). This technological manipulation of one's place of origins is constitutive of the production of a modern mobile world through the 'double helix' of photography and tourism, once kodakized but now also largely visually reinvented and simulated (Löfgren 1999; Osborne 2000; Larsen 2004; Urry and Larsen 2011). There is no doubt that this process freezes local people as objects of the travel desire (Bærenholdt *et al.* 2004). Here, the ethics of mobility become entangled in the inevitable paradox of nostalgia, the angst of the return journey that also haunted the literary scene of Western high modernism (Gibbons 2007: chapter 1). The intentionality of freezing is part of the Odyssean structures migrant agencies produce: Zhang and Weiwei might be mobile subjects but their experience of childhood exile, however difficult, is remembered from a cinematic distance as experiential journey to sites that are both personal and collective (Nora 1989; Huyssen 1995; Urry 2004: 209; Gibbons 2007: 2–3). Both artists created Arcadian worlds from their experiences of living and working in rural or proletarian China. Corresponding to the principles of yin – stereotypically feminized in Chinese militarist nationalism – these domains symbolize the country's 'cultural intimacies', the embarrassing yet endearing sites that are displayed to the world as forms of comprehensive self-stereotyping (Herzfeld 2005: 3; Tzanelli 2008b: chapter 7). Different forms of technology enabled both artists to produce and envisage Chinese modernity through audiovisual projections of explanatory understandings of their identity (Weber 1978a: 11; Tzanelli 2008b: 23). Zhang and Weiwei display a mobile identity as professionals and a travel imaginary and style as artists (Giddens 1991: 18; Wellman 2001). As explained in Chapter 1, blends of art with craft partake in poetic productions of identity, symbolically dissolving highbrow (elite) and lowbrow (folk) divides. Artwork itself turns into social action, allowing Zhang and Weiwei to relinquish their role as passive spectators and valorizing their identity as tourist-like actors (Dann 1977; DeNora 2000, 2003). Where nation-states seek to homogenize symbol creators under the banner of an 'epistemic community' rooted in national land, individual expressions of tourist-like artistic anomie create alternative networks and 'industrial communities' (Blauner 1964: 24 in Hesmondhalgh and Baker 2010: 29).

In the remainder of the chapter I proffer a sociological-anthropological biopic of Zhang's and Weiwei's recent artwork. Both artists looked to pre-industrial contexts to generate a utopian complex of representations in support of an inclusive global memory that debates state-controlled remembrance systems (Herzfeld 2005: 3). Memory here forms an artscape to pluralize national pasts, enabling the technological transposition of rooted landscapes (Appadurai 1981, 1990). A product of both individual and collective manipulation (Connerton 1989; Halbwachs 1992), memory's artscape allows the artist's inner journey to 'make sense as a coming to consciousness' (Clifford 1988: 167). My use of observations from the Greek context is supported by Zhang's role as an adviser in the staging of the Athens 2004 ceremonies. I remain mindful that my epistemological grounding aligns with non-Chinese models of thought, often communicated in this chapter through language. The oscillation between at least three different cosmological planes (a Greek, a Chinese and a Western) can be better understood in the following two sections of the chapter, where I outline the artists' attempts to achieve cultural translatability for their work across different cultural planes.

Out of linguistic limitations rather than political preference I adopt some conceptual tools from those traditions. The use of such tools is firmly embedded in my conviction that there is no such thing as 'pure' tradition, only fixed representations of it: Aristotelian *poesis* was the product of cultural dialogues across the centuries, if indeed there ever was an 'Aristotle'. Epistemologically, my Aristotelian philosophy should be taken as a journey through Hellenic, African, Middle and Far Eastern theories and theosophies that can never be 'recovered' as they were. Its representations as a territorially-bounded 'heritage' of European thought appeals to sanitized discourses of mobility that obscure the workings of power (Jensen and Richardson 2004). My dialogics envisage the presence of plural experiences *within the screen*, fusing the hermeneutics of recovery and suspicion (Dallmayr 2001: 130) into a schema of multidirectional interpretation. Placing experience within the screen frames life narratives for others, inviting artists to share their journeys with the world (Ricoeur 1985, 1993). It is in the interstices of Western and Eastern cosmology, the 'third space of enunciation' (Bhabha 1994: 37), that the two artists perform their labour, material and emotional.

As Archer (1995) contends, human narration produces agency that revises structures of belonging, mapping new imaginative and real trajectories. Zhang and Weiwei deal with this challenge in different ways. The next two sections are dedicated to their artistic trajectory following Beijing 2008, but occasional flashbacks better situate their work politically and culturally. This results in some concluding observations in the final section, centring upon their contribution to a transition of private histories and memories to the global cultural plane.

Yimou Zhang's *diforia*: *wuxia* and mobility complexes

Yimou Zhang's biography and cinematography are fine examples of multiple mobilities – including migration, tourism and visual innovation across different urban and national spaces. Zhang was born in 1950 in the city of Xi'an, Shaanxi province, into a family that became a target of the communist regime. His father was persecuted as an officer in the Kuomitang Army, one of his brothers was accused of being a spy and another fled to Taiwan, whereas Zhang himself was sent first to toil with the peasants and then to a textile factory. His intimate knowledge of Chinese peasantry and proletarian labour informed his artwork as 'an ongoing (re)construction of praxis and space in shared contexts' that theorists associate with conventional and auto-ethnographic tourism (Edensor 2001: 60; Graburn 2001: 151; Graburn 2002: 26). The death of Mao Zedong (1976) and Deng Xiaopeng's decision to reopen the universities found Zhang moving away from this rural environment as a student of Beijing's Film Academy. His engagement as a director with the *wuxia* literary-kinesthetic genre and his ethological development of feminine heroines – *Red Shorhun* (1987), *Ju Dou* (1990), *Raise the Red Lantern* (1991), *The Story of Qiu Ju* (1992) – correspond to this intimate knowledge of peasantry (All Movie, undated). His birthplace, one of China's civilizational birthplaces where 13 feudal dynasties established their dominion, informs his film-making, which transforms national myths into mobile fables. Just like Jackson (see Chapter 2), Zhang's cinematography engages in 'motility', a way of appropriating a field of possibilities relative to the movement so as to use them effectively for his own projects (Kaufman and Montulet 2008: 45; Sheller 2012). Partly a romantic appropriation of landscape and partly a critical intervention of Chinese land and its institutional power, Zhang's past becomes a vehicle of postmodern permutations of Chinese belonging.

I focus here mainly on *Hero* (2002) and *The House of Flying Daggers* (*HFD*, 2004) as his most discussed films with clear visual and kinesthetic links to Beijing 2008. Tying imaginative, virtual and material mobilities, Zhang's *wuxia* films toy with memorial regression that informs national allegory but hybridize these memories. Even if we regard Zhang's poetic ambivalence as individual aesthetic reflexivity (Beck *et al.* 1994; Lash and Urry 1994: 5–6), we must consider how genre *categories* operate as cosmological superscripts and how their modification allows symbolic creators or industrial stakeholders to attract wider audiences (Born 2000; Langford 2005: 9). A member of the so-called 'Fifth Generation' school of film, which included several famous directors,

Zhang changed the global face of Chinese cinema. His insertion into a memory artscape that mediated 'Chinese' martial arts through Western-style combat was pioneered by the Hong Kong cultural industry, which operates outside Chinese knowledge economies (Zhen 2002; Berry 2007: 193–4; Chan 2007). The self-recognition of a group of Beijing apprentices as a 'school' allowed for the synchronization of Confucian pedagogical principles in Chinese technological art with Western culture (also Nederveen Pieterse undated: 4), professionalizing the group. Thus the disciples of this school bridged Chinese social mobility, firmly grounded in class and ethnic hierarchies, with the Western principles of individualism that partook in the professionalization of cinematic craft and its recognition as a form of art (Giddens 1991; Herzfeld 2005: 70).

Though originally known as *Ying Xiong* (Hero of the Earth), *Hero* looks to classics such as *Yellow Earth* (1984, dir. Chen Kaige), and to Hong Kong's commercial cinema to reinvent the *wuxia* genre. The use of an earthly metaphor in the title already communicates the persistence of fixity within the logic of cinematic mobility: it is not just that the movie's 'manicured countryside' (Thrift 1989: 34) is populated by slave peasants, but that it is openly set against the masters of the Chinese land – including the Emperor who is the ultimate hero of the story (see also Urry and Larsen 2011: 109). Zhang's personal ambivalence towards communist appropriations of the Confucian order as a cosmology fixed in time is present in his 2007 film *The Curse of the Golden Flower*. His most recent melodrama *Under the Hawthorn Tree* (2010) critiques the Cultural Revolution for dividing and labelling people on the basis of class under the guise of a love story – possibly an allegorical reference to Zhang's ambivalence towards Chinese rurality as a place of communist exile and a source of inspiration. As critiques of China's cosmetic cosmopolitan policies (Nederveen Pieterse 2006b: 1250) that sidelined the specific needs of the country's polyphonic cultural landscape, education and romantic love became global translatability devices for Zhang's cinematic artwork.

Zhang's shift from documentary-style film-making to spectacular 'mythistory' (myths appealing to historical events) reveals art's role in making real politics (Eliade 1989): realism and romanticism were placed in an autobiographical continuum rather than an opposing schema. It is not coincidental that this shift almost coincided with Zhang's progressive internationalization, popularizing quite specific social instances for global audiences. At the same time, his personal attachment to Chinese cultural ideals did not diminish altogether, possibly as a defence mechanism towards CCP's censorship strategies. On the one hand, in a recent interview (Asian Film Awards, 22–25 March 2010) he stressed Hollywood's continuing influence across the world, conflating American economic and political power with cultural domination, and thus following the CCP-friendly cultural imperialist thesis (Schiller 1991). On the other hand, he stressed Chinese cinema's indebtedness to the Hong Kong industry, reproducing a moral economy of transnational creative labour. In 1995 the government pulled *The Story of Qiu Ju* from the New York Film Festival after finding out that *Gate of Heavenly Peace*, a documentary about the Tiananmen Square massacre, was also programmed (All Movie undated). Communist censorship of Zhang's work shows that the artist offended native political sensibilities.

Zhang's experimentation with the genre of comedy forms a continuation with his later interest in drama. But if folk tragedy acts as an Aristotelian-like critique of communist policies, comedy produces a cosmological framework in favour of a regime keen to romanticize working classness in the place of folk tradition (Murashov 1997: 207; Papathanasiou 2007: 179). In fact, Zhang cast his interest in this genre into a Western educational narrative, explaining that comedy appeals today more to domestic audiences: in past decades the Chinese people suffered more and therefore laughed less (Asian Film Awards, 22–25 March 2010). I term Zhang's allegorical and ambivalent style *diforía*, a poetic practice that allows for reconfiguration of meaning from cultural plane to cultural plane (Tzanelli 2008b: 497). *Diforía* is constitutive of ambivalence – a term identified in post-colonial studies as a discursive play on colonial power (ambivalence as an Oriental characteristic) and in gender studies as a feminine trait (ambivalence as characteristic of feminized strangerhood). As the global cultural plane is populated with multiple audiences we need to distinguish domestic (Chinese) receptions of the message from external ones and speak of *multiforía* instead. *Multiforía* is a way 'of imagining and mak[ing] oneself for oneself' (Kristeva 1991: 13), a code-switching that excludes harmful recipients of one's original message. I will return to Zhang's strategizing below, as it functions in three different ways: as a narrative device in his gendered film-making; as a self-presentational device to power; and as a marketable technique (feminism sold to Westerners).

As a kinesthetic genre, the *wuxia* resembles Western war films, traditionally celebrating the nation through action snapshots rich in emotion. The inextricable connection to national histories of the frontier applies a civilizational veneer to *wuxia* themes, romanticizing the well-meaning outlaw, just like the good outlaw of Western films (Langford 2005: 67). As is the case with famous Western narratives, Zhang's films debate issues around land ownership, regionalism and urbanization (Stanfield 2001). The combination of female strangerhood and the frontier outlaw encodes a double activist discourse in his films, which is symmetrical to contemporary discourses of terrorism. There is a significant connection between terrorism, which 'grew out of the failure of some national liberation movements to … achieve sufficient political potency' (Miller 1980: 1; Tilly 2003: 32), and the early histories of nationalism in which bandits figured as heroes (Herzfeld 1987; Tzanelli 2008b). Terrorism invites the creation of boundaries between legitimate and illegitimate camps (Greisman 1977; Gallant 1999; Tzanelli 2006b), pointing to the existence of 'ever larger political units with an internal monopolization of the legitimate coercive force' (Hess 2003: 351). This political encoding also corroborates with Zhang's *wuxia* inspiration from popular superhero comic-inspired Hollywood movies. Appealing to artistic representations of the lonely hero who departs on a perilous journey against evil forces (often disguised to conceal his everyday identity), Zhang's Chinese bandit genders and racializes Eliasian discourses of civility (Elias 1982; Campbell 2008).

It may be useful to relate Zhang's visual stylistics in *Hero* and *HFD* to Ang Lee's *wuxia* rendition in *Crouching Tiger, Hidden Dragon* (2000) – a confessed influence by the director. By turn this film appears to look to earlier superhero narratives in digital film such as *Iron Monkey* (1993), which was directed by Beijing director Woo-ping Yuen and created by a contingent of Chinese and Hong Kong artists. Partly a Robin Hood fairy tale and partly a choreographed narrative of martial arts, *Iron Monkey* pioneered a new mobility genre that valorized the ancient skill of Eastern fighting. Its innovative uses of technology presented the film's hero as the flying nemesis of institutional corruption, a master of the sky defeating villains who exploit the weak. At the same time, Zhang borrowed from the codes of Western melodrama, which appeals to female and queer audiences (Neale and Krutnik 1990). The tale of aerial threat runs through most of the cinematic subplots in this book, entangling human technologies (from martial arts to military warfare) into the management of the natural world.

The *jianghu* world of martial arts literally means 'rivers and lakes' and its literary development figured wandering heroes. Initially a travel genre, the *wuxia* matched Zhang's double experience as voluntary location hunter and coerced migrant. Zhang's *wuxia* developed in the hubs of the Hong Kong creative industry which provided shelter for several dissident artists. Such touring appeals to hermeneutics of recovery to turn native land into a landscape complete with humans. The famous Chinese *wuxing* colour theory that orders the cosmos on the basis of five elements (wood, earth, metal, water, fire) speaks of a Kantian-like global interconnectedness, but places emphasis on harmony and balance between humans and nature – themes we encounter in Confucian teachings. The *wuxing* union of humans with nature became constitutive of Chinese understandings of agency, whereby nature acts as an organic whole upon the world. This philosophy accommodated the senses, body organs and colours (red, blue, yellow, white, black, green), developing into a unique stylistic complex on which contemporary artscapes capitalize to market China in the West (Zheng 2008; Kommonen 2008). Indeed, it seems that Confucian cosmology is a predecessor of what some proponents of contemporary mobility theory present as a twenty-first-century epistemological innovation: as a 'paradigm' it accounts both for the liquid nature within specific realms but also the concomitant patterns of concentration that create connectivities or promote disconnection and social exclusion (see Graham and Marvin 2001; Urry 2007: 230; Nederveen Pieterse undated: 5).

Wuxing colour-themes cast novel light on Zhang's discussion of rurality as a natural cosmic order destroyed by communist interventions due to intrusions of urban flows. Until his involvement in the Beijing 2008 ceremonies, Zhang made films that talked about his country's struggle against poverty, war and political misrule, and the CCP banned them within China. But today, just as other artists (including Academy Award-winning Tan Dun, pianist Lang Lang, painter-calligrapher Xu Bing) he serves as a cultural ambassador for a regime that cannot shine on the global scene unless it recognizes native talent (Barbosa, 8 August 2008). The stigmatization of Zhang's early cinematic work as anti-communist propaganda might also be rooted in the ambivalence defining genre categories as both popular (hence potentially populist) forms distinct from European definitions of high art (Tudor 1976; Neale 1991) and potent articulations of rooted cosmopolitanisms. The *wuxia* theme of *Hero* and *HFD* informed nation-building across the world: bandit-like personae (Zhang's heroes and heroines) functioned as both central authority's enemy and its collaborators, ensuring that instituted anthropology would later reconfigure them as the original heroes of folk myth, ethnicized human nature or specimens of heritage (Tzanelli 2008a: 100–26).

We may consider *Hero* and *HFD* as late modern technological manifestations of this ethnographic craft that assisted in the making of national traditions. Ethnographic technology defines Zhang's cinematic journeys, 'turning the horns' to the colonial anthropologies of old that consigned specific Orients to the domain of barbarity (Campbell 1964: 26; Blok 1981; Gallant 2002: 98; Herzfeld 2002: 903). As director Zhang would tour the countryside to find the right locations for his films, enacting what we associate with the distant cosmopolitanisms of travel and business mobility. This travelling style is also pronounced in his involvement in a promotional video in support of China's application to host the Summer Olympics in 2008 but also his creation of a live performance for tourists in the Chinese resort of Guilin. The ceremony was celebrated by the national press for its folk music and minority costumes. Such props informed Beijing 2008's opening and closing ceremonies (Encyclopaedia of World Biography, 2007). Though matching the discourses of nationalist primordiality and authenticity, the venture might also be understood as safe utopian regression to Zhang's precarious childhood. But as global art-markets necessitate diversification and nation-states support the valorization of ethnic character through artistic exhibition, Zhang also had recourse to the great Chinese traditions of theatre, painting and poetry. Just as is the case with movies, the shadow theatre was a memory artscape, a cultural practice of worshipping the deities of the netherworld that travelled through China, Indochina, India, Persia and Asia Minor (Tzanelli 2011a: 95). Although ethnic theatre's religious aspect was enmeshed in the cinematic commercialization of art forms, it was argued that celebrity heroes increasingly took on the mantle of religion in commercial contexts (Frow 1998). Zhang's departure from traditional rural storytelling was foretold in his 1996 experimental transfer of Giacomo Puccini's opera *Turandot* to its actual Chinese setting (Forbidden City) for a massive outdoor performance (Eckholm, 1 September 1998). The semi-religious aura of thanatotourist pilgrimage to this part of China matches that of celebrity narratives and heroes across the world.

Despite several offers to direct films outside China, artistically Zhang never left home. However, his memory work does not merely signal an eternal return to the original traumatic site. Rather, it allowed prior knowledge to be processed. Thus it became 'the soil that has to be dug over' to reveal 'deeper hidden strata' of universal social experiences and 'a re-seeing of the strata' (Gibbons 2007: 15–16; Peirce 1998; Benjamin 2005: 576; King 2000: 16–24). This sort of experiential mining, which fuses self-knowledge with discourses of 'travelling' (*contra* Kvale 1997), is auxiliary to tourist policies around the world, especially where memory-work is visually encapsulated by digital means (Beeton 2005; Tzanelli 2007b). *Not One Less* (1999) already suggests a deep emotional attachment to the land through depictions of rural landscape. The film – indicative of Zhang's substitution of intimate with distant vision – debated divisions between China's growing cities and the medieval conditions of its rural areas. Yet, following the conventions of Hollywood melodrama, the film adopted a 'happy ending' resolution also befit for Western comedy (Neale and Krutnik 1990: 133). In most of his films Zhang used Chinese traditionalism to critique communist oppression. His artistic marginalization in China is understood as the reason he eventually changed his openly subversive tactics, creating instead films that appeal to foreign audiences: only through his recognition in Western markets did he achieve recognition at home. Some accuse Zhang of betraying his anti-government beliefs (evident in *Ju Dou*'s post-1989 [Tiananmen massacre] allegory of domestic violence) and giving in to market demands (Eng 2004), but his artwork managed to translate highly specific cosmological genres into something instantly recognizable across the globe.

Recurring themes in *Hero* and *HFD*

Hero and *HFD* recapitulate some themes in Zhang's work while resolving pragmatic problems in its marketing (Alexander 2006). Instead of engaging in detailed plot analysis I endeavour to highlight recurring themes within the films that work to these ends. The first defines the hybrid *wuxia* genre: unlike its Western equivalent that is rooted in chivalric codes of honour, its protagonists come from the lower classes (Gallant 1999). As a result, Zhang's *wuxia* narratives recast national primordiality into the Marxist mould, bypassing communist criticism and injecting novelty into tired Western genres. Both films are ethnographic biopics of characters who organize the anti-statist practices of the communities they come from (de Certeau 1986: 24) while also displaying the usual human weaknesses nationalist propriety attributes to historical others – such as lack of control over desire or greed (Bakhtin 1981: 241). Archetypal femininities determine the stories' course of action, reiterating Zhang's gendered ambivalence as a self-presentational tool: thus in *HFD* Jin (Takeshi Kaneshiro) and Leo (Andy Lau), the outlaw and the policeman, fail to realize their joint goal (expose and eliminate a group of assassins) because of their romantic feelings for a member of the rebel group (Mei).

Both films culminate in the revelation of a female persona as the plot's actual driving force – a woman who is dexterous in martial arts and highly crafty: Mei and Nia (the leader of the assassins) in the *HFD* are liars. The theme of deception and revelation is also strong in *Hero*, where the nameless warrior and the King of Qin proffer three alternative analyses of the same story relating to the King's assassination attempt. Both *Hero* and the *HFD*'s plots are driven by resentment that informs destructive action towards competitors or betraying lovers, turning emotion into a stylistic component of the movies. The theme of deception and revelation (part of the mystery-solving *wuxia*) debates the boundaries between good and evil by gendering and racializing them, thus bridging the gap between Eastern and Western cosmological archetypes (Ricoeur 1967). Suggesting patterns of unequal mobility, the digitization of these folk narratives allowed gender concerns to circulate more widely (Uteng and Cresswell 2008). Both films temporarily displace torture and accusations of treason to debate their demeaning effects on humans – an obsession possibly informed by Zhang's personal experience. Such stylistic-narrativist nodes comprise the coordinates of Zhang's artistic travel, as they are the exotic signposts global audiences can instantly recognize.

Hero visually highlights the diversity of viewpoints, subverting authoritative interpretations of the text (Ricoeur 1974). Appealing to the primacy of the gaze that informs Western cultures (Jay 1993), the red love story of two fabled assassins is succeeded by the confusions of the blue story (a colour also framing the nameless warrior's encounter with the King), the white saving attempt of one lover and some green memory flashbacks – colour themes that excite Western audiences while remaining intelligible to domestic ones. The suggestion that *Hero*'s spectacle allies with Daoism, a way of living 'that finds fullness in absence ... of letting go of struggles [and] the material world' (Kraicer 2002) is reflected in the film in the ways art (calligraphy) and craft (martial arts), reason and emotion become entwined in a deathly game. Such fusions translate into political strategy (symbolized in the ways a chess board foregrounds the

Figure 5.1 Jet Li in *Hero* among Imperial Guards: lucky Chinese red disturbs the blackness, ambiguously fusing the intruder into a sea of warriors.
Credit: Sony/Elite Group/Photofest.

duel between two protagonists in the film's early scenes) and then into ethnic essence (symbolized in the hanging of the calligraphic symbol of land over King Qin's throne).

Zhang's visual stylistics translated into globally palatable ideas of countryside travel through colour and textures without losing their cosmological anchorage: for *Hero* he wandered in the country before choosing Lake Jiuzhaigou for the blue part of the movie and the desert near the border with Kazakhstan for the white, but the green section was digitally manipulated. Distant shots of such isolated areas better turn land to landscape for internal and external tourist gazes alike, injecting travel adventure into the plot: historically, isolated locations such as that of the *HFD*'s bamboo forest used to harbour the exotic bandits of national myth. These colour themes were present in the opening Olympic ceremony: red for the drummers of the opening performance, blue for depictions of the journey to the Seven Seas by the Chinese Muslim General He – another symbol of socio-cultural mobility that was desensitized by the removal of the explorer's ethnic badge. Zhang and Australian director Christopher Doyle's collaboration in *Hero* yielded astounding visual results in complementary rather than conflicting ways: in interviews they explained that whereas Zhang is renowned for his fixed portrayals ('makes still life'), Doyle is renowned for improvisation ('finding the film as he is shooting it') (Mackey, 15 August 2004). Zhang's apprenticeship in drawing and painting has defined his visual style, firmly embedding colour, order and precision in his artwork. Coupling ethnic art with digital craft produced a genre that generated a new Chinese brand in the footsteps of Ang Lee's global success. Branding landscapes nominates them as properties – a phenomenon that Zhang's critical artistic eye deliberately places on an allegorical par with treating women as possessions (Wolff 1984: 55–6; Berger 2008: 102). Digital art emerges once more as a determinant in the global ethics of mobility, especially where gendered fixities or trafficking are regulated by clan leaders – the pinnacle of state-controlled nationalist discourse (Enloe 1990: 45; Bederman 1995; Walby 2006: 124–5; Tzanelli 2008b: 155; Uteng and Cresswell 2008). In fact, here we can connect individual creativity to universal pictures, noting that the CCP's restrictive policies of mobility suggested to modern Chinese citizens that they develop a split view towards movement across time and space: whereas travel has become a status symbol in the public arena, it has also been viewed as a betrayal of one's kinship commitments (and by extension to the seemingly homogenous Chinese 'nation-family' or clan) (Caira 2008: 628). This impacted in unexpected ways on the representational realm, revising the national community's 'Hidden God' in global markets (Goldmann 1964).

Typical *wuxia* stories feature exclusively young male protagonists experiencing tragedies (e.g. losing loved ones), but Zhang's personal touch feminized the genre, gaining thus in transnational feminist audiences. The melodrama conventions (romantic suffering and redemption) that inform both films are easily translatable into Western cultural narratives while also corresponding thematically and stylistically to the work of other renowned Eastern artists such as Kenji Mizoghuchi (1898–1956) and Akira Kurosawa (1910–98)

(Cousins 2011: 133–4). This cultural translatability is reinforced by their ethnic musical style: *Hero*'s composer Tan Dun pioneered alternatives to *Crouching Tiger*'s scores in his exploration of love and longing ('Overture', 'Gone with Leaves') through European instruments such as violin (Coleman, undated), but he also borrowed from epic marching themes that are traditionally used to convey artistically authoritarian violence or the glory of central authority ('At the Emperor's Palace'). Likewise, *HFD*'s soundtrack (Shigeru Umebayashi) mourns in its lyrics the heroine's death (Mei) in fairy tale style, creating an appealing atmosphere for Western audiences. Zhang's decision to use a famous poem by Han dynasty Li Yannian for the film's soundtrack is telling: born into a musical family and becoming court musician during Wu's reign, the poet was later accused of treason (mirroring Zhang's experience) and homosexuality. Choreographed in the film for Zhang Yiyi's (assassin Mei) blind performance in front of officials, the score speaks of a northern beauty foretold to overthrow 'a city or a nation'. The film opens with Yiyi's double performance as a singer and a dancer (first sequence) and a martial artist able to trace movement through sound (second sequence). This double sequence accentuates the poetic clash between Yannian's visual celebrations of beauty with Mei's alleged blindness. Mei's performance follows a combined syn(a) esthetic performance that produces vision laterally as an imaginative force.

Resembling an uncertain critic of the gaze's inability to account for the participation of all senses in tourist experience, Zhang's artwork both endorses and

Figure 5.2 Yiyi-Mei as blind (martial) artist.
Credit: Sony/Elite Group/Photofest.

problematizes Western hierarchies of the senses (Veijola and Jokinen 1994). As a mythical persona, Yiyi is aligned with hegemonic Chinese understandings of beauty but her role within a Westernized narrative of romantic love makes her appealing to Western viewers. Just as in Western environments, Chinese hegemonic orders are intersectionally constructed through variants of gender, age and class and not just race or colour, as some suggested (Dikötter 2008). Just like Zhang's favourite actress, Gong Li, Yiyi is part of his artwork's market window, able to please female audiences across the world in anodyne ways (Friedberg 1993, 1995). Visual tradition is thus understood as a feminine territory but where state policies aspire to protect it from trespassers and foreign influences, Zhang traffics it abroad. The same gendered aesthetics framed Beijing 2008's 'Martial Arts' section, creating an intertextual network in Zhang's work. The inability to distinguish in the *HFD* poem between the auratic (nation), the architectural (city) and the embodied (woman) allows for the articulation of a nostalgic discourse, Chinese-style: in ancient China there were no clear-cut distinctions between urban and rural. Cities functioned instead in a fragmented multicultural imaginary as spaces of intellectual recognition and artistic production (Zhang 1996: 4), foretelling the development of Asian phantasmagoric hubs.

Following this cosmological script, both films articulate a visual pilgrimage in rural China, with *HFD* paying homage to China's bamboo forests (embedding nature into human action) and the country's fields (which isolate the love triangle in enhanced natural colours). Notably, *HFD*'s sole simulated scene shot outside

Figure 5.3 'Memory green': embedding the imaginary of feminized nature (martial arts as ethnic character) into technology.
Credit: Sony/Elite Group/Photofest.

the country in the snow features a Ukranian birch forest. Nature's omnipresence accentuates the absence of what drives movie-making: the machine of the urban spectacle. In this respect, it is significant that *HFD*'s bamboo-green landscape as well as the female rebels' costumes and hats inspired components of the Beijing 2008 ceremonies and matched the design of the Olympic National Stadium (affectionately called the 'Bird's Nest'), globally elevating green to one of China's memory colour themes. It was also Zhang's co-directorship (with Zhang Yigang) of Beijing 2008 that accommodated military displays of ancient drummers dressed in China's national colour (red), the orchestrated participation of 70,000 volunteers projecting Chinese hospitality abroad and the display of the *wuxing*-inspired Fuwa (the Olympic mascots as natural elements and ancient animals). Coupling Chinese mythical creatures with household-like activities (tourist hospitality), presented the actors of the ceremony as members of an enlarged family economy that encourages the development of anthropomorphic metaphors of 'being' a friend or a brother (Lévi-Strauss 1964; Heidegger 1967; Barthes 1993). References to family intimacies found continuation in Beijing 2008's red-inspired 'Memory Tower' section, which included the formation of a torch-like tower by Chinese acrobats to convey Chinese alternatives to Promethean knowledge. The embodied unity of a fictional Chinese family is also present in *Hero*'s red section, which unites art and craft, museumifying tradition for the tourist gaze. These narratives projected a national activist imaginary onto the global plane, legitimizing kinship as an eco-systemic parable of natural belonging (McAdam 1982; Tzanelli 2010b).

Hero never acquired an English website, whereas *HFD* has several in many languages, including an American site that operates both as a commercial node with hyperlinks to photographic galleries, reviews and even sites where one can buy the soundtrack, and as a spectacular journey through China's green-bamboo imaginary. The universally translatable *HFD* (36 award nominations and 16 wins) was more commercially viable in the West than *Hero,* which, nevertheless, entertained instant domestic recognition because of traditional themes only Chinese audiences could understand. *Hero*'s appeal (20 award nominations and 26 wins) outside China can be attributed to its artistic-visual and fairy tale surface that camouflaged it as a piece of exotica befit for the Western gaze – a selling point that probably overdetermined the incorporation of its formulas into Beijing 2008. *Hero*'s Miramax-released DVD version reached Western audiences in 2004 with Quentin Tarantino's advertising support. Tarantino's intervention carried extra weight in light of the earlier release of Miramax-produced *Kill Bill 1* (2003) and *2* (2004), which had developed their plots along the same genre lines as *Hero.* Such support could be construed as an appreciation of Zhang's work, encapsulated in his nickname 'Lao Mouzi' or old schemer/strategist, an ambivalent term appealing to a metaphysics of depth, synonymous in European hermeneutics with the crafty workings of Satan. Personal preferences aside, *Crouching Tiger*'s release four years before, Lee's collaboration with Oscar nominee and ASCAP Award winner Dun, as well as the nomination of Yiyi Zhang as Best Supporting Actress, secured *Hero*'s successful Western marketing.

Figure 5.4 Iconic scene from *Hero*, where the female assassin, dressed in red, is enshrouded in the gold of autumnal decline.
Credit: Sony/Elite Group/Photofest.

The supporting scenario of Zhang's work remained the idea of 'cultural intimacy' (Herzfeld 2005: 3). This potent trope of domesticity, which was theoretically articulated from anthropological research in Greece, is appropriate for an analysis of Zhang's work: as member of a transnational epistemic community Zhang was also involved in the Athens 2004 ceremonies that proffered a linear historical development of the Greek nation from the politically contested 'Greek' antiquity to the present (Tzanelli 2008b: 502–3). Zhang's pyrotechnic narrative of the opening ceremony – a sort of travelogue celebrating Chinese good luck and rebirth that acquired other domestic meanings in the Greek Olympics – illuminated the path from the ancient Forbidden City to the modern National Stadium. But for a politically and artistically informed visitor this pyrotechnic passage through Tiananmen Square might have concealed Zhang's thanatotourist journey to the massacres of 1989 – a move connecting to *Ju Dou*'s allegory and validating Stephen Spielberg's withdrawal from his advisory role in the ceremonies to exercise pressure over China's attitude towards Darfur's genocide. Afterwards Spielberg highlighted the presence of Confucian messages (giving, brotherhood, inner peace, equilibrium and harmony) in Zhang's work (Spielberg, 17 December 2008). It is, of course, precisely such external support that validated his earlier outcry against the communist regime and integrated him into an alternative transnational community of interest. References to collective traumas may function as 'memory screens' in radically opposing ways, 'either enabling a strong memory discourse … or blocking any such public reckoning', by relativizing the commensurabilities of the past (Huyssen 2003: 99; Augé 2004).

Of course, Yimou Zhang's flashbacks and modifications to situated pasts can also be found in the work of other fellow artists from China, but here I focus on another Beijing 2008 contributor who displays more commonalities than we might initially consider: Ai Weiwei. In the following section I place Weiwei's symbolic creativity within the same framework of artistic mobility, to examine how Chinese ideals of global travel are forged.

Ai Weiwei's politics of reproduction

Weiwei's eventual exclusion from China's Olympic enterprise contributed to the ways his artwork globalized pilgrimage to Chinese culture. Son of one of China's most famous poets (Ai Qing) who was imprisoned during the Cultural Revolution, Weiwei spent his childhood in exile in Xinjiang, China's far north-western oil-rich province bordering Kazakhstan, until his father was formally allowed to return to Beijing. After being educated at the Beijing Film Academy (where he founded the art group 'The Stars'), he relocated to the US for a decade. Weiwei's initial involvement in the design of Beijing's Olympic stadium made him internationally famous – an unlucky occurrence, given his eventual repudiation of the project. I use his Olympic involvement as a common reference point in this chapter, because I also endeavour to explore his 'politics of reproduction' as a theme that brings him closer to Western European cosmologies. If anything, the Olympic event itself is haunted by the reproductive politics of city and by nation-building: simultaneously looking back to European customs and protocols of the event and to the organization of Olympic mega-events by previous hosts, it is a fine example of cross-cultural exchange and borrowings even when the organizers claim originality in its delivery. The progressive involvement of film directors, actors and producers in Olympic ceremonies points to reproductions by the makers of such public spectacles. Zhang's inspiration from his own movies in the staging of Beijing 2008 is a case in point.

The politics of Weiwei's artwork complement his digital activism: for a long time he maintained a blog from which he critiqued the government until his arrest on 3 April 2011 on allegations of financial misdemeanours. The vagueness of the accusations pressed on him for financial corruption project native practices (e.g. gambling) to someone who is *de facto* excluded from the Chinese body politic for being vocal about state corruption (also Herzfeld 2009a: 240–1 on similar Roman practices). Widespread associations of theft with unemployment discredit Weiwei's mobility status, associating him instead with economies of waste and excess – all things uncivil that allow some degree of stereotyping of Western tourists in Asian cultures (Tzanelli 2007b: chapter 2). More recent advertisements for the National Stadium as a tourist attraction erase his contribution altogether, stressing architect Li Xinggang's humanistic (but 'scientific') design instead (*Travel China Guide* 2011) while classing the building among the 'top-ten Architectural Wonders in 2007... highly spoken by world-class architects' (Absolute China Tours, undated). The emphasis on science erases the building's cultural specificity, stressing instead how it adheres to the three principles of green, scientific and technological Olympics that address growing global environmental concerns about urban pollution (Urry 2011: 114–5). The wise management of man-made pollution by technological means – a policy discourse that finds variable uses (see Giddens 2009: 185 on Maoist policies) – discards Weiwei's relevant artistic-technological innovation. As was the case with the Elgin Anglo-Greek controversy, Weiwei's *techne* had to give in to hard technology. This replacement partakes in the development of regional warlord- ism (Beijing instead of Chinese hegemonies) while continuing to draw upon the vocabulary of nationalism. As a result, 'socio-ecologic systems' veering towards a world of 'sharply declining physical amenities' manage to erode the social and moral underpinnings of civilization (Giddens 2009: 227, 230; Urry 2010: 148–50). Ironically, this shift reinstates the intrusion of Enlightenment models of progress in non-European regions while downplaying artistic innovation in favour of eco-systemic management.

Blogs and websites supporting the communist regime airbrushed Weiwei's Olympic contribution, presenting him as a difficult individual, a liar and a trouble-maker without a cause. Early on, Weiwei started reciprocating this by discussing the Bird's Nest as an architectural propaganda orchestrated by 'shitty directors' (apparently Weiwei's reference to Zhang and Spielberg) while explaining how his intimate involvement in the project made his self-criticism 'carry more weight' (Chen, 18 August 2007). But Weiwei's involvement in the production of the most recognizable monument after the Great Wall just minutes away from Tiananmen Square speaks the same cultural language Zhang revolutionized in his films by visual means. In 2008 he explained how architecture encodes a generation's interpretive potential, and how the Bird Nest's strength lies in its simplicity with its parts being perfectly integrated in a free-flowing structure. By not separating form from function, which he identified with beauty, Weiwei came close to the historical symbolism of Munich 1972's architecture, which countered the monumentalized neoclassical style of the Nazi and Stalinist eras (Rosenfeld 2000). At the same time, he proffered a critique of the ways mega-events work by re-monumentalizing histories, turning various mobilities into a glorified national narrative. In a reflexive twist, he saw in the shape of the stadium a 'yearning for the rule of reason, but not without passion and dynamism – wanting to show that the head and the heart coexist' (Vulliamy, July 2008: 26). Just as Zhang, Weiwei fused emotion and reason into a distinctive allegory that 'represents the city's strength and ambition' (SexyBeijingTV, 8 August 2008). Not only did this appeal to the distant cosmopolitanism of air travel, it also crafted an ecological discourse we find in social movements.

By reference to Chinese culinary tradition, the Bird's Nest speaks the language of nature mastered by humans (Young 2006: 126), advocating the cosmopolitanism of 'travelling cultures' (Clifford 1992). Weiwei himself cracked this door open by likening the building to the domestic hearth, where strangers are invited to share food with the family (Tzanelli 2010b: 234). Such claims to cosmopolitan belonging can also be detected in Weiwei's *avant gardist* production of 'Remembering', a wall of Chinese text made from children's backpacks. This artwork, which covered the facade of the Haus der Kunst in Munich as a form of mourning for the deceased children from the Sichuan earthquake in May 2008, ensured that China's ideal-typical family travels to the historical hearth of tourism: Europe. Weiwei's humanitarian theme contributes to his self-presentation as a world traveller. This nostalgic travel discourse also informs his October 2010 carpet of 100 million porcelain sunflower seeds hosted by Tate Modern (BBC, 7 April 2011). Weiwei used traditional means and skilled artisans from Southern China, home of the imperial porcelain, to make this work. The hosts of his artwork in London set up direct online communication channels with the public, thus endorsing his blogging practices (YouTube, *Telegraph*, 11 October 2010). Weiwei's fragmented mosaic-like theme in this exhibition is akin to the canvas of the scroll in Beijing's Olympic ceremony that was coloured by China's symbolic future: school children from a variety of ethnic backgrounds (Tzanelli 2010b). Just like Zhang's reproductions of China's rural pasts on the big screen, Weiwei's narratives of familial belonging turn intimate cultural domains into a global public spectacle. By joining global art exhibitions and 'blockbuster exhibitions' characterized by massive media appeal in Western countries (America, Britain), Weiwei articulated his identity as a cosmopolitan traveller. Such global initiatives create transnational artistic nodes akin to that of the *DVC/AD*, producing multiple mobilities (Chia-Ling 2004: 91).

Weiwei's artwork retrieves images of rurality as a commentary on mass production rather than national identity, possibly reliving his own childhood experience of exile. Where Beijing 2008's architectural *anthropopoiesis* (the making of human [Smith, 2007]) is mastered into a tacit form of historical materialism (West 1995: 46), Weiwei's later artwork musters reproductions of nature to contest the auratic project of nationalism. Weiwei's artistic vision provides a set of instruments that enable him to make sense of his own life experiences as a form of activism, asserting his place in global whole (Eyerman and Jamison 1991). Hence, blogging and making art should not be examined as separate endeavours but as forms of social insurgence he can share with other humans from across continents and cultures – a post-national *technopoesis* of sorts. It is in this contingent that we place the production of global activist communities in support of his cause, both in cyberspace and on location (Melucci 1989; Van Aelst and Walgrave 2004; Della Porta and Diani 2006: 73). Ironically, but also understandably, Weiwei is globally celebrated for those works that caused him problems at home: global protesters against his imprisonment in 2011 countered China's Olympic pilgrimage with their *1,001 Chairs for Ai Weiwei*, a peaceful sitting in front of Chinese embassies and consulates in support of his release. The protest, which paid homage to his 2007 documentary at a major arts festival in Kassel, Germany (Sydell, 16 April 2011), became a political pilgrimage to a site (*at the gates* of Chinese embassies, therefore in non-Chinese soil) devoid of its revered token (the artist). The primary protest site invited the crowd to fill exactly 1,001 chairs in reciprocation of Weiwei's cosmopolitan statement. The embodied performance of this rite resembled a religious mass but also the cinematic spectacle, whereby the auditorium was filled with critics demanding reparations for the Chinese government's treatment of the artist (also Graburn 2004 on pilgrimage and strike).

The protests made reference to Weiwei's artwork 'Fairytale', one of his notable pieces at *Documenta 12*, for which 'he flew 1,001 Chinese citizens to Kassel to mill about and experience the town for three months' (Lambeck, 7 April 2011). Such embodied Chinese travel to European sites allowed Weiwei to represent rooted cosmopolitan belonging as folk myth ('fairy tale') without situating this regionally anywhere in China. The German media praised Weiwei for his ability to produce accessible art of 'highly sensual and perceptual quality' through combinations of 'older and contemporary forms' (*ibid.*). Weiwei himself defined the selected Chinese citizens as tourists, mobile subjects sociologists place within the context of modern European consumption and leisure (Dann and Liebmann Parrinello 2009). To be a tourist is to partake in democratized forms of leisure and mobility – hence to be a modern subject. Selecting the town of the Grimm Brothers, two famous fairy-tale authors embedded in European Germanophone traditions, for the enactment of this journey, bound Chinese legends and art to Europe. '1001' acted on this occasion as a metaphor of human uniqueness that matched Western discourses of individualism (Giddens 1991). The choice, explained the artist:

> [i]s due to the fact that what we really want to emphasize is "1", not "1001". Each participant is a single person, and that's why our logo is 1=1000 – that means that in this project 1001 is not represented by one project, but by 1001 projects, as each individual will have his or her own independent experience.
> (Colonnello, 10 August 2007)

Figure 5.5 Circle of Animals/Zodiac Heads, Grand Army Plaza, New York.
Credit: Naveen Selvadurai, Flickr.

Weiwei's more recent work involves the reproduction of twelve bronze animal heads, recreating the traditional Chinese zodiac sculptures which once adorned the fountain of Yuanming Yuan, an imperial retreat in Beijing. The installation is part of an international tour which started in New York, adorned in passing Somerset House's courtyard in London and will traverse three continents (Europe, America and Asia) in a blockbuster exhibition style. The Yuanming Yuan was ransacked in 1860 by French and British troops and the heads were pillaged. The exhibition's sites explain how 'in re-interpreting these objects on an oversized scale, Ai Weiwei focuses attention on questions of looting and repatriation, while extending his ongoing exploration of the '"fake" and the copy in relation to the original' (Circle of Animals/Zodiac Heads 2011). Weiwei politically situated his artwork within the discourse of public art that is not merely addressed to the museum public but generally to those traversing communal places (Somerset House 2011). His personal interest in the zodiac as a collector is translated in this installation into something visually accessible to different cultures and ages, as he explained. Just as Zhang's Chinese recasting of the Western superhero genre, Weiwei understands his art as part of global popular culture: 'When Andy Warhol painted Mao in the 1960s and 1970s, ... it was just this image that people knew, like Marilyn Monroe or somebody. So they might see these zodiac animals like that—like Mickey Mouse. They're just animals' (Circle of Animals/Zodiac Heads 2011).

Containing the exhibition within an imperial courtyard in Somerset House appeared to ritually commemorate Chinese history and deconstruct the auratic pillars of colonial pasts from dominant and subaltern perspectives. At a time when many of the world's leading museums and galleries are strengthening their connections with China by sharing expertise (Gompertz, 11 May 2011), Weiwei contested the political use of museumification through his artistic reproduction of tradition. The selection of the zodiac circle re-allegorizes Beijing 2008's Fuwa narrative: the goods of an imperial retreat are purposely subjected to multiple tourist gazes in an open market (*agora*) of tourists and urban *flâneurs*. Somerset House's courtyard generated a panoptic wall around the artwork but its orchestrated visual exposure on the web and through British news channels contested colonial histories, forging in their place an ideal cosmopolitanism. Thus, the exhibition's spatial stylistics in London (enclosed and panopticized but open to the world) nicely reproduced a collaborative, playful *diforic* message, befit for a former colonial metropolis' urban spectacle.

Why would Weiwei's art become vilified to such an extent by communist authorities? I suggest that we consider the artist's work as an exposure of the regime's 'dirty laundry'. A scandalous nudist appearance among four giggling women in 2011 led to his investigation for spreading pornographic imagery when he was merely doing 'nude art' (Watts, 18 November 2011). Such conceptual clashes (pornography versus nudity) appeal to a Eurocentric hermeneutics, whereby exposure of the human body becomes identified with violations of the national 'body politic', Durkheim's and Herder's take on mechanical solidarity (Tzanelli 2011a: chapter 5). Institutional regulation of pornography was legitimated as a deterrent of 'public decency violations', but given Weiwei's stigmatization as a troublemaker in China the accusation should be considered within the framework of Chinese political censorship. Feminine smiles and giggles in this image connect Weiwei's discourse to Zhang's allegorical cinematography of comic criticism. Exposing one's body to the public gaze is thus another way to convey the vulnerability of those cultural intimacies a valorized regime professes to protect from free-thinking strangers, to remember Leigh Teabing's speech on Magdalene's fate in the *DVC*. The human body and the 'body of social problems' (Bourdieu 1992: 236) each society deems worthy of debate are constitutive of those clashes that define the ethics of multiple mobilities.

Public fora and private aura

Touring is a politically malleable phenomenon: walking the globe in blogospheres and in person is often used by various interest groups to endorse immobile forms and meanings. However, audiences tend to pluralize the meanings of any travel spectacle. Urry, who first conceived of the 'tourist gaze' as an ideal type, notes elsewhere (1996: 193–7) that tourist sites and services may be overdetermined by spatial fixities. The spatial specificity of tourism splits destinations and their meanings into experiences addressed to the romantic traveller and those marketed to mass tourism. Tourist theory might caution us against homogenizing tourist motivations and narratives, but such classifications are imposed on sites by regional and national centres. These centres always seek ways to limit the meaning of artscapes and brand memories tied to art as 'authentic' national sites (Bauman 2000b: 82; Lury 2004). As individual artists, Zhang and Weiwei proffered their own visions of legend, custom and tradition, but always worked towards their global dissemination, thus encouraging an open-ended *multiforic* process in various markets. One might speculate how, on this occasion, communist oppression generates the preconditions for alternative and possibly equally problematic socio-economic visions to blossom, including the absence of any market regulation that characterizes neo-liberal regimes of production and consumption (Berlin 1969: 172; von Hayek 1976; Gray 1984: 129–31; Ryan 1997).

Herein lays the ambivalence in the work of these two artists, who aspire to generate open interpretive frames from personal knowledge of history and legend. The iconic, spectacular dimension of authenticity is associated in tourism with pre-industrial culture, just as it is in Zhang and Weiwei's artwork (Wang 1999). Analyses range from those stressing the systemic emergence of a tourist gaze to those prioritizing emotional engagement with tourist images and *lieux de memoir* 'image-making' as a practice of political valorization (Nora 1989; Crang 1999; Edensor 2005; Savelli 2009). During and after the end of the Olympics, the Chaoyang district where the Olympic Stadium was built emerged as an international superstar in tourism and other recreational activities. The number of tourist visits to the Bird's Nest soared in 2008 and other Olympic cities (Hong Kong, Qingdao, Shanghai) followed suit in tourist development. Domestic media suggested that the 'World Tourist Organization forecast the development of China into the first global tourist destination, the fourth largest original tourism country and the largest domestic tourist market', revealing plans by chief of Beijing Travel Bureau Zhang Huiguang to turn the Bird's Nest and the Water Cube (the stadium for swimming-related athletics) into an Olympic subject park integrating sports, entertainment and culture (Fang, 28 October 2008). Similar predictions were made by the president of the market development committee of the International Olympic Committee, Haiburger, and Liu Deqian, deputy chief of tourist research centre at the Chinese Academy of Social Sciences. Over the same period *China Daily* (Zhuoqiong, 1 October 2008) suggested that the Olympic City had eclipsed traditional tourist attractions during the Golden Week, and presented as evidence Chinese tourists photographing themselves in front of the Bird's Nest. 'We didn't expect the Bird's Nest to become so popular among the Chinese people after the Olympic Games', reported deputy general of the CITIC Consortium Stadium Zhang Hengli to Reuters, claiming that the visitors outside holiday season are between 20,000 and 30,000 per day (Xu and Chisholm, 22 April 2009).

The evidence these agents stress in their reports merges two different phenomena: plural tourist motivations with centralized developmental organization. There is nothing intrinsically Chinese about this: writing before the digital boom, Roche explained how cities hosting the Olympics generate 'mega-event libraries' that decline in volume after the end of the event (1996: 325). But the proliferation of Internet domains in which city-hosts can advertise their staging of such events has altered this pattern, externalizing advertising to multiple global agents in the media industry that have their own interests to promote outside those of the Olympic city's. It remains to be seen whether the book's next case, James Cameron's *Avatar* (2009), is drawn into this representational vortex of the Olympic city (Rio de Janeiro is the 2016 Olympic host), despite Hollywood and Brazilian activism against the Brazilian government's developmental planning. The inclusion of the Stadium in Google's virtual tourism added to the Chinese monument's visual mobility, admitting in the ritual of consumerist worship a global community of tourists-pilgrims (Bauman 1998; Lanfant 2009: 113; Savelli 2009: 141). In conventional pilgrimage the religious community follows a spiritual leader dressed in special attire while voluntarily donating to the sacred site (Graburn 2004: 132). The Bird's Nest tourist rituals apparently involve on-site commercial exchange, the domestic visitors' masquerading in Chinese national team jumpsuits, donations of fake medals and replicas of the Olympic Torch. These rituals are components of a new 'economy of signs and space' which feeds into digital and embodied tourist imaginaries (Lash and Urry 1994: chapter 6). The simultaneous recognition of the Olympic city as a global status symbol and a capitalist node also assisted in reconfigurations of leisure in favour of the rising urban middle classes (Lanfant 2009: 105–6), thus endorsing China's post-Maoist integration into market economy and private entrepreneurship (Xu 2007: 366).

Yimou Zhang and Ai Weiwei became implicated in the production of China's foremost politically allegory, the Beijing 2008 Summer Olympics. Outside this politically charged enterprise both artists appealed to grand Chinese narratives to perform their personal cultural *flânerie* by audiovisual means. Both artists endeavoured to transform ideas of Chinese land to tourist landscape, thus enacting a tourist-like pilgrimage. Blending ethnic art with technological craft (film, documentary and photography) articulated a mobile vision of the rooted worlds from which they emerged as ethnic subjects while also showcasing their creativity as universally translatable poetic narratives. The mobility patterns their art endorsed transformed private cultural domains that entertain auratic status within the Chinese nation (folk and working-class styles) into public figures and forms that can be shared with the world. I would argue that their work became involved in the new vertical mobilities within the field of a broadly defined Chinese art that embraces digital and older crafts alike (Urry 2000: 3–4). But at the same time, these vertical movements of art across different cities and digital networks (Beijing, Hong Kong, Kassel, Berlin, London, New York) worked as strategies for the Chinese state, the city of Beijing and the two artists themselves for 'upward' vertical mobilities in global art and media fields – otherwise put, institutional, collective and individual image-making. In this respect, the people to which Zhang and Weiwei claim to give voice are means to an end that have little to do with traditional frameworks of activist action and philanthropy. The following chapter examines, among other things, some problems generated by fusions between the two, especially when other mobilities also become involved.

6 From deep ecology to thick description

Avatar's (2009) cosmology of protest

Fabulist creativity and political commitment

The reflexive critique and praise James Cameron's blockbuster *Avatar* (2009) has received over the last three years could fill several pages. Economics abound, the film, its digital popular culture, its makers' commitment to a foreign social movement and the tourist milieus it generated evolved in a transnational setting. Tourist and the wider mobility theory provide some good conceptual tools for an analysis of the tropes of authenticity and purity that underline these mobility cocoons, not only at the receiving end (for example, film viewers) but also at the transmitting end (that of its makers) (Linnekin 1991; Urry 1995: 140; Wang 1999; Urry and Larsen 2011: 23). The production and consumption ends of *Avatar* are informed by romantic and pragmatic-economic motivations in more than one way and across different national terrains. The consumption performances of its culture are themselves 'status symbols' (Veblen 1899) and 'cultural capital' (Bourdieu 1984), but they come in the malleable form of signs dispersed across different domains of human memory (Lash and Urry, 1994: chapter 6). The capital sign of my case study is that of the exploitation of human vulnerability (of Pandora's indigenous tribes, of Brazilian communities, and even of Chinese regions neglected by the national centre) that invites multisensory consumption performances (Urry 2007: 56–8). Consumption coordinates are both synchronic and diachronic – in that as a concept consumption refers to the ways colonial mobility channels both encroach in postmodern narratives, inform the symbolic horizons of my work as a historical variable (e.g. stories of New World cannibalism [Obeyesekere 1992: 630; Loomba 2005: 88]) and become a (cyber)ethnographic postulate (e.g. how as a writer I symbolically 'devour' my subject [Fabian 1990; Tzanelli 2012] in ways similar to those employed by movie-makers).

De Pina Cabral (2008: 234–5) notes how Brazil (*Avatar*'s terrestrial political mission) has been characterized throughout its history 'on the one hand by the persistence of its demonic appearance and on the other by the intense domestication of the demonic trope in everyday life'. This produced a bifurcated narrative of identity as otherness, a heterological trope akin to that we encounter in the ill-defined domain of the Caribbean (Sheller 2003, 2004). Foreign observers espoused and globally disseminated this trope to validate representations of specific human types and later on to produce thanatotourist tropes (Dann and Seaton 2001). We might examine Cameron's simulation of Pandoran dwellers as the representational equivalent of demonic exoticism – at once purely Edenic and childlike – but the argument would place excessive emphasis on systemic and structural constraints in artistic representation. The third part of the chapter examines to what extent *Avatar*'s simulation fed back into the global circulation of the Belo Monte controversy by borrowing or contesting these tropes.

The construction of Belo Monte dam in Amazonia – a long-term corporate plan previously hindered by activists – defines the political direction of Brazilian social movements towards environmental conservation and protection of indigenous life. A vital tributary of the eastern Amazon basin, the Xingu River spans 1,700 km from the savannahs of Mato Grosso to the rainforests of Pará. A whole world seems to separate it from the urban developments of the south – Sao Paolo's industrial face and Rio de Janeiro's famous heritage attractions, nightlife and upcoming Olympic development. Neyland (2005) claims that childhood vulnerability (a primary allegory in Western protectionist tropes for the 'Third World') is suspiciously immobile in digital domains, functioning as an image still, so to speak, at once globally exposed and protected by the image-makers. Hutnyk's reiteration of the basic Virilian claim that film criticism no longer has any meaning, rather we have to analyse reality 'in a cinematic way' (Virilio in Hutnyk 1996: 196), coerces us to supersede the role of metaphor in Brazilian-*Avatar* stillness. Cinema always works from image stills in motion, and it is up to image-makers to supplant their craft with fluid narratives of their subject matter, its biographies, needs and aspirations. Of course, Virilian determinism collapses when considered from the standpoint of those who become the object of visual trafficking: they, too, have fully developed intellects and motivations (Maoz 2006; Córdoba Azcárate 2006; Tzanelli 2008b: chapter 4). Enveloped in a deep ecological model, *Avatar*'s activism treats images of tribal societies the same way European totalitarian tyranny idealized histories to promote exclusive racist tribalisms (Argyrou 2005: 79). Paradoxically, Cameron's activism was guided by the same hatred of modernity and the present displayed in the Brazilian context by its anti-totalitarian philanthropic forces. It is too early to assess this paradox given the national centre's dehumanizing programme for development.

I view *Avatar* as a proof of fluidity and fabulist immobility at the same time: the movie came as a response consistent with James Cameron's overall artistic project, but also his self-presentation as a keen world traveller. Just as is the case with Zhang and Weiwei's travel narratives in their national land, Cameron and his associates' journeys to Brazilian lifeworlds figured as human rites conducive to modern mobility cultures. The *Avatar* project merged these mobilities – as a desire for adventure, a bold experiment in visual digital technology, but also a controversial humanitarian intervention in Brazilian environmental policies and politics. An *aficionado* of technology, Cameron has always crafted cinematic narrativity that tapped upon the philosophically complex relationship of human nature with otherness. His artwork has explored the role of the mechanical, the alien or nature in narratives of 'human' (Smith 2007: 95, 105). This overarching theme, which he has explored across three decades with incredible consistency, is also rooted in Western cosmological themes that have evolved into consumption *topoi* (Sheller 2003) and tourist markers (MacCannell 1989). Cameron's determination to support Brazilian protests against harmful development projects thus provides the meta-script of *Avatar*'s project and an opportunity to depart on a 'thick description' (Geertz 1973) of the relationship this particular industry developed with this particular people as well as other communities that capitalized on their association with *Avatar*'s artscape. The *Avatar* project drew upon associations of human exploitation with notions of land as heritage, allowing by turn its indigenous heirs to reclaim it in its digitized and terrestrial forms.

Does Cameron's project disguise the Grand Tourist, imperialist nostalgia in consumerist clothes (Crang 1997: 148–9), or does such criticism mask the political, cultural and emotional complexity of the overall enterprise that cannot be attributed to a single agent? Touring and serving, leisure and work are not mutually exclusive: emotional labour in thin and thick engagement with other cultures can be blended (see Hochschild 1983; Veijola and Valtonen 2007). This chapter outlines the multi-layered and interacting forces of the case in three acts: first, it examines the cinematic and overall digital popular culture of the film without losing sight of its cosmological anchorage and hybridizations. Second, it connects it to the politics of location-hunting and its unintended consequences – notably, the support of tourist enterprise in one country (China) and a social cause in another (Brazil). Finally, it examines the first two in relation to agential choices within the *Avatar* creative industry, focusing in particular on the support of Belo Monte protests by Cameron, Sigourney Weaver and Jon Landau. These acts (cor) responded to what Urry (1995: 174) has identified as the ways in which societies relate to their physical environment, which on this occasion refers to the indigenous people that inhabit it – the primordial face of Brazilian nationhood: stewardship of the land for future generations, exploitation of the land or other resources, scientization of the land as an object of scientific investigation, intervention and regulation, and visual consumption and aesthetic appropriation of landscapes and townscapes. The deep ecology they appeared to promote through activism centring on transpersonal identification clashed with their eco-feminist conviction that the Western (wo)man must promote care and responsibility for particular beings (Argyrou 2005: 58).

A multiplicity of self-presentations and aspirations characterizes the creative agents' actions, including their desire to travel, make art, do business and help others. Within this realm of agential choices, desires and motivations, the *Avatar* industry produced some iconic narratives of political content, granting at the same time the Belo Monte cause in Brazil and Cameron's work with a respectable public face. Without claiming that the *Avatar* makers always reflected *a priori* on the means they used to reach their audiences (a claim impossible to fully validate hermeneutically, even at an artistic level [see Wolff 1984: 99–107]), I consider the poetic circuits generated by their actions and how all parties in the cause responded to them. It is this circular, mutually advantageous but also emotionally creative *logos* (as reasoning process) of the overall *Avatar* phenomenon that makes its critical assessment difficult.

Avatar's audiovisual matrix, I: popular culture

Avatar's digital technology proved to be an obstacle but also its ultimate success. Cameron wrote the first screenplay before entering the creative industry and kept experimenting with new versions, exploring new technologies and looking for new partners until Fox decided to finance the project. The finished project's budget left plenty of room for speculation, with estimates putting its cost somewhere between US$280 and 310 million, with US$150 million for promotion (Barnes, 20 December 2009; Fritz, 20 December 2009). *Avatar* premiered in London on 10 December 2009. It was released internationally on 16 December and in the US and Canada on 18 December 2009, breaking box office records and becoming the highest grossing film of all time in the two northern American countries. It broke the world record held by Cameron's *Titanic* (1997) for 12 years, with a one billion dollars gross profit and an international audience exceeding all expectations in Asian countries, despite its later release in them (Box Office Mojo, 2009). It was nominated for nine Academy Awards, including Best Picture and Best Director and won three for Best Cinematography, Best Visual Effects and Best Art Director (CNN, 2 February 2010).

This success generated additional opportunities for business diversification, further enhancing the *Avatar* sign industry: in late 2011 plans were presented for the construction of an *Avatar* Land, including a theme park built by Walt Disney in the Animal Kingdom section of Orlando's Disney World. Disney won the exclusive global theme park rights to the *Avatar* brand and will commence its construction in 2013 (Barnes, 21 September 2011). The 'triumph of non-human technology over humans', a Weberian thesis propagated in Ritzer and Liska's (1997: 97) influential argument of 'McDisneyization' as a form of post-tourism embedded in consumerist simulacra is both relevant and applicable here. Theorists who see the virtual bound up with spaces, routines and relations of the real world (Shields 1996; Rheingold 2000; Wellman and Haythornthwaite 2002; Germann Molz 2004) are confronted with a concrete example of a post-tourist that comes into being almost simultaneously through a network of virtual and terrestrial practices of seeing, web surfing, visiting and photographing Cameron's utopian hyper-reality.

In 2009 Cameron had promised to transform the story into a trilogy if the box office receipts reached US$1 billion – a promise that materialized when he signed a new contract with Fox Film Entertainment with which he has a long-term relationship. The deal included the non-negotiable clause that Fox will help co-fund with Cameron a non-profit organization, the Avatar Foundation, which will support indigenous rights and the environment, including the fight against global warming. *Avatar 2* and *Avatar 3* will be produced by Cameron and his partner Jon Landau for Cameron's Lightstorm Entertainment (McClintock, 27 October 2010). Although one of the movie's heroines, played by Sigourney Weaver, is killed in the first film, there is the promise that she will return in *Avatar 2* (BBC Entertainment and Arts, 18 September 2011). Although the original release date for *Avatar 2* was 2014, director John Landau revealed that Cameron's decision to shoot it at 60 frames per second (the highest frame rate) from a 3D system for the best CG and performance results will push the release date to 2016 (Gallagher, 11 January 2012). Unsuccessful manipulations of the sea as a site of memory were a hidden theme in *Titanic*, which was released in 2012 in 3D on the hundredth anniversary of the disaster (BBC Entertainment and Arts, 27 March 2012). Travel and natural disaster frame this film's narrative, which is one of Cameron's finest thanatotourist endeavours. The second *Avatar* film revisits some of his interest in sea life: the director explained that the film will move from rainforest to oceanic systems, with most of the movie taking place underwater (Schaefer, 18 October 2011). The emphasis on explorations of ecosystems allows us to examine Cameron's work in terms of overlapping ecologies: a physical ecology of movement, a symbolic one marked by struggle and competition over definitions, and a media ecology overlaying the previous two (Vannini *et al.* 2009: 466). These three ecologies overdetermine Cameron's professional work and cosmology and allow us to construct a thick description of his pilgrimage to the Amazon. In the audiovisual domain the socio-political matrix of *Avatar*'s project produces a 'human poetics of significance', an artistic articulation of human knowledge affected by experience (Smith 2007: 246).

The movie as narrative and digital enterprise

As a trilogy, *Avatar* appears to draw upon Cameron's professional engagement with the *Terminator* genre, which challenged contemporary apocalyptic visions, heralding the destruction of human will in the dawn of techno-rationalism (e.g. Virilio 1991). One of its core ideas, of life transition as a cosmic journey, looks back to his cinematic beginnings with *Xenogenesis* (1978). However, the environmentalist subtext crosses to his interest with sea life and reminds us of *Piranha II: The Spawning* (1981) in which natural predators mark their territory by attacking groups of tourists.

Movies, movie-makers and actors mature as stars through their insertion in signification systems – in Dyer's (1982) words, stars are 'signs', always-already implicated in the cultural politics of their generation. James Cameron is the child of a glorious age, both in politics and cinema: a strange example of self-induced social mobility, he catapulted from a blue-collar social milieu into the Los Angeles entertainment industry where he started a new career (Yahoo Movies, James Cameron, undated). His original background and self-trained beginnings in the industry aside, Cameron ranks today in the circles of professionally-trained American film-makers inspired by the *Nouvelle Vague* movement (first genera-tion: Martin Scorsese, Brian de Palma, Francis Ford Coppola, George Lucas). Dubbed as 'New Hollywood', this generation drew inspiration from the technical principles of European art cinema (Bergman, Godard, Fellini) as infiltrated through John Ford's and Roger Gorman's work (King 2007: 60–1). The European origins of this movement coincide with European democratizations of travel as technologically enabled (air flight) tourism (Parrinello 2001; Dann and Parrinello 2009: 22; Urry and Larsen 2011: 55–6) and an aesthetics of physicality we find in the work of German and Brazilian directors (Cinema Novo) of the same generation (Nagib 2011: 74–5). The folkish and melodramatic aspects of John Ford's work appealed to a popular aesthetics of mobility that reappeared in Cameron's documentaries of sea life and his subtle self-insertions in cinematic diegesis under aliases.

These subtle links between an emergent belief in novel narratives (addressed to elites and general entertainment audiences alike) and technologies across different mobility domains shaped Cameron's career from the 1980s onwards. As screenwriter and director he produced work that drew on war trauma, damaged masculinity (*Rambo*, 1985) and technology-mediated human encounters with alien worlds (*Alien*, 1986; *The Abyss*, 1989; *Terminator 2*, 1991). The discursive constant of physical mobility draws upon ideas of the body as a shared human property but also a marker of the lower classes and the exotic other that can now be experientially understood through physical trials and rites (Nagib 2011: 19, 29). Some of these themes are revisited in the characterization of *Avatar*'s principal actors, as do the visual references to American war histories (e.g. the battles in Hallelujah mountains as reference to famous scenes from *Apocalypse Now*) and a pervasive guilt for the harm Westerners caused to indigenous cultures (see the Na'vi mourning of Hometree's destruction, the anger of natives against the army and even the musical background that envelops the destruction of the moon). Cameron acknowledged that *Avatar*'s exposition of the impersonal nature of mechanized warfare was intended as a critique of America's role in the Iraq war, cautiously noting at the same time that the film is not anti-American (Hoyle, 11 December 2009; Anderson, 10 December 2009; Murphy, 21 December 2009).

Avatar's plot is set in the twenty-second century (2154) in an imagined historical conjunction where a group of army officials and scientists financed by RDA Corporation set foot on a moon called Pandora in the Alpha Centauri star system with a plan to mine its precious mineral 'unobtanium'. RDA is a suggestive allegorical slippage: as an anachronistic pun, it recalls the post-Second World War work of the Research and Development American Corporation (RAND) which addressed issues of US scientific and military security, including terrorism (Tzanelli 2006b: 934). Moving from 'real politics' to the poetics of artistic markets, Cameron's allegory achieved (while recanting) what Chinese artists such as Zhang performed in another censorship environment: to re-narrate an American phallic anxiety of global ridicule that has plagued right-wing policy ever since the public condemnation of Vietnam (Jeffords 1989; Langford 2005: 123–6; Tzanelli 2010b: chapter 2; Tzanelli 2011a: 123–4).

The pursuit of unobtanium threatens the survival of the indigenous Panoran lifeworld – the habitats, customs and memories of the local tribe of Na'vi. The military aims to infiltrate the Na'vi with the help of genetically engineered Na'vi-humanoid hybrid bodies, which enable researchers to interact with natives. A disabled soldier, Jake Sully (Sam Worthington), is selected for this experiment and together with lead scientist Grace Augustine (Sigourney Weaver) attempt the first inter-species contact that leads to Jake's symbolic naturalization into Pandora's cultural biosphere and pacifist Grace's unfortunate death in the heat of a military attack (for the detailed plot, see relevant Wikipedia entry and IMDB). The cinematic narrative is already crafted as a military exploratory journey and a journey of self-discovery that Jake commences as a soldier on an educational mission and completes by going native, like the Borgesian ethnographer Fred Murdock who visits the Amazon to study a tribe for his PhD and becomes acculturated into native life (Borges 1998: 335; Tzanelli 2008b: 178–9). What unfolds thereafter adheres to a familiar post-colonial palimpsest: the destruction of Hometree (the neural root of Na'vi memory), which stands in the way of obtaining unobtanium, signals the destruction of native life.

As digital storytelling *Avatar* partakes in what Baudrillard (1983: 53) sees as the 'death of the real' and the rise of a society that lives through simulations. Nevertheless, it also borrows from the structural sensibility of historical evidence (the assault on ancient American, Asian and European civilizations by more technologically advanced conquerors) to craft a tale of developmental inequality from a futural standpoint (Žižek 1999: 20). Memorial regressions of this sort manifest themselves across cultures, sustaining strategic misremembering that alleviates collective traumas (Habermas 1989b, 1989c; Tzanelli 2010a: 219). In this respect, the cinematic story's content matches the function of thanatotourism. The thanatotourist theme lingers on Cameron's activist enterprise, which draws subtle parallels between the damage inflicted on New World people by past *conquistadores* (e.g. Dann and Seaton 2001) and the potential destruction of remaining indigenous groups by contemporary corporate greed. Internally some narrative norms draw upon Cartesian divides (action versus reflection, good versus evil, community versus corporate power) but externally they function as consumption objects (for the viewer, listener and digital participant). Such divides are eventually superseded through the moral conclusion of the story that indigenous knowledge does not stand at the opposing pole of militarized modernity but constitutes an alternative modernity the director-traveller can render intelligible to others (Nederveen Pieterse 2004: 110). However, before viewers arrive at this conclusion they have to plough their way through a Cartesian minefield.

Throughout the film Cameron maps a clash between brainless macho militarists and humanist scientists, thoughtless actors and thoughtful listeners observing before they act – in short, evil and good. There is also a submerged gender order in which subordinate masculinities serve as narrative vehicles for experiential authenticity and self-knowledge whereas the Na'vi tribes are viewed as in desperate need of protection. *Avatar*'s hero, Jake, regains his damaged masculinity through new technologies of humanoid hybridization, whereas the female scientist (Grace) dies in her attempt to prevent Pandora's total obliteration. Jake's personal story appeals to a discourse on the social model of disability, rarely present in science fiction films that are usually framed by fast action and able-bodied heroes. In this Cameron displays a form of reflexivity – intuitively or not – towards Cartesian functionalism which views the body as a machine in need of repair to conform to societal norms and expectations of 'able-bodiness' (Paley 2002; Oliver and Sapey 2006). Jake's functional limitations make him half-human in the eyes of his fellow soldiers but a perfect motivational subject for the *Avatar* interplanetary experiment. By extension, they fit into Cameron's activist cinematic repertoire, as the social model of disability belongs to the 1960s' activist history. Controversially, overcoming disability stands only partially as an attack on army machismo from the standpoint of a disempowered subject. Jake re-asserts his masculinity through innovative uses of science and technology: leaving one's body to inhabit as mind another bodily site addresses existentialist issues in a developmental fashion that matches the Western implication in disabling and damaging (while supporting) different cultures. Jake's persona appeals to new conceptions of male identity centring on soft power, associated with science savants. We need to recall how the soldier empowerment has been representing a 'parallel restoration of American nationhood' since the defeat of the Vietnamese enemy, replayed in films such as *Rambo* (1982) and *First Blood Part II* (1984), or in later cinematic successes such as *Patriot Games* (1992), *Saving Private Ryan* (1998) and *The Manchurian Candidate* (2004) (Langford 2005: 126–7).

Hero archetypes we encountered in Cameron's earlier movies are either revised or reinstated in the film (e.g. the contemplative and conscientious Jake Sully clashes with Arnold Schwarzenegger's *Terminator* but Grace Augustine resembles Sarah Connor's caring persona in *Terminator* and Ellen Ripley's scientific role in *Alien*). Cameron has always allegorized in his cinematography intersectional inequalities (Tzanelli 2011a: chapter 5), portraying mostly female subordinate types as resilient heroes *contra* earlier Cinema Vague narratives, for example, in which hardship endurance is monopolized by male heroes. *Avatar* attacks the workings of power by artistic and discursive means. Artistically, it borrows from first-person(al) narratives we encounter in melodrama, matching them with subplot formulas that appeal to mixed gender audiences (the love between a human and a humanoid into the film's symbolic core of interracial fusion). Discursively, it matches Cameron's less reflexive techno-fetishism that is both progressive (the story's military and corporate leadership and hence the masters of *Avatar* simulations are white, able-bodied and masculine) and conformist. The scientific predicament of matching human minds with Na'vi bodies revisits the gap between experience and feelings of exclusion and their externalized articulation (as in cinematic iconographies). The incubation of human Avatar carriers in sterilized spaces is visualized with CGI shots of Na'vi bodies, reminding us of the role photography played in the scientific anthropological study of human 'types' and 'races' in colonial times (Banks 2001: 28; Pinney 1997: 28).

In this way Cameron introduces the philosophical question of internal perception 'as invested with a cognitive, affective and teleological character, which exemplifies it as a social, and not merely biological or neurophysiological activity' (Wartofsky in Smith 2007: 112). The film's developmental angle focuses on familiar binaries set by science ('Here I am', Jake informs us when he lands on Pandora,

Figure 6.1 Jake in front of his Avatar incubator: the film mediates the Cartesian divide
between mind and body through futuristic technologies.
Credit: 20th Century Fox/Photofest.

'doing science'), gender (women are either dispensable military subordinates or
sensitive scientists) and whiteness (not a single Western authority figure is black)
in relation to the condition under which multiple mobilities take place. The
Western visitor's aspiration to 'control Na'vi bodies with Western minds' borrows
from old colonial tropes that present nativeness as embodied and inviting technological manipulation by the colonizer. Some irony defines scenes where Western
technology is employed both externally, as a cinematic tool (Computer-Generated
Imaging for the film) and internally as a scopic narrative (CGI of Hometree and
the Na'vi in the mission's spacecraft), revising McLuhan's (1964) identification
of the message in the medium. Through such visual plays *Avatar* suggests
that strategic alliances of military, industrial and scientific communities make a
cross-over into civilian and political sectors 'to create *a global administration of
fear*', capable of merging reality with virtuality (Virilio 1990). Cameron's pen and
lens enable a hermeneutics of recovery, because it looks back to actual human
pasts to understand a present allegorized in the movie as the future of human
memory (Giddens 1987; Stoller 1992; Dallmayr 2001: 40; Banks, 2001: 7–9).

Jake, who occupies an interstitial place as an inside critic and a designated
cosmic traveller mediates bureaucratic treachery. As an *Avatar* subject he records
his daily impressions on the mission's spacecraft computer, allowing the administrative machine to gain insight into his mind while using his body. His digital travelogue borrows from the ambivalent motivations of backpack and adventure
tourism, a form of leisure activity increasingly associated with pedagogical pursuits,
the thrill of a new challenge but also humanitarian convictions (Cohen 2011).
This ambivalence resides in Jake's professional identity (as an experimental

Figure 6.2 A digital projection of 'Hometree' in the human mission's spacecraft: CGI is in *Avatar* both a cinematic tool and a diegetic conundrum.
Credit: 20th Century Fox/Photofest.

subject and a corporate spy) that is called into question by his accumulating knowledge about the indigenous humanoids. The ambivalence, which is ethical in nature, will reappear in Cameron's digital intimations on his Amazonian journeys, which are rife with personalized intimations on social 'geographies of power' (Balibar 1990; Massey 1993; Florida 2003). Jake's fictional journey, habitually described by Pandorans and himself as 'dream walking', has a subconscious peripatetic nature befit of Western psychoanalysis (Freud 1965a), largely critiqued for its implication in primitivist generalizations and male occulocentrism alike (Irigaray 1974; McClintock 1995). His digital intimations substitute the complex relationship between analyst and analysand in their breakthrough moment: 'Everything is backwards now. Like out there is the true world and here is the dream. I can barely remember my own life. I don't know who I am any more', he confesses in a reel reality fashion when he has already bonded with Pandorans. Jake's experiential journey is both personal and collective, mapping the rocky road of a Western scientific heritage centring on the study of 'human'. Unlike the standard Oedipal tale of psychoanalysis, *Avatar*'s allegory murders the child to mark the passage of humanity to adulthood (Leclaire 1998); and unlike the optimism of human sciences such as psychoanalysis, it mourns the death as a collective loss – the very loss with which Christian philanthropy defines some activist action in the developing world.

Coupling empowerment and agency with technology often disturbs gender orders in the story, calling instead for further, intersectional considerations of character development: throughout the film Jake's outlook is paired with that of a female scientist displaying a rebellious attitude (Grace Augustine is a keen smoker, completely absorbed by her research and not mincing her words) but also a conscience (she is a pacifist, supportive of Pandora's eco-systemic future). But it is precisely Grace's considerate anti-corporate nature that marks her as a modern woman – a Western woman nevertheless who can partake in the scientific mastery of indigenous environments and bodies. Cameron's new digital polity fosters activity and the mastery of nature in two epochally articulated forms: Pandoran tacit knowledge and Western technologically mediated knowledge (Dyson 1998: 49; Gauntlett 2011). Once again technological innovation is juxtaposed with corporeal nature to both illustrate the separation of the Western mind (that can think and act even outside human bodies in Avatar environments) from nature while also idealizing an indigenous (feminized) nature in the eyes of global audiences. Cameron's allegory maps a form of cosmopolitan citizenship that debates the institution of scientific regimes in which *techne* (as technological production) and *physis* (female nature) occupy different domains. Weaver's casting as Grace capitalized on her previous role as the by-the-book officer assigned to the commercial space Nostromo (Ellen Ripley in Ridley Scott's *Alien* [1979]). But Grace's persona also borrows from all the subsequent films of the tetralogy – among which *Aliens* (1986) was directed by Cameron and received several Academy Award nominations, including Weaver's nomination as Best Actress (Biography.com, 'James Cameron', undated). Other relevant roles by Weaver include her casting as primatologist Dian Fossey in *Gorillas in the Mist* (1988) for which she received a Best Actress Oscar nod; as Queen Isabella in Ridley Scott's disastrous *1492: The Conquest of Paradise* (1992); as a guilt-ridden woman over the death of a child in *A Map of the World* (1999); and as a New Yorker helping a fire captain construct eulogies for his fallen men in the 9/11-inspired *The Guys* (2003). In 2007 she replaced David Attenborough's voice-over in the BBC-produced documentary *Planet Earth* (Discovery, 2007), which also complements her role in *Avatar* (for a complete biographical note see Yahoo! Movies, Sigourney Weaver, undated; Biography.com, Sigourney Weaver, undated).

As a compassionate scientist Grace forms an alliance with Jake who is the story's primary digital actor. Traveller to an Edenic world envisaged and depicted by armchair anthropologists and colonial visionaries in the past, he is on a double pedagogical mission, at once political and existential. His journey of 'going native' commences with his initial ritual incorporation into the tribe by native medicinal ingestion, but continues until the end of the first film when he emerges as a fully recognized Pandoran citizen by Western technological means (e.g. use of guns against the corporate machine). The narrative reminds us of Parrinello's (2001) argument that the technological body operates as a natural artefact rather than alien prosthesis, assisting in the wellness of the traveller. Jake's matriculation is completed when he leaves his human body to inhabit a humanoid-native one during an Omaticayan ritual, thus fully replacing Western simulation with Pandoran reality. The Cartesian dualism is resolved: Pandora is both a world 'out there' to be learned and conquered and a universe within to be discovered and recognized as part of the conscious Western Self (Szerszynski and Urry 2006).

In this context, Neytiri's (Zoe Saldana) mother, Mo'at (C.C.H. Pounder), is right to suggest to Jake that her daughter's tour to Pandoran culture 'will cure his insanity' – that is, his lack of situated knowledge that such dualisms are redundant ('Neytiri calls me *skxawng*. It means moron' he writes in his digital diary). Dialogues on Pandora are rife with epistemological clarifications for the benefit of the viewers who are given a crash course on the philosophical value of ocular metaphors: 'I see you' means I see 'into you', Jake assures us, acting as a translator of native Pandoran cosmology but in fact articulating a commonly accepted Western view that ties vision to knowledge from the Renaissance to the age of terrorist surveillance (Jay 1993). However, even the restoration of a harmonious order in Pandoran Eden presents aboriginal conservatism as both natural and civilized, as it falls back to ideas of naturalized relationships like the one between a father and his child (Spurr 1993: 34). For example, the old colonial pattern is reversed when Neytiri openly considers 'Sky People' (Western incomers) ignorant like children, but not removed from *Avatar*'s philosophical core.

The philosophy of the inner eye also permeates the lyrics of the score 'I see you', written by Simon Franglen, Thaddis Harrell and James Horner (*Avatar*'s music composer and conductor). The lyrics operate at two interlocked levels, speaking of earthly love but also a spiritual connection reminiscent of philosophical blends from Eastern and Western religions. Written in a dialogical style, it focuses on the confession of someone who sees himself through his interlocutor's eyes 'living new life, flying high' while the 'love shines the way into paradise – so I offer my life as sacrifice'. As the score re-articulates the plot discursively, we may safely assume that the confessor is Jake and his addressee Neytiri, the living proof that civilizations can fuse ('I live through you and you through me') rather than clash. The selection of a female voice (2006 *X Factor* winner Leona Lewis, renowned for her solo love song performance) for the score enhances the intimate tone of the song. The idea of flight permeates the lyrics, accounting for a spiritual uplifting equivalent to the Neoplatonic conception of *anaforá* (relocation to the realm of Ideas) (Tzanelli 2008b: chapter 6; Herzfeld 1986: 43–4). Cameron's note about the *Avatar* score on the official CD release focuses on the story's epistemological conundrum through uses of a vocabulary at once compatible with traditional conceptions of intercultural pedagogy and postmodern technological consumption:

> Our goal in making *Avatar* was to transport you to … the primeval world that has existed in our dreams since before history began. To watch *Avatar*, especially in 3D, is to dream lucidly, with our eyes wide open. The music had to match the images with its own power to transport us to another world of powerful emotions. … The music is both classic, in its orchestral power, but also connects us to the soul of the Na'vi through the use of indigenous rhythms and vocals. The raw intimacy of the human voice is unequalled in creating the heartbreak of Hometree destruction. These arching solo vocals give way to the might of low strings and superb high brass writing, as the orchestra sweeps us into battle, and through the tumult of defeat and ultimate salvation.
>
> (*Avatar* CD, 2009)

Contemporary audiovisual consumption supports a kind of 'digital *dreamtime* that connects current relationships with those of the dead' (Miller 2009: 8) and makes *Avatar*'s simulated aboriginal inheritance more real than reality – in that it evokes feelings of loss and the joy of salvation to its consumers. The epic music is a form of neo-pilgrimage to a multicultural space that draws upon recorded ethnic technologies of immense market value in the global leisure trade (Graburn 1983). Such a visually spectacular film would normally be matched with upbeat scores to better translate action to music and lyrics. But James Horner's soundtrack adopts a counterintuitive approach that betrays his own love for modernized folk style and Cameron's less explored artistic melancholy. Horner recorded parts of the score with a small chorus singing in Na'vi in 2008, working at the same time with ethnomusicologist Wanda Bryant to invent the right tunes for the alien culture (Marketsaw, 2 April 2008). *Avatar*'s archplot of human development encloses a form of 'structural nostalgia' (Herzfeld 2005: 150) for a world lost to human (post)modernity – a world nevertheless accessible in its original (cinematic) form. Here Baudrillard's (1981) simulation theory takes precedence over social realities, staging alternative cosmological visions that might resemble actual civilizational forms but never identify with them. The multi-award winning composer's creations are deliberately utopian, picking up from his previous collaboration with Cameron (*Alien*, *Titanic*) without replicating them.

Starry twinkles, strange whistles and strings familiar to fans of Celtic music are matched with African rhythms and vocals 'rooted in rainforests and savannas' (for a review see Diver, 21 December 2009). In James Horner's hybrid rhythms we discern African and South American styles that dominate what Cameron earmarks as the story's climax (McKee 1999: 48): Jake's mastery of flight ('Climbing up "Inkimaya – The Path to Heaven"' and 'Jake's First Flight', *Avatar* CD, 2009). Although these moments operate within the cinematic narrative as an indigenous rite of passage (van Gennep 1906), for audiences they remain a form of voluntary audiovisual travel to a simulated world (Turner 1974). Rendered in similar blends of indigenous and classical rhythms 'The Destruction of Hometree' is an elegiac score bound to the 'Shutting Down Grace's Lab' theme following through low keys escalating to modern epic tones. These epic tones are present in Cameron's previous films. *Avatar*'s audiovisual matrix is thus producing a pedagogical journey for aesthetically reflexive audiences (Beck *et al.* 1994; Lash and Urry 1994: 5–6) that can experience performative catharsis as 'time outside work' (Urry 1996: 120).

Unlike Jake (the story's anthropologist-explorer), Colonel Miles Quaritch (Stephen Lang), the film's impersonation of evil, considers the Avatar programme a bad joke run by 'a bunch of limp dick science majors'. His attitude as a military leader of the programme resembles Koro's cautioning note to his young apprentices in *Whale Rider* (2002). Koro, the tribal leader of the community, cautions his apprentices that their 'dicks will drop' if they fail to learn the old Maori ways. The likeness in dialogue has a structural rationale that may also point to Cameron's epistemic connections in New Zealand. Quaritch personifies a form of

Western heritage associated with hard power: his dismissive attitude towards hard-earned knowledge appeals to institutional frameworks of science he does not comprehend – unlike his corporate ally, Parker Selfridge (Giovanni Ribisi), who is ethologically defined as a harsh pragmatist unwilling to value intercultural respect over profit. Although the binary formula itself is commonplace in Hollywood film-making, Quaritch's association of socio-cultural illiteracy with science and technology suggests that there are humans who behave like ruthless machines. Cameron's portrayal of Quaritch updates the patterns of Vietnam films of the 1980s (e.g. *Platoon* [1986] or the Cameron-directed *Aliens* [1986]), in which combat officers 'were typically portrayed as irrelevant, incompetent or downright crazy' (Langford 2005: 128–9), as well as combat film trends stressing the deficit of military accountability (Neale 1991: 48). Quaritch's use of bodily metaphors of emasculation enhances his masculine uncouthness and the audience's dislike of his ethics. Just as Grace projects a particular version of modern human subject who is hungry for knowledge, Quaritch's uncouthness reflects a conservative communitarian logic of ethno-nationalist belonging prioritizing mateship as a form of kinship (Herzfeld 1992): 'I take care of my own', he says to Jake. Hence, matching Koro's Maori tribalism with Quaritch's *habitus* reflects Cameron's anti-colonial commitment to non-evolutionist cross-cultural comparisons. Quaritch recruits Jake as his own Pandoran intelligence, explaining that if he discharges his duties successfully he 'will get his legs back'. Soon Jake finds out that aligning his vision with either camp comes at a price: 'Outcast; betrayer; alien. I was in the place the eye does not see', he comments when his Pandoran brothers and sisters accuse him of espionage and expel him from their community. Cameron portrays a radical critique of the alliances forged between military and corporate power that refer back to real American war histories.

It is in the heat of the colonel's invasion of Pandora that Grace, a representative of humanitarian science, will be killed but in the intimate confines of the Pandoran ecosystem that she will ascend to Eywan Afterlife. Following portrayals of women scientists in horror films in which nature is feminized and science controls nature, Grace debates the prevalence of gender orders in Western societies (Connell 1987; Jackson 2011). Her very name toys with the heritage of European writings from Plato to Augustine that provided a particular philosophical definition of human as the being aspiring to benevolent progress and perfection (Augustine 1948; Cassirer 1968; Tzanelli 2011a: chapter 5). These ideas enabled a relationship between humanist values and science to flourish during the Enlightenment, and formed the basis of what we know today as the 'dialectical imagination' (Jay 1993; Adorno and Horkheimer 1991). Within the Pandoran context they provide the contours of a religious-like system that is rooted less in faith and more in the experience of unity of consciousness with other beings as manifestations of Eywa, the metaphysical Being that ties humanoids to ancestral Na'vi Time (Heidegger 1967).

This ontological basis of sharing in experience echoes similar cases across centuries and religions (Muslim, Jewish, Christian, Taoist, Buddist and Hindu) that in contemporary secular milieus have transformed into commercialized tourist pilgrimage (Graburn 1983, 2001, 2004). Experience guides *Avatar*'s 'deep ecological' model that ties humanoids to nature and which clashes with Western anthropocentrism that places the natural world at the service of humans (Ezzy 2005). The separation of humans from nature is the product of religion that in Western milieus eventually replaced Christian belief with scientism – including environmental scientism that recognizes the material value of balanced ecosystems for the future of humanity (Orr 2005). The Augustinian science of *Avatar* oscillates between the 'metaphysics of culture' and a pragmatism geared towards alien nature, recasting this philosophy in a popular cultural grammar: nature belongs to the realm of simulacra, whereas God(dess) is the original truth. Cameron's neo-pilgrimage retains its Western cosmological overtones, especially in its audiovisual representations of native healing chants that echo Christian religious music. This influence is combined with a distinctive Eastern mystique reminiscent of religious thaumaturgy, forming an Oriental(ist) matrix.

Incidentally, the scenes in which we watch Omaticayans pray for Grace's healing bear striking similarity to the first scene of Beijing 2008's opening ceremony, tying thus Western and Eastern cosmologies through their ritual representation for a global audience. The term 'Na'vi' (Hebrew *navi* = prophet) presents the movie's Na'vi 'panentheism' as a sort of middle ground between pantheism and theism, the acknowledgment that God is everywhere and everything (the pinnacle of some Eastern religions) and that there is only one Master-God we cannot reach immediately (see Michaelson, 22 December 2009). Revising Robertson's (1992: 183) recognition of a 'deep history of globality' in the spread of world religions, we may view *Avatar*'s religious sphere in terms of an enlarged interspecies consciousness in which nevertheless Na'vi humanoids stand for nature and humans for culture. In this respect, Cameron's cinematic para-theologization – mediated in his visualization of the humanoid encounter with Eywa or Jake's initiation into Na'vi cosmology – stands at a familiar epistemological crossroads as an anthropocentric meta-narrative, a 'double hermeneutics' or phaneroscopic process (Giddens 1987; Peirce 1998). His very selection of 'Avatar' (Sanskrit for dialogically reflected image) as a cinematic title bridges the gap between simulation and unattainable reality by new technological means.

Cameron's distant shots of the Hallelujah region on Pandora introduce a detached vision that Jake and Neytiri personalize through their flight. This matches their proximate experience of Pandora's memoryscape – Jake's introduction to the Utaya Motui or Trees of Voices that preserve Na'vi ancestry. Historically, the mastery of distant CGI fluidity originates in the Chinese and Hong Kong cinema of the 1970s. This cinema marked the coming of the occulocentric digital age in which technologies of Western 'Sky People' became a reality (Cousins 2011: 458). In this respect, the Na'vi term for human incomers is another reflection on the coming of a technological postmodernity from which Cameron speaks. These two complementary visions actualize *Avatar*'s neo-pilgrimage that simulates visits to sacred sites and sights for cinematic viewers. By analogy to conventional visits to natural sites, the film produces 'popcorn tourism' with extensions in *Avatar*'s Wikipedia and Internet site, where web travellers can expand their knowledge on Pandoran customs, flora and fauna. This cosmic simulation borrows from discourses of heritage: there is a notable shift from landscape shots to land, signalling a reversal of Urry's (2004) critical schema that applies to other instances of cinematic tourism (Tzanelli 2007b: chapter 4).

Within the cinematic story this shift remains tied to ideas of community and extended family (tribe), the rightful custodians of Pandoran ecology. The deep connection of the 'People' (another term borrowed in the cinematic script from political philosophy) to the forest reveals to Jake and Grace a network of energy, free-flowing from nature to culture and back again. It is indigenous environmental knowledge that beats the colonial-cum-corporate machine with a coordinated attack between humanoids and animals, and native technology (armoury and the use of native poisons) that defeats the Western technocratic war machine. By extension, it is the future of an Omaticayan heritage traumatized by colonial greed (impersonated by Neytiri, Pandora's female leading progeny) that retaliates (she kills Quaritch). Neytiri's revenge responds to Quaritch's double atrocity against her father, Eytukan (Wes Studi), whom he murders, and the destruction of the sacred Hometree, which plays in the story a key mnemonic role as an imagological idea.

The fact that Neytiri's mother figures in the story as the Omaticayan interpreter of Eywa genders Pandoran hermeneutics and places them in the experiential regime. It was mentioned before that feminine imagery is characteristic of Cameron's work. The Na'vi appearance is one of Cameron's most intimate artistic conceptions: it was based on a dream his mother had some time ago about a 16-feet tall blue-skinned woman the director connected to the appearance of Hindu deities (Svetkey, 15 January 2010 in Wikipedia, 'Avatar', undated). The conception was included in his first screenplay in the mid-1970s, which served as treatment for the finished product (Ordoña, 13 December 2009). Aesthetic preference aside, the Na'vi stand in the visual narrative as a racialized metaphor – the first in Cameron's cinematography, which was previously populated with white heroines. Resembling ancient goddesses, Cameron's magnified feminized and racialized humanoids are skilful and athletic, appealing to depictions of the indigenous body in actual colonial histories of the globe.

In other interviews the director also admitted that he was inspired by science fiction readings from his childhood and that he aimed to update Edgar Rice Burrough, Yet Cameron's recreation of the classic story is shaped by Rudyard Kipling and Joseph Conrad's writings, which appeal to the colonial European tradition. The civilizational clash *Avatar* portrays resembles the one in *Dances with Wolves* (Boucher, 14 August 2009). Thus Cameron's renditions of European heritage remain gendered and racialized: his work appeals to Freudian narratives of the fatherly Law as the foundation of civilization, one of Cameron's early influences via George Lucas' *Star Wars* (Lacan 1994: 34–5). Freud (1965b) called such substitutions of images for an idea 'screen memories,' arguing that they should be seen as part of the linguistic apparatus of human experience. Their role is to foreclose traumatic experiences humans keep at bay because

Figure 6.3 Racializing and gendering Otherness: Neytiri's athletic depiction appears to draw on surviving images from actual colonial repositories.
Credit: 20th Century Fox/Photofest.

they cannot bear their burden. As a visual symbol, Hometree articulates Omaticayan culture. Parallels with the collapse of the American cosmos in the 9/11 tragedy are submerged in Cameron's digitopian art that turns Hometree into a replacement discourse in Manhattan's bruised cityscape. Huyssen (2003: 162–3) recognizes in this Islamic attack the obliteration of the modern(ist) sublime, in which even bin Laden's icon partakes. The terrorist destruction of modernity from above finds an ironic encoding in the *skxawng*-ness of 'Sky People', who ultimately destroy their own modernity with their iconoclastic actions. In this respect, unobtanium is an allegory of what invaders cannot appropriate and thus destroy instead: an intact, native essence of 'home' that now survives only in simulacra of disaster and semi-religious ceremonies of mourning (Connerton 1989).

Everything is reversed in *Avatar*: for example, Tsu'tei (Laz Alonzo) calls Jake and his People 'demons' (by analogy to the demon of Islamic terrorism). But at the same time, the sky is the domain of miracles for Pandoran culture (by analogy to Western technologies of the sky). Torek, the dangerous lynopteryx Jake eventually tames like a true descendant of Neytiri's great-grandfather is also the master of sky and Pandora's 'dark shadow'. Jake describes himself as a 'stone-cold aerial hunter', a 'demon in a false body', living up to Pandoran conceptions of the metaphysical world. Belonging to the past and the present of human-humanoid civilizations, the Sky (a domain of visual knowledge) is both demonized and claimed as heritage. The same oscillation characterizes Hometree as an image and an idea that introduces in the cinematic narrative the theme of War from a distant historical perspective (Western political heritage). We might trace the historical treatment for Cameron's cinematic script in Australasian instances of post-colonial nation-building that demonized the Oriental other – an early manifestation of Islamophobia with roots in European history. The Battle of Gallipoli (25 April 1915) against the Turks is a notable instance of great diachronic importance both for Australians and New Zealanders – Cameron's digital collaborators in the *Avatar* project. Its thanatotourist potential contributes to *Avatar*'s 'time warp' in that it transposes painful collective memories into commodified artzones, enacting a transnational urban palimpsest.

The proliferation of Gallipoli pilgrimage sites and legends in Australia and New Zealand generated a global tourist industry viable to the day. Of particular relevance here is Lone Pine, a site of carnage in 1915 from which seeds were allegedly transported and planted at the War Memorial Site in Melbourne (Moorehead 1973). Although there is no way to demonstrate that trees planted around Australia are descendants of the original Pine Tree (Slade 2003: 790–1), its significance as a myth of founders and family fathers is indisputable (Bakhtin 1981: 13). Various Australian film-makers have used it in their reproduction of so-called ANZAC mythologization and some disconnected it from the original Gallipoli context (Thompson 1994: 195–6). The original Battle has also found an analogical reproduction in New Zealand, where coastal parts of Wellington physically resemble the original geographies of the Gallipoli Peninsula. The sacralization of this imagined *topos* was tied to the antithesis of pure national antiquity (strategically tied to ideas of European Christian civilization) embodied by the Oriental Turkish enemy. Cameron seems to have constructed his own Occidentalist counter-polemic on these mythical premises (MacKenzie 1993; Carrier 1995). The death of Hometree signifies the destruction of native memory, an event that, coupled with the death of Neytiri's father and clan leader, triggers ceremonial mourning. Hometree signifies the disruption of patrilineage and the commencement of enshrinement that promotes cinematic thanatotourism (MacCannell 1973; Couroucli 2008). At the same time, enshrinement is the film's visual contribution to radical developmental discourse: Gallipoli is not present in the film as such, but scenes of war destruction appeal to political cinema's library to produce a critical text. The audiovisual resonance of Hometree's fall appeals to dystopian forms matching earlier critiques of American neo-colonial greed in *Apocalypse Now* (1979).

Asked about the scene's resemblance to the 9/11 attacks on the World Trade Centre, Cameron said that he was 'surprised at how much it did look like [it]', leaving further speculation to film critics (Hoyle, 11 December 2009). But as Peter Jackson's *Twin Towers* has been a crucial moment in *Avatar*'s realization, we can safely assume that the resemblance was intentional. Quaritch's unprovoked attack on Pandoran indigenous enclaves in pursuit of unobtanium is also followed by a statement echoing President Bush's post-9/11 interview on the ensuing War on Terror: 'We will fight Terror with Terror ... We will blast a crater in their racial memory so deep that they won't come within 1,000 clicks of this place ever again,' Quaritch shouts before the attack on Pandora. As I explain in the third section of the chapter, Cameron's recruitment of Arnold Schwarzenegger in the

Figure 6.4 The human forces on Pandora unleash tremendous firepower in an epic battle against the Na'vi. The visual diegesis of aerial technology, the magnificent landscape and gunfire are references to *Apocalypse Now* (1979).
Credit: 20th Century Fox/Photofest.

anti-Belo Monte activism has been anything but coincidental. Schwarzenegger's appearance in science fiction films debating military manipulations of memory (*Total Recall* 1990, dir. Paul Verhoeven) but also heroic responses to the onset of terrorist threat on the iconic American family (*Collateral Damage* 2002, dir. Andrew Davis) relate to *Avatar*'s development archplot and humanist cosmology in more than one way. The director's cautious commentary on his film might have to do with the fate several post-9/11 movies (including *Collateral Damage*) had because of their discursive connections to America's 9/11 trauma. Because they reproduced the fantasy of threat too soon after the World Trade Centre tragedy, they were banned or made available to the public only several months after 9/11 (e.g. *The Siege, Big Trouble, Sidewalks of New York, Gangs of New York* and *Windtalkers*) (Žižek 2002; Sharpe 2002; O'Brien *et al.* 2005; Meeuf 2006).

It is not coincidental that for *Avatar*'s visual effects Cameron hired Weta Digital, the company owned by Wellington-born Jackson, whose epistemic network was discussed in Chapter 2. Cameron admits that the first time he thought *Avatar* might materialize as a project was after the release of *King Kong* and the *Lord of the Rings* trilogy, when 'Gollum came alive. And to me, that was the moment … when I said, if they can do that, "Avatar" is possible' (Murphy, 21 December 2009). Weta's visual effects supervisor on all these projects was Joe Letteri, who won Academy Awards for his work on *The Two Towers, The Return of the King* and *King Kong* (he was also Oscar-nominated for *I, Robot*) (Wakefield, 19–25 December 2009). To complete the colossal task of finishing all special effects on time other companies were brought on board, including Industrial Light and Magic, a pioneer in creating CGI explosions. The huge amount of data that had to be stored and catalogued on two different continents (Los Angeles, US and Wellington, New Zealand) necessitated the creation of a cloud-computing system by Microsoft. The whole industry's infrastructure relied on the creation of a community of digital craft in urban milieus that revised traditional artistic and organizational frameworks (Urry 2007: 239–42). Evans and Wustler (2000: 217) note how new networking technologies deconstruct contemporary organizations, replacing face-to-face co-presence where tacit knowledge is involved. Cameron and Jackson are examples of such commercialized artistic 'knowledgeability' (Giddens 1984; Polanyi 1966), enabling otherwise distant urban creative labour to communicate efficiently across time and space (on communications between LA and Wellington see Boucher, 14 August 2009). Not only did they articulate *Avatar*'s CGI vision, they connected it to two cities that figured as 'global digital articulations' (also Sassen 2002) through this enterprise.

Microsoft's cloud-computing system, which would play a role in Cameron's future digital enterprise, was named Gaia. Cameron's relationship with Microsoft started in 2002. His documentary unit, Earthship Productions, was relying on Microsoft technologies in the creation of the marine-focused 3-D *Ghosts of the Abyss*, released in 2003, and would continue to employ Microsoft technologies in the production of *Aliens of the Deep*, released in 2005 (Siegel, 5 February 2010). It could be argued that the deep ecological narrative of this work was also reflected in Gaia's naming, which was propagated in an earlier science fiction CGI film *Final Fantasy: The Spirits Within* (2001, dirs Hironobu Sakaguchi, Motonori Sakakibara) that was based on a popular video games series. Gaia (Greek 'earth') was in this metaphysical tale the semi-religious essence of earth, a notion akin to Cameron's Eywan allegory of humanoid interconnectedness with the Pandoran nature-Goddess. Microsoft's initiative crosses the boundary from nature to technology through configurations of a supposedly global 'ecosystem' as a mechanical self-regulation system in technological terms (Argyrou 2005: 76). The use of Gaia's name in this context puns out as irony given the digital manipulation of nature in this system. Cameron himself does not recognize the film as an inspiration, and it may be more productive to consider both cinematic scripts as incarnations of twenty-first-century humanity's 'Hidden God' (Goldmann 1964): both allegorize on digital platforms human greed, environmental destruction and a clash between humanist science and mindless militarism.

Again, *Avatar*'s technological articulation corresponds cosmologically to the film's artistic content. The digital combination of images and ideas from multiple exotic domains, allows for the *technopoetic* staging of civilizational pasts (Dyson 1998; Hand and Sandywell 2002: 209). The staging itself does not conform to the purifying principles we encounter in ethno-nationalist discourse but allows for a cosmetic hybridization in which politics occupy space as allegories of the human condition (Nederveen Pieterse 2006a; Christians and Carey 1981 in Vannini *et al.* 2009: 463). Otherwise put, *Avatar*'s utopian audiovisual space operates as a meeting point for actual material or intangible memory sites (e.g. Nora 1989) that were or still are of cultural significance somewhere in the human cosmos. Simulating geographically situated experience in Pandoran sites speaks a cosmopolitan idiom, producing a global *mélange* representative of local identities around the world (Nederveen Pieterse 2004: 92–83; Hannerz 1990). At the same time, the audiovisual outcome of the enterprise produces a distinctive digital utopia that stands quite apart from familiar memory sites. The actual filming of *Avatar* reflected digitopic hybridity, combining CGI characters and live environments: Cameron claims that about 60 per cent of the film consists of CG elements, with the remaining 40 per cent involving traditional miniatures and live action (Thompson, 9 January 2007). The live action photography, which started in Wellington in 2007, involved prior training of the actors in character activities such as archery, horseback riding and hand-to-hand combat. The cast was also sent to the Hawaiian tropical rainforests to become familiar with the story's setting before shooting on the soundstage (Starpulse, 9 November 2009). The training projects the digitopic mastery of natural environments as a cultural fusion of science and art, with landscape being mediated by experts 'including the myth-making of the tourist industry' (Pine 1998 in Jamal *et al.* 2003: 155).

Website and computer games commerce

A quick visit to the film's website (Avatarmovie.com, undated) will shed further light on Cameron's digitopia in which we become ocular masters of an alien world open for exploration and adaptation to our needs (Friedberg 1995; Fruehling Springwood 2002). Indigenous specificity has been used by cultural industries as a valuable commodity (Nash 1977; Greenwood 1977), but the idea is here that a digitally fabricated ecosystem does not put any existing community under such pressure.

On this one may add a note on the video game franchise – yet another addition to the global trade in fixities such as indigeneity: the game was created by Ubisoft Montreal, which was chosen by Cameron in 2007 for this purpose. Subsequently, Cameron decided to include some of Ubisoft's vehicle and creature designs in the film. *James Cameron's Avatar: The Game* was released on December 2009 for most home video game consoles (PS3, Xbox 360, Wii, Nintendo DS, iPhone), Microsoft Windows and PSP (Relax News, 12 December 2009). The game singles out the cinematic themes of war and indigenous skill, allowing players to be soldiers for either side, therefore crossing the border from detached observation to militant action. Fast-trackness and event speed sideline but do not remove reflections on the game's cosmological context in favour of visual consumption (Patton 1996: 17). As soldier, the player is equipped with firearms such as assault rifles, shotguns, grenade launchers and flamethrowers, and has to eliminate fast and resilient enemies usually charging towards the player from afar. As an Avatar s(he) is limited to only one Avatar-issued machine gun and various primitive weapons such as bows, crossbows and melee weapons. The environment reacts differently to the character: many plants will attack the soldier, while the Avatar can walk past them unharmed. Again, this suggests that players can only transform into successful actors when they learn to navigate the indigenous environment, just like their movie counterparts. This second-order simulation extends to the fact that 'experience points' are converted to credits and used in the *Conquer* minigame. Alien landscapes are not merely to be viewed but also tamed and understood through digitally mediated experience (Strain 2003: 250; de Lauretis 1984: 119).

The website is organized under a similar rationale: from the outset the idea of indigeneity assumes the place of an intimate entity, ready to be displayed on a 'digital window' in the form of a domestic environment for virtual visitors (Friedberg 1993; Tzanelli 2008b: chapter 4). We must remember how the idea of domestic intimacy, better protected within the bosom of the family unit, partakes in production domains of the tourist industries but also consumption rituals of tourist visitors (Larsen *et al.* 2006). Family and feminine intimacy travel across time and space as ideas, utopias, commodities and collective agents. *Avatar*'s developmental archplot toys with the possibility of irrevocable loss of these utopias, which are represented by Neytiri, her mother and their connection to environments in danger by ruthless corporate invaders. At the same time, it is Neytiri and her mother who display the skills and eagerness to engage in inter-cosmological communications, not their male counterparts. Ideologically playful in its tools, narratives and commerce, *Avatar*'s website allegorizes the socio-cultural face of disorganized capitalist practices in the mediascapes of late modernity (Lash and Urry 1987).

The start page follows the flow of a viewer's narrative, blending in the introductory trailer the fantastic (movie scenes) with work 'behind the scenes' (shootings, digital manipulation, directing). Front and back stages thus deliberately merge, following the simulatory design of the project: aware that the backstage we are offered is carefully produced we function as post-tourists, aware of the consumerist game (Ritzer and Liska 1997; MacCannell 2001). The site is cleverly designed as a bifurcated path to active knowledge: one digital path leads us to the site of *Avatar*'s industry, which is complete with DVD, music CD and Blu-ray offers but also computer and iPhone games and tune selections. The other path leads us to what is marked on the start page as the 'Join the Home Tree Initiative', a 'worldwide effort to plant one million trees and receive an official Home Tree Initiative certificate'. This page provides a short video in which Cameron and Landau caution against the depletion of natural resources, inviting visitors to sign a form and become active participants in the joint Avatar-Earth Day Network initiative. A separate page provides the names of signatories, thus constructing a community of environmentalist interest (Szerszynski 1997) within an industry promoting consumer products. Binding cosmetic cosmopolitan practices to activism partakes in practices of 'demediating mediation' (Strain 2003) while also granting both market leaders and their consumers/audiences with a common purpose.

The initiative nicely reproduces one of *Avatar*'s subplots in which mobility is critically discussed as the property of intersectional privilege: geographical distance assumes the place of (Jake's) disability and technology acts as a liberating force. As Fischer *et al.* have noted (2008: 523), in our late modern world '"presence" is our ability to exert influence at the other end of our communication link' increasingly through avatars, YouTube videos and simulated images. Manipulating media in multiple ways, such leadership retains an exquisite ambivalence of purpose. Thus the messages of *Avatar*-Amazon Watch's matrix are expanded within the second path, which offers web surfers the same options (product consumption or activist education) again, implicitly suggesting that there is a way to marry corporate enterprise with the common good. I will return to this point in the following section of the chapter, which explores in detail the 'Pandoras on Earth' initiative.

At this stage in our virtual journey the commercial node is already turning real ideological contexts into adjacent fabulist subtexts: the link to 'Pandorapedia' helps visitors to discover the planet in more detail as an ecosystem with distinctive flora and fauna and its own race of humanoids with specific behaviours, customs and cosmology. A perfect simulation of developmental anthropology, Pandorapedia classifies species, sites and beings, and hence copies what administrative anthropology achieved in colonial and interwar times: to turn different lifeworlds into a global consumer spectacle (Tzanelli 2011a: chapter 6; Law 2010: chapter 2 on the racist extensions of this exercise). The 'Hometree' section is a particularly good example of this phenomenon: providing both information on the trees' structure and function and a selection of simulated folk songs that frame public and domestic activities in Omaticayan society, it replicates the archive of the global human sciences and its crypto-racist content (Foucault 1997a; Derrida 1998). The link to a Pandoran dictionary mirrors Frazer's folklore enterprise, because it couples armchair anthropology with leisure travel: what in 1907 was for Frazer 'not so much a science as a pleasant hobby' (Urry 1993: 24) has transformed in Cameron's digitopia into a new form of round-the-world travel (Germann Molz 2004).

It may be suggested that digital articulation of ideas in Na'vi borrows from traditional conceptions of human communication within national polities. 'Articulation' is borrowed here from the lexicon of music to convey the formulation of transitions and continuities between multiple notes or sounds. Just like Said's (1993) contrapuntal thesis, it promises to transform the mediation of different viewpoints into a methodology of knowledge (Chowdry 2007: 103), ingesting different ethnic idioms into the technological machine that institutes dominant forms of speech (various national languages around the world). Articulation's allusion to the act of bending one's joints (Latin *articulation* from *artus*, Greek *árthosis* = connection, joint, from *arthrõnõ* = verbally articulate) also corroborates the embodied dimensions of nationhood (Tzanelli 2011a: chapter 5). Just like *Avatar*'s developmental archplot, the digital dictionary propagates quasi-functionalist views on humanoid culture and habitats, re-presenting them as unique biological creations bestowed with some sort of racial-cum-linguistic purity web travellers and designers rescue from oblivion (Walsh 1967: 130–1).

Avatar's simulated authenticity extended to the invention of an alien language with its own exotic phonetics, lexicon and syntax. This language, which is today part of the film's online wiki, is the invention of Paul Frommer, Professor at the Marshall School of Business at the University of Southern California, who holds a PhD in linguistics. In terms of inception the enterprise echoes Tolkien's fully fledged languages of Middle Earth that embellish the *LOTR* website, but Cameron openly admits to have drawn 'xenolinguistic' inspiration from extraterrestrial genres such as those pioneered in *The Day the Earth Stood Still* (1951) and *Star Wars*' (1997–2008) pseudo-Orientalist vocabularies. Frommer's Na'vi linguistic typology commenced in 2005, and used as structural foundation his mentor's (Bernard Comrie) work and his own wide-ranging knowledge of Malay, Persian, Hebrew and even Mandarin Chinese, as well as his previous workbook *Looking at Languages* (complete with a student exercise in deciphering 'Klingon', which first attracted Cameron's attention) (Zimmer, 4 December 2009). Cameron's original suggestions of words phonetically resembled Polynesian, making the overall idea hybrid but rooted in identifiable cultural forms (Nederveen Pieterse 2006a: 661). The language had to be accessible to the actors who had to articulate it with varied degrees of proficiency but also to the growing pool of Na'vi fans that access the wiki and the website (Kozinets 1999, 2001). Frommer also translated into Na'vi four sets of song lyrics originally written by Cameron in English and helped vocalists with their pronunciation during James Horner's score recordings.

We may tie xenolinguistic hybridity to the film's archplot: Frommer's project complements the imminent destruction of Pandoran purity by human modernity (pointedly, machines are placed in the service of the evil side, whereas the benevolent indigenous humanoids appear to display no interest in them – a slide that might suggest unintentional folklorization of a species otherwise presented as inquisitive). The Na'vi accents in the movie and the film's soundtrack adhere to a Pan-African theme anti-Orientalist scholars would immediately condemn as politically problematic (Said 1978). The encoding of cultural fusions in art has been controversial since time immemorial, with some scholars of hybridity stressing the roots of the term in pure cultural forms ascribed to First-World primivitist interest in institutions of difference (Nederveen Pieterse 2006a; Tomlinson 2007). After Sapir's (1929) recognition of language as constitutive of the cultural context in which it is born, anthropology proceeded to focus on the properties of 'verbal art' as an aspect of emergent communicative events in which interlocutors act as 'co-creators' (Bauman 1977). But as *Avatar*'s xenolinguistics adhere to simulated cultural narratives, the co-creation of Na'vi in virtual spaces becomes mediated by technology – as did the playful communications of the cinematic crew in this fantastic language during filming. Indeed, Cameron's experimental replication of *Star Wars* fan culture has been successful, with reported global followers of Na'vi in 2011 (UBC, 28 July 2011). The official digital compendium follows recent transformations in encyclopaedic and dictionary cultures, democratizing the consumption of *Avatar* and further ramifying its representational appeal in lieu of the film's capitalist node (Hardt and Negri 2000). Such democratizations replace old *technopoetic* practices rooted in national spheres and safeguarded by nation-states with the disorganized *technopoetic* enterprise of the Internet that better accommodates transnational and transcultural communities of interest (Rheingold 2000; Urry and Larsen 2011: 99). The following sections highlight how the Internet enabled the virtual co-existence of communities associated with the *Avatar* enterprise, even when these communities projected different goals and motivations.

Avatar's audiovisual matrix, II: popular protest as *autopoetic* simulation

Tracing the overarching cinematic plot in the commitment *Avatar*'s creative leaders displayed to ideals stretching beyond those of narrowly defined politics necessitates a focus on the role social imagology plays in the circulation of cinematic images within a more or less defined terrain of activist meaning (Habermas 1989d). Herzfeld (2005: 27–31) explores this at length in relation to 'iconicity', the power of semblances to furnish negotiable models of 'national characters' in terms of essentialized gender styles and actions. Just as in his production of the cinematic archplot, Cameron's digital activism capitalized on the fragility of social essentialisms, challenging and reifying stereotypical gender performances in search of effective social action. Such performances matched the 'carnivalesque' (Bakhtin 1968: 255–7) of Brazilian social movements, in that they allowed *Avatar* activists to speak and enact instantly recognized tropes of human decency against the 'shamelessness' of corporate capital (Andretta 2003; Della Porta and Diani 2006: 75). Borrowing from the civil language of a world in which they move as professionals, they actualized a 'subversive mimesis' (Cahn 1984) of systemic power to attack the Belo Monte project from within. The very consumerist tools used in *Avatar*'s popular culture were inserted into an activist network to render the principal cinematic agents' political pilgrimage to the Amazon with acceptable political meaning.

This pilgrimage retained its tourist flair but constructed a polemic against the eradication of indigenous culture in favour of technocratic progress, thus joining fates with transnational organizations in the battle against state-backed developmental plans in the Amazon. These organizations are Amazon Watch, which is based in San Francisco, California and collaborates with Brazilian professionals, and International Rivers, another international network based in Berkeley, California. Belo Monte is already affecting indigenous communities living along what is known as the Xingu's 'Big Bend'. About 1,000 indigenous people from the Xikrín, Juruna, Arara, Xipaia, Kuruaya, Kayapó and other ethnic groups live in this region. Amazon Watch organized collection of donations in support of Kayapó demands for demarcation of ancestral territories. Attacks by ranchers and illegal settlers on the Kayapó and Juruna are regular incidents and not properly addressed by the Federal Government. Interestingly, the support for the demarcation of the Kapot Nhinore ancestral territory of the Kayapó and Juruna indigenous peoples in the upper Xingu in the Brazilian state of Mato Grosso, via the Instituto Raoni, a foundation headed by a chief, is constructed on mergers of heritage and legacy that support biopolitical representations of the land online (Amazon Watch, 2012). From a cultural point of view, the joint *Avatar*-Amazon Watch activist project allowed the industry's *technopoetic* ethos to become *autopoetic* in a Habermassian (hermeneutic) rather Luhmannian (systemic) fashion (Tzanelli 2007a: 255). It has become more commonplace for activism to amass its organizational tools and human networks in digital domains that defy time-space problems (Cere 2002). It is this malleability of cyberspace that allowed *Avatar* actors to suggest to a pool of global fans by *technopoetic* means (videos, photos and press interviews posted on *Avatar*'s blog) that they can figure as actors rather than spectators of an eco-systemic disaster in a faraway land (Yar 2000: 1–3).

I therefore argue that the political commitment some actors (Sigourney Weaver, Arnold Schwarzenegger) and makers (James Cameron and Jon Landau) expressed in Brazil's radical movements for eco-systemic conservation can be better read against *Avatar*'s ideological simulacra. Artistic poetics is thus constitutive of the political beliefs held by them, because it supplemented their action with a dramaturgical stage in which social realities were ordered and narrated (Melucci 1995; Sasoon 1984; Donati 1992). The environmental dimension of their activism is reminiscent of the left-wing narrative that liberal artists express in the American star system. Charity work transforms fame into positive agency, adding to audiences' 'quest for *mediated* identity, where being a celebrity is morally justified' (Tolson 2001: 456 in Earl 2008: 412). The 'postmodern assault' (Miller 2009: 6) has allowed liberalism to triumph over holistic socialist traditions (see Lindholm 1997) without nevertheless eliminating left-wing utopianism: American liberal traditions fostering individual self-presentation continue to supplement the spirit and the causes of collectively orientated activism originating in European socialist cosmologies of giving. Angelina Jolie's UNCHR's humanitarian debut in the context of *Lara Croft*'s filming in 2001, and Tim Robbin's and UNICEF Goodwill Ambassador Susan Sarandon's stance against the war in Iraq (*Washington Post*, 13 February 2003; Morales, 3 April 2009) are relevant examples. Sarandon's leftist Christian humanism is also compatible with Cameron's confessions in televised appearances. His political views are clearly expressed in a televised debate with Oprah Winfrey for whose complimentary comments on *Avatar* he reciprocated by creating an Oprah-Na'vi. Drawing upon the deep resonance of the Na'vi greeting 'I see you', Oprah asked Cameron if he is a spiritual person. Cameron's response turns Sarandon's humanist action into a pagan discourse:

> I guess I must be, because this film represents a lot of ideas and feelings I have as an artist … and the idea that we are all connected to each other as human beings … when I became a scuba diver, I really realized *how great nature's imagination* is. This film was an attempt to kind of bottle that.
> (*Avatar* Blog, 19 January 2010; italics mine)

Cameron's deep ecological philosophy is knit into a dystopian view of earth as a 'blue planet' slowly destroyed by its own inhabitants and finds better resonance with humanitarian interventions of female public personae. But it also potentially harbours an ecofacistic logic that prioritizes regulated living for nature's sake, which can be easily conflated with indigenous ecosystems. Ironically, his activism runs the risk of completing a vicious circle in which advocacy of the native right to self-regulation and difference might also support introvert ideologies of land as heritage, anti-cosmopolitan ethics or the neo-colonial rationale of Westernization (Argyrou 2005: 78). Following Bourdieu's (1984) theory of practice, Crossley (2003) suggests that activist and artistic movements overlap significantly. Artists and activists are socio-culturally disposed towards a particular type of social action that questions social norms and values and grants them with a form of pedagogical agency constitutive of bourgeois radicalism. He views this 'radical *habitus*' as manifestation of the 'submerged networks' and 'abeyance structures' that keep radicalism in constant flow through various mobility channels (*op. cit.* 45). Where historical evolution seeks to abolish history 'by relegating to the past, that is to the unconscious, the lateral possibles that it eliminated' (Bourdieu 1998: 56), artistic activism resurrects the past in creative ways to remind us of our obligation to bring *doxic* imperatives to the sphere of discourse (Tzanelli 2007a: 254; Habermas 1996).

Even if market imperatives govern Hollywood artists' public self-presentation, *technopoetic* reproductions of a *mélange* of histories of oppression and genocide appeal to normative imperatives, exceeding commercial demands (Huyssen 2000) and enabling further emotional investment in activist projects and corrective self-reflexivity (Husserl 1972; Heidegger 1967). Honneth's (1979; 1991: 32–72) elaboration on the Habermassian distinction between the *praxis* of intersubjective interaction and the *poesis* of engagement with objects already reconsiders cultural creativity in relation to what literary theorists such as Goldmann dubbed *vision du monde*, a world vision human subjects uphold and upon which they are educated to act (Karatsinidou 2005: 57; Lukács 1968). The voices of Honneth's work draw upon the Marxist paths of European postwar philosophy to differentiate Marxist teleological singularities on the basis of salvation and self-salvation narratives (Goldmann 1980; Jay 1993). These narratives correspond to the twin self-presentational paradigm social movement theorists explored both in the context of situationist and interactionist theories of action. The analytical line we cross from explorations of commercial strategies to humanitarian policies in the creative industries of Hollywood may be so fine that even its agents need special tools to outline them to others and to themselves, even in moments of self-advertising.

Cameron's liaison with anthropologists and environmental activists makes sense in this light: his digital and terrestrial work on Belo Monte broadcast his emotional investment in the project, the same way the habitual involvement of Brazilian activists in caring professions presents their 'taste for contention' as pedagogy (Crossley 2003: 53; Rootes 1995). I will return to the role of caring professionalism in Brazilian activism. For the moment, I want to draw attention to Cameron's confession that his pen and his camera are driven by a mystical connection to the environment as much as the plight of its indigenous people.

This continuity produces an eco-systemic discourse that goes back to the beginnings of Enlightenment humanism, when religious metaphysics was brushed aside in favour of a secular soteriology we find in Frankfurt School dialectics (Benjamin 1992 [1968]: 247). Much has been said about the tendency to superimpose Western European models of social movement theory onto the Brazilian context (Reiter 2010: 154). However, both the historical roots of professional Brazilian activism and Cameron's biographical record suggest a sound link with the histories and cosmologies of Europe's radical artistic *habitus* – in particular, Enlightenment's romantic transmutation into a discourse on land and landscape via the nationalist ideologies of the continent (also Herzfeld 1987 on the relationship between anthropological and nationalist trajectories). These very ideologies connected romantic pursuits to consumerist spirit in early modernity. In the current late modern context these ideologies contribute to the production of the new digital world travellers because they equip them with novel tools to articulate their nostalgic discourses (Bauman 2000a; Germann Molz 2004; Urry 2003, 2004; Campbell 2005; Herzfeld 2005).

Post-industrial digital iconographies fed into Cameron's artistic imagination for similar reasons. It is not coincidental that to create the interiors of the human mining colony on Pandora, production designers visited the Noble Clyde Bodreaux oil platform in the Gulf of Mexico during June 2007 to photograph, measure and film its every aspect and replicate it with photorealistic CGI on screen. Several hundred photos and detailed written descriptions of the Bodreaux were translated into real and virtual sets at a studio in New Zealand (Comingsoon.net/Noble Link, 12 January 2008). The double-deck drilling rig operates with underwater robots in depths humans cannot reach (see Shell, 28 January 2010). These *Avatar* shots share in visual resonance with the Orc machinery in the *Twin Towers* but emphasize instead contemporary technology and its impending social risks – today, a standard globalization thesis matching Cameron's narrative focus on global interdependency (see Beck 1999). The idea of sustainable biodiversity is also compatible with American Democratic policy – hence, with the liberal Hollywood context in which Cameron belongs as a transnational professional. In fact, he advertised his initiative as such:

> We're in a century right now in which we're going to start fighting more and more over less and less. The population ain't slowin' down, oil will be depleted – we don't have a great Plan B for energy in this country right now, notwithstanding Obama's attempts to get people to focus on alternative energy. We've had eight years of the oil lobbyists running the country.
>
> (Ordoña, 13 December 2009)

The transition from fabulism to politics is a haphazard business that globalization theorists do not always explore in compatible ways across the field. The *Avatar* project could be read as a difficult marriage between the two planes, a scapal paradox pointing to multidirectional mobilities and clashes of ideals, ideas and action (Appadurai 1990). The generation of a series of videos for the dissemination of *Avatar*-led activism against the construction of Belo Monte dam that threatens to destroy indigenous ecosystems and human ecologies alike appears to draw upon the cinematic archplot, whereby human progress and development build upon destruction. It is to Cameron's credit that he did not limit his cosmological convictions to cosmetic strategies. However it became difficult to acknowledge representational distinctions between the real, the visual and the virtual in his activism, as he repeatedly merged them to promote his merchandise online (also Virilio 1989).

I will explore the virtual presence of Cameron's initiative to bring different mobility pathways together. Once again, we have to perform as the digital tourist (Prideaux 2002: 319) to achieve this: returning to *Avatar*'s twin digital path, we now opt for the 'Home Tree Initiative', and come across a video taster from *A Message from Pandora* (2010), a special feature produced by James Cameron about the battle to stop the Belo Monte Dam on the Xingu. *Avatar*'s contribution links virtually to the action taken by Amazon Watch and International Rivers. The start shot is foregrounded by the traveller's desire, which figures as the voice of a male technological God (Cameron) looking on earth from the vantage point of a turbo prop aircraft taking off. 'I always wanted to go to the Amazon', he says. The camera cuts to a medium shot of the director, who continues: 'It's the last bastion of nature. It's so vast and biodiverse (*a plan of Amazon rivers and a steamboat full of people appear on screen*) and rich even in its present state (*a new cut to bulldozers working the ground*) when 20 per cent of it has been destroyed and another 20 per cent has been degraded'. Bulldozing produces a visual spectacle of environmental violation that by turn provides a familiar colonial metonymy of rape of the indigenous terrain by foreign invaders (Handler 1988: 14; Herzfeld 1987: 173; McClintock 1995: 187). Artistically, the traditional 'buddy movie' genre (Mulvey 2006: 346–7) gives way to a scopophilic one, in which Cameron 'the man' is both the 'bearer of the Look' and its emotional object. Cameron's romantic gaze is translated into a performance. This is related back at home as more than an 'aesthetically consumed experience' commonly identified with Amazonia eco-tourism but less than a nationalist declaration of territorialized 'uniqueness' (Adler 1989; Wheeler 1997; Jamal *et al.* 2003: 150–1).

As Cameron proceeds to discuss the imminent eco-systemic disaster, an intimate shot of indigenous life and Cameron's presentation at the International Sustainability Forum set the political scene clearly. The softly spoken monologue continues to have the confessional tone of a female travel diary: 'I thought: I need to go down there – and I need to speak to the people directly,' Cameron continues, while we view his first handshaking with indigenous people from above, as if we are now simultaneously judging and interpreting his humanitarian mission (Bauman 1987). At this stage we witness the display of the cultural-ideational apparatus on which Cameron makes sense of his own life experiences as a gateway to the Belo Monte controversy (Swindler 1986; Eyerman and Jamison 1991). As a defender of other people's land, Cameron fully assumes the place of his digital Jake. Welcomed by an indigenous woman in Brazilian

('Our newest warrior!'), his face is coloured red, and we know that like Jake, he has entered a phase of initiation into a different cosmos and a new political cause.

The video presentation assumes the qualities of a thanatotourist pilgrimage in that it foretells the death of yet another civilization in the name of progress. Treating his initiation to it with respect allows Cameron to place himself among those living humans that are imminently to be declared a dead culture plunged into oblivion (Lane 2000: 59). Death is being treated in his documentary as a social relation that ought to be articulated artistically as something more than a material or biological fact, if the cinematographer truly aspires to 'go native' (Butler 1999: 97–8). 'It was heart-breaking – these were people whose life was going to be altered irrevocably,' he proceeds to explain while the camera presents us with scenes of indigenous people at work. 'For these people, it's the end of the world as they know it – and they react accordingly,' says a tear-inducing Cameron while we admire indigenous people in traditional outfits: 'They are there, with their spears and their arrows, saying that they will fight.'

This video-recorded rite of initiation seals a deal of patronage in search of recognition and grants a reputable 'public face' to this private (p)act (Campbell 1964: 218). What is recorded and broadcast is the meeting point of two different value fields in a virtual transnational sphere: protagonists in this drama are a blend of indigenous and cinematic leadership that have a vital role to play in this spiritual exchange as community mediators. Within the narrative Cameron begins to function as an unexpected 'godfather' for his guests but also a virtual replacement of Jake 'humble to stand there amongst so strong leaders' – a Jake-director intimating that 'his world' does not understand. A simulacrum of his own making, Cameron declares to the people with the help of a local translator: 'We made a commitment.' Deliberately or not, Cameron adopts in this video the conventions of melodrama, modelling this intercultural encounter as a 'weepy' travel romance between a visitor and his host, which stimulates the viewer's body (Dyer 1992: 121). His sensory carnivalesque challenges the camera's hierarchy of the senses, producing a touring viewer in an Avatar-like body that can associate emotionally with indigenous groups beyond the ethereal gaze of a blockbuster hit (Veijola and Jokinen 1994). Here we can read the dialectic of Enlightenment within contemporary mobility genres (visual, virtual and embodied) as an act that redeems modern European aesthetic narratives of human creativity in religion's stead (Wolff 1984: 58; 1987: 3). As a student of the cinematic art, a virtuoso of the action sci-fi genre but also a sensitive human being, Cameron speaks in codes that can appeal to most contemporary viewers. But the same well-meaning gesture might contribute to socio-cultural essentializations, ultimately generating recognisable categories akin to Orientalist formulae (Bondi 2005: 63). The ethic of professional mobility that emerges from this audiovisual spectacle peaks the ambivalent language of volunteer tourism as an adventurous lifestyle as much as it propagates activist empathy (Hall and Williams 2002; Hall and Müller 2004; Simpson 2005; Benson 2011).

Aesthetic considerations aside, *Avatar* activism fronts a 'repertoire of collective action', a constellation of tactics and strategies developed over time and used by groups that want to act collectively online (Tilly 1984b; Van Laer and Van Aelst 2010: 231). In a subsequent scene that confirms my initial hypothesis we encounter Sigourney Weaver and Joel D. Moore (Norm Spellman): 'It's interesting, the parallel of what's going on here with what went on in the movie (*at this point we watch scenes from* Avatar) and it's one of the reasons why Jim got so passionate and involved' (*here the documentary cuts to scenes from the destruction of Hometree*). These virtual flashbacks are intended as critical pedagogy. Just as the Jake persona outlines the contours of a heroic character determined to bridge rifts and restore harmony and order in the cosmos (Campbell 2008: 169), Cameron shoulders a heavy burden by admitting that since *Avatar*'s inception: 'I knew it was going to be an environmentally themed film … I was going to Brazil and ended up living on … *Avatar*'. Upon this confession Jake pops in the video again to shout among the Omaticaya: 'This is our land!' As 'a cybernetic war of persuasion and dissuasion', this is a brilliant piece of cinematography, because it turns the function of 'informational spectrums' (Der Derian 1999: 223) on its head to craft distant humanitarian activism. Social scientists note that similar televised initiatives appeal to charity-prone *flâneurs* who engage in the alleviation of distant suffering (Chouliaraki 2008: 232; Kyriakidou 2008). The end of the video allows Cameron to change the ethnographic traveller's hat for that of the North American entrepreneur, with a concluding note that the *Avatar* collector's edition is soon to be released with the full documentary on Belo Monte (see Zukin 2003 on the variety of performances that bring together different mobilities).

At the same time, the page contains a link to 'Stop the Belo Monte Monster Dam!' for the collection of signatures against the project, as well as a transitional page to Amazon Watch's website, where we watch more natives talking about their woes. There we are also introduced to anthropologists Christian Poirier and Terry Turner who fight against Amazonian exploitation (Amazon Watch-Avatar, undated). Perfect reproductions of the cinematic narrative, the clips attempt to amend the damage done to the ethos of reality through simulations addressed to cinematic-digital viewers (Der Derian 1999: 224). In this respect – and against the Amazon Watch videos – Cameron's video works backwards to grant the movie with interpretive depth: from the primitivist background of Pandora's generic tribe it transposes us to the specific socio-political context in which the Amazonian communities live (Lane 2000: 58). If in their Omaticayan guise the Amazonian tribes were nothing other than Tasaday mummies (Baudrillard 1994: 8), in *Avatar*'s and Amazon Watch's videos they have a face, a voice and a cause specific to their land and to Brazil's national politics. At the same time, Cameron's work offers an apologetic corrective to anthropology's collaborations with colonial administration – a tale that academic supporters of the 'cultural imperialism' thesis transpose in contemporary market circuits onto cultural industries (Schiller 1991; Herman and McChesney 1997; MacKay 2004: 61). Let us re-enact the story, the *Avatar*-Amazon Watch activists suggest, but consider anthropological collaborations with cultural industries beneficial to indigenous futures, because they fill in the deplorable void of bureaucratic indifference within a nation-state that prioritizes profit over the wellbeing of its disenfranchised subjects (Herzfeld 1992: chapter 1).

Sigourney Weaver's video on the same controversy gestures towards a similar humanitarian narrative, prompting viewers to sympathize with the cause. However, her actual role complements rather than overlaps with that of Cameron-Jake's. Whereas Cameron casts himself as an explorer-actor, Weaver recedes in the background, leaving thus her authoritative voice to function hermeneutically as a moral time traveller: she is the 'true' embodiment of *Avatar*'s thick description. Weaver becomes the resurrected phantom of Grace the scientist, who's seen the 'other side' and returns to tell a story even before *Avatar 2*'s release. Having established herself professionally as a feminist icon (see *Alien*'s tough Ripley persona), Weaver's presence also alludes to relevant American movements. I follow Weaver's narrative in conjunction with BBC Radio 4's programme on Belo Monte as a fairly accurate genealogical record of *Avatar*'s thick description and primary material on the events. They are dressed in a smooth background music that is ethnic and very inviting. The music and the images produce a virtual environment, a soundscape that bestows upon *Avatar*'s aural, vocal and visual aspects a hard realist core specific to Brazilian memory.

Weaver translates a New Google Earth Animation on Belo Monte into a conventional documentary (Amazonwatch.org, 15 August 2011). She explains that the Belo Monte project has tapped into a protected area, hosting a mosaic of rare plants and animals and a network of indigenous and conservation areas. Xingu River, which passes through these areas, is important for the Amazon as it sustains the livelihoods of over 25,000 indigenous people from 18 ethnic groups. But the Brazilian Government is planning to construct the three largest hydroelectric dams in the world in the heart of this tropical rainforest. The US$17 billion project threatens the biodiversity of the area because it will divert the flow of the Xingu to generate electricity, flooding over 640,000 km, cutting off the flow of the river, and leaving populations without access to water, fish or means of transport. The dam will not even generate clean energy, as at the bottom of its reservoirs methane will be released from decomposing vegetation – a greenhouse gas 25 times more potent than carbon dioxide. Much of the dam's energy will go to dirty mining industries that generate few jobs in the region, but the diversion of the river will also alter the habitats of animals and fish, condemn some rare species to extinction and allow uncontrolled growth of mosquitoes carrying deadly diseases such as malaria. *Avatar*'s utopian Pandora is related to the dying Amazonian utopia by default: the traditional way of life for some tribes. Just as is the case with *Avatar*'s developmental archplot, the coming of a heavily industrialized modernity will give with one hand to snatch with the other.

The digital discourse translates situated ethics (the meaning of land for the Amazon's people) into morality as propagated by the 1948 Universal Declaration of Human Rights – a 'bible' that influenced contemporary considerations of cultural-as-intellectual property (Eagle Merry 2003). Paradoxically, as corporate and moral enterprise the *Avatar* matrix subscribes to this discourse while turning the rights to land use and ownership into globally marketed landscape. Weaver's clip connects to a series of videos posted on International Rivers' (2012) website that borrow from *Avatar*'s music. But while on *Avatar*'s website we watch a face-painted woman speaking directly to lens ('They are playing games with these lands, the lands of my people'), on International Rivers' we learn that this woman is Sheyla Juruna, leader of Juruna community in Boa Vista, Pará. Once more, Christian Poirier is recruited to explain the background of indigenous gatherings and the meaningful absence of a government that 'treats [its people] like they are nothing'. A fast-changing stream of portraits flickers through the film: Edison Lobao, Minister of Mines and Energy, and Dilma Roussef, President of Brazil, are tagged like criminals as the narrative gives way to sharp drum sounds. The clip's audiovisual matrix suggests that Brazil is ruled by a corrupt bureaucratic state.

Yet Weaver's nostalgic prologue prepares us for some hard facts to dispel any listener's delusions: she explains that pushing these people out of their habitats will coerce them to move into cities, where they are likely to compete for jobs with other migrants (another crucial revelation cut off by the testimony of a Brazilian man that begs English translation). Out of necessity these indigenous populations that will not find jobs may turn to logging, which contributes to deforestation. But as the dam will probably flood a considerable portion of the nearby city of Alta Mira, it will also displace more than 20,000 people from its fringes. It is not hard to see how this disorganized restratification will turn friends and former neighbours to foes, ripping some urban sociospheres apart in the same way it will destroy tribal lifeworlds (Albrow 1997; Sassen 2001; Herzfeld 2009). Reminiscent of traditional strain theory, Weaver's discourse opens cracks to Brazil's civilizational façade, allowing listeners and viewers to imagine spatial rearrangements that reconstruct class and racial inequalities (Marcuse 1996). Indigenous people and the disenfranchised urban poor partake in the same chronotopic discourse of federal planning and environmental development – otherwise put, they are recognized as polluted and pollutant subjects worthy to occupy times and spaces outside the nation's sanitized modernity (Bakhtin 1981: 84; Blanton 2011: 78). With the influx of new digital and industrial mobilities, Alta Mira is at risk of generating new zones of exception while sustaining old problems of poverty and violence, reminiscent of Rio de Janeiro's notorious *favelas* (Diken and Laustsen 2005; Ellison and Burrows 2007). Weaver's discursive snapshots on the future of Alta Mira come closer to the painful audiovisual diegesis of *Citade de Deus* (*City of God*, 2002, dir.s Fernando Meirelles and Katia Lund), a film that gives a realist account of Brazil's social divisions (Nagib 2007) rather than Cameron's cinematic airflight.

Weaver, not Cameron, is designated to sketch the background of activism for Xingu that stretches back to 1989, when Sting and Xingu tribal groups succeeded in creating enough worldwide protest to cancel the project and prompt the World Bank to stop financing similar projects. The threat returned in 2002 with renewed plans to flood the river that propelled indigenous groups to resume their action. Weaver's narrative is backed by a distinctive background noise that signifies upheaval, enhancing the realist feel of her story, which forges a link to the 2010 contingency, when Brazil's Federal Environmental Agency granted a licence for the Belo Monte complex against recommendations of its own technical staff. The protesting noise returns in this key moment of the narrative and is matched with appropriate ethnic music. This audiovisual frame debates in a discreet but powerful way what Herzfeld (2002) has explored as the 'absent presence' of indigenous voices that should claim centrality in scholarly discourses of Western civilization, and what de Sousa Santos (2000 in Barreira 2011: 154; de Sousa Santos 1999a, 1999b) describes as the 'sociology of absences', the ability of institutional frameworks to erase or amplify disenfranchised voices:

> The Brazilian Government is likely to build additional dams … in the future with large social and environmental impacts … also in Bolivia, Peru, and Ecuador.… Scientists, indigenous people and anthropologists quest[ion the] environmental, social and financial risks and suggest clean alternatives: wind and solar energy. The rivers are the lifeblood of the Amazon … You can help defend the Xingu and the rivers of the Amazon by taking action now, visiting the links on the screen, and sending a message to the Brazilian government.

The ideological organization of centralized state campaigning in support of such projects centred upon the typical argument that generating energy resources calls for amiable alliances with corporate enterprise. State alliances with what I shall term 'corporate developmentalists' are part of those histories of Brazilian governance that ensured the country's much-debated political transition from a 25-year military dictatorship (1964–89) to a neo-liberal democracy. This transition defined institutional organization in three interconnected spaces: the military, the political and the bureaucratic (Nervo Codato 2006). These interconnected domains incidentally underline Cameron's developmental archplot in which Pandoran natives and Western free minds alike are symbolically devoured by a Western military *getulismo* (authoritarianism). In the federalized Brazil's case, they harboured a fragmented governance model in which administrative maladjustment and the overall ill-defined functional boundaries between branches of the state became sources of infinite conflict, prompting bureaucrats to strengthen their ties with external 'allies' and 'clients'. As a result, regional policies harboured a disorganized capitalism in more recent years, allowing the amplification of problems such as the continuity between (liberal) ideological discourse and (crypto-authoritarian) political practice, as well as a 'deficit in citizenship' (*ibid.*). At the same time the onset of industrialization and increased urbanization transposed in big cities old citizenship struggles originating in the age of slavery.

The overall situation produced its own nemesis in two distinctive patterns of mobility: the first encouraged clientelist connections with non-Brazilian agents that could enhance the profile of localities. The second encouraged the emergence of social movements whose militant groups came from the educated, professional strata of society (e.g. academia). Brazil's NGOs initially fostered collaborations between the Church, the universities and political parties. This certainly places Brazilian histories in the glocalized context of the 1960s' affluent West. Today such NGOs rely mostly on external funding – possibly a moot point in the alliances between Brazilian activists and the *Avatar* fundraisers. In any case, the cultivation of a philanthropic ethic placing emphasis on the protection of vulnerable groups, sustainable development of international networks, human rights and the environment (Barreira 2011: 153) and geared towards ideological alliances between Christianity and Marxism in Brazilian activism (Garrison 1996: 250) is compatible with the *Avatar*-Amazon Watch ethic, placing the overall case in a Western cosmological context.

It does not take much to understand how the institutional argument of 'poor energy resources' as a sign of underdevelopment in a fiercely competitive global market was received in activist enclaves. In the Belo Monte context the bureaucratic desire to keep all mobility channels open with the 'developed' world became a key component in the production of 'official fears' and the assumption of an 'architectural' role in the management of Brazilian national space by a now almost corporatized state (Bauman 1992: 178; 2004: 8). But it also produced its own nemesis in indigenous action that displayed centrifugal characteristics as a form of activism: mobility outside the national sphere is good, when the nation's rulers continue to act in dictatorial economic styles. Both institutional policies and the excess of symbolic capital that characterizes the symbiotic humanitarian relationship between native and Western activism allowed the makers of *Avatar* to plan ahead for the second film in the 'trilogy' with a training trip to the Brazilian rainforest now underway. Speaking at the Second International Forum on Sustainability in late March 2011, Cameron stressed that the trip would help the cast to learn about the natives and what 'real jungle life' is like (Child, 28 March 2011). 'Avatar is a film about the rainforest and its indigenous people,' he clarified, reasserting thus continuities between the land, its people and his own digital landscapes.

This unlikely conflation was also validated by the presence of Arnold Schwarzenegger on an excursion to Xingu River. His impersonation of some iconic popular characters applies a cosmetic varnish to his identity as Governor of California – a political role which has become essential for the maintenance of his celebrity aura (Frow 1998; Street 2004). Meeting five members of the Amazonian Caiapo tribe at a restaurant with some journalists allowed him to reiterate that their timely encounter would have allowed him to make a better film. His Belo Monte activism will find continuation in a 3D 'experiential' documentary about indigenous struggles against the Belo Monte Dam. Today Cameron is known among natives as *krampremp-ti*, a 'man who is a friend of the jungle' (Child, 28 March 2011). The report suggests that at least the front stage of this highly politicized symbiosis (of directors, actors and tribe leaders) has a solid basis that is both instrumental and emotional, ensuring the future global circulation of Brazilian thanatotourist practices.

This meeting of two so different worlds speaks the benign language of charitable contact, while plunging us into the heart of developmental darkness: Amazon Watch's decision to release into the public domain a series of photographs depicting Cameron and Weaver leading the 2010 protests in Brazil among various native activists, confirms the power of digital technology to reproduce the fantasy of a Na'vi indigeneity that rebels in liaison with Westerners against the 'gardening state' and its corporate connections (Bauman 1992). Just as other *Avatar* activist products, the photographs became part of middle-class activist storytelling that resonates with other vernacular arts (Heywood 2004: 49; Earl 2008: 412). Simulations of cinematically produced imagery in recent protests around the world (see, for example, the ubiquitous use of the Guy Fawkes mask from *V for Vendetta* [2005] by groups such as Anonymous in recent Greek protests against multiple austerity measures) suggest that we combine 'strain theory' approaches with an examination of the ways the new media inform 'habitats of meaning', intersecting glocalized contexts organized by social movements, the state and the market (Löfgren 1989; Hannerz 1996; Hannerz and Löfgren 1994). *Avatar* activism transformed the Borgesian tale of Murdock's journey into a thanatotourist environment that reproduces a node of Western knowledge, the library of Yale – from which Weaver graduated. The coincidence is rife with moral meaning: always from the standpoint of privileged spectatorship, Western art stands stereotypically 'effeminate', perhaps surrounded by digital toys, but, just like Ripley, never quite ready to study the alien before eliminating it (Baudrillard 1994: 10–12).

At the moment of this global media recording of Hollywood's encounter with Amazonian tribes, *Avatar's* developmental archplot runs a full circle, actualizing Sahlins' (1972) suggestion that the economy of the market translates the idea of pure reciprocity into rational exchange. Artistic simulations of 'the behaviour of [what modernity has cast as] the underdeveloped (including the adoption of Marxist tenets)' in the confines of the market is disguised as a human ecology of energy crises and mechanical warfare to convey an 'esoteric aureole to the triumph of an esoteric culture' (Baudrillard 2006: 462). The oscillation in *Avatar's* audiovisual narratives of Belo Monte between a hermeneutics of suspicion (dictating that we think about dark motives and underhand dealings) and recovery (dictating to consider histories of New World colonialism [Ricoeur 1970: 520]) highlights the emotional dimension of creative labour and establishes some unexpected links between highly acclaimed workers in creative industries and the 'subordinate (gender and racial) orders' of their cinematography and their humanitarian action (Rollins 1996; Doezema 2001).

The Nietzschean term *ressentiment* partly captures the emotional complexity of artistic action, in that visible activism allows positive artistic interventions in Brazil to claim digital mobility as 'good [digital-artisanal] agency' (Hirsch 1972; Hesmondhalgh and Baker 2010: 46). From an industrial viewpoint, the craft of digital reproduction still stands at the fringes of established understandings of art, easily succumbing in our case to accusations of crypto-pornographic trading in folk simulacra (Attwood 2002: 95). The fantasy of contaminated pornographic consumption, which historically refers to fears about working-class men as beings 'brutish, animal-like and voracious' (Kipnis 1996: 175), complements Cameron's public projections of indigeneity as an intimate cultural terrain, ready to be devoured by millions of eyes and millions of dollars. Here artistic performance is emotional labour of immense value, in that it places creativity on a par with everyday discourses of being a benevolent (if imperfect) human with which we all can identify (Williams 1958; Tzanelli 2008b: 149; Hesmondhalgh and Baker 2010: 60–1; Tzanelli 2011a: 93). The fusion of futuristic sci-fi, travel and crime genres informing *Avatar*'s digital activism borrows from Brechtian alienation tropes, turning minority groups into political subjects and objects of affection at the same time (but see also Nagib's [2011: 157–73] analysis of *Delicate Crime*).

This type of pornographic-like mobility of cultural imagery in support of a radical cause is very difficult to assess, because it both uses and challenges cultural hierarchies supplementary of state violence in Brazil (Wicke 1993; Morley 1995). The 'thanks' extended to Cameron by indigenous tribes clashed with film critiques as a racist fantasy and even the indignation of businessmen in the Amazonian city of Alta Mira, who according to the BBC suspect that the motivations of media business go deeper than we might think (Hirsch, 12 May 2011). Interestingly, Western reporters also had to model their investigations on the digital Jake to conduct and relate their haphazard *flânerie* to global audiences. On a meta-level, social science scholars might consider how digital activism effectively simulates the cosmopolitan paradox of knowledge economies: Western technology always appears to control communication tools, to invite alternative indigenous worldviews to partake in global audiovisual mobilities. Ironically, it is the disorganized system of global mobility that allowed *Avatar*'s neotribal community to reach these Brazilian tribes, breaking the spatial boundaries of previous decades. Articulations of the cause were mostly managed by Western neotribal and Brazilian tribal leaders, but this is one of the missions of public communication: '[it] must bring "dialogic, contesting voices" into the centre of the common domain' (Murdock 1999: 16). If habitats of meaning were diffused in the Belo Monte controversy, then public communication had a valuable role to play 'in cultivating relevant interpretative and evaluative resources' (Titley 2003: 5).

The question of whether *Avatar*'s developmental agents needed this involvement to gain in public recognition, or Brazilian activism actually gained from the involvement of Hollywood celebrities fronting the protest photos that populate today Flickr collections lingers (Amazon Watch–International Rivers, 12 April 2010). 'Image-making' as instant recognition method might have locked Hollywood professionals and indigenous activists into a game of interdependency, whereby cinematic simulation sets a social precedent to follow. Photographs of demonstrations are testimony to 'high threshold' action on the part of Hollywood agents, complementing the 'low threshold' Internet-supported action of petition signatories (Van Laer and Van Aelst 2010: 235–7). Artistic self-narrations and presentations in *Avatar* activism could thus be contextually constructed as ethical in spite of their aesthetically reflexive aspects that political moralists tend to exclude from 'real political action' (Ezzy 1997: 428). It is perhaps more useful to examine such photos as an *autopoetic* mechanism, with Jake-Cameron and Grace-Weaver fronting claims of the rebelling (Pandoran) crowds in Brazilian and Western spaces. The extension of *Avatar*'s simulations to the activist domain did not necessarily displace politics and agency onto the aesthetic realm but reasserted the rational basis of emotional commitment humans of all creeds, classes and races might display in a post-Enlightenment public sphere (Hess 1999 in Hesmondhalgh and Baker 2010: 62).

Beyond the typical tale of global recognition, through their alliance with *Avatar*-Amazon Watch and International Rivers activism, the tribes achieved the production of a lasting collective image within the national domain as a trafficked-by-necessity culture facing extinction – a valuable commodity ready to be *exchanged* now with better service provision by the central bureaucrats that sidelined their needs in search of profit-making. If anything, the *Avatar*-Amazon Watch-International Rivers initiative managed to postpone once more the Belo Monte project – this time, with the ruling of Brazilian judge Carlos Castro Martins, who recognized that industrial work in the region would interfere with the natural flow of the Xingu river, affect local fish stocks and harm indigenous families that live from fishing (BBC, 29 September 2011). All communities engage in simulacra of sociality on the lens and the big screen these days, projecting outwards images of intimacy (Baudrillard 1988). Western *technopoetics* are neatly mirrored in the 'cultural poetics' of everyday interactions (Herzfeld 2005: 25), dispelling the illusions of grand scale some globalization theory might sustain. It is worth considering this politically valuable process of 'image-making' in relation to what Banks (2001: 56) explores as photographs: '[they] do not serve as the opening tokens in exchange relationships, but they most certainly serve to maintain relationships'. Image mobility allows for new hermeneutic constellations to inhabit liquid modernity – hence for new citizenship claims to emerge (Albrow 1996; Hand and Sandywell 2002). In such mobility systems, lands and their people achieve the status of national heritage as simulated landscapes. But the suspect methods, means and consequences of such digital flows cannot be anticipated, as the concluding section suggests.

Hunting for tourist signs

Most cinematic tourism commences with the encapsulation of the natural and socio-cultural dimensions of landscapes around the world – an act tapping into questions of (in)tangible heritage (Yudhisthir 2004). *Avatar* publicized an array of political issues regarding the ways new media routes reinvent cultural roots through simulated signposting (MacCannell 1989; Clifford 1997). Such *onomatopoeia*, the poetics of naming and claiming (Barthes 1979), hybridizes forms originating in Enlightenment divides between culture and technology (Wiggershaus 1994: 202–3). However, Cameron's hybridization in *Avatar* that simulates 'humans' through their insertion into humanoid bodies with alien DNAs (Ordoña, 13 December 2012) also produces a circular logic, whereby non-real entities, ideas and customs replace reality through their enactment of and incorporation into other worlds (Milton 1993). This ontological circuit is also part and parcel of an *autopoeia* that partakes in real policy-making. *Avatar*'s envisaged tourist mobilities stand then at yet another crossroads between landscape *onomatopoieia* (showcasing human actors as artists or entrepreneurs) and *autopoieia* of digital custom and habitats (flagging simulation while obscuring human agency and creativity) (Urry and Larsen 2011: 110).

The renaming of Southern Sky column in Zhangjiajie, Hunan province in China as 'Hallelujah' after the floating Pandoran Mountains is an example of global image mobility that partakes in tourism growth (Anders, 14 January 2010). After having inspired the visual design of the simulated Pandoran landscapes in 2008, Southern Sky gained an ambivalent status in China. In January 2010 hundreds of locals in ethnic Tujia costumes launched an official ceremony to rename the mountains (Agarwal, 26 January 2010). This marks an agential shift from staged authenticity rituals to the production of a simulated authentic stage quite independently from the actions of *Avatar*'s makers (MacCannell 1973, 1989: chapter 1; Tzanelli 2007b: chapter 3). As mentioned in Chapter 5, a similar initiative that marked the prelude of Beijing 2008 was staged in Guilin by one of China's metropolitan artists, Yimou Zhang. Such performative reproduction from the margins makes sense as a form of social poetics that ensures the global trade in ethnic fixities, where mobility is better organized by the national centre. Filtering Zhang's ethnic narratives through Western simulated tales of natural wilderness granted the act with some authenticity. In Hunan the municipal government was prompted to adopt the slogan 'Pandora is far but Zhangjiajie is near' to induce tourism in the region (BBC, 26 January 2010). Li Ping, an official with the Zhangjiajie branch of the China International Travel Service made sure that global reporting included a note on the 25-minute *Avatar* shots in the region, thus amplifying the fabulist capital of the Chinese region.

The Zhangjiajie scenic spot in the newly baptized Hallelujah area is the core area of the World Heritage Wulingyuan zone in Zhangjiajie city, and therefore a protected area in need of global advertising. However, ideoscapal and mediascapal clashes were almost inevitable in a capitalist node shared by so many different interest groups. A local rumour that developed into global gossip suggested that *Avatar*'s later withdrawal from Chinese cinemas aimed to make way for domestic films such as *Confucius* (2010), which silenced state practices of forced land evictions in China. *Avatar*'s civilizational allegory invoked these social dramas in the Na'vi downfall at the altar of technological postmodernity, constructing links between Western and Eastern ideological circuits reminiscent of other cinematic successes. It is understandable why, just as the Jur tribes of the Amazon, Zhangjiajie regional groups opted to ally with Western cinematic apparatuses: as practice and policy, image-making was possible only outside the national domain.

Unlike the Chinese initiative in the tourist sector, Brazilians are yet to turn their involvement in Cameron's industry into a similar enterprise. The custodianship of their ecological heritage proves both an asset and a burden, given the conservation issues tourist expansion poses. Even heritage policies aside, the needs of Amazonian people appear to be different and differentiated even within the region, with urban enclaves prioritizing industrial development and tribal habitats hinging on traditional lifestyles. Adding to these priorities external activist planning further complicates the picture, nevertheless shedding more light on the ethics of mobility. Inevitably, the chapter concludes with questions surrounding the archetypical ethical conundrum of developmental action: does privileged-professional intervention limit or enhance indigenous action (Hobart 1993)? Is it merely self-serving or is it sincere action on behalf of the weak? Can we speak of corporate humanism that educates viewers? These issues were read against old racial-primitivist ideologies at the time of *Avatar*'s release, conflating artistic and political action in ways begging further qualification (Newitz, 18 December 2009). At the same time, it could be claimed that *Avatar*'s multiple mobilities reproduced the 'white (wo)man's burden' and duty to save the dispossessed from suffering – what Sahlins (1996) also recognized as a form of Western Christian sadness in anthropological philanthropy. The Amazonian tribes in question are one skin colour darker than privileged metropolitan Brazilians and different from Western professionals. But this begs further investigation elsewhere.

Bibliography

100% New Zealand, 2 (undated) 'Peter Jackson'. Available at: www.newzealand.com/travel/media/features/film&television/film&television_nz-film-maker-peter-jackson_feature.cfm (accessed 9 December 2010).

100% Pure New Zealand (18 May 2008) Prince Caspian brings Narnia back to New Zealand. Available at: www.newzealand.com/travel/about-nz/features/narnia/prince-caspian.cfm (accessed 9 December 2010).

100% Pure New Zealand, 1 (undated) New Zealand director making Narnia sequel. Available at: www.newzealand.com/travel/media/features/personalities/04_nov_17_film_lionwitchwardrobe_feature.cfm (accessed 9 December 2010).

1Up.com (undated) 'Cracking the Code: The Konami Code'. Available at: www.1up.com/features/cracking-code-konami-code (accessed 12 March 2012).

A Message from Pandora (undated) Take Action to Defend Pandoras on Earth. Available at: http://messagefrompandora.org/ (accessed 3 February 2012).

A Traveller's Guide to London (2006) 'See the London sights featured in the *Da Vinci Code*'. Available at: www.offtolondon.com/davinci_tours.html (accessed 1 December 2006).

Absolute China Tours (undated) 'Bird's Nest (National Stadium of Beijing Olympics)'. Available at: www.absolutechinatours.com/Beijing-attractions/National-Stadium.html (accessed 22 April 2011).

Adams, D. (2011) *The Music of* The Lord of the Rings *Films*, New York: Harper Collins.

Aden, R. (1999) *Popular Stories and Promised Lands*, Tuscaloosa: Alabama University Press.

Adler, J. (1989) 'Travel as performed art', *American Journal of Sociology*, 94(6): 1366–91.

Adler, J. (1992) 'Mobility and the creation of the subject', *Proceedings of the International Colloquium, International Tourism: Between Tradition and Modernity*, Nice: France.

Adorno, T. (1991) *The Culture Industry: Selected Essays on Mass Culture*, London: Routledge.

Adorno, T.W. and Horkheimer, M. (1993) *The Dialectic of Enlightenment*, New York: Continuum.

Agarwal, A. (26 January 2010) 'Chinese want to rename peaks "Hallelujah Mountains" following Avatar success', *News Track India*. Available at: www.newstrackindia.com/newsdetails/145455 (accessed 4 September 2012).

Agnew, J. (2007) 'No borders, no nations: Making Greece in Macedonia', *Annals of the Association of American Geographers*, 97(2): 398–422.

Ahmed, S. (2004) *The Cultural Politics of Emotion*, London: Routledge.

Aitken, S. and Dixon, D. (2006) 'Imagining geographies of film', *Erduke*, 60: 326–36.

Al Jabri, M.A. (1999) *Arab-Islamic Philosophy*, Austin, TX: University of Texas.

Alba, R.D. (2000) 'Assimilation's quiet tide', in Stephen Steinberg (ed.) *Race and Ethnicity in the United States*, Oxford: Blackwell.

Albertsen, N. and Diken, B. (2003) 'Artworks' networks – field, system or mediators?', *Department of Sociology On-line Papers*. Available at: http://comp.lancs.ac.uk/sociology.soc105bd.html (accessed 30 March 2012).

Albrow, M. (1996) *The Global Age*, Cambridge: Polity.

Albrow M. (1997) 'Travelling beyond local cultures: Socioscapes in a global city', in J. Eade, *Living the Global City*, London: Routledge.

Alexander, J.C. (2006) 'Cultural pragmatics: social performance between ritual and strategy', in J.C. Alexander, B. Giesen and J.L. Mast (eds) *Social Performance, Symbolic Action, Cultural Pragmatics and Ritual*, Cambridge: Cambridge University Press.

Alexander J.C. and Smith, P. (2001) 'The strong program in cultural theory: elements of structural hermeneutics', in J. Turner (ed.) *Handbook of Social Theory*, New York: Kluwer.

Ali, S. (2012) 'The sense of memory', *Feminist Review*, 100: 89–105.

All Movie (undated) 'Zhang Yimou Biography'. Available at: www.allmovie.com/artist/zhang-yimou-117624/bio (accessed 17 April 2011).

Altman, R. (1999) *Film Genre*, London: BFI.

Amazon Watch (2012) 'Xingu urgent action fund'. Available at: https://amazonwatch.org/donate/xingu-urgent-action-fund?utm_source=Amazon+Watch+Newsletter+and+Updates&utm_campaign=df40907973-xingu_20120308&utm_medium=email (accessed 11 March 2012).

Amazon Watch-Avatar (undated) 'Stop the Belo Monte monster dam'. Available at: http://amazonwatch.org/work/belo-monte-dam (accessed 3 February 2012).

Amazon Watch–International Rivers (12 April 2010) 'Belo Monte dam, Xingu river', International Rivers Flickr Photostream. Available at: www.flickr.com/photos/internationalrivers/4522089264/ (accessed 4 September 2012).

Americans in France (2006) 'Sightseeing tours – Da Vinci Code tours'. Available at: www.americansinfrance.net/TravelPlanner/Da-Vinci-Code-Tours.cfm (accessed December 2006).

Amoamo, M. and Thompson, A. (2010) '(Re)imagining Maori tourism: representation and cultural hybridity in postcolonial New Zealand', *Tourist Studies*, 10(1): 35–55.

Anders, C.J. (14 January 2010) '*Avatar*'s designers speak: Floating mountains, AMP suits and the dragon', *IO9.com*. Available at: http://io9.com/5444960/avatars-designers-speak-floating-mountains-amp-suits-and-the-dragon (accessed 29 January 2012).

Anderson, B. (1991) *Imagined Communities*, London: Verso.

Anderson, J. (10 December 2009) 'Alternate world, alternate technology', *The New York Times*. Available at: www.nytimes.com/2009/12/13/movies/13avatar.html?pagewanted=all (accessed 30 January 2012).

Andretta, M. (2003) 'Making transnational social movements work', *Social Movements and Contentious Politics in a Democratising World*, seminar paper.

Ang, I. (1996) *Living Room Wars*, New York: Routledge.

Anita, A. (26 January 2010) 'Chinese want to rename peaks "Hallelujah Mountains" following *Avatar* success', *Real Bollywood*. Available at: www.realbollywood.com/2010/01/chinese-rename-peaks-hallelujah-mountains-avatar-success.html (accessed 13 May 2012).

Antoniou, D. (2003) 'Muslim immigrants in Greece', *Immigrants and Minorities*, 22(2): 155–74.

Appadurai, A. (1981) 'The past as a scarce resource', *Man*, 16(2): 201–19.

Appadurai, A. (1990) 'Disjuncture and difference in the global cultural economy', *Public Culture*, 2(2): 1–24.

Appadurai, A. (1996) *Modernity at Large*, Minneapolis: University of Minnesota Press.

Archer, M. (1995) *Realist Social Theory*, Cambridge: Cambridge University Press.

Argyrou, V. (2005) *The Logic of Environmentalism*, Oxford: Berghahn.

Aristotle (1996) *Poetics*, London: Penguin.

Árnarson, Á. (2007) 'Fall apart and put yourself together again: the anthropology of death and bereavement counselling in Britain', *Mortality*, 12: 48–65.

Asian Film Awards (22–25 March 2010) 'Zhang Yimou: Hong Kong's "crucial" role in China film', *Hong-Kong Filmart*. Available at: www.youtube.com/watch?v=otG-lDU V7ew (accessed 27 March 2011).

Ateljevic, I. (2000) 'Circuits of tourism: Stepping beyond the "production/consumption" dichotomy', *Tourism Geographies*, 2: 369–88.

Attwood, F. (2002) 'Reading porn: the paradigm shift in pornography research', *Sexualities*, 5(1): 91–105.

Attwood, F. (2006) 'Sexed up: theorizing the sexualisation of culture', *Sexualities*, 9(1): 77–94.

Augé, M. (2004) *Oblivion*, Minneapolis: University of Minnesota Press.

Augustine (1948) 'Concerning the nature of the good', in W. Jones (ed.) *Basic Writings of Saint Augustine*, New York: Random House.

Avatar Blog (19 January 2010) 'James Cameron to Oprah: "I see you"'. Available at: http://avatarblog.typepad.com/avatar-blog/2010/01/james-cameron-to-oprah-i-see-you. html (accessed 25 January 2012).

Avatarmovie.com (undated) Available at: www.avatarmovie.com (accessed 2 February 2012).

Azcárate, M.C. (2006) 'Between local and global, discourses and practices: rethinking ecotourism development in Celestún (Yucatán, México)', *Journal of Ecotourism*, 5(1): 97–111.

Bærenholdt, O., Haldrup, M., Larsen, J. and Urry, J. (2004) *Performing Tourist Places*, Aldershot: Ashgate.

Bakhtin, M.M. (1968) *Rabelais and His World*, Cambridge, MA: MIT.

Bakhtin, M.M. (1981) *The Dialogic Imagination*, Austin, TX: Texas University Press.

Bakhtin, M.M. (1984) *Problems of Dostoevski's Poetics*, Manchester: Manchester University Press.

Balibar, E. (1990) 'The nation form: history and ideology', *Review*, 13: 329–61.

Banks, M. (2001) *Visual Methods in Social Research*, London: Sage.

Barbosa, D. (8 August 2008) 'Gritty renegade now directs China's close-up', *New York Times*. Available at: www.nytimes.com/2008/08/08/sports/olympics/08guru. html?pagewanted=all (accessed 13 May 2012).

Barclay, B. (2003) 'Exploring Fourth Cinema', in *Reimagining Indigenous Cultures: The Pacific Islands*, Summer Institute: Hawaii.

Barker, M. (2009) 'Changing lives, challenging concepts: some findings and lessons from *The Lord of the Rings* project', *International Journal of Cultural Studies*, 12(4): 375–93.

Barker, M. and Mathjis, E. (2007) *Watching The Lord of the Rings*, New York: Peter Lang.

Barnes, B. (20 December 2009) '"Avatar" is No. 1 but without a record', *The New York Times*. Available at: www.nytimes.com/2009/12/21/movies/21box.html (accessed 28 January 2012).

Barnes, H. (21 September 2011) 'James Cameron unveils plans for Avatar land attraction', *The Guardian*. Available at: www.guardian.co.uk/film/2011/sep/21/james-cameron-avatar-land-attraction (accessed 25 January 2012).

Barnet, R. (1994) *Global Dreams*, New York: Simon and Shuster.

Barreira, I.A.F. (2011) 'Social movements, culture and politics in the work of Brazilian sociologists', *Latin American Perspectives*, 38(3): 150–68.

Barth, F. (ed.) (1969) *Ethnic Groups and Boundaries*, Boston: Little, Brown & Co.

Barthes, R. (1979) *The Eiffel Tower and Other Mythologies*, New York: Hill and Wang.

Baudrillard, J. (1983) *Simulations*, New York: Semiotext.

Baudrillard, J. (1988) *Selected Writings*, Stanford, CA: Stanford University Press.

Barthes, R. (1993) *Mythologies*, London: Vintage.

Baudrillard, J. (1994) *Simulacra and Simulation*, Ann Harbour: University of Michigan Press.

Baudrillard, J. (1997) *The Consumer Society*, London: Sage.

Baudrillard, J. (2006) 'The precession of simulacra', in M.G. Durham and D. Kellner (eds) *Media and Cultural Studies*, Malden: Blackwell.

Baum, T. (2007) 'Human resource in tourism', *Progress in Tourism Management*, 28: 1383–99.

Bauman, R. (1977) *Verbal Art as Performance*, Illinois: Waveland.

Bauman, Z. (1987) *Legislators and Interpreters*, Ithaca, NY: Cornell University Press.

Bauman, Z. (1989) *Modernity and the Holocaust*, Cambridge: Polity.

Bauman, Z. (1991) *Modernity and Ambivalence*, Cambridge: Polity.

Bauman, Z. (1992) *Intimations of Postmodernity*, London: Routledge.

Bauman, Z. (1998) *Globalization*, New York: Columbia University Press.

Bauman, Z. (2000a) *Community*, Cambridge: Polity.

Bauman, Z. (2000b) *Liquid Modernity*, Cambridge: Polity.

Bauman, Z. (2003) *Liquid Love*, Cambridge: Polity.

Bauman, Z. (2004) 'Stalin', *Cultural Studies—Critical Methodologies*, 4(1): 3–11.

Bauman, Z. (2005) *Liquid Life*, Cambridge: Polity.

Baym, N.K. (2000) *Tune in, Log On*, Thousand Oaks, CA: Sage.

BBC (26 January 2010) 'China renames "Avatar" mountain in honour of film'. Available at: http://news.bbc.co.uk/1/hi/8480954.stm (accessed 26 February 2012).

BBC (25 October 2010) 'New Zealanders rally behind Hobbit shoot', *BBC News Entertainment and Arts*. Available at: www.bbc.co.uk/news/entertainment-arts-11617860 (accessed 9 December 2010).

BBC (7 April 2001) 'Profile: Ai Weiwei'. Available at: www.bbc.co.uk/news/world-asia-pacific-12997324 (accessed 16 April 2011).

BBC (29 September 2011) 'Brazil judge halts job on Belo Monte Amazon dam'. Available at: www.bbc.co.uk/news/world-latin-america-15102520 (accessed 26 February 2012).

BBC Coventry and Warwickshire (25 October 2011) 'Shakespeare signs covered in protest of Anonymous film'. Available at: www.bbc.co.uk/news/uk-england-coventry-warwickshire-15440882 (accessed 23 April 2012).

BBC Entertainment and Arts (18 September 2011) 'Sigourney Weaver Avatar 2 role confirmed'. Available at: www.bbc.co.uk/news/entertainment-arts-14964191 (accessed 22 January 2012).

BBC Entertainment and Arts (27 March 2012) 'James Cameron returns from dive for Titanic 3D premiere'. Available at: www.bbc.co.uk/news/entertainment-arts-17523013 (accessed 28 April 2012).

BBC News (18 February 2003) 'Mona Lisa smile secrets revealed'. Available at: http://news.bbc.co.uk/1/hi/entertainment/2775817.stm (accessed 30 March 2012).

BBC News (7 May 2009) 'Demons "harmless", say Vatican'. Available at: http://news.bbc.co.uk/1/hi/entertainment/8037538.stm (accessed 10 March 2012).

BBC Newsbeat (24 April 2012) 'Kazakhstan thanks Borat for boosting tourism'. Available at: www.bbc.co.uk/newsbeat/17826000 (accessed 2 May 2012).

Beck, U. (1992) *Risk Society*, London: Sage.

Beck, U. (1999) *World Risk Society*, Cambridge: Polity.

Beck, U. (2000) 'The cosmopolitan perspective: sociology of the second age of modernity', *British Journal of Sociology*, 51: 79–105.

Beck, U. (2002) 'The cosmopolitan society and its enemies', *Theory, Culture and Society*, 19: 17–44.

Beck, U. and Beck-Gernshein, E. (1995) *The Normal Chaos of Love*, Cambridge: Polity.

Beck, U., Giddens, A. and Lash, S. (1994) *Reflexive Modernization*, Cambridge: Polity.

Becker, H.S. (1982) *Art Worlds*, Berkeley and Los Angeles: University of California Press.

Becker, H.S., Faulkner, R.R. and Kirshenblatt-Gimblett, B. (2006) 'Introduction', in H.S. Becker, R.R. Faulkner and B. Kirshenblatt-Gimblett (eds) *Art from Start to Finish*, Chicago, IL: University of Chicago Press.

Bederman, G. (1995) *Manliness and Civilization*, Chicago, IL: University of Chicago Press.

Beeton, S. (2005) *Film-Induced Tourism*, Toronto: Channel View.

Bell, C. (2002) 'The big OE: young New Zealand travelers as secular pilgrims', *Tourist Studies*, 2(2): 143–58.

Bell, C. and Lyall, J. (2002) *The Accelerated Sublime*, Westport, CT: Praeger.

Benhabib, S. (1992) *Situating the Self*, New York: Routledge.

Benjamin, W. (1973) *Understanding Brecht*, London: Fontana.

Benjamin, W. (1989) 'The work of art in the age of mechanical reproduction', in D. Richter (ed.) *The Critical Tradition*, New York: St. Martin's Press.

Benjamin, W. (1992) *Illuminations*, London: Fontana.

Benjamin, W. (2005) 'Excavation and memory', in M. Jennings, H. Eiland and G. Smith (eds) *Walter Benjamin*, II, London: Belknap Press.

Benson, A.M. (2011) *Volunteer Tourism*, New York: Routledge.

Ben-Ze'ev, E. and Lomsky-Feder, E. (2009) 'The canonical generation: trapped between personal and national memories', *Sociology*, 43(6): 1047–66.

Berger, J. (2008) *Ways of Seeing*, London: Penguin.

Berlin, I. (1969) *Four Essays on Liberty*, Oxford: Oxford University Press.

Bernal, M. (1991) *Black Athena: The Afroasiatic Roots of Classical Civilisation, The Fabrication of Ancient Greece*, I–II, London: Vintage.

Bernal, M. (1995) 'Greece: Aryan or Mediterranean? Two contending historiographical models', in Sylvia Federici (ed.), *Enduring Western Civilisation*, Connecticut: Praeger.

Bernstein, E. (2001) 'The meaning of the purchase: desire, demand and the commerce of sex', *Ethnography*, 2(3): 389–420.

Berry, C. (2007) 'Chinese cinema', in P. Cook (ed.) *The Cinema Book*, London: BFI and Palgrave-Macmillan.

Bhabha, H.K. (1994) *The Location of Culture*, London: Routledge.

Binkley, S. (2000) 'Kitsch as a repetitive system: a problem for the theory of taste hierarchy', *Journal of Material Culture*, 5(2): 131–52.

Biography.com (undated) 'James Cameron'. Available at: www.imdb.com/name/nm0000116/bio (accessed 4 September 2012).

Biography.com (undated) 'Sigourney Weaver'. Available at: www.biography.com/people/
   sigourney-weaver-17179376 (accessed 18 December 2011).
Blakeslee, S. (27 November 2000) 'The mystery of Mona Lisa's smile linked to flickering
   eyes', *New York Times* (in *San Francisco Chronicle*). Available at: http://library.think-
   quest.org/13681/data/links/mlsmile.htm (accessed 30 March 2012).
Blanton, R. (2011) 'Chronotopic landscapes and environmental racism', *Linguistic
   Anthropology*, 21(1): 76–93.
Bloch, E. (1986) *The Principle of Hope*, Oxford: Blackwell.
Bloch, M. and Parry, J. (1982) *Death and the Regeneration of Life*, Cambridge: Cambridge
   University Press.
Blok, A. (1981) 'Rams and billy-goats: A key to the Mediterranean code of honor', *Man*
   (NS), 16: 427–40.
Bly, L. (21 October 2004) 'Tourists get into "Da Vinci" mode', USA Today. Available at:
   www.usatoday.com/travel/destinations (accessed 10 October 2006).
Body, Mind, Spirit Journeys (2006) 'France: Mary Magdalene and Black Madonna
   Pilgrimage', May 12–25, 2007' Available at: www.bodymindspiritjourneys.com/
   markpinkham_france-may07.htm (accessed 1 December 2006).
Bok, S. (1978) *Lying*, Sussex: The Harvester Press.
Bondi, L. (2005) *Working the Spaces of Neoliberalism*, Oxford and New York: Wiley-
   Blackwell.
Bonstead-Bruns, M. (2007) 'Sociology of work', in G. Ritzer (ed.) *Blackwell Encyclopedia
   of Globalization*, New York: Wiley-Blackwell.
Book Browse (2001) 'A conversation with Dan Brown, author of *The Da Vinci Code*'.
   Available at: www.bookbrowse.com/author_interviews/full/index.cfm/author_number
   /226/dan-brown (accessed 11 March 2012).
Boorstin, D. (1962) *The Image*, Harmondsworth: Penguin.
Borges, J.L. (1998) *Collected Fictions*, New York: Viking.
Born, G. (2000) 'Inside television: television research and the sociology of culture',
   Screen, 41(4): 68–96.
Boucher, G. (14 August 2009) 'James Cameron: Yes, 'Avatar' is "Dances with Wolves"
   in space … sorta', *San Francisco Times*. Available at: http://herocomplex.latimes.
   com/2009/08/14/james-cameron-the-new-trek-rocks-but-transformers-is-gimcrackery
   (accessed 29 January 2012).
Bourdieu, P. (1977) *Outline of a Theory of Practice*, Cambridge: Polity Press.
Bourdieu, P. (1984) *Distinction*, Cambridge: Harvard University Press.
Bourdieu, P. (1992) 'The practice of reflexive sociology'. in P. Bourdieu and L.J.D.
   Wacquant (eds) *An Invitation to Reflexive Sociology*, Chicago, IL: University of
   Chicago Press.
Bourdieu, P. (1993) *The Field of Cultural Production*, Cambridge: Polity.
Bourdieu, P. (1998) *Practical Reason*, Cambridge: Polity.
Bourdieu, P. and Wacquant, L.J.D. (eds) (1992) *An Invitation to ReflexivemSociology*,
   Chicago, IL: University of Chicago Press.
Bovingdon, E. (20 June 2011) 'Town turns blue to celebrate film release', *Yahoo! Movies*.
   Available at: http://uk.m.yahoo.com/w/ygo-frontpage/lp/story/uk/41893/coke.bp?ref_
   w=frontdoors&.ysid=XW1ZX_2t8L4k51mRo99bzlrr&.intl=gb&.lang=en-gb (accessed
   27 April 2012).
Bowles, M.J. (2003) 'The practice of meaning in Nietzsche and Wittgenstein', *Journal of
   Nietzsche Studies*, 26(1): 14–24.

Bowles, S. (27 October 2008) 'First look: "Angels & Demons" will fly faster than "Da Vinci"', *USA Today*. Available at: www.usatoday.com/life/movies/news/2008-10-27-angels-demons_N.htm (accessed 7 March 2012).

Box Office Mojo (2005) 'The Chronicles of Narnia: The Lion, the Witch and the Wardrobe'. Available at: http://boxofficemojo.com/movies/?id=narnia.htm (accessed 23 April 2012).

Box Office Mojo (2009) 'Avatar, All Time Box Office'. Available at: www.boxofficemojo.com/alltime/world/ (accessed 28 January 2012).

Box Office Mojo (2009) 'Greece'. Available at: http://boxofficemojo.com/intl/greece/?yr=2009&p=.htm (accessed 2 May 2012).

Boyd, D. and Ellison, N. (2007) 'Social network sites: definition, history and scholarship', *Journal of Computer-mediated Communication*, 13(1). Available at: http://jcmc.indiana.edu/vol13/issue1/boyd.ellison.html (accessed 13 May 2012).

Braidotti, R. (1992) 'On the feminist female subject or from she-self to she-other', in G. Bock and S. James (eds) *Beyond Equality and Difference*, London: Routledge.

Brandist, C. (2002) *The Bakhtin Circle*, Virginia: Pluto.

Brewster, C. and Brewster, K. (2006) 'Mexico city 1968: sombreros and skyscrapers', in A. Tomlinson and C. Young (eds) *National Identity and Global Sports Events*, New York: SUNY.

BringThemBack.org (2010) Available at: www.bringthemback.org/default.aspx (accessed 29 April 2012).

British Tours Ltd. (2006) 'See the London sights featured in Dan Brown's bestselling novel'. Available at: www.britishtours.com/davincicodetours.html (accessed 1 December 2006)

Brodsky-Porges, E. (1981) The Grand Tour: travel as an educational device, 1600–1800', *Annals of Tourism Research*, 8(2): 171–86.

Brookley, R.A. and Booth, P. (2006) 'Restricted play: synergy and the limits of interactivity in *The Lord of the Rings: The Return of the King* video game', *Games and Culture*, 1(3): 214–30.

Brooks, D. (2000) *Bobos in Paradise*, London: Simon & Schuster.

Brown, D. (undated) 'The official Dan Brown web site'. Available at: www.danbrown.com/#/home (accessed 11 March 2012).

Brown, D. (2001) *Angels and Demons*, London: Corgi.

Brown, D. (2004) *The Da Vinci Code*, London: Random House.

Bunnell, E. (2010) 'Headlines: not necessarily a bad thing', *Saint Thomas Times Journal*. Available at: www.stthomastimesjournal.com/ArticleDisplay.aspx?e=1640616 &archive=true (accessed 16 March 2012).

Burlingame, J. (5 October 2006) 'Harry Gregson-Williams: A 21st century man', *BMI*. Available at: www.bmi.com/musicworld/entry/335000 (accessed 23 April 2012).

Burnham, D. (2005) 'Kant's aesthetics', in J. Fieser and B. Dowden (eds) *Internet Encyclopaedia of Philosophy*. Available at: www.iep.utm.edu/kantaest/#SH2a (accessed February 2010).

Büscher, M., Urry, J. and Witchger, K. (2011) *Mobile Methods*, London: Routledge.

Butler, B. (2006) 'Heritage and the present past', in C. Tilley (ed.) *Handbook of Material Culture*, London: Sage.

Butler, J. (1993) *Bodies that Matter*, London: Routledge.

Butler, J. (1997) *The Psychic Life of Power*, Stanford, CA: Stanford University Press.

Butler, R. (1995) 'Introduction', in R. Butler and D. Pearce (eds) *Change in Tourism*, London: Routledge.

Butler, R. (1999) *Jean Baudrillard*, London: Sage.

Butler, R. (2007) 'Subversive bodily acts', in S. During (ed.) *The Cultural Studies Reader*, Abingdon: Routledge.

Buzard, J. (1993) *The Beaten Track*, Oxford: Clarendon.

Cahn, M. (1984) 'Subversive mimesis', in M. Spariosu (ed.) *Mimesis in Contemporary Theory*, London: John Benjamins.

Caira, M. (2008) 'The concept of migration and clandestinity in the Chinese culture', *Social Science Information*, 47(4): 623–8.

Campbell, C. (2005) *The Romantic Ethic and the Spirit Of Modern Consumerism*, Oxford: Blackwell/Alcuin Academics.

Campbell, J. (1964) *Honour, Family and Patronage*, Oxford: Oxford University Press.

Campbell, J. (2008) *The Hero with a Thousand Faces*, California: New World.

Carrier, J. (ed.) (1995) *Occidentalism*, Oxford: Oxford University Press.

Cassirer, E. (1968) *The Individual and the Cosmos in Renaissance Philosophy*, Philadelphia: University of Pennsylvania Press.

Castells, M. (1989) *The Informational City*, Oxford: Blackwell.

Castells, M. (1996) *The Rise of the Network Society*, Oxford: Blackwell.

Castells, M. (1997) *The Information Age*, II: *The Power of Identity*, Oxford: Blackwell.

Castells, M. (2000) 'Towards a sociology of the network society', *Contemporary Sociology*, 29: 693–9.

Castoriadis, C. (1987) *The Imaginary Institution of Society*, Cambridge, MA: Cambridge University Press.

Caves, R.E. (2002) *Creative Industries*. Cambridge: Harvard University Press.

CBS News (12 November 2004) '"Da Vinci Code" tourist letdowns'. Available at: www.cbsnews.com/2100-500174_162-652625.html (accessed 13 May 2012).

CBS News (13 March 2006) 'Mining Da Vinci'. Available at: www.cbsnews.com/stories/2006/03/10/listening_post/main1390534.shtml (accessed 1 January 2007).

CBS News (19 June 2008) 'Fans Line Up For "Angels & Demons" Tours'. Available at: www.cbsnews.com/stories/2008/06/19/earlyshow/leisure/boxoffice/main4193975.shtml (accessed 2 September 2008).

CBS News, *The Early Show* (November 2004) by Richard Roth.

Cere, R. (2002) 'Digital counter-cultures and the nature of electronic social and political movements', in Y. Jewkes (ed.) *Dot.cons: Crime, Deviance and Identity on the Internet*, Tavistock, Devon: Willan.

Chalfen, R. (1999) 'Interpreting family photography as pictorial communication', in J. Prosser (ed.) *Image-Based Research*, London: Falmer.

Chan, F. (2007) 'In search of a comparative poetics: cultural translatability in transnational Chinese cinema', unpublished thesis, University of Nottingham.

Chaney, D. (2002) *Cultural Change and Everyday Life*, Basingstoke: Palgrave.

Chatterjee, P. (1993) *The Nation and its Fragments*, Princeton, NJ: Princeton University Press.

Chen, Peijin (18 August 2007) 'Ai Weiwei hates his Bird's Nest', *Shanghaiist*. Available at: http://shanghaiist.com/ai_weiwei_hates.php (accessed 18 April 2011).

Chhabra, D. (2005) 'Defining authenticity and its determinants: toward an authenticity flow model', *Journal of Travel Research*, 44: 64–73.

Chhabra, D., Healy, R. and Sills, E. (2003) 'Staged authenticity and heritage tourism', *Annals of Tourism Research*, 30(3): 702–19.

Chia-Ling, L. (2004) 'Art exhibitions travel the world', in M. Sheller and J. Urry (eds) *Tourism Mobilities*, London: Routledge.

Child, B. (25 October 2010) 'The Hobbit relocation row sparks street protests in New Zealand', *The Guardian*. Available at: www.guardian.co.uk/film/2010/oct/25/the-hobbit-protests-new-zealand (accessed 18 December 2010).

Child, B. (29 October 2010) 'Extra claims she was rejected for Hobbit role for looking "too brown"', *The Guardian*. Available at: www.guardian.co.uk/film/2010/nov/29/extra-too-brown-the-hobbit (accessed 17 December 2010).

Child, B. (28 March 2011) 'James Cameron plans *Avatar 2* training trip to Brazilian rain-forest', *The Guardian*. Available at: www.guardian.co.uk/film/2011/mar/28/james-cameron-avatar-2-brazil (accessed 26 May 2012).

China National (17 May 2006) 'China to beat Cannes for first premiere of *"Da Vinci Code"*'. Available at: www.chinadaily.com.cn/china/2006-05/17/content_593514.htm (accessed 1 January 2007).

Chouliaraki, L. (2008) 'The media as moral education: mediation as action', *Media, Culture and Society*, 30(6): 831–52.

Chowdry, G. (2007) 'Edward Said and contrapuntal reading: implications for critical interventions in international relations', *Millennium*, 36(1): 101–16.

Circle of Animals/Zodiac Heads (2011) 'A historic outdoor public sculpture exhibition by the acclaimed Chinese artist'. Available at: www.zodiacheads.com/?page_id=17 (accessed 12 May 2011).

Clark, S. (2001) *Captain Corelli's Mandolin*, London: Headline.

Clifford, J. (1983) 'On ethnographic authority', *Representations*, 1(2): 118–46.

Clifford, J. (1986) 'On ethnographic analogy', in J. Clifford and G. Marcus (eds) *Writing Culture: The Poetics and Politics of Ethnography*, Berkeley: University of California Press.

Clifford, J. (1988) *The Predicament of Culture*, Cambridge: Harvard University Press.

Clifford, J. (1992) 'Travelling cultures', in L. Grossberg, C. Nelson and P. Treichler (eds) *Cultural Studies*, New York: Routledge.

Clifford, J. (1997) *Routes*, Cambridge: Harvard University Press.

Clogg R. (1992) *A Concise History of Modern Greece*, Cambridge: Cambridge University Press.

Cloke, P. and Perkins, H.C. (1998) '"Cracking the Canyon with the Awesome Foursome": representations of adventure tourism in New Zealand', *Environment and Planning D: Society and Space*, 16(2): 185–218.

CNN (2 February 2010) 'List of Academy Award nominations'. Available at: http://articles.cnn.com/2010-02-02/entertainment/academy.award.nominations.list_1_crazy-heart-colin-firth-avatar-district-sapphire?_s=PM:SHOWBIZ (accessed 28 January 2012).

Cohen, E. (1973) 'Nomads from affluence: notes on the phenomenon of drifter tourism', *International Journal of Comparative Sociology*, 14(1–2): 89–103.

Cohen, E. (1996) 'A phenomenology of tourist experiences', in Y. Apostolopoulos, S. Leivadi and A. Yannakis (eds) *The Sociology of Tourism: Theoretical and Empirical Investigations*, London: Routledge.

Cohen, E. (2003) 'Backpacking: diversity and change', *Tourism and Cultural Change*, 1(2): 95–111.

Cohen, I.J. (1989) *Structuration Theory*, London: Macmillan.

Cohen, S. (2002) 'Paying one's dues: the music business, the city and urban regeneration', in M. Talbot (ed.) *The Business of Music*, Liverpool: University of Liverpool Press.

Cohen, S. (2005) 'Screaming at the moptops: convergences between tourism and popular music', in D. Crouch, R. Jackson and F. Thompson (eds) *The Media and the Tourist Imagination*, New York: Routledge.

Cohen, S.A. (2011) 'Lifestyle travellers: backpacking as a way of life', *Annals of Tourism Research*, 38(4): 117–33.

Coleman, C. (undated) 'How swift is Thy Score', *Tracksounds*. Available at: www.track-sounds.com/reviews/hero_tan_tun.htm (accessed 24 April 2011).

Collard, A. (1989) 'Investigating "social memory" in a Greek context', in E. Tonkin, M. McDonald and M. Chapman (eds) *History and Ethnicity*, London and New York: Routledge.

Colonnello, N. (10 August 2007) 'An interview with Ai Weiwei', *ArtZine*. Available at: www.artzinechina.com/display_vol_aid499_en.html (accessed 4 September 2012).

Comingsoon.net/Noble Link (12 January 2008) '*Avatar* designs based on drilling rig'. Available at: www.comingsoon.net/news.php?id=40855&offset=20 (accessed 30 January 2012).

Connell, R.W. (1987) *Gender and Power*, Stanford, CA: Stanford University Press.

Connell, R.W. (1995) *Masculinities*, Berkeley, CA: University of California Press.

Connerton, P. (1989) *How Societies Remember*, Cambridge: Cambridge University Press.

Conversi, D. (2001) 'Cosmopolitanism and nationalism', in A. Leoussi (ed.) *The Companion Guide to Nationalism*, New Brunswick: Transactions.

Cooper, J.C. (2009) *An Illustrated Encyclopedia of Traditional Symbols*, London: Thames and Hudson.

Córdoba Azcárate, M. (2006) 'Between local and global, discourses and practices; rethinking ecotourism development in Celestún (Yucatán, Mexico)', *Journal of Ecotourism*, 5(1–2): 97–112.

Cosgrove, D. (1993) 'Landscapes and myths, gods and humans', in B. Bender (ed.) *Landscape*, Oxford: Berg.

Cosgrove, D. and Jackson, P. (1987) 'New directions in cultural geography', *Area*, 19(2): 95–101.

Couldry, N. (2003a) 'Media meta-capital: extending the range of Bourdieu's field theory', *Theory and Society*, 32(5/6): 653–77.

Couldry, N. (2003b) *Media Rituals*, New York: Routledge.

Couroucli, M. (2008) 'Sharing nostalgia in Istanbul; Christian and Muslim pilgrims to St George's Sanctuary', CNRS-Université Paris X International Conference, Columbia University, New York, 14–15 February.

Cousins, M. (2011) *The Story of Film*, Edinburgh: Pavillion.

Cowan, J. (1990) *Dance and the Body Politic in Northern Greece*, Princeton, NJ: Princeton University Press.

Craig, C.J., Turcotte, J.F. and Coombe, R. (2011) 'What's feminist about open access? A relational approach to copyright in the academy', *Feminists@law*, 1(1): 1–35.

Crang, P. (1997) 'Performing the tourist product', in C. Rojek and J. Urry (eds) *Touring Cultures*, London and New York: Routledge.

Crang, M. (1999) 'Knowing, tourism and practices of vision', in D. Crouch (ed.) *Leisure/Tourism Geographies*, Oxford: Blackwell.

Cresswell, T. (2001) 'The production of mobilities', *New Formations*, 43(1): 11–25.

Crossley, N. (2002) *Making Sense of Social Movements*, Buckingham: Open University Press.

Crossley, N. (2003) 'From reproduction to transformation: social movement fields and the radical habitus', *Theory, Culture and Society*, 20(6): 43–68.

Crouch, D. (ed.) (1999) *Leisure/Tourism Geographies*, Oxford: Blackwell.

Crouch, D. and Desforges, L. (2003) 'The sensuous in the tourist encounter: the power of the body in tourist studies', *Tourist Studies*, 3(1): 5–22.

Crouch, D. and Lübbren, N. (eds) (2003) *Visual Culture and Tourism*, Oxford: Berg.

Crouch, D., Jackson, R. and Thompson, F. (eds) (2005) *The Media and the Tourist Imagination*, New York: Routledge.

CTV News (1 June 2009) 'Vardalos heads to Greece for "My Life in Ruins"'. Available at: www.ctv.ca/CTVNews/undefined/20090601/Vardalos_Movie_090601 (accessed 2 May 2012).

Culler, J. (1988) *Framing the Sign*, Oxford: Blackwell.

Cunningham, S. (2005) 'Creative enterprises', in J. Hartley (ed.) *Creative Industries*, Oxford: Blackwell.

Curtis, L.P. (1971) *Apes and Angels*, New York: Smithsonian Institution Press.

D'Costa, G. (2010) 'Traditions and reception: interpreting Vatican II's Declaration', *New Blackfriars*, 484–503.

Da Vinci Code Tours (2006). Available at: http://davincicodetours.co.nz/ (accessed 1 November 2006).

Daily Mail (5 May 2009) 'Low-cut Ayelet Zurer steals the show from Tom Hanks and Ewan McGregor at Angels & Demons world premiere in Rome' (editorial). Available at: www.dailymail.co.uk/tvshowbiz/article-1177538/Low-cut-Ayelet-Zurer-steals-Tom-Hanks-Ewan-McGregor-Angels-amp-Demons-world-premiere-Rome.html (accessed 8 March 2012).

Daily Times (13 October 2007) 'Shooting at Acropolis for the first time'. Available at: www.dailytimes.com.pk/default.asp?page=2007/10/13/story_13-10-2007_pg9_5 (accessed 30 April 2012).

Dallmayr, F. (2001) *Beyond Orientalism*, New Delhi: Rawat.

Dann, G.M.S. (1977) 'Anomie, ego-enhancement and tourism', *Annals of Tourism Research*, 4: 184–94.

Dann, G.M.S. (2001) 'Slavery, contested heritage and thanatotourism', *International Journal of Tourism Hospitality and Administration*, 2(3/4): 1–29.

Dann, G.M.S. (2002) 'The tourist as a metaphor of the social world', in G.M.S. Dann (ed.) *The Tourist as a Metaphor of the Social World*, Wallingford: CABI.

Dann, G.M.S. and Liebman Parrinello, G. (2009) 'Introduction', in G.M.S. Dann and G. Parrinello (eds) *The Sociology of Tourism*, UK: Emerald.

Dann, G.M.S. and Seaton, A.V. (2001) 'Slavery, contested heritage and thanatourism', in G.M.S. Dann and A.V. Seaton (eds) *Slavery, Contested Heritage and Thanatourism*, New York: Haworth Hospitality Press.

Davis, J. (1992) *Exchange*, Buckingham: Open University Press.

Daye, M. (2005) 'Mediating tourism: an analysis of the Caribbean holiday experience in the UK national press', in D. Crouch, R. Jackson and F. Thompson (eds) *The Media and the Tourist Imagination*, New York: Routledge.

Davis, M. (2008) *Freedom and Consumerism*, Aldershot: Ashgate.

De Beauvoir, S. (2007) 'The independent woman', in S. During (ed.) *The Cultural Studies Reader*, Abingdon: Routledge.

De Certeau, M. (1985) 'What we do when we believe', in M. Blonsky (ed.) On Signs: A Semiotic Reader, Baltimore: John Hopkins University Press.

De Certeau, M. (1986) *Heterologies*, Manchester: Manchester University Press.

De Certeau, M. (1988) *The Writing of History*, New York: Columbia University Press.

De la Fuente, E. (2007) 'The "new sociology of art": putting art back into social science', *Cultural Sociology*, 1(3): 409–25.

De Lauretis, T. (1984) *Alice Doesn't*, Bloomington: Indiana University Press.

De Lauretis, T. (2007) 'Upping the anti (sic.) in feminist theory', in S. During (ed.) *The Cultural Studies Reader*, Abingdon: Routledge.

De Peuter, J. (1998) 'The dialogics of narrative identity', in M.M. Bell and M. Gardiner (eds) *Bakhtin and the Human Sciences*, London: Sage.

De Pina Cabral, J. (2008) 'Sarakatsani reflections on the Brazilian Devil', in M. Mazower (ed.) *Networks of Power in Greece*, London: Hurst.

De Sousa Santos, B. (1995) *Towards a New Common Sense*, New York: Routledge.

De Sousa Santos, B. (1999a) 'Towards a multicultural conception of human rights', in M. Featherstone and S. Lash (eds) *Spaces of Culture*, London: Sage.

De Sousa Santos, B. (1999b) *Towards a New Common Sense*, New York: Routledge.

Debord, G. (1995) *Society and the Spectacle*, New York: Zone.

Delanty, G. (1995) *Inventing Europe*, Basingstoke: Macmillan.

Delanty, G. (2000) *Citizenship in a Global Age*, Buckingham: Open University Press.

Delanty, G. (2006) 'The cosmopolitan imagination: critical cosmopolitanism and social theory', *The British Journal of Sociology*, 57(1): 25–47.

Delanty, G. and O'Mahony, P. (2002) *Nationalism and Social Theory*, London: Sage.

Della Porta, D. and Diani, M. (2006) *Social Movements*, 2nd edition, Oxford: Blackwell.

DeNora, T. (2000) *Music and Everyday Life*, Cambridge: Cambridge University Press.

DeNora, T. (2003) *After Adorno*, Cambridge: Cambridge University Press.

Der Derian, J. (1999) 'The conceptual cosmology of Paul Virilio', *Theory, Culture and Society*, 16(5/6): 215–27.

Derrida, J. (1976) *Of Grammatology*, Baltimore: John Hopkins University Press.

Derrida, J. (1997) *Writing and Difference*, London: Routledge.

Derrida, J. (1998) *Archive Fever*, Chicago, IL: University of Chicago Press.

Derrida, J. (2002) *Ethics, Institutions and the Right to Philosophy*, New York: Rowman and Littlefield.

Desforges, L. (2000) 'Traveling the world: identity and travel biography', *Annals of Tourism Research*, 27(4): 926–45.

Diken, B. and Laustsen, C.B. (2005) *The Culture of Exception*, London: Routledge.

Dikötter, F. (2008) 'The racialization of the globe: an interactive interpretation', *Ethnic and Racial Studies*, 31(8): 1478–96.

Diver, M. (21 December 2009) 'James Horner Avatar: Music from the motion picture', *BBC Music*. Available at: www.bbc.co.uk/music/reviews/vxm5 (accessed 23 January 2012).

Doane, M.A. (1991) *Femmes Fatales*, New York: Routledge.

Doeringer, P.B. and Piore, M. (1971) *Internal Labor Markets and Manpower Analysis*, Lexington, MA: Heath.

Doezema, J. (2001) 'Ouch! Western feminists' "wounded attachment" to the "Third World prostitute"', *Feminist Review*, 67(1): 16–38.

Donati, P.R. (1992) 'Political discourse analysis', in M. Diani and R. Eyerman (eds) *Studying Collective Action*, London: Sage.

Double Helix Games (30 September 2008) *Silent Hill Homecoming*. (Konami Digital Entertainment), Scene: Staff credits.

Douglas, M. (1993) *Purity and Danger*, London: Routledge.

Drake, M. (2003) 'Representing "old countries": the strategic representation of culture as heritage in the Asia-Europe summit meetings', in S. Lawson (ed.) *Europe and the Asia-Pacific Culture*, London: Routledge/Curzon.

Dudley, A. (1992) 'Adaptation', in G. Mast, M. Cohen and L. Braudy (eds) *Film Theory and Criticism*, Oxford: Oxford University Press.

Duhaime.org (undated) 'Legacy'. Available at: www.duhaime.org/LegalDictionary/L/Legacy.aspx (accessed 10 December 2010).

Durkheim, E. (1997 [1893]) *The Division of Labour in Society*, New York: Free Press.

Dürr, E. (undated) 'Island purity as global imaginary', EASA Conference, 2006, AUT: New Zealand.

Duval, D.T. (2007) *Tourism and Transport*, Wallingford: CABI.

Duvenage, P. (1999) 'The politics of memory and forgetting after Auschwitz and apartheid', *Philosophy and Social Criticism*, 25(3): 1–28.

Dyer, R. (1982) *Stars*, London: BFI.

Dyer, R. (1992) 'Coming to terms: gay pornography', in R. Dyer, *Only Entertainment*, London: Routledge.

Dyer, R. (1993) 'White' in R. Dyer, *Matters of Image*, London: Routledge.

Dyer, R. (2006) 'Stereotyping', in M.G. Durham and D.M Kellner (eds) *Media and Cultural Studies*, Oxford: Blackwell.

Dyson, E. (1998) *Release 2.1: A Design for Living in a Digital Age*, London: Penguin.

Eade, J. (1992) 'Pilgrimage and tourism at Lourdes, France', *Annals of Tourism Research*, 19: 18–32.

Eade, J. (2001) *Placing London*, Oxford: Berghahn.

Eagle Merry, S. (2003) 'Human rights law and the demonization of culture (and anthropology along the way)', *Political and Legal Anthropology Review*, 26(1): 55–76.

Eagleton, T. (2000) *The Idea of Culture*, Oxford: Blackwell.

Earl, B. (2008) 'Literary tourism: constructions of value, celebrity and distinction', *International Journal of Cultural Studies*, 11(4): 401–17.

Eckholm, E. (1 September 1998) 'A spectacular tale in its mythic home', *New York Times*. Available at: www.nytimes.com/1998/09/01/arts/a-spectacular-tale-in-its-mythic-home-turandot-enters-the-forbidden-city.html (accessed 20 April 2011).

Edensor, T. (2001) 'Performing tourism, staging tourism: (re)producing tourist space and practice', *Tourist Studies*, 1(1): 59–81.

Edensor, T. (2004) 'Automobility and national identity: representation, geography and driving practice', *Theory, Culture and Society*, 21(4/5): 101–20.

Edensor, T. (2005) 'Mediating William Wallace: audio-visual technologies in tourism', in D. Crouch, R. Jackson and F. Thompson (eds) *The Media and the Tourist Imagination*, New York: Routledge.

Edmunds, J. and Turner, B. (2002) *Generations, Culture and Society*, Buckingham: Open University Press.

Egan, K. and Barker, M. (2006) 'Rings around the world: notes on the challenges, problems and possibilities of international audience projects', *Particip@tions*, 3(2). Available at: www.participations.org/volume%203/issue%202%20-%20special/3_02_eganbarker.htm (accessed 4 September 2012).

Eisenstein, E. (1979) *The Printing Press as an Agent of Change*, Cambridge: Cambridge University Press.

Eleftherotypia History (2010) *The Junta Trials* (special issue), Athens: Eleftherotypia.

Eliade, M. (1989) *The Myth of the Eternal Return, or Cosmos and History*, London: Arkana.

Elias, N. (1982) *The Civilizing Process: State Formation and Civilization*, II, Oxford: Blackwell.

Elliot, A. and Urry, J. (2010) *Mobile Lives*, London: Routledge.

Ellison, N. and Burrows, R. (2007) 'New spaces of (dis)engagement? Social politics, urban technologies and the rezoning of the city', *Housing Studies*, 22(3): 295–312.

Encyclopaedia of World Biography (2007) 'Zhang Yimou'. Available at: www.encyclopedia.com/topic/Zhang_Yimou.aspx#1 (accessed 20 April 2011).

Eng, R.Y. (2004) 'Is Hero a paean to authoritarianism?', Asia Media Archives. Available at: www.asiamedia.ucla.edu/article.asp?parentid=14371 (accessed 25 April 2011).

Enloe, C. (1990) *Bananas, Beaches and Bases*, Berkeley, CA: University of California Press.

Erickson, R. (2006) *Crime in an Insecure World*, Cambridge: Polity.

Erskine, T. (2002) '"Citizen of nowhere" or "the point where circles intersect"? Impartialist and embedded cosmopolitans', *Review of International Studies*, 28: 457–78.

Evans, M. (1997) 'Public and private: women and the state', in M. Evans (ed.) *Introducing Contemporary Feminist Thought*, Cambridge: Polity.

Evans, P. and Wustler, T. (2000) *Blown to Bits*, Boston: Harvard Business School Press.

Evans-Pritchard, E.E. (1937) *Oracle, Witchcraft and Magic Among the Azande*, Oxford: Clarendon.

Evans-Pritchard, E.E. (1940) *The Nuer*, Oxford: Oxford University Press.

Eyerman, R. and Jamison, A. (1991) *Social Movements*, Cambridge: Polity.

Ezzy, D. (1997) 'Subjectivity and the labour process: conceptualising "good work"', *Sociology*, 31: 427–44.

Ezzy, D. (2005) 'I am the mountain walking', in L. Angeles, E.R. Orr and T.V. Dooren (eds) *Pagan Visions for Sustainable Future*, Woodbury: Llewellyn Publications.

Fabian, J. (1983) *Time and the Other*, New York: Columbia University Press.

Fabian, J. (1990) *Power and Performance*, Wisconsin: University of Wisconsin Press.

Fairburn, M. (1989) *The Ideal Society and its Enemies*, Auckland: Auckland University Press.

Fairclough, N. (1992) *Discourse and Social Change*, Cambridge: Polity.

Fang, A. (28 October 2008) 'Post-Olympic tourism revs up in Beijing', *China Economic Net*. Available at: http://en.ce.cn/Insight/200810/28/t20081028_17206540.shtml (accessed 22 April 2011).

Faubion, J. (1993) *Modern Greek Lessons*, Princeton, NJ: Princeton University Press.

Featherstone, M. (1991) 'The body in consumer culture', in M. Featherstone, M. Hepworth and B.S. Turner (eds) *The Body*, London: Sage.

Fensel, D., Hendler, J., Lieberman, H. and Wahlster, W. (eds) (2002) *Semantic Web Technology*, Cambridge, MA: MIT.

Ferry, I. (20 April 2006) 'Master class Silent Hill', Encranlarge.com. Available at: www.ecranlarge.com/article-details_c-interview-282.php (accessed 16 March 2012).

Filmtracks (5 October 2009) 'Angels and Demons'. Available at: www.filmtracks.com/titles/angels_demons.html (accessed 14 March 2012).

First Great Western (December 2006) 'Break the code', p. 51.

First Great Western (December 2006) 'See the film, visit the set...', p. 26.

Fischer, M. (2004) 'Integrating anthropological approaches to the study of culture: the "hard" and the "soft"', *Cybernetics and Systems*, 35(2/3): 147–62.

Fischer, M., Lyon, D. and Zeitlyn, D. (2008) 'The Internet and the future of social science research', in *The Sage Handbook of Online Research Methods*, London: Sage.

Florida, R. (2003) *The Rise of the Creative Class*, Melbourne: Pluto.

Fodor's (undated) 'Travel the roads taken by characters in the best-selling novel'. Available at: www.fodors.com/wire/archives/000902.cfm (accessed 1 November 2006).

Forster, E.M. [1910] (1931) *Howard's End*, Harmondsworth: Penguin.

Fortes, M. (1969) *Kinship and the Social Order*, Chicago, IL: Aldine de Guyter.

Foucault, M. (1997a) *The Archaeology of Knowledge*, London: Routledge.

Foucault, M. (1997b) 'The birth of biopolitics', in P. Rabinow (ed.) *Michel Foucault: Ethics*, New York: New Press.

Fox Searchlight (undated) 'My Life in Ruins'. Available at: www.foxsearchlight.com/mylifeinruins (accessed 4 May 2012).

Freedman, D. (2008) *The Politics of Media Policy*, Cambridge: Polity.

Fretts, B. (11 April 2003) 'My big fat Greek life', *Entertainment Weekly*. Available at: www.ew.com/ew/article/0,,254097,00.html (2 May 2012).

Freud, S. (1965a) *The Interpretation of Dreams*, New York: Avon Books.

Freud, S. (1965b) *The Psychopathology of Everyday Life*, New York: Norton.

Friedberg, A. (1993) *Window Shopping*, Berkeley, CA: University of California Press.

Friedberg, A. (1995) 'Cinema and the postmodern condition', in L. Williams (ed.) *Viewing Positions*, Brunswick, NJ: Rutgers University Press.

Friedman, J. (1994) *Cultural Identity and Global Process*, London: Sage.

Fritz, B. (20 December 2009) 'Could 'Avatar' hit $1 billion?', *Los Angeles Times*. Available at: http://latimesblogs.latimes.com/entertainmentnewsbuzz/2009/12/could-avatar-hit-1-billion.html (accessed 28 January 2012).

Frow, J. (1998) 'Is Elvis a God? Cult, culture, questions of method', *International Journal of Cultural Studies* 1(2): 197–210.

Fruehling Springwood, C. (2002) 'Framing, dreaming and playing in Iowa: Japanese mythopoetics and agrarian utopia', in S. Coleman and M. Crang (eds) *Tourism: Between Place and Performance*, Oxford: Berghahn.

Gabriel, B. (2004) 'The unbearable strangeness of Being', in B. Gabriel and S. Ilcan (eds) *Postmodernism and the Ethical Subject*, Montreal: McGill-Queen's University Press.

Gallagher, B. (11 January 2012) 'Avatar 2 release pushed to 2016 says John Landau', MovieWeb. Available at: www.movieweb.com/news/avatar-2-release-pushed-to-2016-says-jon-landau (accessed 18 January 2012).

Gallant, T.W. (1999) 'Brigandage, piracy, capitalism, and state-formation: transnational crime from a historical world-systems perspective', in J.McC. Heyman (ed.) *States and Illegal Practices*, Oxford and New York: Oxford Berg.

Gallant, T.W. (2002) *Experiencing Dominion*, Notre Dame, IN: University of Notre Dame Press.

Gauntlett, D. (2011) *Making is Connecting*, Cambridge: Polity.

Garrison, J.W. (1996) 'Practical notes: Brazilian NGOs from grassroots to national civic leadership', *Development and Practice*, 6: 250–4.

Geertz, C. (1973) *The Interpretation of Cultures*, New York: Basic Books.

Geertz, C. (1980) *Negara*, Princeton, NJ: Princeton University Press.

Gelder, K. (2006) 'Epic fantasy and global terrorism', in E. Mathijs and M. Pomerance (eds) *From Hobbits to Hollywood*, Amsterdam: Rodopi.

Gellner, E. (1983) *Nations and Nationalism*, Oxford: Blackwell.

Germann Molz, J. (2004) 'Playing online and between the lines', in M. Sheller and J. Urry (eds) *Tourism Mobilities*, London: Routledge.

Gibbons, J. (2007) *Contemporary Art and Memory*, London: I.B. Tauris.

Giddens, A. (1984) *The Constitution of Society*, Berkeley: University of California Press.

Giddens, A. (1987) *Social Theory and Modern Sociology*, Cambridge: Polity.

Giddens, A. (1990) *The Consequences of Modernity*, Cambridge: Polity.

Giddens, A. (1991) *Modernity and Self-Identity*, Cambridge: Polity.

Giddens, A. (1992) *The Transformation of Intimacy*, Cambridge: Polity.

Giddens, A. (2009) *The Politics of Climate Change*, Cambridge: Polity.

Gilroy, P. (1993) *The Black Atlantic*, London: Verso.

Glass, R. (2004) *Authors Inc*, New York: New York University Press.

Gledhil, C. (1997) 'Klute 1: A contemporary film noir and feminist criticism', in E.A. Kaplan (ed.) *Women in Film Noir*, 3rd edition, London: BFI.

Glogg, R. (1992) *A Concise History of Modern Greece*, Cambridge: University of Cambridge Press.

Gluckman, M. (1963) 'Gossip and scandal', *Current Anthropology*, 4(3): 307–16.

Goffman, E. (1961) *Asylums*, New York: Anchor.

Goffman, E. (1975) *Frame Analysis*, Harmondsworth: Penguin.

Golding, P. and Murdock, G. (2000) 'Culture, communications and political economy', in J. Curran and M. Gurevitch (eds) *Mass Media and Society*, 3rd edition, London: Arnold.

Goldmann, L. (1964) *The Hidden God*, London: Routledge.

Goldmann, L. (1980) *Method in the Sociology of Literature*, Oxford: Blackwell.

Gompertz, W. (11 May 2011) 'Art world missing Ai Weiwei', BBC. Available at: www.bbc.co.uk/blogs/thereporters/willgompertz/2011/05/art_world_missing_ai_weiwei_1.html (accessed 12 May 2011).

Gourgouris, S. (1996) *Dream Nation*, Stanford, CA: Stanford University Press.

Graburn, N.H.H. (1977) 'Tourism: the sacred journey' in V. Smith (ed.) *Hosts and Guests*, Philadelphia: University of Pennsylvania Press.

Graburn, N.N.H. (1983) *To Pray, Pay and Play*, Aix en-Provence: Centre des Hautes Etudes Touristiques.

Graburn, N.H.H. (2001) 'Relocating the tourist', *International Sociology*, 16(2): 147–58.

Graburn, N.H.H. (2002) 'The ethnographic tourist', in G.M.S. Dann (ed.) *The Tourist as a Metaphor of the Social World*, Wallingford: CABI.

Graburn, N.H.H. (2004) 'The Kyoto tax strike: Buddism, shinto and tourism in Japan', in E. Badone and S.R. Roseman (eds) *Intersecting Journeys*, Chicago, IL: University of Illinois.

Graham, S. and Marvin, S. (2001) *Splintering Urbanism*, London: Routledge.

Graml, R. (2004) '(Re)mapping the nation: Sound of Music tourism and national identity in Austria, ca 2000', *Tourist Studies*, 4(2): 137–59.

Gramsci, A. (1971) *Selections from the Prison Notebooks of Antonio Gramsci*, London: Lawrence and Wishart.

Gray, A. (2003) *Research Practice for Cultural Studies*, London: Sage.

Gray, J. (1984) *Hayek on Liberty*, Oxford: Blackwell.

Graydanus, S.D. (undated) 'The achievement of Peter Jackson's *The Lord of the Rings*', Decentfilms.com *(Catholic World Report)*. Available at: http://decentfilms.com/articles/lotr_achievement (accessed 8 April 2012).

Great Buildings Online (2008) 'Pyramide Du Louvre'. Available at: www.greatbuildings.com/buildings/Pyramide_du_Louvre.html (accessed 1 September 2008).

Greenwood, D.J. (1997) 'Culture by the pound', in V. Smith (ed.) *Hosts and Guests*, Philadelphia: University of Pennsylvania Press.

Gregory, E. (1998) *H.D. and Hellenism*, Cambridge: Cambridge University Press.

Greisman, H. (1977) 'Social meanings of terrorism', *Contemporary Crises* 1: 303–18.

Greydanus, S.D. (undated) 'Faith and fantasy: Tolkien the Catholic, The Lord of the Rings, and Peter Jackson's film trilogy', *Decent Films Guide*. Available at: www.decentfilms.com/articles/faithandfantasy (accessed 4 September 2012).

Guardian (27 February 2006) 'Da Vinci Code author begins copyright battle'. Available at: http://books.guardian.co.uk/danbrown/story/0,1719147,00.html (accessed January 2007).

Guardian (17 November 2006) 'Pan's People' (editorial). Available at: www.guardian.co.uk/film/2006/nov/17/2 (accessed 15 December 2010).

Guardian (28 March 2007) 'Authors loose appeal over Da Vinci Code plagiarism'. Available at: www.guardian.co.uk/uk/2007/mar/28/danbrown.books (accessed 30 June 2009).

Gudeman, S. (1986) *Economics as Culture*, London: Routledge Kegan Paul.

Guest, I. (1990) *Behind the Disappearances*, Philadelphia: University of Pennsylvania Press.

Guibernau, M. and Hutchinson, J. (eds) (2004) *History and National Destiny*, Oxford: Blackwell.

Guns, C. (6 April 2006) 'On the red pyramid, Carol Spier as production designer and exploring Society of Horror Films'. Available at: www.sonypictures.com/movies/silenthill/productiondiary/archives/2006/04/on_the_red_pyra.php (accessed 16 March 2012).

Haas, P. (1992) 'Knowledge, power and international policy coordination', *International Organization*, 46(1): 1–35.

Habermas, J. (1972) *Knowledge and Human Interests*, Boston: Beacon Press.

Habermas, J. (1989a) *The Structural Transformation of the Public Sphere*, Oxford: Polity Press.

Habermas, J. (1989b) *The Theory of Communicative Action*, I, Boston, MA: Beacon Press.

Habermas, J. (1989c) *The New Conservatism*, Cambridge, MASS: MIT.

Habermas, J. (1989d) *The Theory of Communicative Action*, II, Boston, MA: Beacon Press.

Habermas, J. (1996) *Between Facts and Norms*, Cambridge: Polity.

Halbwachs, M. (1992) *On Collective Memory*, Chicago, IL: University of Chicago Press.

Haldrup, M. and Larsen, J. (2010) *Tourism, Performance and the Everyday*, London: Routledge.

Halgreen, T. (2004) 'Tourists in the concrete desert', in M. Sheller and J. Urry (eds) *Tourism Mobilities*, London: Routledge.

Hall, C. and Müller, K. (2004) *Tourism, Mobility, and Second Homes*, Toronto: Channel View.

Hall, M. and Williams, A. (2002) *Tourism and Migration*, Irvine: Springer.

Hall, S. (1992) 'The question of cultural identity', in S. Hall, D. Held and D. McGrew (eds) *Modernity and its Futures*, Oxford: Polity.

Hall, S. (1996) 'Cultural studies and its theoretical legacies', in S. Hall, D. Morley and K.H. Chen (eds) *Stuart Hall*, London: Routledge.

Hamilakis, Y. and Yalouri, E. (1995) 'Antiquities as symbolic capital in modern Greece', *Archaeological Dialogues*, 6(2): 115–59.

Hand, M. (2012) *Ubiquitous Photography*, Cambridge: Polity.

Hand, M. and Sandywell, B. (2002) 'E-topia as cosmopolis or citadel', *Theory, Culture and Society*, 19(1–2): 197–225.

Handel, J. (20 October 2010) 'Hobbit union boycott lifted', *The Hollywood Reporter*. Available at: www.hollywoodreporter.com/news/hobbit-union-boycott-lifted-jackson-31680?page=show (accessed 19 November 2010).

Handler, R. (1985) 'On dialogue and destructive analysis', *Journal of Anthropological Research*, 41: 171–82.

Handler R. (1988) *Nationalism and the Politics of Culture in Quebec*, Madison: University of Wisconsin Press.

Hannam, K., Sheller, M. and Urry, J. (2006) 'Editorial: mobilities, immobilites and moorings', *Mobilities*, 1(1): 1–22.

Hannerz, U. (1990) 'Cosmopolitans and locals in world culture', *Theory, Culture and Society*, 7(2): 237–51.

Hannerz, U. (1996) *Transnational Connections*, London: Routledge.

Hannerz, U. and Löfgren, O. (1994) 'The nation in the global village', *Cultural Studies*, 8: 198–207.

Hanson, A. (1989) 'The masking of the Maori: cultural invention and its logic', *American Anthropologist*, 91(4): 890–902.

Hardt, M. (1996) 'Introduction', in M. Hardt and P. Virno (eds) *Radical Thought in Italy*, Minneapolis: University of Minnesota Press.

Hardt, M. and Negri, A. (2000) *Empire*, Cambridge, MA: Harvard University Press.

Harrison, D. (2005) 'Contested narratives in the domain of world heritage', in D. Harrison and M. Hitchcock (eds) *The Politics of World Heritage*, Clevedon: Channel View.

Harrison, T.M. and Barthel, B. (2009) 'Wielding new media in Web 2.0: Exploring the history of engagement with the collaborative construction of media products', *New Media and Society*, 11(1–2): 155–78.

Harvey, D. (1999) *The Limits to Capital*, London: Verso.

Hayes, B. (2006) 'Unwed numbers', *American Scientist*, 94: 12–15.

Heelan, H.A. (16 December 2004) 'Loved the book? Go there, literally, with a literary tour', Frommers.com. Available at: www.frommers.com/articles/2523.html (accessed 16 December 2006).

Heidegger, M. (1967) *Being and Time*, Oxford: Blackwell.

Held, D. (1995) *Democracy and the Global Order*, Cambridge: Polity.

Hennion, A. and Latour, B. (1993) *La Passion Musicale*, Paris: Editions Métalié.

Henry, S. and Milovanovic, D. (1996) *Constitutive Criminology*, London and Thousand Oaks, CA: Sage.

Heritage, S. (15 December 2009) 'Who killed off the Golden Compass?', *Guardian Film Blog*. Available at: www.guardian.co.uk/film/filmblog/2009/dec/15/golden-compass-sam-elliot-catholic-church (accessed 26 April 2012).

Herman, E.S. and McChesney, R.W. (1997) *The Global Media*, London: Cassell.

Herod, A. (2012) 'Scales of globalization', in G. Ritzer (ed.) *Encyclopaedia of Globalization*, Oxford and New York: Wiley-Blackwell.

Herzfeld, M. (1983) 'Semantic slippage and moral fall: the rhetoric of chastity in rural Greek society', *Journal of Modern Greek Studies*, 1(1): 161–72.

Herzfeld, M. (1985) *The Poetics of Manhood*, Princeton, NJ: Princeton University Press.

Herzfeld, M. (1986) *Ours Once More*, New York: Pella.

Herzfeld, M. (1987) *Anthropology through the Looking-Glass*, Cambridge: Cambridge University Press.

Herzfeld, M. (1991) *A Place in History*, Princeton, NJ: Princeton University Press.

Herzfeld, M. (1992) *The Social Production of Indifference*, Oxford: Berg.

Herzfeld, M. (2001) *Anthropology*, Oxford: Blackwell.

Herzfeld, M. (2002) 'The absent presence: discourses of crypto-colonialism', *South Atlantic Quarterly*, 101(4): 899–926.

Herzfeld, M. (2004) *The Body Impolitic*, Chicago, IL: University of Chicago Press.

Herzfeld, M. (2005) *Cultural Intimacy*, 2nd edition, New York and London: Routledge.

Herzfeld, M. (2006) 'Practical Mediterraneanism', in W.V. Harris (ed.) *Rethinking the Mediterranean*, Oxford: Oxford University Press.

Herzfeld, M. (2007) 'Global kinship: anthropology and the politics of knowing', *Anthropological Quarterly*, 80(2): 313–23.

Herzfeld, M. (2008) 'The ethnographer as theorist', in M. Mazower (ed.) *Networks of Power in Modern Greece*, London: Hurst.

Herzfeld, M. (2009a) *Evicted from Eternity*, Chicago, IL: University of Chicago Press.

Herzfeld, M. (2009b) 'The cultural politics of gesture', *Ethnography*, 10(2): 131–52.

Hesmondhalgh, D. (2007) *The Cultural Industries*, 2nd edition, London: Sage.

Hesmondhalgh, D. and Baker, S. (2010) *Creative Labour*, London: Routledge.

Hess, H. (2003) 'Like Zealots and Romans: terrorism and the empire in the 21st century', *Crime, Law and Social Change*, 39: 339–57.

Hewison, R. (1987) *Heritage Industry*, London: Methuen.

Hewison, R. (1989) 'Heritage: an interpretation', in D. Uzzel (ed.) *Heritage Interpretation*, I, London: Belhaven.

Heyer, P. (1993) *American Architecture*, New York: John Wiley and Sons.

Heywood, S. (2004) 'Informant disavowal and the interpretation of storytelling revival', *Folklore*, 115: 45–63.

HFCO (undated) 'My Life in Ruins'. Available at: www.hfco.gr/716F0611.en.aspx (accessed 12 December 2007).

Hidden DVD Easter Eggs (February 2012) Available at: www.hiddendvdeastereggs.com (accessed 17 March 2012).

Hinch, T. (1998) 'Tourists and indigenous hosts: divergent views on their relationship with nature', *Current Issues in Tourism*, 1(1): 120–4.

Hirsch, P.M. (1972) 'Processing fads and fashions: an organization-set analysis of cultural industry systems', *American Journal of Sociology*, 77: 639–59.

Hirsch, T. (12 May 2011) 'Costing the Earth – The real Avatar', BBC Radio 4. Available at: www.bbc.co.uk/iplayer/episode/b010y0t5/Costing_the_Earth_The_Real_Avatar/ (accessed 15 February 2012).

Hobart, M. (ed.) (1993) *An Anthropological Critique of Development*, London: Routledge.

Hobson, B. and Lister, R. (2002) 'Citizenship', in B. Hobson, J. Lewis and B. Siim (eds) *Contested Concepts in Gender and Social Politics*, Cheltenham: Edward Elgar.

Hochschild, A. (1983) *The Managed Heart*, Berkeley: University of California Press.

Holden, D. (1972) *Greece Without Columns*, London: Faber and Faber.

Honneth, A. (1979) 'Communication and reconciliation: Habermas' critique of Adorno', *Telos*, 39: 45–69.

Honneth, A. (1991) *The Critique of Power*, Cambridge, MA: MIT.

Honneth, A. (1995) *The Struggle for Recognition*, Cambridge: Polity.

hooks, b. (1992) 'Eating the other: desire and resistance', in b. hooks (ed.) *Black Looks*, Boston: South End Press.

hooks, b. (1993) 'The oppositional gaze', in M. Dianara (ed.) *Black American Cinema*, London: Routledge.

Horst, H.A. (2009) 'Aesthetics of the self: digital mediations', in D. Miller (ed.) *Anthropology and the Individual*, Oxford: Berg.

Howard, R. (21 April 2009) 'Angels & Demons: It's a thriller, not a crusade', *Huffington Post*. Available at: www.huffingtonpost.com/ron-howard/iangels-demonsi-its-a-thr_b_189053.html (accessed 10 March 2012).

Hoyle, B. (11 December 2009) 'War on Terror backdrop to James Cameron's Avatar', *The Australian*. Available at: www.theaustralian.com.au/news/arts/war-on-terror-backdrop-to-james-camerons-avatar/story-e6frg8pf-1225809286903 (accessed 30 January 2012).

Hughes, C.R. (2006) *Chinese Nationalism in the Global Era*, London: Routledge.

Hunkin, J. (5 February 2007) 'Adamson back in NZ to shoot next *Narnia* film', *The New Zealand Herald*. Available at: www.nzherald.co.nz/movies/news/article.cfm?c_id=200&objectid=10422515 (accessed 24 April 2012).

Husserl, E. (1972) *Experience and Judgement*, Evanston: Northwestern University Press.

Hutnyk, J. (1996) *The Rumour of Calcutta*, London and New Jersey: Zed.

Huyssen, A. (1995) *Twilight Memories*, London: Routledge.

Huyssen, A. (2000) 'Present pasts: media, politics, amnesia', *Public Culture*, 12(1): 21–38.

Huyssen, A. (2003) *Present Pasts*, Stanford, CA: Stanford University Press.

IGN Film Force (16 February 2005) '*Narnia* Shooting Ends. And post-production begins'. Available at: http://uk.movies.ign.com/articles/588/588270p1.html (accessed 24 April 2012).

IMDB (2006) 'Silent Hill'. Available at: www.imdb.com/title/tt0384537/ (accessed 16 March 2012).

IMDB (2009) 'Avatar (2009)'. Available at: www.imdb.com/title/tt0499549/ (accessed 17 February 2012).

IMDB (2009) 'Driving Aphrodite'. Available at: www.imdb.com/title/tt0865559/ (accessed 30 April 2012).

Inglis, D. and Robertson, R. (2005) 'The ecumenical analytic: "globalization", reflexivity and the revolution in Greek historiography', *European Journal of Social Theory*, 8(2): 99–122.

Ingold, T. (1993) 'The temporality of landscape', *World Archaeology*, 25(2): 152–73.

Ingold, T. (2000) *The Perception of the Environment*, London: Routledge.

International Rivers (2012a) 'Mission'. Available at: www.internationalrivers.org/ (accessed 26 February 2012).

International Rivers (2012b) 'Stop the monster dam: Urgent action for the Xingu and its people'. Available at: www.causes.com/causes/77274-amazon-watch/actions/1531518 (accessed 28 February 2012).

Introvigne, M. (2012) 'Angels and Demons from the book to the movie FAQ – Do the Illuminati really exist?', CESNUR. Available at: www.cesnur.org/2005/mi_illuminati_en.htm (accessed 11 March 2012).

Irigaray, L. (1974) *Speculum of the Other Woman*, Ithaca: Cornell University Press.

Jackson, J.K. (2011) 'Doomsday ecology and empathy for nature: women scientists in "B" horror movies', *Science Communication*, 33(4): 533–55.

Jacobson, R. (1971) 'The dominant', in L. Matejka and K. Pomorska (eds) *Readings in Russian Poetics*, Cambridge, MA: MIT.

Jamal, T., Everett, J. and Dann, G.M.S. (2003) 'Ecological rationalization and performance resistances in natural area destinations', *Tourist Studies*, 3(2): 143–69.

Jameson, F. (2005) *Archaeology of Global Futures*, London: Verso.

Jardine, L. and Brotton, J. (2000) *Global Interests*, London: Reaktion.

Jay, M. (1973) *The Dialectical Imagination*, Berkeley: University of California Press.

Jay, M. (1993) *Downcast Eyes*, Berkeley: University of California Press.

Jeffords, S. (1989) *Hard Bodies*, Brunswick, NJ: Rutgers University Press.

Jenks, C. (1993) *Culture*, London and New York: Routledge.

Jewkes, Y. (2005) 'Men behind bars: "doing" masculinity as an adaptation to imprisonment', *Men and Masculinities*, 8: 44–63.

Jones, D. and Smith, K. (2005) 'Middle-earth meets New Zealand: authenticity and location in the making of the Lord of the Rings', *Journal of Management Studies*, 42(5): 923–45.

Just, R. (1995) 'Cultural certainties and private doubts', in W. James (ed.) *The Pursuit of Certainty*, London: Routledge.

Kaldor, M. (1996) 'Cosmopolitanism versus nationalism: the new divide?', in R. Caplan and J. Feiffer (eds) *Europe's New Nationalism*, New York: Oxford University Press.

Kaplan, A. (1986) *Sea Changes*, London: Verso.

Karatsinidou, C. (2005) *The Regeneration of Meaning* (in Greek), Athens: Indictos.

Karatzogianni, A. (2011) 'WikiLeaks affects: ideology, conflict and the revolutionary virtual', in A. Karatzogianni and A. Kuntsman (eds) *Digital Cultures and the Politics of Emotion*, Basingstoke: Palgrave Macmillan.

Kaufmann, V. and Montulet, B. (2008) 'Between social and spatial mobilities', in W. Ganzler, V. Kaufmann and S. Kesserling (eds) *Tracing Mobilities*, Burlington: Ashgate.

Kellner, D. (2002) 'Theorizing globalization', *Sociological Theory*, 20: 285–305.

Kellner, D. (2006) 'The Lord of the Rings as trilogy', in E. Mathijs and M. Pomerance (eds) *From Hobbits to Hollywood*, Amsterdam: Rodopi.

Kellogg, W.A., Carroll, J.M. and Richards, J.T. (1991) 'Making reality a cyberspace', in M. Benedikt (ed.) *Cyberspace: First Steps*, Cambridge: MIT Press.

Kien, G. (2008) 'Technography=technology+ethnography', *Qualitative Inquiry*, 14(7): 1101–9.

King, N. (2000) *Memory, Narrative, Identity*, Edinburgh: Edinburgh University Press.

King, N. (2007) 'Hollywood', in P. Cook, *The Cinema Book*, London: BFI.

Kipnis, L. (1996) *Bound and Gagged*, New York: Grove Press.

Knorr Cetina, K. (2007) 'Microglobalization', in I. Rossi (ed.) *Frontiers of Globalization Research*, New York: Springer.

Kohn, N. and Love, L. (2001) 'This, that and the other: fraught possibilities of the souvenir', *Text and Performance Quarterly*, 21(1): 1–17.

Kommonen, K. (2008) 'Narratives of Chinese color cultures in business contexts', Department of Languages and Communication: Helsinki School of Economics.

Konami Computer Entertainment Tokyo, Inc. (23 May 2003) *Silent Hill 3*. (Konami of America, Inc.) PlayStation 2. Available at: http://en.wikipedia.org/wiki/Konami_Computer_Entertainment_Tokyo#Konami_Computer_Entertainment_Tokyo (accessed 16 March 2012).

Kozinets, R. (1999) 'E-tribalized marketing? The strategic implications of virtual communities of consumption', European Management Journal, 17(2): 252–64.

Kozinets, R.V. (2001) 'Utopian enterprise: articulating the meaning of *Star Trek's* culture of consumption', *Journal of Consumer Research*, 28(2): 67–88.

Kraicer, S. (2002) 'Absence as spectacle', *Asia Week*. Available at: www.chinesecinemas.org/hero.html (accessed 26 April 2011).

Kristeva, J. (1991) *Strangers to Ourselves*, New York: Columbia University Press.

Kuhn, A. (1995) *Family Secrets*, London: Verso.

Kunkle, K. (14 May 2006) 'A "Da Vinci Code" tour sampler', *The Oregonian.* Available at: www.oregonlive.com/travel/oregonian/index.ssf?/base/travel/ (accessed 1 November 2006).

Kvale, J. (1997) *The Research Interviewer as a Traveller* [Den kvalitativa forskningsintervjun], Lund: Studentlitteratur.

Kyriakidou, M. (2008) 'Rethinking media events in the context of a global public sphere: exploring the audience of global disasters in Greece', *Communications*, 33(3): 273–91.

Lacan, J. (1994) *The Four Fundamental Concepts of Psychoanalysis*, London: Vintage.

LaCapra, D. (1988) *History and Memory after Auschwitz*, Ithaca, NY: Cornell University Press.

Laing, D. (1978) *The Marxist Theory of Art*, Sussex: Harvester Press.

Lambeck, P. (7 April 2011) 'Chinese artist Ai Weiwei has special connection to the West', *Deutsche Welle*. Available at: www.dw-world.de/dw/article/0,,14971397,00.html (accessed 28 April 2011).

Lane, R.J. (2000) *Jean Baudrillard*, London and New York: Routledge.

Lanfant, F.M. (2009) 'Roots of the sociology of tourism in France', in G.M.S. Dann and G. Liebmann Parrinello (eds) *The Sociology of Tourism*, UK: Emerald.

Langdon, J. (1992) *Wordplay*, Boston: Houghton Mifflin Harcourt.

Lange, M. (2007) 'Voices from the Kalahari', in K. Tomaselli (ed.) *Writing in the Sand*, New York: Altamira Press.

Langford, B. (2005) *Film Genre*, Edinburgh: Edinburgh University Press.

Larsen, J. (2004) '(Dis)connecting tourism and photography, corporeal and imaginative travel', *Journeys*, 5: 20–42.

Larsen, J. (2005) 'Families seen photographing: the performativity of tourist photography', *Space and Culture*, 8: 416–34.

Larsen, J., Urry, J. and Axhausen, K.W. (2006) 'Networks and tourism: mobile social life', *Annals of Tourism Research*, 34(1): 244–62.

Larson, W. (1993) 'Literary modernism and nationalism in post-Mao China', in W. Larson and A. Wedell-Wedellsbror (eds) *Inside Out*, Aarhus: Aarhus University Press.

Lash, S. and Urry, J. (1987) *The End of Organised Capitalism*, Madison, WI: University of Wisconsin Press.

Lash, S. and Urry, J. (1994) *Economies of Signs and Space*, London: Sage.

Law, I. (2010) *Racism and Ethnicity*, London: Pearson Education.

Lawn, J. and Beaty, B. (2006) 'On the brink of a new threshold of opportunity: the Lord of the Rings and New Zealand cultural policy', in E. Mathijs (ed.) *The Lord of the Rings*, London: Wallflower.

Lax, S. (2004) 'The internet and democracy', in D. Gauntlett and R. Horsley (eds) *Web Studies 2*, 2nd edition, New York: Oxford University Press.

Lazaridis, G. (2001) 'Trafficking and prostitution: the growing exploitation of migrant women in Greece', *The European Journal of Women's Studies*, 8(1): 67–102.

Leclaire, S. (1998) *A Child is Being Killed*, Stanford, CA: Stanford University Press.

Lemke, T. (2001) 'The birth of bio-politics: Michel Foucault's lecture at the Collège de France on neo-liberal governmentality', *Economy and Society*, 30(2): 190–207.

Lennon, J. and Foley, M. (2000) *Dark Tourism*, London: Continuum.

Leontis, A. (1995) *Topographies of Hellenism*, Ithaca, NY and London: Cornell University Press.

Leotta, A. (2012) *Touring the Screen*, Chicago, IL and Bristol: Intellect.

Lévi-Strauss, C. (1964) *Totemism*, London: Merlin Press.

Lin, J. (2002) 'Dream factory redux: mass culture, symbolic sites and redevelopment in Hollywood', in J. Eade and C. Mele (ed.) *Understanding the City*, Oxford: Blackwell.

Lindholm (1997) 'Logical and moral problems of postmodernism', *Journal of the Royal Anthropological Institute*, 3(4): 747–60.

Linnekin, J. (1991) 'Cultural invention and the dilemma of authenticity', *American Anthropologist*, 93(2): 446–9.

List of Konami Code Games (undated) Wikipedia. Available at: http://en.wikipedia.org/wiki/List_of_Konami_code_games (accessed 12 March 2012).

Lister, R. (1997a) *Citizenship*, Basingstoke: Macmillan.

Lister, R. (1997b) 'Citizenship: towards a feminist synthesis', *Feminist Review*, 57(1): 28–48.

Lister, R., Williams, F. and Anttonen, A. (2007) *Gendering Citizenship in Western Europe*, Bristol: Policy.

Live Journal (24 March 2009) 'Hans Zimmer – Angels & Demons soundtrack review'. Available at: http://disjecta.livejournal.com/362422.html (accessed 11 March 2012).

Löfgren, O. (1989) 'The nationalisation of culture', *Ethnologica Europaea*, 19(1): 5–24.

Löfgren, O. (1999) *On Holiday*, Berkeley: University of California Press.

Loizos, P. and Papataxiarchis, E. (1991a) 'Introduction', in P. Loizos and E. Papataxiarchis (eds) *Contested Identities*, Princeton, NJ: Princeton University Press.

Loizos, P. and Papataxiarchis, E. (1991b) 'Gender, sexuality, and the person in Greek culture', in P. Loizos and E. Papataxiarchis (eds) *Contested Identities*, Princeton, NJ: Princeton University Press.

Loomba, A. (2005) *Colonialism/Postcolonialism*, London: Routledge.

Lord of the Rings (LOTR) Official Website (undated). Available at: www.lordoftherings. net (accessed 16 April 2012).

Lowenthal, D. (1985) *The Past is a Foreign Country*, Cambridge: Cambridge University Press.

Luhmann, N. (1990) 'Weltkunst', in N. Luhmann, F.D. Bunsen and D. Baecker (eds) *Unbeobachtbare Welt*, Bielefeld: Cordula Haux.

Luhmann, N. (1992) *Die Wissenschaft der Gesselschaft*, Frankfurt am Main: Surkamp Verlag.

Luhmann, N. (1999) 'The concept of society', in A. Elliott (ed.) *Contemporary Social Theory*, Oxford: Blackwell.

Lukâcs, G. (1968). *History and Class Consciousness*, London: Merlin.

Lury, C. (2004) *Brands*, London: Sage.

Lyon, D. (1994) *The Electronic Eye*, Minneapolis: University of Minnesota Press.

MacCannell, D. (1973) 'Staged authenticity: arrangements of social space in tourist settings', *American Journal of Sociology*, 79(3): 589–603.

MacCannell, D. (1989) *The Tourist*, London: Macmillan.

MacCannell, D. (2001) 'Tourist agency', *Tourist Studies*, 1(1): 23–37.

Mackay, H. (2004) 'The globalization of culture?', in D. Held, (ed.) *A Globalizing World?*, London: Open University Press.

Mackenzie, J.M. (1993) 'Occidentalism: counterpoint and counter-polemic', *The Journal of Historical Geography*, 19(3): 339–44.

Mackenzie, J.M. (1997) *Empires of Nature and the Nature of Empires*, East Linton: Tuckwell Press.

Mackey, R. (15 August 2004) 'Cracking the color code of 'Hero''', *The New York Times*.

Macmaster, N. and Lewis, T. (1998) 'Orientalism: from unveiling to hyperveiling', *Journal of European Studies*, 28, 121–35.

MacRobbie, A. (2006) 'Feminism, postmodernism and the real "me"', in M.G. Durham and D. Kellner (eds) *Media and Cultural Studies*, Malden: Blackwell.

Maffesoli, M. (1996) *The Time of the Tribes*, London: Sage.

Malinowski, B. (1922) *Argonauts of the Western Pacific*, II: *The Language of Magic and Gardening*, London: Allen and Unwin.

Malinowski, B. (1948) *Magic, Science and Religion, and Other Essays*, Boston: Beacon.

Mann, C. and Stewart, F. (2000) *Internet Communication and Qualitative Research*, London: Sage.

Mannheim, K. (1968) *Ideology and Utopia*, New York: Harcourt, Brace and World.

Mannheim, K. (2003) 'The dynamics of spiritual realities', in J. Tanner (ed.) *The Sociology of Art*, London: Routledge.

Maoz, D. (2006) 'The mutual gaze', *Annals of Tourism Research*, 33: 221–39.

Marcuse, P. (1996) 'Space and race in the post-Fordist city: the outcast ghetto and advanced homelessness in the United States today', in E. Mingione (ed.) *Urban Poverty and the Underclass*, Oxford: Blackwell.

Marketsaw (2 April 2008) 'Na'vi Alien Language incorporated in 'Avatar' music soundtrack'. Available at: http://marketsaw.blogspot.com/2008/04/navi-alien-language-incorporated-in.html (accessed 1 February 2012).

Martín-Barbero, J. (2000) 'Transformations in the map: identities and culture industries', *Latin American Perspectives*, 27(4): 27–48.

Marx, K. (1976) *Capital*, I, Harmondsworth: Penguin.

Massey, D. (1993) 'Power-geometry and a progressive sense of place', in B. Curties, G. Robertson and L. Tickner (eds) *Mapping the Futures*, London: Routledge.

Massey, D. (1994) *Space, Place and Gender*, Cambridge: Polity.

Mathijs, E. (2006) 'Popular culture in global context: The Lord of the Rings phenomenon', in E. Mathijs *(ed.) The Lord of the Rings*, London: Wallflower.

Mauss, M. (1954) *The Gift*, London: Free Press.

Mayne, J. (1995) 'Paradoxes of spectatorship', in L. Williams (ed.) *Viewing Positions*, Brunswick, NJ: Rutgers University Press.

McAdam, D. (1982) *Political Process and the Development of Black Insurgency*, Chicago, IL: University of Chicago Press.

McAdam, D. (1988) *Freedom Summer*, New York: Oxford University Press.

McAdam, D. and Paulsen, R. (1993) 'Specifying the relationship between social ties and activism', *The American Journal of Sociology*, 99(3): 640–67.

McClintock, A. (1991) 'No longer in future heaven: women and nationalism in South Africa', *Transition*, 51: 104–23.

McClintock, A. (1995) *Imperial Leather*, New York: Routledge.

McClintock, P. (27 October 2010) 'James Cameron's 5-year plan', *Variety*. Available at: www.variety.com/article/VR1118026416 (accessed 28 January 2012).

McGrath, G. (30 May 2006) 'A Paris Da Vinci Code tour', *Times*. Available at: http://travel.timesonline.co.uk (accessed 10 October 2006).

McGregor, A. (2000) 'Dynamic texts and the tourist gaze: death, bones and buffalo', *Annals of Tourism Research*, 27(1): 27–50.

McKee, R. (1999) *Story*, London: Methuen.

McKevitt, C. (1991) 'San Giovanni Rotondo and the shrine of Padre Pio', in J. Eade and M.J. Sallnow (eds) *Contesting the Sacred*, London: Routledge.

McLean, S. (2009) 'Stories and cosmogonies: imagining creativity beyond "nature" and "culture"', *Cultural Anthropology*, 24(2): 213–45.

McLuhan, M. (1962) *The Guttenberg Galaxy*, London: Routledge and Kegan Paul.

McLuhan, M. (1964) *Understanding the Media*, New York: McGraw.

Meethan, K. (2002) *Tourism in Global Society*, Basingstoke: Palgrave.

Meethan, K. (2003) 'Mobile cultures? Hybridity, tourism and cultural change', *Tourism and Cultural Change*, 1(1): 11–28.

Meeuf, R. (2006) 'Collateral damage, terrorism, melodrama, and the action film on the eve of 9/11', *Jump Cut*, 48. Available at: www.ejumpcut.org/archive/jc48.2006/CollatDamage/index.html (accessed December 2009).

Melosi, D. (2000) 'Changing representations of the criminal', *British Journal of Criminology*, 40(2): 296–320.

Melucci, A. *(1989) Nomads of the Present*, London: Hutchinson Radius.

Melucci, A. (1995) 'The process of collective identity', in H. Johnston and B. Klandermas (eds) *Social Movements and Culture*, Minneapolis: University of Minnesota Press.

Michaelson, J. (22 December 2009) 'The meaning of Avatar: Everything is God (A response to Ross Douthat and other naysayers of "pantheism"', *Huffington Post*. Available at: www.huffingtonpost.com/jay-michaelson/the-meaning-of-avatar-eve_b_400912.html (accessed 22 January 2012).

Miége, B. (1987) 'The logics at work in the new cultural industries', *Media, Culture and Society*, 9(2): 273–89.

Miège, B. (1989) *The Capitalization of Cultural Production*, New York: International General.

Mignolo, W.D. (2002) 'The enduring enchantment (or the epistemic privilege of modernity and where to go from here)', *The South Atlantic Quarterly*, 101(4): 927–54.

Miller, A.H. (1980) *Terrorism and Hostage Negotiations*, Boulder, CO: WestviewPress.

Miller, D. (1987) *Material Culture and Mass Consumption*, Oxford: Blackwell.

Miller, D. (2009) 'Individuals and the aesthetic order', in D. Miller (ed.) *Anthropology and the Individual*, Oxford: Berg.

Milton, K. (1993) 'Land or landscape: rural planning policy and the symbolic construction of the countryside', in M. Murray and J. Greer (eds) *Rural Development in Iceland*, Aldershot: Avebury.

Minca, C. and Oakes, T. (2006) 'Travelling paradoxes', in T. Oakes and C. Minca (eds) *Travels in Paradox*, Lanham: Rowman and Littlefield.

Mitchell, W.J.T. (1994) *Landscape and Power*, Chicago, IL: University of Chicago Press.

Mizstal, B. (2003) *Theories of Social Remembering*, Maidenhead: Open University Press.

Molotch, H. (2004) 'How art works: form and function in the stuff of life', in R. Friedland and J. Mohr (eds) *Matters of Culture*, Cambridge: Cambridge University Press.

Moorehead, G. (1973) *Gallipoli*, London: Andre Deutsch.

Morales, T. (3 April 2009) 'Sarandon to Bush: Get real on war', CBS News. Available at: www.cbsnews.com/stories/2003/02/14/earlyshow/living/main540658.shtml (accessed 12 February 2012).

Morgan, N., Pritchard, A. and Piggott, R. (2003) 'Destination branding and the role of the stakeholders: the case of New Zealand', *Journal of Vacation Marketing*, 9(3): 285–99.

Morley, D. (1995) 'Theories of consumption in media studies', in D. Miller (ed.) *Acknowledging Consumption*, London: Routledge.

Morley, D. (2000). *Home Territories*, London: Routledge.

Morley, D. and Robins, K. (1995) *Spaces of Identity*, London: Routledge.

Moskos, C. (1999) 'The Greeks in the United States', in Richard Clogg (ed.) *The Greek Diaspora in the Twentieth Century*, London: St Martin's Press.

Mulgan, I. (1967) *Report on Experience*, Auckland: Oxford University Press.

Mulvey, L. (2006) 'Visual pleasure and narrative cinema', in M.G. Durham and D.M. Kellner (eds) *Media and Cultural Studies*, Oxford: Blackwell.

Murashov, I. (1997) 'Bakhtin's carnival and oral culture', in C. Adlam, R. Falconer, V. Makhlin and A. Renfrew (eds) *Face to Face*, Sheffield: Sheffield Academic Press.

Murdock, G. (1999) 'Rights and representations: public discourse and cultural citizenship', in J. Gripsrud (ed.) *Television and Common Knowledge*, London: Routledge

Murphy, M. (21 December 2009) 'A few questions for James Cameron', *The New York Times*. Available at: http://carpetbagger.blogs.nytimes.com/2009/12/21/a-few-questions-for-james-cameron/ (accessed 30 January 2009).

Murray, J. (29 October 2010) 'Mallard flags Hobbit dissent', 3news.NZ. Available at: www.3news.co.nz/Mallard-flags-Hobbit-dissent/tabid/419/articleID/183707/Default.aspx (accessed 9 December 2011).

My Life in Ruins (2009) poster. Available at: www.echobridgeentertainment.com/uploads/90305EPK.pdf (accessed 30 April 2012).

Nagib, L. (2007) *Brazil on Screen*, London: I.B. Tauris.

Nagib, L. (2011) *World Cinema and the Ethics of Realism*, New York: Continuum.

Nakashima, R. (4 November 2010) 'Hobbit money sought as MGM files for bankruptcy', 3news.NZ. Available at: www.3news.co.nz/Hobbit-money-sought-as-MGM-files-for-bankruptcy-/tabid/418/articleID/184793/Default.aspx (accessed 19 December 2010).

NarniaWeb.com (29 March 2008) 'The official movie companion, book review'. Available at: www.narniaweb.com/2008/03/the-official-movie-companion-book-review (accessed 24 April 2012).

Nash, D. (1977) 'Tourism as a form of imperialism', in V. Smith (ed.) *Hosts and Guests*, Philadelphia, PA: University of Philadelphia Press.

Neale, S. (1991) 'Aspects of ideology and narrative in American war film', *Screen*, 32(1): 35–57.

Neale, S. and Krutnik, F. (1990) *Popular Film and Television Comedy*, London: Routledge.

Nederveen Pieterse, J. (2004) *Globalization and Culture*, Lanham: Rowman & Littlefield.

Nederveen Pieterse, J. (2005) 'Paradigm making while paradigm breaking: Andre Gunder Frank', *Review of International Political Economy*, 12(3): 383–6.

Nederveen Pieterse, J. (2006a) 'Globalization as hybridization', in M.G. Durham and D. Kellner (eds) *Media and Cultural Studies*, Malden: Blackwell.

Nederveen Pieterse, J. (2006b) 'Emancipatory cosmopolitanism: towards an agenda', *Development and Change*, 37(6): 1247–57.

Nederveen Pieterse, J. (undated) 'Oriental globalization: past and present'. Available at: www.jannederveenpieterse.com/pdf/NP%20Orient%20Glob%20PP.pdf (accessed 11 April 2012).

Negus, K. (1995) 'Where the mystical meets the market: creativity and commerce in the production of popular music', *The Sociological Review*, 43(2): 316–41.

Nervo Codato, A. (2006) 'A political history of the Brazilian transition from military dictatorship to democracy', *Revista Sociologia e Politica*, 2, trans. by M. Adelman (25: 83–106).

Neumann, M. (1988) 'Wandering through the museum: experience and identity in a spectator culture', *Borderlines*, 12: 1–27.

Newitz, A. (18 December 2009) 'When will white people stop making movies like "Avatar"?', I09. Available at: http://io9.com/5422666/when-will-white-people-stop-making-movies-like-avatar (accessed 13 May 2012).

Neyland, D. (2005) *Privacy, Surveillance and Public Trust*, London: Macmillan.

Nietzsche, F.W. (1980) *On the Advantage and Disadvantage of History for Life*, Indianapolis, IN: Hacket.

Nietzsche, F.W. (1996) *On the Genealogy of Morals*, Oxford: Oxford University Press.

Nora, P. (1989) 'Between memory and history: Les Lieux de Memoire', *Representations*, 26(2): 7–25.

Nussbaum, M. (2010) 'Kant and cosmopolitanism', in G.W. Brown and D. Held (eds) *The Cosmopolitan Reader*, Cambridge: Polity.

Nussbaum, M. and Cohen, J. (eds) (1996) *For Love of Country*, Boston, MA: Beacon.

NZPA (1 November 2010) 'Hobbit drama- Govt comes out on top', 3news.NZ. Available at: www.3news.co.nz/Hobbit-drama---Govt-comes-out-on-top/tabid/419/articleID/183996/Default.aspx (accessed 19 December 2012).

O'Brien, M. (2008) *A Crisis of Waste?*, New York: Routledge.

O'Brien, M., Tzanelli, R., Yar, M. and Penna, S. (2005) 'The spectacle of fearsome acts: crime in the melting p(l)ot in *Gangs of New York*', *Theoretical Criminology*, 13: 17–35.

O'Connor, M. and Airey, R. (2007) *Symbols, Signs and Visual Codes*, London: Southwater.

O'Hanlon, C. (2006) 'A conversation with Douglas W. Jones and Peter G. Neumann', *Queue*, 4(9). Available at: www.deepdyve.com/lp/association-for-computing-machinery/

a-conversation-with-douglas-w-jones-and-peter-g-neumann-YFx3TwZ4nh (accessed 18 March 2012).

O'Regan, T. (1990) 'Maori control of the Maori heritage', in P. Gathercole and D. Lowenthal (eds) *The Politics of the Past*, Cambridge: Cambridge University Press.

Oakley, A. (1998) 'Gender, methodology and people's way of knowing: some problems with feminism and the paradigm debate in social research', *Sociology*, 32(4): 707–31.

Obeyesekere, G. (1992) '"British cannibals": contemplation of an event in the death and resurrection of James Cook, explorer', *Critical Enquiry*, 18(3): 630–54.

Oliver, M. and Sapey, B. (2006) *Social Work with Disabled People*, London: Palgrave Macmillan.

Ong, A. and Nomini, D. (1997) *Ungrounded Empires*, New York: Routledge.

Ong, W. (1987) *Oralidad y Escriptura*, Mexico City: FCE.

Ordoña, M. (13 December 2009) 'Eye-popping 'Avatar' pioneers new technology', *San Francisco Chronicle*. Available at: www.sfgate.com/cgi-bin/article.cgi?f=/c/a/2009/12/11/PK4B1B0EHD.DTL&type=movies (accessed 29 January 2012).

Orr, E.R. (2005) 'The ethics of paganism: the value and power of the sacred relationship', in L.D. Angeles, E.R. Orr and T.V. Dooren (eds) *Pagan Visions for a Sustainable Future*, Woodbury: Llewellyn Publications.

Osborne, P. (2000) *Travelling Light*, Manchester: University of Manchester Press.

Osterman, L. (21 October 2005) 'Why no Easter eggs?', Larry Osterman's Blog. Available at: http://blogs.msdn.com/b/larryosterman/archive/2005/10/21/483608.aspx (accessed17 March 2012).

Paley, J. (2002) 'The Cartesian melodrama in nursing', *Nursing Philosophy*, 3(3): 189–92.

Panoramas (2006) 'The [Da Vinci Code] locations'. Available at: www.panoramas.dk/da-vinci-code/ (accessed 11 November 2006).

Papastergiadis, N. (2003) *The Turbulence of Migration*, Cambridge: Polity.

Papastergiadis, N. (2005) 'Hybridity and ambivalence: places and flows in contemporary art and culture', *Theory, Culture and Society*, 22(4): 39–64.

Papathanasiou, S. (2007) *Alexandros Papadiamantis and the Grammi tou Orizontos* [in Greek], Thessaloniki: Mygdonia.

Paris Muse (2006) 'Explore the "Da Vinci Code"'. Available at: www.parismuse.com/about/news/da-vinci-code.shtml (accessed 1 December 2006).

Paris through Expatriate Eyes (2006) 'Cracking the Da Vinci Code at the Louvre'. Available at: www.paris-expat.com/tours/davinci_code.html (accessed 1 December 2006).

Parkhurst Ferguson, P. (1994) 'The flâneur on and off the streets of Paris', in K. Tester (ed.) *The Flâneur*, London: Routledge.

Parrinello, J. (2001) 'The technological body in tourism: research and praxis', *International Sociology*, 16(2): 205–19.

Parsons, T. and Smelser, N.J. (1957) *Economy and Society*, London: Routledge and Kegan Paul.

Pateman, C. (1989) *The Disorder of Women*, Cambridge: Polity.

Patke, R.S. (2000) 'Benjamin's arcades project and the postcolonial city', *Diacritics*, 30(4): 2–14.

Patton, P. (1996) *Deleuze*, Oxford: Blackwell.

Payvdad News (16 March 2007) 'Iranian Academy of Arts to submit UNESCO declaration against "300"'. Available at: www.payvand.com/news/07/mar/1224.html (accessed 24 April 2012).

Peaslee, R.M. (2010) '"The man from New Line knocked on the door": Tourism, media power, and Hobbiton/Matamata as boundaried space', *Tourist Studies*, 10(1): 57–73.

Peaslee, R.M. (2011) 'One ring, many circles: the Hobbiton tour experience and a spatial approach to media power', *Tourist Studies*, 11(1): 37–53.

Peirce, C.M. (1998) 'Harvard lectures on pragmaticism', in N. Houser and C. Kloesel (eds) *The Essential Peirce*, I, Bloomington: Indiana University Press.

Pellauer, D. (2007) *Ricoeur*, New York: Continuum.

Pensky, M. (1989) 'On the use and abuse of memory: Habermas, anamnestic solidarity and the Historikerstreit', *Philosophy and Social Criticism*, 15: 351–80.

Peristiany, J.G. (ed.) (1965) *Honour and Shame*, London: Weidenfeld and Nicolson.

Perkins, H.C. and Thorns, D.C. (2001) 'Gazing or performing? Reflections on Urry's tourist gaze in the context of contemporary experience in the Antipodes', *International Sociology*, 16(2): 185–204.

Pinney, C. (1997) *Camera Indica*, London: Reaktion.

Plummer, K. (1995) *Telling Sexual Stories*, London: Routledge.

Polanyi, M. (1966) *The Tacit Dimension*, New York: Doubleday.

Porteous, D. (1996) *Environmental Aesthetics*, London: Routledge.

Prentice, R. and Guerin, S. (1998) 'The romantic walker? A case study of users of iconic Scottish landscape', *Scottish Geographical Magazine*, 108(2): 180–91.

Prideaux, B. (2002) 'The cybertourist', in G.M.S. Dann (ed.) *The Tourist as a Metaphor of the Social World*, Wallingford: CABI.

Przeclawski, K., Bystrzanowski, J. and Ujma, D. (2009) 'The sociology of tourism in Poland', in G.M.S. Dann and G. Parrinello (eds) *The Sociology of Tourism*, UK: Emerald.

Putnam, R. (1993) *Making Democracy Work*, Princeton, NJ: Princeton University Press.

Qiongli, W. (2006) 'Commercialization of digital storytelling: an integrated approach for cultural tourism, the Beijing Olympics and wireless VAS', *International Journal of Cultural Studies*, 9(3): 383–94.

Radio New Zealand (21 May 2006) 'Samoa's government censor bans Da Vinci Code film'. Available at: www.rnzi.com/pages/news.php?op=read&id=24194 (accessed 10 May 2012).

Radner, H. (2005) 'In search of authenticity: the "global" popular and "quality" culture – the case of *The Lord of the Rings* trilogy and *Pavement*', *Journal of Multidisciplinary International Studies*, 2(2): 1–13. Available at: http://epress.lib.uts.edu.au/journals/index.php/portal/article/view/109/68 (accessed 12 April 2012).

Read, D. (2006) 'Kingship algebra expert system', *Social Science Computing Review*, 24(1). Available at: www.deepdyve.com/lp/sage/kinship-algebra-expert-system-kaes-a-software-implementation-of-a-DavpWwtJIt (accessed 14 May 2012).

Reijnders, S. (2011) 'Stalking the count: Dracula, fandom and tourism', *Annals of Tourism Research*, 38(1): 231–48.

Reiter, B. (2010) 'What's new in Brazil's "new social movements"?', *Latin American Perspectives*, 38(1): 153–68.

Relax News (12 December 2009) '"Avatar" in four different formats", *The Independent*. Available at: www.independent.co.uk/arts-entertainment/films/news/avatar-in-four-different-formats-1839073.html (accessed 4 February 2012).

Religion Facts (2008a) 'The Council of Nicea and the Da Vinci Code'. Available at: www.religionfacts.com/da_vinci_code/nicea.htm (accessed 12 March 2012).

Religion Facts (2008b) 'The Louvre Pyramids and *The Da Vinci Code*'. Available at: www.religionfacts.com/da_vinci_code/louvre_pyramids.htm (accessed 12 August 2008).

Ren, C. (2011) 'Non-human agency, radical ontology and tourism realities', *Annals of Tourism Research*, 38(3): 358–81.

Rheingold, H. (2000) *The Virtual Community*, Cambridge, MA: MIT.

Richardson, T. and Jensen, O.B. (2004) 'The Europeanisation of spatial planning in Britain: new spatial ideas for old territories?', ESRC/UACES Study Group on the Europeanisation of British Politics and Policy-Making, Sheffield, 23 April 2004. Available at: http://aei.pitt.edu/1733/1/richardson.pdf (accessed 4 September 2012).

Ricoeur, P. (1967) *The Symbolism of Evil*, New York: Harper and Row.

Ricoeur, P. (1970) *Freud and Philosophy*, New Haven: Yale University Press.

Ricoeur, P. (1974) *The Conflict of Interpretations*, Evanston: Northwestern University Press.

Ricoeur, P. (1981) *Hermeneutics and the Human Sciences*, New York: Cambridge University Press.

Ricoeur, P. (1984–8) *Time and Narrative*, I-II, New York: Columbia University Press.

Ricoeur, P. (1993) *Oneself as Another*, Chicago, IL: University of Chicago Press.

Ricoeur, P. (2004) *Memory, History, Forgetting*, Chicago, IL: University of Chicago Press.

Ritzer, G. (2010) *Globalization*, Oxford: Wiley-Blackwell.

Ritzer, G. and Liska, A. (1997) '"McDisneyization" and "post-tourism": contemporary perspectives on contemporary tourism', in C. Rojek and J. Urry (eds) *Touring Cultures*, London and New York: Routledge.

Robertson, R. (1992) *Globalization*, London: Sage.

Roche, M. (1996) 'Mega-events and micro-modernization', in Y. Apostolopoulos, S. Leivadi and A. Yannakis (eds) *The Sociology of Tourism*, London: Routledge.

Rojek, C. (2000) *Leisure and Culture*, Basingstoke: Macmillan.

Rojek, C. (2001) *Celebrity*, London: Reaktion.

Rollins, J. (1996) 'Invisibility, consciousness of the Other and ressentiment among black domestic workers', in C. McDonald and C. Sirianni (eds) *Working in the Service Society*, Philadelphia: Temple University Press.

Rootes, C. (1995) 'A new class? The higher educated and the new politics', in L. Mahen (ed.) *Social Movements and Social Classes*, London: Sage.

Rosenfeld, G.D. (2000) *Munich and Memory*, Berkeley and Los Angeles: University of California Press.

Ryan, A. (1997) 'Liberalism', in R.E. Goodin and P. Pettit (eds) *A Companion to Contemporary Political Philosophy*, Oxford: Blackwell.

Ryan, M. and Kellner, D. (1990) *Camera Politica*, Bloomington, IN: Indiana University Press.

Sacred Destinations (undated) 'St Sulpice-Paris'. Available at: www.sacred-destinations.com/france/paris-st-sulpice (accessed 4 September 2012).

Sacred Earth Journeys (2006) 'On the trail of the Da Vinci Code'. Available at: www.scaredearthjourneys.ca/TOURS/sacred-Davinci-des.htm (accessed 11 November 2006).

Sahlins, M. (1972) *Stone Age Economics*, Chicago, IL: Aldine.

Sahlins, M. (1985) *How Natives Think*, Chicago, IL: University of Chicago Press.

Sahlins, M. (1996) 'The sadness of sweetness: the native anthropology of Western cosmology', *Current Anthropology*, 37(3): 395–415.

Said, E. (1978) *Orientalism*, London: Penguin.

Said, E. (1993) *Culture and Imperialism*, London: Vintage.

Samoa Observer (21 May 2009) 'Chief censor bans movie Angels and Demons'. Available at: www.samoaobserver.ws/index.php?option=com_content&view=article&id=8309:chief-censor&catid=1:latest-news&Itemid=50 (accessed 10 March 2012).

Sandywell, B. (2011) *Dictionary of Visual Discourse*, Surrey: Ashgate.

Sapir, E. (1929) 'The status of linguistics as science', *Language*, 5: 207–14.

Sasoon, J. (1984) 'Ideology, symbolic action and rituality in social movements: the effects of organizational forms', *Social Science Information*, 23: 861–73.

Sassen, S. (2000) 'New frontiers facing urban sociology at the Millennium', *British Journal of Sociology*, 51: 143–60.

Sassen, S. (2001) *The Global City*, New Jersey: Princeton University Press.

Sassen, S. (ed.) (2002) *Global Networks, Linked Cities*, London: Routledge.

Sassen, S. (2003) 'Globalization or denationalization?', *Review of International Political Economy*, 10(1): 1–22.

Satherley, D. (29 October 2010) 1: 'Hobbit bill becomes law', 3news.NZ. Available at: www.suite101.com/content/peter-jacksons-hobbit-movie-invokes-industrial-protests-a301440 (accessed 19 December 2010).

Satherley, D. (29 October 2010) 2: 'Labor MP slams Hobbit law change', 3news.NZ. Available at: www.3news.co.nz/Labour-MP-slams-Hobbit-law-change/tabid/423/articleID/183695/Default.aspx (accessed 19 December 2010).

Savelli, A. (2009) 'Tourism in Italian sociological thought and study', in G.M.S. Dann and G. Parrinello (eds) *The Sociology of Tourism*, UK: Emerald.

Sayer, A. (2000) 'Moral economy and political economy', *Studies in Political Economy*, 61(2): 79–103.

Schaefer, S. (18 October 2011) 'James Cameron teases "Avatar 2" plot & setting details', *Screen Rant*. Available at: http://screenrant.com/james-cameron-avatar-2-plot-setting-sandy-136853/ (accessed 22 January 2012).

Schiller, H. (1991) 'Not yet the post-imperialist era', *Critical Studies in Mass Communication*, 8: 13–28.

Schrøder, K. (1994) 'Audience semiotics, interpretive communities and the "ethnographic turn" in media research', *Media, Culture and Society*, 16(2): 337–47.

Schrøder, K., Dotner, K., Kilne, S. and Murray, C. (2003) *Researching Audiences*, London: Arnold.

Schweiger, D. (6 May 2008) 'E-notes: Harry Gregson-Williams returns to "Narnia" with "Prince Caspian"', *IfMagazine*. Available at: http://web.archive.org/web/200806 05224419/http://www.ifmagazine.com/feature.asp?article=2820 (23 April 2012).

Scotsman.com (7 May 2006) 'Da Vinci Code soundtrack "too tense" for children'. Available at: www.scotsman.com/lifestyle/film/da-vinci-code-soundtrack-too-tense-for-children-1-1411621 (accessed 14 March 2012).

Scott Provan, J. (2009) 'Sudoku: strategy versus structure', *American Mathematical Monthly*, October, 1-10. Available at: http://stat-or.unc.edu/research/Current%20 Reports/techpdf/TR_08_04.pdf (accessed 28 March 2012).

Seaton, A.V. (1996) 'Guided by the dark: from thanatopsis to thanatourism', *Journal of Heritage Studies*, 2(4): 234–44.

Seaton, A.V. (1999) 'War and thanatotourism: Waterloo, 1815–1914', *Annals of Tourism Research*, 26(1): 130–59.

SexyBeijingTV (8 August 2008) 'Ai Weiwei: Olympic Bird's Nest & Beyond'. Available at: www.youtube.com/watch?v=hddG7u1hlOU (accessed 26 April 2011).

Shapiro, J. (4 November 2011) 'Shakespeare – a fraud? Anonymous is ridiculous', *The Guardian*. Available at: www.guardian.co.uk/film/2011/nov/04/anonymous-shakespeare-film-roland-emmerich (23 April 2012).

Sharpe, M. (2002) 'The sociopolitical limits of fantasy: September 11 and Slavoj Žižek's theory of ideology', *Cultural Logic*. Available at: http://clogic.eserver.org/2002/sharpe. html (accessed 1 December 2009).

Sharpley, R. (2004) 'Islands in the Sun: Cyprus', in M. Sheller and J. Urry (eds) *Tourism Mobilities*, London: Routledge.

Shaw, G. and Williams, A. M. (2004) *Critical Issues in Tourism*, 2nd edition, Oxford: Blackwell.

Shell (28 January 2010) 'Shell Perdido: Buster Stewart, Noble Clyde Boudreaux drilling foreman', YouTube. Available at: www.youtube.com/watch?v=AJXjWeGFKO4 (accessed 30 January 2012).

Sheller, M. (2003) *Consuming the Caribbean*, New York: Routledge.

Sheller, M. (2004) 'Demobilizing and remobilizing Caribbean paradise', in M. Sheller and J. Urry (eds) *Tourism Mobilities*, London: Routledge.

Sheller, M. (2012) 'Mobilities', in G. Ritzer (ed.) *Encyclopaedia of Globalization*, New York: Wiley-Blackwell.

Sheller, M. and Urry, J. (2006) 'The new mobilities paradigm', *Environment and Planning A*, 38: 207–26.

Shields, R. (1991) *Places on the Margin*, London: Routledge.

Shields, R. (1996) *Cultures of the Internet*, London: Sage.

Shohat, E. (1992) 'Notes on the "post-colonial"', *Social Text*, 31/32: 99–113.

Shohat, E. and Stam, R. (1994) *Unthinking Eurocentrism*, London and New York: Routledge.

Shore, H. (undated) Official Site Video, National Film Board of Canada. Available at: www.howardshore.com (accessed 14 April 2012).

Sibley, B. (2006) *Peter Jackson*, London: Harper Collins.

Siegel, J. (5 February 2010) 'Cameron says Microsoft's role in Avatar was crucial', Microsoft Services. Available at: www.microsoft.com/microsoftservices/en/us/article_Microsoft_Role_In_Avatar.aspx (accessed 1 February 2012).

Siegel, T. (6 March 2009) 'Catholic controversy doesn't bug Sony', *Variety*. Available at: www.variety.com/article/VR1118000940?refCatId=1019 (accessed 10 March 2012).

Silent Hill 3 (2003) Available at: www.translatedmemories.com/bookpgs/Pg94-95.jpg (accessed 16 March 2012).

Silver, I. (1993) 'Marketing authenticity in Third World Countries', *Annals of Tourism Research*, 20: 302–18.

Simpson, K. (2005) 'Broad horizons? Geographies and pedagogies of the gap year'. unpublished PhD thesis, University of Newcastle. Available at: www.ethicalvolunteering.org/downloads/final.PDF (accessed 3 March 2012).

Sinclair, D. (1992) 'Land: Maori view and European response', in M. King (ed.) *Te Ao Harihuri: Aspects of Maoritanga*, Auckland: Reed.

Sinclair, J., Jacka, E. and Cunningham, S. (1996) 'Peripheral vision', in J. Sinclair, E. Jacka and S. Cunningham (eds) *New Patterns in Global Television*, Oxford: Oxford University Press.

Singh, A. (7 May 2009) 'Angels and Demons: Vatican breaks silence to review film', *Telegraph*. Available at: www.telegraph.co.uk/news/celebritynews/5290910/Angels-and-Demons-Vatican-breaks-silence-to-review-film.html (accessed 10 March 2012).

Slade, P. (2003) 'Gallipoli thanatotourism: the meaning of ANZAC', *Annals of Tourism Research*, 30(4): 779–94.

Smith, A.D. (1981) *The Ethnic Revival in the Modern World*, Cambridge: Cambridge University Press.

Smith, A.D. (1984) 'National identity and myths of ethnic descent', *Research in Social Movements, Conflict, Change*, 7: 95–130.

Smith, A.D. (1995) *Nations and Nationalism in a Global Era*, Cambridge: Polity.

Smith, A.D. (1999) *Myths and Memories of the Nation*, Oxford: Oxford University Press.

Smith, A.D. (2000) *The Nation in History*, Hanover, NH: University Press of New England.

Smith, D. (15 May 2005) 'So you thought Sudoku came from the Land of the Rising Sun...', *The Observer*. Available at: www.guardian.co.uk/media/2005/may/15/press andpublishing.usnews (accessed 28 March 2012).

Smith, H. (18 October 2007) 'Acropolis to star in film debut', *The Guardian* Film Blog. Available at: http://blogs.guardian.co.uk/film/2007/10/acropolis_to_star_in_film_debut. html (accessed May 2008).

Smith, P. (2008) 'The Balinese Cockfight decoded: reflections on Geertz, the strong programme and structuralism', *Cultural Sociology*, 2(2): 169–86.

Smith, R. (2007) *Being Human*, New York: Columbia University Press.

Sobchack, V. (1992) *Address of the Eye*, Princeton, NJ: Princeton University Press.

Somerset House (2011) 'Ai Weiwei: Circle of animals/zodiac heads'. Available at: www. somersethouse.org.uk/visual-arts/ai-weiwei-circle-of-animals-zodiac-heads (accessed 12 May 2011).

Sontag, S. (1990) *On Photography*, New York: Doubleday.

Spiegelman, A. (1999 [1988]) 'Commix: an idiosyncratic historical and aesthetic overview', *Print*, 42(6): 61–73, 195–6.

Spielberg. S. (17 December 2008) 'Person of the year 2008', *Time-CNN*. Available at: www.time.com/time/specials/packages/article/0,28804,1861543_1865103_18 65107,00.html (accessed 20 April 2011).

Spivak, G. (1992) *Thinking Academic Freedom in Gendered Post-Coloniality*, Cape Town: University of Cape Town Publishing.

Spivak, G. (1999) *A Critique of Postcolonial Reason*, Cambridge, MA: Harvard University Press.

Spode, H. (2009) 'Tourism research and theory in German-speaking countries', in G.M.S. Dann and G. Parrinello (eds) *The Sociology of Tourism*, UK: Emerald.

Spooner, B. (1986) 'Weavers and dealers: authenticity and Oriental carpets', in A. Appadurai (ed.) *The Social Life of Things*, Cambridge: Cambridge University Press

Spurr, D (1993) *The Rhetoric of Empire*, London: Durham University Press.

Stanfield, P. (2001) *Hollywood, Westerns and the 1930s*, Exeter: University of Exeter Press.

Starpulse (9 November 2009) 'James Cameron's jungle expedition for "Avatar" stars'. Available at: www.starpulse.com/news/index.php/2009/11/09/james_cameron_s_ jungle_expedition_for_av (accessed 1 February 2012).

Stavrou Karayanni, S. (2004) *Dancing Fear and Desire*, Canada: Wilfrid Laurier University Press.

Steiner, C. (1995) 'The art of the trade: on the creation of value and authenticity in the African art market', in G. Marcus and F. Meyer (eds) *The Traffic in Culture*, Berkeley: University of California Press.

Steiner, J. (2001–6) Available at: www.jeffsteiner.com/Jeff-Steiner.php (accessed 22 December 2006).

Stevenson, N. (2002) *Cultural Citizenship*, Buckingham and Philadelphia, PA: Open University Press.

Stoller, P. (1992) *The Taste of Things Ethnographic*, Philadelphia, PA: University of Pennsylvania Press.

Strain, E. (2003) *Public Places, Private Journeys*, Brunswick, NJ: Rutgers University Press.

Strang, V. (1997) *Uncommon Ground*, New York: NUP.

Strathern, M. (1983) 'The kula in comparative perspective', in J.W. Leach and E. Leach (eds) *The Kula*, Cambridge: Cambridge University Press.

Strathern, M. (1988) *The Gender of the Gift*, Berkeley: University of California Press.

Strathern, M. (1996) 'Cutting the network', *Journal of the Royal Anthropological Institute*, 2: 517–35.

Strathern, M. (2004) 'The whole person and its artifacts', *Annual Review of Anthropology*, 33: 1–19.

Street, J. (2004) 'Celebrity politicians: popular culture and political representation', *BJPIR*, 6: 435–52.

Sudoku (undated) Wikipedia entry. Available at: http://en.wikipedia.org/wiki/Sudoku#History (accessed 28 March 2012).

Sutton, D. (2000) *Memories Cast in Stone*, Oxford and New York: Berg

Svetkey, B. (15 January 2010) 'Avatar: 11 burning questions', *Entertainment Weekly*. Available at: www.ew.com/ew/gallery/0,,20336893,00.html (accessed 29 January 2012).

Swindler, A. (1986) 'Culture in action: symbols and strategies', *American Sociological Review*, 20: 305–29.

Sydell, L. (16 April 2011) 'Art and consequence: a talk with China's controversial Ai Weiwei', NPR.

Szerszynski, B. (1996) 'On knowing what to do: environmentalism and the modern problematic', in S. Lash, B. Szerszynski and B. Wynne (eds) *Risk, Environment and Modernity*, London: Sage.

Szerszynski, B. (1997) 'The varieties of ecological piety', *Worldviews*, 1: 37–55.

Szerszynski, B. and Urry, J. (2006) 'Visuality, mobility and the cosmopolitan: inhabiting the world from afar', *British Journal of Sociology*, 57(1): 113–31.

Tannenbaum, F. (1966) *Peace by Revolution*, New York: Columbia University Press.

Taylor, J.P. (2001) 'Authenticity and sincerity in tourism', *Annals of Tourism Research*, 28(1): 7–26.

Telegraph (17 June 2008) 'Vatican bans "godless" Da Vinci Code sequel Angels & Demons from Rome churches'. Available at: www.telegraph.co.uk/news/2139472/Vatican-bans-%27godless%27-Da-Vinci-Code-sequel-Angels-andamp-Demons-from-Rome-churches.html (accessed 1 September 2008).

The Hobbit on Facebook (2011–12) Available at: www.facebook.com/TheHobbitMovie (accessed 13 April 2012).

The Hobbit, Production Video 1 (5 November 2011). Available at: www.youtube.com/watch?v=NWBQqVgkGuc&feature=related (accessed 14 April 2012).

The Hobbit, Production Video 5 (23 December 2011) Available at: www.youtube.com/watch?v=dY1JmJw8EBg (accessed 12 April 2012).

The Hobbit, Production Video 6 (1 March 2012) Available at: www.youtube.com/watch?v=QjYn845i08A&feature=relmfu (accessed 14 April 2012).

The Numbers (22 July 2009) Available at: www.the-numbers.com/charts/daily/2009/20090722.php (accessed 2 May 2012).

The Religion of Islam (10 February 2007) 'Da Vinci Code broken?'. Available at: www.islamreligion.com/articles/426/ (accessed 1 September 2008).

Theatre Royal Drury Lane (2011) The Lord of the Rings. Available at: www.lotr.com/home (accessed 3 May 2011)

TheOneRing.net (25 April 2008) 'Guillermo Del Toro chats with TORN about "The Hobbit" film'. Available at: www.theonering.net/torwp/2008/04/25/28747-guillermo-del-toro-chats-with-torn-about-the-hobbit-films (accessed 15 December 2010).

Thompson, A. (1994) *Anzac Memories*, Melbourne: Oxford University Press.

Thompson, A. (9 January 2007) 'Cameron sets live-action, CG epic for 2009', *The Hollywood Reporter*. Available at: http://web.archive.org/web/20070110054929/http://www.hollywoodreporter.com/hr/content_display/film/news/e3i1c5a3d24ccc0c11be5f736c8e625bd90 (Accessed 1 February 2012).

Thompson, J. (1995) *The Media and Modernity*, Cambridge: Polity.

Thompson-Carr, A. (2012) 'Aoraki/Mt Cook and the Mackenzie basin's transition from wilderness to tourist place', *Journal of Tourism Consumption and Practice*, 4(1): 30–58.

THR.com (23 December 2009) 'Peter Jackson on the Hobbit'. Available at: www.youtube.com/watch?v=ZjUOa6xbwCI (accessed 9 April 2011).

Thrift, N. (1989) 'Images of social change', in C. Hamnett, L. McDowell and P. Sarre (eds) *The Changing Social Structure*, London: Sage.

Thrift, N. (2007) *Non-Representational Theory*, London: Routledge.

Tilly, C. (1984a) *Big Structures, Large Processes, Huge Comparisons*, New York: Russell Sage Foundation.

Tilly, C. (1984b) 'Social movements and national politics', in C. Bright and S. Harding (eds) *Statemaking and Social Movements*, Ann Arbor: University of Michigan Press.

Tilly, C. (2003) *The Politics of Collective Violence*, Cambridge: Cambridge University Press.

Titley, G. (2003) 'Cultivating habitats of meaning: broadcasting, participation and interculturalism', *Irish Communications Review*, 9. Available at: www.icr.dit.ie/volume9/articles/Titley.pdf (accessed 15 May 2012).

Todorova, M. (1997) *Imagining the Balkans*, Oxford: Oxford University Press.

Toffler, A. (1980) *Future Shock*, NY: William Morrow and Co.

Tolkien, J.R.R. (1999) *The Lord of the Rings*, London: Harper Collins.

Tolstoy, L. (1960 [1896]) *What is Art?*, New York: Macmillan.

Tomashevsky, B. (1965) 'Thematics', in L.T. Lemmon and M. Reis (eds) *Russian Formalist Criticism*, Lincoln: University of Nebraska Press.

Tomlinson, J. (1999) *Globalization and Culture*, Chicago, IL: University of Chicago Press.

Tomlinson, T. (2007) *The Culture of Speed*, London: Sage.

Towner, J. (1985) 'The Grand Tour: a key phase in the history of tourism', *Annals of Tourism Research*, 12(3): 293–333.

Travel China Guide (2011) 'National Stadium'. Available at: www.travelchinaguide.com/attraction/beijing/national-stadium.htm (accessed 22 April 2011).

Tsagarousianou, R., Tambini, D. and Bryan, C. (eds) (1998) *Cyberdemocracy*, London: Routledge.

Tuan, Y.F. (1974) *Topophilia*, New York: Columbia University Press.

Tudor, A. (1976) 'Genre and critical methodology', in B. Nichols (ed.) *Blurred Boundaries*, Bloomington, IN: Indiana University Press.

Tudor, A. (1989) *Monsters and Mad Scientists*, Oxford: Blackwell.

Turner, B.S. (1982) 'The discourse of the diet', *Theory, Culture and Society*, 1(1): 23–32.

Turner, S. (2002) 'Cinema of justice', *Illusions*, 33: 9–11.

Turner, V. (1974) 'Liminal to liminoid, play flow and ritual: an essay in comparative symbolology', *Rice University Studies*, 50: 53–92.

TVNew Zealand (21 October 2010) 'Close up: The battle for the Hobbit'. Available at: www.youtube.com/watch?v=XoUN2AGxrnA (accessed 9 April 2011).

Tzanelli, R. (2004a) 'Constructing the "cinematic tourist": the "sign industry" of *The Lord of the Rings*', *Tourist Studies*, 4(1): 21–42.

Tzanelli, R. (2004b) '"Europe" within and without: narratives of American cultural belonging *in* and *through My Big Fat Greek Wedding* (2002)', *Comparative American Studies*, 2(1): 35–59.

Tzanelli, R. (2004c) 'Giving gifts (and then taking them back): identity, reciprocity and symbolic power in the context of *Athens 2004*', *The Journal of Cultural Research*, 8(4): 425–46.

Tzanelli, R. (2006a) '"Reel" Western fantasies: portrait of a tourist imagination in *The Beach* (2000)', *Mobilities*, 1(1): 121–42.

Tzanelli, R. (2006b) 'Capitalising on value: towards a sociological understanding of kidnapping', *Sociology*, 40(5): 929–47.

Tzanelli, R. (2007a) 'Solitary amnesia as national memory: from Habermas to Luhman', *International Journal of Humanities*, 5(4): 253–60.

Tzanelli, R. (2007b) *The Cinematic Tourist: Explorations in Globalization, Culture and Resistance*, London: Routledge.

Tzanelli, R. (2008a) 'Cultural intimations and the commodification of culture: sign industries as makers of the "public sphere", *The Global Studies Journal*, 1(3): 1–10.

Tzanelli, R. (2008b) *Nation-Building and Identity in Europe*, Basingstoke: Palgrave Macmillan.

Tzanelli, R. (2008c) 'The nation has two voices: *diforia* and performativity in *Athens 2004*', *European Journal of Cultural Studies*, 11(4): 489–508.

Tzanelli, R. (2009) *The 'Greece' of Britain and the 'Britain' of Greece*, Saarbrücken: Verlag Dr Müller.

Tzanelli, R. (2010a) 'Islamophobia and Hellenophilia: Greek myths of post-colonial Europe', in S. Sayyid and A.K. Vakil, *Thinking Through Islamophobia*, New York: Columbia Univeristy Press.

Tzanelli, R. (2010b) 'Mediating cosmopolitanism: crafting an allegorical imperative through *Beijing 2008*', *International Review of Sociology*, 20(2): 215–41.

Tzanelli, R. (2011a) *Cosmopolitan Memory in Europe's 'Backwaters'*, Oxford: Routledge.

Tzanelli, R. (2011b) 'Ill-defined heritage: exploring Thessaloniki's selective agenda', *The Global Studies Journal*, 4(4): 193–218.

Tzanelli, R. (2012) 'Domesticating sweet sadness: Thessaloniki's *Glyká* as a travel narrative', *Cultural Studies—Critical Methodologies*, 12(2): 159–72.

Tziovas, D. (1986) *Nationalism of the Demoticists and its Impact on the Literary Theory*, Amsterdam: Hakkert.

UBC (28 July 2011) 'Language of Avatar under study'. Available at: https://news.ok.ubc.ca/2011/07/28/language-of-avatar-under-study (accessed 12 February 2012).

UNESCO (undated) 'Acropolis, Athens'. Available at: http://whc.unesco.org/en/list/404 (accessed 3 May 2012).

UNHCHR (2005) Decision 1 (66): New Zealand, 27/04/2005, CERD/C/DEC/NZL/1. Available at: www.unhchr.ch/tbs/doc.nsf/%28Symbol%29/CERD.C.DEC.NZL.1.En?Opendocument (accessed 15 December 2010).

Urry, J. (1993) *Before Social Anthropology*, Chur, Switzerland: Harwood Academic Publishers.

Urry, J. (1995) *Consuming Places*, London: Routledge.

Urry, J. (1996a) 'Changing economics of the tourist industry', in Y. Apostolopoulos, S. Leivadi and A. Yannakis (eds) *The Sociology of Tourism*, London: Routledge.

Urry, J. (1996b) 'Tourism, culture and social inequality', in Y. Apostolopoulos, S. Leivadi and A. Yannakis (eds) *The Sociology of Tourism*, London: Routledge.

Urry, J. (2000) *Sociology Beyond Societies*, London: Routledge.

Urry, J. (2001) 'Globalising the tourist gaze', *Department of Sociology On-line Papers*. Available at: www.lancs.ac.uk/fss/sociology/papers/urry-globalising-the-tourist-gaze. pdf (accessed 1 January 2011).

Urry, J. (2002) *The Tourist Gaze*, 2nd edition, London: Sage.

Urry, J. (2003) *Global Complexity*, Cambridge: Polity.

Urry, J. (2004) 'Death in Venice', in M. Sheller and J. Urry (eds) *Tourism Mobilities*, London and New York: Routledge.

Urry, J. (2007) *Mobilities*, Cambridge: Polity.

Urry, J. (2011) *Climate Change and Society*, Cambridge: Polity.

Urry, J. and Larsen, J. (2011) *The Tourist Gaze 3.0*, London: Sage.

Uteng, T.P. and Cresswell, T. (2008) *Gendered Mobilities*, Aldershot: Ashgate.

Van Aelst, P. and Walgrave, S. (2004) 'New media, new movements? The role of the Internet in shaping the "anti-globalization" movement', in W. van de Donk (ed.) *Cyberprotest*, London: Routledge.

Van Gennep, A. (1906). *Rites of Passage*, Chicago, IL: University of Chicago Press.

Van Laer, J. and Van Aelst, P. (2010) 'Cyber-protest and civil society: the Internet and action', in Y. Jewkes and M. Yar (eds) *The Handbook of Internet Crime*, Devon: Willan.

Vannini, P., Hodson, J. and Vannini, A. (2009) 'Toward a technography of everyday life', *Cultural Studies—Critical Methodologies*, 9(3): 462–76.

Vardalos, N. (2006) *The Dialogue* (with Mike DeLuca), Horshu LLC.

Vardalos, N. (8 June 2009) '"Women don't go to the movies" – Huh?', *Huffington Post*. Available at: www.huffingtonpost.com/nia-vardalos/women-dont-go-to-the-movi_ b_212888.html (accessed 4 May 2012).

Vardiabasis, N. (2002) *Story of a Word* (in Greek), Athens: Livani.

Vatican (City State) (2012) 'Sistine Chapel (virtual tour)'. Available at: www.vatican.va/ various/cappelle/sistina_vr/index.html (accessed 18 March 2012).

Veblen, T. (1899) *The Theory of the Leisure Class*, New York: Macmillan.

Veijola, S. and Jokinen, E. (1994) 'The body in tourism', *Theory and Society*, 11: 125–51.

Veijola, S. and Valtonen, A. (2007) 'The body in tourism industry', in A. Pritchard, N. Morgan, I. Ateljevic and C. Harris (eds) (2003) *Tourism and Gender*, Wallingford: CABI.

Vertovec, S. and Cohen, R. (eds) (2002) *Conceiving Cosmopolitanism*, Oxford: Oxford University Press.

Virilio, P. (21 October 1984) 'Cyberwar, god and television', *C-Theory*.

Virilio, P. (1989) *War and Cinema*, London and New York: Verso.

Virilio. P. (1990) *Popular Defence and Ecological Struggles*, New York: Semiotext.

Virilio, P. (1991) *The Aesthetics of Disappearance*, New York: Semiotext.

Virilio, P. (1995) *The Vision Machine*, Bloomington: Indiana University Press/BFI.

Virilio, P. (1997) *Open Sky*, New York: Verso.

VisitScotland.com (2006) 'Rosslyn Chapel tours: Scotland'. Available at: www.visitscotland.com/sitewide/davincicode (accessed 11 November 2006).

Von Hayek, F. (1976) *The Mirage of Social Justice (II)*, London: Routledge and Kegan Paul.

Vulliamy, E. (July 2008) 'The Nest Generation', *The Observer Sport Monthly*.

Wagner, R. (1975) *The Invention of Culture*, Englewood Cliffs: Prentice-Hall.

Wakefield. P. (19–25 December 2009) 'Close encounters of the 3D kind', *The New Zealand Listener*, no. 3632. Available at: www.listener.co.nz/issue/3632/features/14597/ close_encounters_of_the_3d_kind_.html (accessed 1 February 2012).

Walby, S. (1990) *Theorising Patriarchy*, Oxford: Blackwell.

Walby, S. (1994) 'Is citizenship gendered?', *Sociology*, 28(2): 379–95.

Walby, S. (2006) 'Gender approaches to nations and nationalism', in G. Delanty and K. Kumar (eds) *The Sage Handbook of Nations and Nationalism*, London: Sage.

Wall, D. and Yar, M. (2010) 'Intellectual property crime and the Internet', in Y. Jewkes and M. Yar (eds) *Handbook of Internet Crime*, Devon: Willan.

Walsh, W.H. (1967) *Philosophy of History*, New York: Harper & Row.

Walter, T. (2008) 'The sociology of death', *Sociology Compass*, 2(1): 317–36.

Wang, N. (1999) 'Rethinking authenticity in tourist experience', *Annals of Tourism Research*, 26(2): 349–70.

Wang, N. (2000) *Tourism and Modernity*, Oxford: Pergamon.

Washington Post (13 February 2003) 'Iraq: anti-war voices (with Susan Sarandon)'. Available at: www.washingtonpost.com/wp-srv/liveonline/03/special/world/sp_world_sarandon021303.htm (accessed 12 February 2012).

Watts, J. (18 November 2011) 'Ai Weiwei investigated over nude art', *The Guardian*. Available at: www.guardian.co.uk/artanddesign/2011/nov/18/ai-weiwei-investigation-nude-art (accessed 2 April 2012).

Weaver, A. (2005) 'Interactive service work and performative metaphors: the case of the cruise industry', *Tourist Studies*, 5: 2–27.

Weber, M. (1978a) *Economy and Society*, Berkeley, CA: University of California Press.

Weber, M. (1978b) *Selections in Translation*, Cambridge: Cambridge University Press.

Weber, M. (1985) *The Protestant Ethic and the Spirit of Capitalism*, London: Unwin Hyman.

Weedon, C. (1987) *Feminist Practice and Poststructuralist Theory*, Oxford: Blackwell.

Wellman, B. (2001) 'Physical place and cyberplace: the rise of networked individualism', in M. Tanabe, P. van den Beseelaar and I. Ishidar (eds) *Digital Cities II*, Berlin: Springer.

Wellman, B. and Haythornthwaite, C. (eds) (2002) *The Internet and Everyday Life*, Oxford: Blackwell.

Wellman, B., Quan-Hasse, A. and Boase, J. (2003) 'The social affordances of the Internet for networked individualism', *Journal of Computer-mediated Communication*, 8(3). Available at: http://jcmc.indiana.edu/vol8/issue3/wellman.html (accessed 15 May 2012).

West, D. (1995) 'The contribution of continental philosophy', in R.E. Goodin and P. Pettit (eds) *A Companion to Contemporary Political Philosophy*, Oxford: Blackwell.

Weta (2008) *The Crafting of Narnia*, New York: Harper One.

Wheeler, B. (1997) 'Here we go, here we go, he we go eco', in M.J. Stabler (ed.) *Tourism and Sustainability*, Wallingford: CABI.

White, H. (1973) *Metahistory*, Baltimore: Johns Hopkins University Press.

White, H. (1978) *Tropics of Discourse*, Baltimore: Johns Hopkins University Press.

Wicke, J. (1993) 'Through a gaze darkly: pornography's academic market', in P. Church Gibson and R. Gibson, *Dirty Looks*, London: BFI.

Wiggershaus, R. (1994) *The Frankfurt School*, Cambridge: Polity.

Wikipedia (undated) 'Avatar (2009 film)'. Available at: http://en.wikipedia.org/wiki/Avatar_(2009_film) (accessed 12 February 2012).

Williams, R. (1958) *Culture and Society*, London: Chatto and Windus.

Williams, R. (1965–61) *The Long Revolution*, Harmondsworth: Penguin.

Williams, R. (1974) *The Country and the City*, New York: Oxford University Press.

Williamson, K. (8 June 2006) 'Critical mass' *Calgary Sun*. Available at: www.calgarysun.com/cgi-bin/publish.cgi?p=141769&x=articles&s=showbiz (accessed 10 January 2007).

Williamson, M. (2006) *The Lure of the Vampire*, London: Wallflower Press.

Williamson, V. (27 October 2010) 'Peter Jackson's Hobbit movie invokes industrial protests', *Suite 101*. Available at: www.suite101.com/content/peter-jacksons-hobbit-movie-invokes-industrial-protests-a301440 (accessed 10 December 2010).

Wills, J.E. (2001) *1668: A Global History*, London: Granta.

Wolff, J. (1984) *The Social Production of Art*, New York: New York University Press.

Wolff, J. (1987) 'The ideology of autonomous art', in R. Leppert and S. McClary (eds) *Music and Society*, Minneapolis: University of Minnesota Press.

Wood, R. (1986) *Hollywood – From Vietnam to Reagan*, New York: Columbia University Press.

Woods, P.A. (2005) *From Gore to Mordor*, London: Plexus.

Xu, (Hua) J. (2007) 'Brand-new lifestyle: consumer-oriented programmes on Chinese television', *Media, Culture and Society*, 29(3): 363–76.

Xu, P. and Chisholm, M. (22 April 2011) 'China tourists twig to Beijing's Bird's Nest', *Reuters*. Available at: www.reuters.com/article/2009/04/22/us-china-birdsnest-id USTRE53L10L20090422 (accessed 22 April 2011).

Yahoo! Movies (undated) 'James Cameron: Biography'. Available at: http://movies. yahoo.com/person/james-cameron/biography.html (accessed18 December 2011).

Yahoo! Movies (undated) 'Melina Mercouri'. Available at: http://movies.yahoo.com/ movie/contributor/1800059812/bio (accessed 1 December 2009).

Yahoo! Movies (undated) 'Sigourney Weaver: Biography'. Available at: http://movies. yahoo.com/person/sigourney-weaver/biography.html (accessed 18 December 2011).

Yalouri, E. (2001) *The Acropolis*, Oxford: Berg.

Yar, M. (2000) 'From actor to spectator: Hannah Arendt's "two theories" of political action', *Philosophy and Social Criticism*, 26(2): 1–27.

Yar, M. (2005) 'The global "epidemic" of movie "piracy": crime-wave or social construction?', *Media, Culture and Society*, 27(5): 677–96.

Yar, M. (2008) 'The rhetorics and myths of anti-piracy campaigns: criminalization, moral pedagogy and capitalist property relations in the classroom', *New Media and Society*, 10(4): 605–13.

Young, C. (2006) 'Munich 1972: re-presenting the nation', in A. Tomlinson and C. Young (eds) *National Identity and Global Sports Events*, New York: SUNY.

YouTube, *Telegraph* (11 October 2010) 'Ai Weiwei's sunflower seeds at the Tate'. Available at: www.youtube.com/watch?v=m7UcuYiaDJ0&feature=related (accessed 26 October 2011).

Yudhisthir, R.I. (2004) '"Tangible" and "intangible" heritage: are they really Castor and Pollux?', *Indian National Trust for Art and Cultural Heritage –INTACH Vision 2020*, New Delhi, India. Available at www.unesco.ch/typo3conf/ext/dam_frontend/pushfile. php?docID=3181 (accessed November 2008).

Yuval-Davis, N. and Webner, P. (1999) *Women, Citizenship and Difference*, London: Zed.

Zanker, R. and Lealand, G. (2003) 'New Zealand as Middle Earth: local and global popular communication in a small nation', *Popular Communication*, 1: 65–72.

Zeitlyn, D. (2001) *Reading in the Modern World, Writing and the Virtual World*, Canterbury: CASC Monographs. Available at: http://casc.anthropology.ac.uk/ CASCMONOG/RRRweb (accessed 8 February 2011).

Zeitlyn, D. (2003) 'Gift economies in the development of open source software: anthropological reflections', *Research Policy* (special issue: Open Source Software Development), University of Kent at Canterbury. Available at: http://lucy.ukc.ac.uk/dz/ (accessed 29 March 2012).

Zhang, Y. (1996) *The City in Modern Chinese Literature and Film*, Stanford, CA: Stanford University Press.

Zhen, N. (2002) *Memoirs from the Beijing Film Academy*, Durham: Duke University Press.

Zheng, Q. (2008) 'Feng shui and traditional Chinese architecture' (lecture), Huazhong Normal University, Wuhan.

Zhuoqiong, W. (1 October 2008) 'Bird's Nest takes gold in tourist stakes', *China Daily*. Available at: www.chinadaily.com.cn/china/2008-10/01/content_7071700.htm (accessed 22 April 2008).

Zimmer, B. (4 December 2009) 'On language: Skxawng!', *The New York Times*. Available at: www.nytimes.com/2009/12/06/magazine/06FOB-onlanguage-t.html (accessed 22 December 2011).

Žižek, S. (1999) *The Ticklish Subject*, New York: Verso.

Žižek, S. (2002) *Welcome to the Desert of the Real!*, New York: Verso.

Zukin, S. (2003) 'Home-shopping in the global marketplace', paper presented to 'Les sens du mouvement' colloquium, Cerisyla-Salle, Normandy.

Filmography

Angels and Demons (2009) DVD, dir. R. Howard, Sony Pictures.

Avatar (2010) DVD Blu-Ray, dir. J. Cameron, 20th Century Fox.

The Da Vinci Code (2006) DVD, dir. R. Howard, Sony Pictures.

Driving Aphrodite/ My Life in Ruins (2009) DVD, dir. D. Petrie, Search Foxlight.

The Guillermo Del Toro Collection (2007) DVD, dir. G. Del Toro, Optimum World (US).

Hero (2004) DVD, dir. Y. Zhang, Miramax.

House of Flying Daggers (2004) DVD, dir. Y. Zhang, Dolby.

Lord of the Rings (The) (2004) Extended DVD trilogy set, dir. P. Jackson, New Line.

Silent Hill (2006) DVD, dir. C. Guns, Pathé/20th Century Fox.

Index